JEWISH CONTINUITY IN AMERICA

ALSO BY ABRAHAM J. KARP

AUTHOR

New York Chooses a Chief Rabbi (1955)

A History of the United Synagogue of America (1964)

The Jewish Way of Life (1965)

Golden Door to America: The Jewish Immigrant Experience (1976)

To Give Life: The UJA in the Shaping of the American Jewish Community (1980)

The Jewish Way of Life and Thought (1981)

Haven and Home: A History of the Jews in America (1985)

Haye Haruah shel Yahadut Amerika (in Hebrew) (1985)

Mordecai M. Noah—First American Jew (1987)

From the Ends of the Earth: Judaic Treasures of the Library of Congress (1990)

A History of the Jews in America (1997)

EDITOR

Conservative Judaism: The Legacy of Solomon Schechter (1963)

The Jewish Experience in America, 5 vols. (1969)

Texts and Studies Series in American Jewish History, 6 vols., coeditor with Moshe Davis (in Hebrew) (1970–1984)

Beginnings—Early American Judaica (1975)

The Jews in America: A Treasury of Art and Literature (1994)

TRANSLATOR

Five from the Holocaust (1974)

JUDAIC STUDIES SERIES

Leon J. Weinberger

GENERAL EDITOR

JEWISH CONTINUITY
IN AMERICA

Creative Survival in a Free Society

ABRAHAM J. KARP

THE UNIVERSITY OF ALABAMA PRESS

Tuscaloosa and London

Library of Congress Cataloging-in-Publication Data

Karp, Abraham J.
    Jewish continuity in America : creative survival in a free
society / Abraham J. Karp.
    p. cm. — (Judaic studies series)
    Includes bibliographical references and index.
    ISBN 0-8173-0923-3 (cloth)
    1. Judaism—United States—History. 2. Judaism—History—Modern
period, 1750– 3. Rabbis—United States. 4. Conservative
Judaism—United States—History. I. Title. II. Series: Judaic studies
series (Unnumbered)
    BM205 .K38 1998
    296'.0973—ddc21
                                                              98-8951

British Library Cataloguing-in Publication data available

CONTENTS

Preface   ix

Acknowledgments   xiii

Introduction: Quest for a Viable Identity   1

PART ONE: THE SYNAGOGUE IN AMERICA

1. The Synagogue in America: A Historical Typology   17

2. The Americanization of Congregation Beth Israel, Rochester   45

PART TWO: THE AMERICAN RABBINATE

3. Expanding the Parameters of the Rabbinate: Isaac Leeser of
    Philadelphia   109

4. From Campus to Pulpit: Simon Tuska of Rochester   122

5. American Rabbis for America: Solomon Schechter
    Comes to the Seminary   132

6. New York Chooses a Chief Rabbi: Jacob Joseph of Vilna   145

PART THREE: A PLURALISTIC RELIGIOUS COMMUNITY

7. The Tripartite Division: How It Came to Be   193

8. A Century of Conservative Judaism   204

    Postscript: Between Fear and Faith   259

    Notes   267

    Glossary   291

    Index   293

PREFACE

Jewish life in North America almost came to an end before it began. No sooner had the twenty-three Jewish refugees fleeing the Portuguese reconquest of Recife, Brazil, set foot in New Amsterdam in late summer 1654 than the governor of the colony, Peter Stuyvesant, asked permission from the Dutch West India Company "to request them to depart." Fortunately, word of his request reached leaders of the Jewish community in Amsterdam, who immediately petitioned the company, arguing that such a decree would be "of no advantage to the general Company but rather damaging" to it, reminding the directors that "many of the Jewish nation are principal shareholders of the Company." Just a half year after the arrival, on April 26, 1655, the company instructed Stuyvesant, "The people may travel and trade to and in New Netherlands and live and remain there."[1]

The Jews did remain, and more came in ever-increasing numbers. New Amsterdam became New York. In time New York became the city with the largest Jewish population, by far, in the long history of the Jewish people, and the Jews of the United States became the largest Jewish community in the world.

The incident in New Amsterdam was the first and last direct overt threat from *without* to Jewish survival in America, but threats to survival coming from *within* have been many. The ease of assimilation into America's free and open society led W. M. Rosenblatt, a perceptive observer of the American scene, to conclude in 1872 that "within fifty years . . . the grandchildren, at the latest, will be indistinguishable from the mass of humanity which surrounds them. . . . Of that ancient people only the history of their peril and their suffering will remain, and the change that came over them in an enlightened age."[2] Two decades later, Rabbi Jacob David Willowsky expressed it conditionally, "If we do not bestir ourselves now, I am sore afraid that there will be no Jews left in America in the next generation."[3]

American Jews, like other Jews before them, have lived within a paradox of faith and fear—the faith that they are an eternal people, and the fear that their generation may be the last. The survival of every Jewish community has been conditional. The studies in this volume describe the creative response of individual Jews and organized groups to the ongoing threats to Jewish continuity. For every generation of American Jews the Jewish survival of the next generation has been its highest priority.

The introductory essay, "Quest for a Viable Identity," enlarges on Winthrop S. Hudson's observation in his *Religion in America:* "The adherents of Judaism were compelled to live in two worlds at the same time, to maintain the integrity of their faith while meeting the demands for coexistence within a non-Jewish culture and society. . . . Such dual allegiance was not easy to maintain. . . . It became doubly difficult when the coercion of the ghetto was relaxed. Still it could be and was done, even in America where the temptation to abandon a dual allegiance was greatest."[4]

Observers of the American Jewish religious scene point to three components that have developed in America to a degree unique in the Jewish religious historical experience: the centrality of the synagogue; the influence of the rabbinate; and the pluralistic nature of the Jewish religious community. The three became the catalysts for the ongoing endeavor to secure the allegiance of the coming generation.

THE SYNAGOGUE

The two chapters of the section "The Synagogue in America" are studies in the changes in the synagogue responding to new realities faced in America: benign assimilation, denominationalism, separation of church and state, the melting pot construct, cultural pluralism, and ethnic assimilation with religious differentiation. The first chapter is a chronological retelling of the ongoing restructuring of the synagogue to best meet the needs of a changing constituency while retaining its basic form and mission. The second is a pioneering study of one of the earliest east European immigrant congregations—its autobiography, as it were— drawn from its minute books. These accounts, written in Yiddish, record 845 meetings during the congregation's "forty years in the wilderness," as it attempted, under all manner of conflicting pressures, to balance the need for the retention of traditionalism and the increasing demands for change.

THE RABBINATE

Simha Assaf, in a study of the central and east European rabbinate, writes, "The rabbinate occupied a place of prime importance in the life of our people."[5] Nowhere is this more true than in America, for here, no matter what functions the rabbi was called on to fulfill, none was more important than to serve as an "intramural missionary," to win anew every rising generation to loyalty to faith and people. To do so demanded extra measures of faith, will, and devotion on the part of the individual aspirant and the community.

The chapter on the Rev. Isaac Leeser describes his pioneering efforts in extending the parameters of the rabbinic office far beyond what they had been elsewhere. The determined quest for rabbinical training by a graduate of the University of Rochester, class of 1856, years before there were rabbinical seminaries in this country, unfolds in "From Campus to Pulpit." "American Rabbis for America" tells of the successful attempt by the American Jewish cultural and monied establishment at the turn of the century to bring to America one of the best-known Jewish scholars, Solomon Schechter, to lead the Jewish Theological Seminary of America. Its mission was to be to train American rabbis for the rapidly growing east European immigrant community—a grand act of noblesse oblige out of concern for the spiritual needs of "other people's children." "New York Chooses a Chief Rabbi," the section's major study, is an account of the "other people"—i.e., leaders and members of the Orthodox congregations on New York's Lower East Side—joining, in 1887, to bring from eastern Europe a noted rabbi and declare him their chief rabbi. They were confident in their faith that his presence, authority, and influence would help solve all manner of problems plaguing the immigrant community, as they publicly expressed it in a broadside distributed on New York's Lower East Side by the Association of the American Hebrew Congregations, April 1888: "Many are they who stray like sheep. . . . Their fathers and grandfathers were as Orthodox as we. Is it not our duty to prevent our children and grandchildren from straying like them?"[6]

A PLURALISTIC RELIGIOUS COMMUNITY

In 1886, Judah D. Eisenstein informed the readers of the Orthodox newspaper, *New Yorker Yiddische Zeitung*, "Judaism in America is divided into three factions or parties: Orthodox, Conservative and Reform; that is to say, those who believe in the old tradition, those who steer a middle course, and those who take an extreme position."[7] This section's opening essay describes how this tripartite division came to be.

The relationship between the three parties has been in varying degrees, at different times, complementary and competitive. There was general recognition—though rarely stated—that all profited from the existing pluralism. The variety of patterns of religious observance and ideology offered a far larger number of American Jews congenial affiliation in the Jewish community than a monolithic system would have permitted. Each of the factions benefitted from the numerical strength of the whole.

Each was significantly affected by the presence of the others, none more so than the centrist movement, Conservative Judaism, which shared fluid boundaries with both of the others—hence the study "A Century of Conservative Judaism." In the competition for membership, the movements rose to high creativity, offering in eloquent expositions their distinctive vision and program for the securing of the Jewish future in America.

The three major studies deal with events in the religious life of the eastern European Jewish immigrant community. Why this emphasis on this segment of American Jewry? Although nearly 90 percent of America's Jews are of east European ancestry, the religious history of this community has been largely neglected in American Jewish historiography.

The singular spiritual qualities of this community have been little known or appreciated. Henrietta Szold, who met and taught Russian Jewish immigrants in Baltimore and New York at the turn of the century, did appreciate these qualities and celebrated them in her introductory essay to *The Russian Jew in the United States:* "To say what the Russian Jew is and can be is to prophesy the course of the twentieth century. . . . The Russian Jews will use the institutions created by [the German and Sephardic Jews before them] as the stock on which to engraft their intenser fervor, their broader Jewish scholarship, a more enlightened conception of Jewish ideals, and a more inclusive interest in world Jewish questions."[8] These qualities revitalized existing institutions and enterprises and created new ones for American Jewry's ongoing endeavor to secure its future.

The chapters that follow present case studies of activities in the American Jewish religious community—some of individuals, some of organized groups, one of a religious movement—all in service of communal survival through creative continuity. The accounts are almost wholly drawn from primary source material. These historical studies were done more in consonance with the anthropologist's eye than the philosopher's mind—appropriate to the study of a religious community given more to deed than to creed.

ACKNOWLEDGMENTS

My deepest gratitude goes to friends and colleagues Professors Milton R. Konvitz of Cornell University, Jonathan D. Sarna of Brandeis University, and Leon J. Weinberger of the University of Alabama for their reading of the manuscript and for their insightful comments and helpful suggestions.

Studies in this volume were published over a span of more than three decades. They are reprinted by permission:

"Quest for a Viable Identity" (as "Survival in a Free Society"), © Abraham J. Karp, in *Haven and Home: A History of the Jews in America,* Schocken Books, 1985, pp. 360–373;

"Overview: The Synagogue in America: A Historical Typology," in *The American Synagogue: A Sanctuary Transformed,* ed. Jack Wertheimer, © 1987 by the Jewish Theological Seminary of America; printed in paperback by the University Press of New England;

"Isaac Leeser of Philadelphia," in *Quest for Faith, Quest for Freedom,* ed. Otto Reimherr, © 1987 by Associated University Presses, Inc.;

"Simon Tuska Becomes a Rabbi," *Publications of the American Jewish Historical Society,* © 1960 by the American Jewish Historical Society, vol. 50, no. 2 (December 1960): 79–97;

"Solomon Schechter Comes to America," *American Jewish Historical Society Quarterly,* © 1963 by the American Jewish Historical Society, vol. 53, no. 1 (September 1963): 42–62;

"New York Chooses a Chief Rabbi," *Publications of the American Jewish Historical Society,* © 1955 by the American Jewish Historical Society, vol. 44, no. 3 (March 1955): 129–198; and

"A Century of Conservative Judaism in the United States," in *1986 American Jewish Year Book,* © 1986 by the American Jewish Committee and the Jewish Publication Society of America.

JEWISH CONTINUITY IN AMERICA

Introduction

Quest for a Viable Identity

Emancipation and enlightenment permitted the Jews to enter the modern world. Nowhere have they experienced these more fully than in America, where they have come to accept them as both a right and a mandate. It has been in America that Jews have undergone the fullest testing of their will and ability to retain their corporate identity in a free and open society. American Jews, as participants in Jewish history and the American experience, have had to weigh the demands of each on their personal and communal life.

In America, common citizenship tended to erase distinctions of creed and nationality. Whereas in Europe, assimilation had demanded an act of disassociation from one's own group—usually apostasy—in America one would become assimilated into the larger community unless one expressed, in word or deed, identification with the community into which he or she was born.

Assimilation was facilitated by many factors in America: no governmental designation of "Jew," small isolated communities, continued movement of immigrants uninhibited by communal or family restraints, no ancestral memories evoked by neighborhood, no webs of social relationships extending over generations. The maverick spirit, the social mobility of a frontier society, and the overriding ideology of a unified America, which later observers termed the melting pot, further facilitated smooth entry into the larger society. In the context of such an America, the Jews who wished to retain their Jewishness had to fashion an identity that would be acceptable to America and that would prove vital to themselves. In this enterprise, they could look to the solution in a similar challenge worked out by Jews in Europe entering the modern world.

EUROPEAN PRECEDENTS

Jews of western Europe learned early in their experience of enlightenment and emancipation that the society that was beginning to open its doors to them was asking that they justify their continued corporate existence and that the national state that was haltingly extending civic and political rights was asking for a public group identity that would fit comfortably into the body politic and would be compatible with fullest loyalty to the nation. These twin demands were given dramatic expression in the Swiss clergyman Reverend Johann Caspar Lavater's challenge to Moses Mendelssohn in 1769 to refute Christianity or accept it and by Napoleon's twelve questions to the Assembly of Jewish Notables convened in 1806, which asked: Can Jews abiding in their Jewishness be full participants in the life of the modern state? More pointedly, Lavater suggested the need for Jews to justify their continued existence, and Napoleon pointed to the need for a new definition of Jewish corporate identity. The response to the latter challenge was direct and immediate. Abraham Furtado, president of the assembly, well expressed it: "We no longer are a nation within a nation." Joseph Marie Portalis *fils*, a commissioner of Napoleon, described it: "The Jews ceased to be a people and remained only a religion."

Their new definition as a "religious community," the emancipated Jews felt certain, would make their status more comprehensible and more acceptable to their neighbors. But the need to explain, to justify continued Jewish existence persisted. Of what benefit is it to the nation, of what value to the Jew? Why should the modern world tolerate Jewish survival? Why should a Jew remain a Jew?

Ideological justification for Jewish survival in the modern world was formulated by Reform Judaism in Germany early in the nineteenth century. Seizing on the then-popular theory—which nationalism made emotionally acceptable and intellectually respectable—that each people is endowed with a unique native genius, Rabbi Abraham Geiger applied it to the Jews. The ancient Greeks, he noted, possessed a national genius for art, philosophy, and science. The Jewish people, he asserted, are likewise endowed with a *religious* genius, which it is obligated to use in service to humankind. Rabbi Samuel Holdheim, among others, expressed what came to be known as the Mission Idea: "It is the destiny of Judaism to pour the light of its thoughts, the fire of its sentiments, the fervor of its feelings, upon all the souls and hearts on earth. . . . It is the Messianic task of Israel to make the pure law of morality of Judaism the common possession and blessing of all the peoples on earth."[1]

The Mission Idea, which held that Israel is a *religious community* charged with the divine task to bring the knowledge of the One God and the message of ethical monotheism to the world, made Jewish group survival acceptable in the modern national state. It provided the ideological justification for continued communal existence: the world needs this "priest-people" and its "God-ordained mission" of spiritual service; the Jew, as a Jew, in undertaking this divine mission fulfills the noblest of purposes in life, service to humankind.

THE MELTING POT

The challenge posed by emancipation and enlightenment was altered in the New World by the new context of Jewish existence. In the European experience emancipation was the end product of a long struggle, in part a victory won, in part a gift granted. The declaration that announced American nationhood proclaimed liberty not as a gift but as an unalienable right. In the unfolding social and cultural climate of the New World there were, in theory, no doors barring entry into mainstream America; one assimilated into the larger society, unless one chose voluntarily to retain an individual group identity.

Throughout the nineteenth century, the melting pot concept (although the term was used only in the twentieth) demanded cultural assimilation of immigrants. As early as 1782, Michel Guillaume Jean de Crèvecoeur noted, "He is an American, who leaving behind him all his ancient prejudices and manners, receives new ones from the new mode of life he has embraced, the new government he obeys, and the new rank he holds. . . . Here individuals of all nations are melted into a new race of men."[2] In 1845 Ralph Waldo Emerson wrote in his journal: "In this continent-asylum of all nations . . . all the European tribes . . . will construct a new race, a new religion, a new state."

Later, the Anglo-Jewish writer Israel Zangwill, in his play *The Melting Pot* (1908), would apply this concept to the Jewish experience in America. A young Russian-Jewish composer is writing an "American" symphony, celebrating an America where a new nation is being forged. The symphony completed and performed, David Quixano speaks his vision: "America is God's crucible, the Great Melting Pot, where all races of Europe are melting and reforming . . . Celt and Latin, Slav and Teuton, Greek and Syrian, black and yellow, Jew and Gentile. . . . How the great Alchemist melts and fuses them with his purging flame! . . . Here shall they all unite to build the Republic of Man and the Kingdom of God. Peace, peace unto ye unborn millions fated to fill this giant continent— the God of our children give you Peace."[3]

This was America as perceived by immigrant Jews. It demanded of them that they divest themselves of their distinctive ways and absorb and adopt the language, the values, the ways of native American culture. It was an enticing invitation, an opportunity to rise above minority status and become members of God's new Chosen People—the American nation. If it was difficult for immigrants to cast off the known and the habitual that provided them with stability in the new and threatening environment, it was easy and alluring for their children to wash away the marks of Old World peculiarity and become *Americans.*

The same America that called for ethnic and cultural assimilation accepted religious differentiation. The retention of a particular religious identity was viewed as a contribution to the well-being of a nation that was a gathering of peoples. The sense of continuity and security the immigrants needed to feel at home in their new home could be provided by a transplanted church. For the sake of national unity the nation willed the immigrant to take on new political loyalties, new cultural ways, but for the sake of social well-being it permitted religious diversity.

Organized religion was esteemed in nineteenth-century America because, as Louis B. Wright concluded, it was the most effective "of all the agencies utilized by man in maintaining traditional civilization on the successive frontiers in America."[4] It was not lost on the Jews, newly arrived in America, that here churches and other religious institutions were favored, that those who supported them were respected, and that the synagogue was viewed as an American religious institution. They therefore maintained the synagogue not only in support of their own Jewish interests but also as an expression of patriotic obligation. Dr. Jacob de la Motta expressed it at the dedication of the Mikveh Israel synagogue in Savannah, Georgia, in 1820: "Were we not influenced by religious zeal, a decent respect to the custom of the community in which we live should actuate us to observe public worship."[5]

Building a house of worship in America was not so much an act of piety as an expression of good citizenship; maintaining it was bearing witness to America as a land of freedom and opportunity.

Identity as a religious community established the appropriate corporate status for Jewish survival in America; justification for that survival required an ideology with roots in Jewish ideals and experience, as well as a promise of service to America and the world. The Mission Idea of Reform Judaism served well the western European immigrant Jew. It lifted the difficult and anxiety-filled experience of relocation to an enterprise of high, selfless purpose. It fit in well with the rhetoric used to vindicate America's national expansion in the language of "mission" and "manifest destiny."

The rabbinic conferences that formulated the ideology of Classic Reform affirmed these emphases. The Philadelphia Conference of 1869 stressed the messianic goal of Israel, defining the dispersion of the Jews in terms of divine purpose; the Pittsburgh Conference of 1885 proclaimed: "We consider ourselves no longer a nation, but a religious community." Such a status enabled the Jews to retain communal identity while becoming integrated into the American nation.

The Jewish religious community proclaimed itself a partner and coworker with other religious denominations in "doing God's work" and allied itself with progressive forces outside the religious establishment. The Pittsburgh Conference stated: "We acknowledge that the spirit of broad humanity of our age is our ally in the fulfillment of our mission, and therefore we extend the hand of fellowship to all who operate with us in the establishment of the reign of truth and righteousness of men."[6]

As a religious community whose dominant ideology was the Mission Idea, and that sought alliances with the forces of "broad humanity," it was closer in spirit and practices to liberal Christianity than to traditional Judaism. There were, of course, factors that bound Jews of all persuasions one to another, factors such as national and historic identity, but these were precisely those which Reform chose to suppress. By the end of the nineteenth century American Jews had evolved a public identity that, they were certain, America would understand and accept: a religious community in a larger setting of cultural assimilation.

By the beginning of the twentieth century, it became apparent that, while such an identity might be acceptable to America, it could not serve Jewish survival needs. It deprived Judaism of the cultural-national vitality that gave it viability, and it made no provision for the growing number of Jews who defined their Jewish identity as cultural rather than religious.

The first serious call for a redefinition of identity came from a venerated leader of Reform Judaism, Rabbi Bernhard Felsenthal. In his "Fundamental Principles of Judaism," published in the first issue of the Zionist periodical the *Maccabean* (November 1901), he states: "*Judaism* and *Jewish Religion* are not synonymous. . . . *Jewish religion* is only part of *Judaism*. . . . Judaism is the sum of all ethnological characteristics which have their roots in the distinctively Jewish national spirit. . . . The Jewish People is the fixed, the permanent, the necessary substratum, the essential nucleus. Judaism is not a universal religion. There would be no Judaism without Jews."[7]

Felsenthal shifted the definition of identity from religious concepts to the living community of Jews. To be sure, Judaism contains "certain universal elements, certain absolute and eternal truths," but "Judaism does not limit itself to these universal elements." It requires "a certain characteristic ritual, certain established national days of consecration, certain defined national symbols and ceremonies." Survival demands an acceptance of Jewish distinctiveness and the fostering of those elements of culture and nationality which constitute the "national Jewish religion." How does a national religion serve larger humanity? Felsenthal suggested that as each national religion strengthens its inner wisdom and truth, and "exerts beneficial influence upon its particular nation, it also adds to the adornment of all humanity."

The realities of American life led Felsenthal to accept the organization of American Jewry as a religious community, with the synagogue as its central institution. But, he reminded, "The Jews are *not only* a religious community, and Judaism is *not only a religion.*" As implementation of his broader definition of Judaism, he urged commitment to Zionism and greater emphasis on Jewish culture and folkways. What was crucial to him was that the Jews, organized as a religious community, accept a broad cultural-national definition of Judaism and that this be reflected in the life—purpose, programs, activities—of the congregation and community.[8]

From the camp of traditional Jewry in the first decades of the twentieth century came a voice calling for reassertion of *national* Jewish identity. Israel Friedlaender, professor at the (Conservative) Jewish Theological Seminary and a founder of the Young Israel movement in Orthodoxy, argued that a religion divorced from nationality and culture was false to authentic Judaism and could therefore neither save nor survive. If Judaism is to continue in America, he argued, "it must break the narrow frame of a creed and resume its original function as a culture, as the expression of the Jewish spirit and the whole of Jewish life. The Jew must have the courage to be different, to think his own thoughts, to feel his own feelings, to live his own life . . . but with the consciousness that only in this way does he fulfill his destiny, for the benefit of mankind." Friedlaender envisioned a Judaism "that does not confine itself to synagogues and hospitals, but endeavors to embrace the breadth and width of modern life." He urged a reassessment of the possibilities of Judaism in the American environment—a Judaism comprised of national and cultural as well as religious elements. "The true American spirit," he observed, "understands and respects the traditions and associations of other nationalities." The American idea of liberty "signifies liberty of conscience, the full, untrammeled development of the soul." Judaism owes it not only to itself but to America to become the center "of the spiritual life of the Jewish people in the dispersion," for in doing so it will become "a most valuable and stimulating factor in the public and civic life." Friedlaender questioned the melting pot concept as being truly reflective of the American spirit and rejected the implication that "Americanization" demands cultural assimilation. He laid the foundation for what was later termed "cultural pluralism" by pointing to the receptivity of America to national cultures and to the contribution that an ethnic culture, sustained and developed, would make to American civilization.[9]

Both Felsenthal and Friedlaender recognized that the realities of American life mandated that American Jewry be organized as a religious community, but they argued for a definition that was based not on American models but on the Jewish historic tradition. Religious leaders could plead for attention to inner Jewish spiritual and cultural needs, but immigrant Jews and their children had a higher priority, the need to be accepted by America—an America still conceived as a melting pot. What was needed was a new image of America—an America that would ap-

prove of a distinctive Jewish identity and welcome Jewish cultural creativity and expression.

CULTURAL PLURALISM

The danger to Jewish survival in the melting pot vision of America
was noted by two secular ideologists, Chaim Zhitlowsky and Horace M.
Kallen. Each, from his own viewpoint, called the concept inimical to
American civilization.

Zhitlowsky, the leading proponent of secular Yiddish cultural life in
America, argued that the melting pot was neither desirable nor possible,
for it robbed American civilization of the richness that variety bestows,
and the ethnic groups in response to their own needs would turn from
such an America. He called on America to harbor the "united nationalities of the United States." He proposed a "nationality-brotherhood,"
where "each individuality unfolds and brings out into the open all the
richness with which its soul may be blessed by nature."[10]

Such a peaceful, creative unity of national cultures would lead to
mutual enrichment. The individual nationalities would become channels
that would carry to their homelands, and thus to the world, the most
precious gift America could give, a model for a United States of the
World. His was a secular restatement of the mission idea in the context
of America. To the Jews it proclaimed that retaining their cultural national identity was a service to America, helping America to fulfill its
world mission. Zhitlowsky failed because he made the vehicle of national
expression the Yiddish language, but he prepared the immigrant generation for acceptance of the practical application of cultural pluralism.

It was Kallen, Harvard-educated disciple of William James, who gave
currency to the concept "cultural pluralism." His article "Democracy
Versus the Melting Pot" appeared in the *Nation* on February 18 and 25,
1915, its argument that true democracy demands a vision of America
other than a melting pot. Kallen concluded his seminal essay with "the
outlines of a possibly great and truly democratic common-wealth":

> Its form would be that of the federal republic; its substance a democracy
> of nationalities, cooperating voluntarily and autonomously through
> common institutions in the enterprise of self-realization through the
> perfection of men according to their kind. . . . "American civilization"
> may come to mean . . . multiplicity in a unity, an orchestration of man-
> kind. As in an orchestra every type of instrument has it specific *timbre*
> and *tonality* . . . so in society, each ethnic group may be the natural in-
> strument, its temper and culture may be its theme and melody and the
> harmony and dissonances and discords of them all may make the sym-

phony of civilization . . . and the range and variety of the harmonies may become wider and richer and more beautiful.[11]

As Kallen later stated, his vision of America grew out of his Jewish cultural milieu. In his 1910 essay, "Judaism, Hebraism, Zionism," he had declared his commitment "to the persistence of a 'Jewish separation' that shall be national, positive, dynamic and adequate." Critical of those who would take from the Jewish group its group identity and uniqueness, he rejected Reform's recasting the nature of corporate Jewish existence. Kallen's concept of cultural pluralism, his vision of an America enriched by its distinctive ethnic groups, provided justification for continued Jewish communal life. What Zhitlowsky was saying to his immigrant, Yiddish-speaking, European-oriented audiences, Kallen was advocating for the "Americanized" Jew: the individual's need of life-giving cultural sustenance within his own ethnic group and the benefit of such corporate cultural activity to the nation.

In American Jewish life, the period between the two world wars was the era of cultural pluralism, in which Jewish life underwent significant change. The "Americanizing" settlement houses were replaced by Jewish community centers. The communal Talmud Torah become the most prominent and successful Jewish educational institution. Hebrew, Zionist, and Yiddish culture found expression in synagogue, center, school, and summer camp programs. In response to the new definition of Judaism and the new understanding of American democracy, synagogues began to transform themselves from "houses of worship" to "synagogue-centers," offering a broad spectrum of activities "for every member of every family."

JUDAISM AS A CIVILIZATION

The chief philosopher of the redefinition of Judaism was Mordecai M. Kaplan, and the title of his magnum opus, *Judaism as a Civilization,* sums up his definition. Judaism is "the evolving religious civilization of the Jewish people." The Jewish people is the enduring, creative constant. Civilization includes "peoplehood, history, language, music, literature and art." The motive force of this civilization is religion, and like the civilization itself, religion is evolving, growing, changing. Yet basic forms persist: "The conservation of form with the reconstruction of meaning has been the history of the Jewish civilization."[12] The citizen of a modern state, Kaplan argued, "is not only permitted but encouraged to give allegiance to two civilizations; one, the secular civilization of the country in which he lives, and the other the Christian which he has inherited from the past."[13] Thus the American Jew lives at one and the same time in two civilizations, that of America and that of his group.

Kaplan felt no need to offer justification for Jewish group survival because "if Jewish life is a unique way of experience, it needs no justification."[14] But the need for justification was felt, nonetheless, and it was provided by Kaplan's most gifted disciple, Rabbi Milton Steinberg. In *To Be or Not to Be a Jew,* Steinberg made an eloquent plea for *living in two civilizations.* He recognized that Jews "are accustomed to the circumstance that Americans will be identified with minority churches. After all, every religious denomination in our country is of such a character vis-à-vis the total population." But the Jew, he argued, is "associated with a cultural tradition as well." Thus, the American Jew has two cultural traditions, the primary American and the ancillary Jewish. To the question: "Can a person live happily, without stress and strain, in two cultures?" Steinberg answered, "yes," and proposed that "out of such husbandry of the spirit may well emerge a cultural life richer than any the human past has heretofore known." Steinberg offered yet another justification of Jewish group survival, one that foreshadowed the emphasis on the fulfillment of the individual that would characterize American society in the twentieth century and beyond: "If the only effects . . . were to bolster the shaken morale of the Jews and to enrich their personalities with the treasures of a second heritage, the whole effort would have justified itself from the point of view of American interests. Quite obviously America will be benefitted if its Jews, who constitute one segment of its citizenry, respect themselves, if they are psychologically adjusted rather than disaffected, if they are richer rather than poorer in spirit."[15]

Kaplan's concept of Judaism as a religious civilization came to be accepted as "normative" in Conservative Judaism. It also influenced Reform's own redefinition of Judaism as "the historical religious experience of the Jewish people." From Felsenthal, Friedlaender, and others, the survivalist American Jew had learned that Judaism demanded a definition deeper in tradition and broader in meaning than a "religious community." The concept of cultural pluralism made the broader definition proposed by Kaplan acceptable in the American context.

BEYOND CULTURAL PLURALISM

Kallen concluded his essay with the query: "But the question is, do the dominant classes in America want such a society?" With the wisdom of hindsight, we can assert that the more relevant question would have been, "Do the ethnic groups want such a society, which would continue their ethnic identity?" Hindsight permits us also to provide the answer: The children of the "ethnic" immigrants did not want to remain "ethnics."

Cultural pluralism had its able ideologists and zealous devotees, but it was becoming clear that America as a "nation of nationalities" was being rejected by those most affected. The proponents of cultural pluralism then seized on a felicitous sentence of the historian of immigration, Marcus L. Hansen, and gave it the status of a sociological law: "What the son wishes to forget, the grandson wishes to remember." If the second generation rejected cultural pluralism and ethnic identity, the third generation, more secure and at home in America, less in need to "Americanize," would retain or reestablish ethnic identity. C. Bezalel Sherman points out, however, "Alone of all the white ethnic groups do American Jews supply proof for the correctness of the Hansen thesis. Only among them do the grandchildren manifest a greater desire to be part of the community than the children of immigrants."[16] Will Herberg offers an explanation: "We can account for this anomaly by recalling that the Jews came to this country not merely as an immigrant group but also as a religious community; the name 'Jewish' designated both. . . . When the second generation rejected its Jewishness, it generally, though not universally, rejected both aspects at once. . . . The young Jew for whom the Jewish immigrant-ethnic group had lost all meaning because he was an American and not a foreigner could still think of himself as a Jew, because to him being a Jew now meant identification with the Jewish religious community."[17] Part of the "religious revival" that marked American life in the decades following World War II, third-generation Jews did not return to the *folkways* of their immigrant forefathers, but they did return to the *faith* of their grandparents.

Sherman noted, "Contrary to secularist prophecy, America has manifested no desire to become a nationality state, and religion has shown no inclination to die, a lesson not lost on the acculturated Jew."[18] Quite the opposite: "Acculturation" spurred Jews to retain their particularistic identity, to affiliate and participate in that which the American culture esteemed—their religious heritage.

The melting pot still operated, but not as had been theorized. As minorities entered it, their ethnic distinctiveness was indeed melted away, but their religious tradition—Protestant, Catholic, Jewish—was stressed. America became, as Herberg termed it, "the land of the three great faiths."

No one accepted this terminology with greater alacrity than did the Jew. American Jewry, viewed as a religious community, was lifted out of the constellation of ethnic minorities: from the status of 3 percent of the population to one-third of the nation. Symbols of this new status abounded in mid-century. A minister, a priest, and a rabbi sat on the dais at civic functions, including the inauguration of a president; radio and television apportioned time to each of the three faiths. Small wonder that American Jews accepted once again the identity of the religious community. (They delighted most of all in the use of the term "Judeo-Christian heritage." This concept raised the Jew to full partnership—and senior partner at that!)

It was noted, however, that the posture of a religious community did not reflect a true religious revival, such as transforms the life of the individual. It was more an expression of organization and form than a way of life or commitment.

American Jewry designated itself a religious community, while at the same time holding on to its own self-identification as a people. The establishment of the state of Israel, and the ready identification of American Jewry with its destiny, indicated an identity beyond that of a "faith" group.

DUAL-IMAGE IDENTITY

What had developed was a new corporate posture that we may term a *dual-image identity.* Having neither an initiator nor an ideologist, it was fashioned by the folk wisdom of the people. In simple words it says: Before the world, in our relationship with the larger society and with other groups, we retain the identity of a *religious community.* Internally, in our understanding of ourselves, in assessing our needs, in ordering our priorities, in fashioning our institutions, we are a *people,* possessed of our own unique *civilization.* When we address America, we do so as one of its religious communities; in relating to other Jewish communities, we do so as a component segment of a world people and civilization.[19]

This dual-image identity persisted into the new image of America that emerged in the sixties and seventies, a land of *ethnic identity.*

Once again, the Jewish community seems to be the exception. In the midst of a serious crisis that beset the Christian religious establishment, Jews retained the posture of a religious community. Jewish seminaries expanded their student bodies, and a new one, the Reconstructionist, was founded; synagogues have retained their membership to a remarkable degree. There was little evidence that American Jews were anxious to call themselves an ethnic minority. There was a significant increase in the influence and activities of local Jewish federations and community councils and of the Council of Jewish Federations and Welfare Funds on the national scene. This might have seemed a move from religious to communal identification. But, as in the 1920s, when the congregations became miniature communities in function, so in the 1970s the community councils were becoming expanded congregations. In their relations with the larger community they present the posture of representing a religious group, and they sponsor programs of culture and education that heretofore had been deemed the province of the synagogues. The dual-image identity was maintained in the "decades of the ethnics." American Jews utilized structure and symbols recognized as religious to express their national, "peoplehood" identity.

American Jews, from the beginning, have attempted to fashion a corporate identity that would make for their full integration into the American nation, while at the same time retaining their identification with the people civilization called Israel. They drew optimism for the possibility of such an identity from America's commitment to political federalism, which posits multiple political associations and loyalties. They saw this as giving legitimacy to a pluralistic society and argued that religious, ethnic, cultural pluralism was not only permissible but mandatory if America was to be a truly democratic society. Their quest for a corporate identity that would make for group survival began with all emphasis on "objective public identity" but has become increasingly influenced by the need to give fullest expression to "self-identity."

Practical viability has been given higher priority than ideological consistency—as in the separation of form and content in the dual-image identity. Long-range hazards have been mitigated by apparent present well-being. American Jews have been so intent in their faith that "America is different" that they have rarely sought to assess their situation in the context of world Jewish experience or consider seriously lessons that could be drawn from the accounts of other communities in similar question. They continue to believe, buoyed by the historic memory, as Arthur A. Cohen noted, that the American tradition and the American environment made it possible for the Jew to become an American without ceasing to be a Jew.

Church historian Winthrop S. Hudson notes that for two thousand years Jews have been faced with the challenge "to maintain the integrity of their faith while meeting demands for coexistence within a non-Jewish culture and society." It was a difficult task to accomplish, especially in the modern era of emancipation and enlightenment, but it was done "even in America where the temptation to abandon a dual allegiance was greatest."

Because American Jews are heirs to a two-millennial experience in the world and a tricentennial experience in America of bearing "the burden of both commitments," they can make a signal contribution to America. Says Hudson: "Perhaps one of the greatest contributions of Judaism to the United States will be to help other Americans understand how the United States can be a truly pluralistic society in which the pluralism is maintained in a way that is enriching rather than impoverishing, a society of dual commitments which need not be in conflict but can be complementary. . . . From the long experience of Judaism, Americans of other faiths can learn how this may be done with both grace and integrity."[20]

There has been in America a turning away from group concerns to the needs of the individual. Formerly, the group, be it ethnic or religious, would justify its existence by demonstrating its worth to American institutions; today, a group is esteemed to the degree by which it enhances the life of its individual members. The sentiment is abroad that America's real strength is rooted in the well-being, psychological as well as physical, of its individual citizens.

The pledge and promise of America was *life, liberty,* and *the pursuit of happiness.* The first was secured by economic expansion and opportunity; the second was assured by democratic institutions; the third, the pursuit of happiness, remains the continuing challenge. There is a growing feeling that this challenge can best be met by religioethnic groups that nurture the well-being of the individual. To the extent, then, that the Jewish community in America provides its members those components of religious vision, cultural expression, and group association that strengthen purpose and fulfillment, it contributes to the preservation of a pluralist and democratic America. To strengthen such a group, to enhance its effectiveness, can only contribute to America's well-being. American Jews can thus view their participation in the Jewish enterprise as both a response to their own individual and community needs and a civic contribution to the nation in which they have found both haven and home.

PART ONE

The Synagogue in America

From the beginning of Jewish communal life in America, the synagogue has been the chosen instrument for the expression and transmission of Jewish identity. It became the central institution for establishing and enhancing Jewish association, for inculcating Jewish knowledge, and for the fostering of Jewish loyalties. Hebrew University Professor Ernst Simon has observed that, whereas in the European Jewish experience inertia has assured Jewish identity, in America inertia makes for assimilation. In America, a positive Jewish identity requires an active effort of affiliation or association. Each generation has to be re-won for Judaism, and the institution charged with that responsibility has been the synagogue.

Historian Salo Wittmayer Baron reported in his *The Jewish Community:* "The religious congregation has been the mainstay of all organized Jewish life. . . . The synagogue has continued to attract the relatively most constant and active participation of a large membership. . . . Despite our highly agnostic age it must be remembered that total congregational membership in the United States vastly exceeds, numerically, Jewish membership in purely philanthropic undertakings."[1]

1 The Synagogue in America

A Historical Typology

Little more than half a year after the first Jews arrived in New Amsterdam, the Reverend Johann Megapolensis of the Reformed Dutch Church wrote to his superiors in Amsterdam, on March 18, 1655: "Last summer some Jews came here from Holland. . . . Now again, in the spring some have come . . . and report that a great many of that lot would yet follow and then build here their synagogue."[1] The Reverend's apprehensions that the handful of immigrant Jews, the first of their people on the North American continent, planned to form a congregation, were well-founded. Governor Peter Stuyvesant complained to the directors of the Dutch West India Company, owners of the colony, on June 10, 1656, that "the Jewish nation . . . have many times requested of us free and public exercise of their abominable religion." He urged that this not be granted, for "giving them liberty, we cannot refuse the Lutherans and the Papists."[2] A year earlier, in July 1655, in reply to a petition by the recently arrived Jews to "purchase a burying place for their nation," the council of the colony noted, "that inasmuch as they did not wish to bury their dead in the common burying ground, there would be granted them when the need and occasion thereof arose, some place elsewhere of the free land belonging to the Company,"[3] and on February 22, 1656, two members of the council were "authorized to point out to the petitioners a little hook of land situated outside of this city for a burial place."[4]

Within a year of their arrival, the Jews of New Amsterdam had already joined together for their common religious needs, the first of which was consecrated ground for burial. Congregation Shearith Israel, mother synagogue of American Israel, may well be right in dating its inception to the year of arrival, 1654. The first congregation's initial holding, as in the case of many of the congregations that followed, was a cemetery. As the Reverend Mr. Megapolensis feared, many were to follow the first arrivals and "did build here their synagogue" for worship, for religious celebration, and for the transmission, retention, and fostering of Jewish loyalties.

The establishment of a congregation was not always a profession of religious piety, nor was the building of a synagogue evidence of a desire to worship. For many, the act was primarily an expression of Jewish identity or a response to what was believed to be an American "demand."[5] The definition and function of the American synagogue were forged within the parameters of Jewish needs and American demands, changing in response to the changing religious needs of the American Jew and in conformity both to the possibilities for public expression of corporate Jewish religious life that America afforded and to the perceived limitation upon it that America imposed.

SYNAGOGUE COMMUNITY

In colonial America, synagogue and community were synonymous, and the congregation served all communal needs. "No colonial American Jewish community ever sheltered more than one permanent synagogue," Jacob R. Marcus has noted, "and the local synagogue virtually exercised a monopolistic control over every Jew within its ambit."[6] It was able to do so because it alone provided for the basic needs of the recently arrived or native Jew: companionship with fellow Jews, a place to worship when piety or other sentiments demanded it, circumcision for a son and a wedding service for a daughter, kosher meat for the table and a proper burial in consecrated ground, and the opportunity to give or to receive charity. Hannah, the widow of Moses Louzanda, remained on the pension rolls of Shearith Israel from 1756 through 1774, and Levi Michaels petitioned "the President and Elders of the Synagogue in the City of New York" in 1764 for "a sum of money, upon loan, as you in your wisdom shall see meet" to enable him to return to Montreal. In 1762 Abraham I. Abrahams was engaged by the congregation "to keep a publick school . . . to teach the Hebrew language and translate the same into English, also to teach English, reading, writing, and cyphering." Seven years later he described his tenure as "having served this congregation in the capacity of a Ribbi [sic]" (the term designates teacher, for there were no ordained rabbis in America until the middle of the nineteenth century).[7] The chief religious functionary was the reverend minister (called *hazzan*), who led the services, officiated at religious ceremonies (although permission to officiate at a marriage had to be granted by the lay leaders), and on occasion would be permitted to preach. The governance of the congregation in all its aspects was firmly in the hands of lay leaders, who kept a tight rein.

For the immigrant Jew, the synagogue provided the comforting continuity of familiar liturgy and ritual and the security of the company of fellow Jews who would care and provide for one's family in time of need or loss. In a society that was splintering into a religious pluralism, the synagogue was becoming part of the religious landscape, its adherents clothed with an identity coherent and acceptable to the host community. Marcus suggests that "in its hegemonic aspect the colonial American synagogue did parallel contemporary Protestantism" as it moved "toward the integration of [its] communicants into one rounded-out religious, social, and eleemosynary whole."[8] What permitted the local synagogue to exert "monopolistic control" was the place and power of the church in colonial America. Franklin Hamlin Littell notes that the major religious factor in colonial America was the established church and that even in the early years of the Republic, the great Virginians, Washington, Jefferson, et al., "were all committed to the cause of organized religion . . . the large majority as taxpayers and patrons of the state church."[9] The Jews, seeking acceptance, laboring at integration, took instruction and example from their Protestant neighbors, choosing the synagogue as the institution that would establish their community; indeed, they regarded congregation and community as synonymous.

No more than a half dozen congregations served colonial Jewry. They were small and far apart. Almost one hundred miles separated the nearest two, New York's Shearith Israel and Philadelphia's Mikveh Israel. Although separated by distance, they were united by their shared Jewish identity, by a similar Sephardi synagogue rite, and by family and business ties. One congregation could freely turn to another in time of need, whether it was for aid in building a synagogue, for the loan of a Torah or other ritual objects, or for guidance in religious matters. This unity found symbolic expression when four of the six—the Hebrew congregations in the cities of Philadelphia, New York, Richmond, and Charleston—united in an "Address . . . to the President of the United States," George Washington, in 1790. Only the most northern congregation in Newport, Rhode Island, and the most southern, in Savannah, Georgia, framed their own letters. The Jewish communities spoke through their congregations, which were the sole communal institutions.

The mother congregation, as we have noted, was Shearith Israel, New York. The earliest extant minute books disclose that by 1728 it was a fully functioning organization presided over by a "Parnaz and Two Hatanim" and served by three functionaries:

The Hazzan Mosses Lopez de fonseca shall be obliged to attend at the Sinogog at the customary hours twice every weekday, and three times on the Sabbath and feasts. . . . Semuel Bar Meyr a Cohen of this Kahall shall be obliged to kill at severall places and Sufficiently for the whole Congregation. . . . Valentin Campanall Shamaz shall be obliged to attend at the Sinogog and shall call the Yehidimz that they may assemble togeathere at the usual hours . . . he shall keep the Synagog candlesticks &

lamp clean and make the candles also shall keep the sestern supplyed with watter.[10]

The hazzan, *bodek* (ritual inspector), and *shamash* (beadle) were paid £50, £20, and £16, respectively, and were supplied with firewood and *matzot* (unleavened Passover bread). The congregation met in a house on Mill Street, "commonly known by the name of the Jews' synagogue."[11]

Dr. Alexander Hamilton, of Annapolis, Maryland, on a visit to the New York synagogue on Rosh Hashanah, 1744, wrote:

> I went in the morning with Mr. Hog to the Jews' sinagogue where was an assembly of about 50 of the seed of Abraham chanting and singing their doleful hymns, dressed in robes of white silk. Before the rabbi, who was elevated above the rest, in a kind of desk, stood the seven golden candlesticks transformed into silver gilt. They were all slipshod. The men wore their hats . . . and had a veil of some white stuff which they sometimes threw over their heads in their devotion; the women, of whom some were very pritty, stood up in a gallery like a hen coop. They sometimes paused or rested a little from singing and talked about business.[12]

The colonial synagogue represented continuity. It replicated in form and function the Jewish houses of worship on the European continent—adopting the same prayers, garb, melodies, and decorum, or lack thereof. It was that, and more. Already in colonial days it was part of the American religious landscape. When Rabbi Haim Isaac Carigal, emissary from Hebron, preached in the Newport, Rhode Island, synagogue on Shavuot, 1773, the twenty-five Jewish families were joined at the service by neighbors, including Governor Joseph Wantan and judges Oliver and Auchmuty. The dedication of a new synagogue in Charleston, South Carolina, on September 19, 1774, was attended by Governor William Moultrie and civil and military officers of the state and city. The South Carolina *State Gazette* noted: "From the style of the building and the splendor of its ornaments, we can perceive that, that injured people . . . have realized their promised land . . . in the blessed climes of America. The shackles of religious distinctions are now no more . . . they are permitted to the full privileges of citizenship, and bid fair to flourish and be happy."[13]

The Jews perceived that in America "religious distinctions" expressed by the synagogue were not bars to "privileges of citizenship." To the contrary, the synagogue served as a symbol of the Jews' at-homeness in America. In 1788 the Jews of Philadelphia solicited contributions for building a synagogue from "worthy fellow Citizens of every religious Denomination . . . flattering themselves that their worshipping Almighty God in a way and manner different from other religious societies will never deter the enlightened citizens of Philadelphia, from generously subscribing."[14] They were correct in their surmise. Benjamin Franklin was the first to respond with a generous £5, and he was joined by a who's who of the community.

The small size of the Jewish communities in colonial America permitted only single congregations, all following the Sephardic (Spanish and Portuguese) rite. As established churches became prevalent, community and congregation were seen as identical. Functionally, the total needs of Jewish life were provided for by the congregation, which in turn exerted considerable discipline over its membership. The synagogue as an institution of religion afforded the immigrant community an accepted and respected vehicle for its integration into the larger society.

RITE CONGREGATIONS

During the first half of the nineteenth century, while the Jewish population of the world doubled in size, that of the United States increased twenty-five fold, from some two thousand to fifty thousand. Migration from central and western Europe provided the numbers and helped diversify the rapidly growing network of Ashkenazi synagogues. By midcentury, the ten synagogues of the early 1800s had grown to almost ninety. New York City alone could boast of twenty, Philadelphia, five. Their rite varied with country of origin, as noted in the Lyons–De Sola *Jewish Calendar of 1854.*[15] New York's synagogues ranged from the Portuguese *minhag* (rite) Shearith Israel to seven following the Polish minhag, seven the German, and one the Bohemian; in addition, one was described as a Netherlandish congregation. As identified by their min hag, the five synagogues of Philadelphia were Portuguese, German (two), Polish, and Netherlandish. The *Calendar* also discloses that communal function was becoming diversified. No fewer than forty-four societies served the charitable and educational needs of New York Jewry; Philadelphia listed seventeen; and Cincinnati, served by two Polish and two German congregations, supported eleven societies and schools.

Factors external and internal to Jewish life were responsible for the proliferation and diversification of synagogues. In the 1830s Francis Grund described the role of religion in America: "Religion has been the basis of the most important American settlements; religion kept their little community together, religion assisted them in their revolutionary struggle. . . . The Americans look upon religion as a promoter of civil and political liberty; and have, therefore, transferred to it a large portion of the affection which they cherish for the institutions of their country."[16]

The immigrant Jew quickly perceived that religion and religious institutions were highly esteemed in America, that those associated with these institutions were respected as "good citizens," and that religious diversity was viewed as a mandate of democracy. Thomas Jefferson stated to Jacob de la Motta that in religion the maxim is "divided we stand, united, we fall."[17] The diversity that the synagogue brought to the religious scene was a service to democracy. Hence, to build and maintain a synagogue was a response to the American as well as to the Jewish call to duty. Wherever Jewish and American interests fortified each other, American Jews responded with enthusiasm.

American church bodies, whether Episcopalian, Presbyterian, Lutheran, Methodist, or Baptist, reflected differences not only in religious ideology but also in European national origins. The immigrant Jews took example and did the same. The rite synagogues afforded the immigrant the needed comfort and security of the known, the habitual. Continuity of ritual and familiar liturgical melodies sung by *landsleit* (fellow immigrants from the same town or region) eased the trauma of migration and resettlement. The first Ashkenazi congregation, Rodef Shalom of Philadelphia, came about naturally, when in 1795 a group of Jews felt more comfortable praying "according to the German and Dutch rules" than the Sephardi rite of Mikveh Israel. The older congregation accepted this division as natural and right.[18] This was not the case in New York's first Ashkenazi synagogue, B'nai Jeshurun. In May 1825, fifteen members of Shearith Israel requested that they be permitted to conduct their own services in the synagogue. The request was summarily turned down by the trustees, who stated that they could not "recognize any society or association for religious worship distinct from Congregation Shearith Israel." Nonetheless, the petitioners were determined to found a new congregation, explaining: "We have a large portion of our brethren who have been educated in the German and Polish minhag, who find it difficult to accustom themselves to what is commonly called the Portuguese minhag."[19] They also argued that increasing immigration and dispersal of places of residence would soon make another synagogue necessary. The leaders of the mother congregation never replied to the seceders; unhappy with the defection, they would not wish them well, but, recognizing the inevitable, they knew that to protest would be futile.

Once begun, the process of congregation building, aided by growing immigration, continued. In 1828, a group of German, Dutch, and Polish Jews left B'nai Jeshurun, which styled itself as an English synagogue recognizing the authority of London's Great Synagogue and its rabbi, to found Anshe Chesed. Eleven years later, a group of Polish Jews left both synagogues to form Shaarey Zedek, which in turn was abandoned by a group of its congregants who organized Beth Israel in 1843.

The professional traveler I. J. Benjamin II describes the situation well: "The Portuguese claimed a sort of patronage—over the immigrants. . . . Accordingly, the immigrants founded a new synagogue. Those of English origin . . . introduced the London minhag with a sermon and discussion of congregational matters in English. The Germans . . . could not endure the English; the Poles could not endure the Germans; so there was soon division and separation in all directions. New York spread ever more rapidly; distances became too great, the synagogues too small."[20]

Most separations were acrimonious, occasioned by disagreement on a point of ritual or liturgical usage, social distinctions, ethnic loyalties, or personal peeves. What made possible this volatility and viability of the new congregations was the congregationalism that marked American religious life, legitimizing secession, and a constantly increasing immigration from numerous countries.

The same group that had left Shearith Israel to found B'nai Jeshurun in 1825 left it twenty years later to form Shaaray Tefilah. The immediate cause of the rupture was a contested election of trustees, which reached the state supreme court. On leaving, the dissidents were accompanied by the Reverend Samuel M. Isaacs, hazzan of B'nai Jeshurun, and its *shamash* (sexton), B. M. Davis. The religious rites, rituals, liturgy, and order of services remained identical in both congregations. Like its parent congregation, it remained fully Orthodox, worshipping "according to the rites of the Polish and German Jews."[21]

Isaac Leeser described Jewish religious life in 1844:

> We have no ecclesiastical authorities in America, other than the congregations themselves. Each congregation makes its own rules for its government, and elects its own minister, who is appointed without any ordination, induction in office being made through his election. . . . As yet we have no colleges or public schools of any kind, with the exception of one in New York, . . . one in Baltimore and another in Cincinnati, and Sunday schools . . . in New York, Philadelphia, Richmond, Charleston, Columbia, S.C., Savannah, and Cincinnati. . . . In all our congregations where the necessity demands it, there are ample provisions made for the support of the poor.[22]

Leeser anticipated an expansion of educational endeavors "as soon as we become more numerous," and his optimism was bolstered by the fact that, although "in the southern and western states the arrival of Israelites [was] but recent," there were already congregations in Mobile, New Orleans, Louisville, Cincinnati, Cleveland, and St. Louis.[23] The Israelites were becoming more numerous; they were settling in the cities and towns of the south and west and establishing congregations to answer their communal needs.

In the smaller communities, one congregation served the needs of all. Since the great majority of the Jews in these communities were immigrants from Germany, the congregational articles of incorporation often provided, as did those of Congregation Beth El of Detroit, that the

"Divine . . . services shall be held according to the German Ritual (Minhag) and not be changed." The congregation had been organized in 1850 at the urging of a pious woman, Sarah Cozens. That year twelve Jews founded the Beth El Society and brought Samuel Marcus from New York to serve as rabbi, cantor, teacher, *shohet* (ritual slaughterer), and *mohel* (circumciser) at an annual salary of $200. He instituted services, opened a Hebrew-German-English day school and organized the *Hevra Bikur Cholim* (society to visit the sick) to care for the sick and the dying. In 1854 he was succeeded by Dr. Liebman Adler, who had arrived from Germany and to whose duties was added preaching in German, all for a salary of $360. Dr. Isaac M. Wise, who had recommended Dr. Adler, was pleased to publish in the *Israelite* extracts of Beth El's constitution and bylaws adopted in 1856, translated from the original German:

1. An Israelitish congregation . . . should be one great family. . . .
3. [It] is obliged to establish and support regular and public divine worship . . . by warm, earnest and cordial participation. . . .
4. The education of the young in all its branches, especially in religion, is a duty involving the whole congregation. . . .
5. An appropriate, dignified and religious treatment of the dead is likewise a duty of the congregation.
6. [as is] The support of the poor co-religionists . . .
7. The congregation shall, in all its religious institutions, pay due attention to the progress of the age, and maintain the respect due to customs or laws handed down to us by our pious fathers. In case of innovation, this congregation shall attempt to remain in unity with the majority of the American congregations, and shall always attempt to produce uniformity in the American synagogue.[24]

Wise hails this permission for modest reform as "fairly opening the way to the *Minhag America* [the American rite]," a uniform prayer book for American synagogues, and sees in article 7 an expression of commitment to a united synagogue body, synod, and college.[25]

THE REFORM TEMPLE

In the second half of the nineteenth century the Reform movement began to make serious inroads. Within three decades it had enlisted the great majority of the leading congregations and grew ever more radical with each triumph. "The number of reform congregations prior to the Civil War was small," Leon A. Jick notes, but "by 1870, there were few congregations in America in which substantial reforms had *not* been introduced and in which an accelerating program of radical revision was *not* in process." The war had brought to a virtual end the large-scale immigration from Germany, which had trebled the Jewish population from 50,000 in 1850 to 150,000 in 1860. Few immigrants "who might have reinforced the ranks of traditionalism" arrived in the 1860s and 1870s; those who had arrived earlier were caught up in an assimilatory process that "the nationalist fervor generated by the war" had accelerated and that expressed itself through religious reform. "Respectability and Americanization were the goals; decorum, reform of ritual, and English were the means."[26] As Joseph Krauskopf noted, "From the moment that the American-born element began to make itself felt, it could not reconcile its mode of thought and its higher aspirations with the musty ghetto religious practices."[27]

In 1824, forty-seven members of the Charleston, South Carolina, Beth Elohim congregation petitioned for synagogal reforms. Rebuffed, they founded the Reformed Society of Israelites a year later, adopted articles of faith, worshipped from their own prayer book, with heads uncovered, to the accompaniment of instrumental music. The society lasted only eight years, but when Beth Elohim built a new synagogue, it voted "that an organ be erected in the Synagogue to assist in the vocal parts of the service." At the synagogue's dedication, the Reverend Gustav Poznanski advocated "the reformed practice of conducting certain portions of the service in the vernacular."[28]

American Reform Judaism was, however, an imported product. Thus in 1842 in Baltimore, a group of German immigrants, influenced by the Hamburg (Germany) Reform Temple, protested the Orthodoxy of the existing congregation and formed the *Har Sinai Verein,* "the first American synagogue founded *ab initio* on a Reform basis."[29] On Shavuot of that year, following refusal of the loan of a Torah scroll by the mother congregation, the Torah portion was read from a printed Bible. The new congregation used the Hamburg temple prayer book at its Rosh Hashanah services, singing hymns from its hymnal to the accompaniment of a parlor organ. Its "most learned member," Max Sutro, "reader, preacher and teacher of the congregation," questioned whether it should observe the Tisha B'Av day of mourning for the destruction of the temple in Jerusalem for fear that "Christian fellow-citizens . . . [seeing us] mourning the destruction of Jerusalem [would conclude] that we are longing to return there and that our patriotism for our present homeland cannot be a true, genuine and fervent one."[30]

A dozen years later, the now radical Reform congregation did hold a service on the "Anniversary of the Destruction of Jerusalem," but it was not a service of lamentation—it was one of commemoration and celebration. As its rabbi, David Einhorn, explained in his prayer book *Olath Tamid,* "The one temple in Jerusalem sank into the dust, in order that countless temples might arise to thy honor and glory."[31]

One such temple was Har Sinai in Baltimore; another was Emanu-El in New York, founded in 1845. Its road to Reform was gradual. In its first prayer room, "the front seats were set apart for use of men, and those at the back for use of the women," and a volunteer choir was established.[32] Leo Merzbacher (called "Mr." in the early minutes) was engaged as rabbi and G. M. Cohen as cantor at salaries of $200 per annum. The rabbi's discourse was central to the service. The congregation took offense when he failed to preach and requested that he give notice in advance if circumstances prevented him from speaking. He was also asked to introduce hymns in German at the services and to supply the board with a list of the prayers to be said on the forthcoming High Holidays. In the spring the board inquired of the rabbi how the Purim service might be conducted *mit kirchliche Hinsicht* (with becoming churchly respect). At the first annual meeting a committee was appointed to assist the Reverend Dr. Merzbacher with liturgical reforms.

Two and one-half years after its founding, having purchased a church building, Emanu-El began its program of reform: it introduced an organ to accompany the choir, the triennial cycle of Torah reading, and a confirmation service for boys and girls; at the same time, it abolished "old-fashioned, useless ceremonies, such as reading a portion of the Law by a so-called Bar Mitzvah boy, making a *mi-sheberach* (public blessing) for one called to hear the Law read, and eventually the calling up to the reading of the Law."[33] The weekday elementary school was replaced by a religious school that met on Saturday and Sunday. In 1849, the rabbi was directed to prepare a ritual for services in German and English. Five years later, the rabbi and a committee prepared a revised prayer book, and this was followed by the abolition of the wearing of a *tallit* (prayer shawl) and the second-day observance of the festivals. Americanization also prompted the adoption of English as the language of the pulpit. "Patriotic in all things," the chronicler of Emanu-El explains, "they desired that the language of the land should be heard in their shrine, and Dr. Merzbacher was asked to speak in English at times . . . and a committee was appointed to secure an English lecturer." Mr. R. J. De Cordova, a popular professional lecturer, was engaged to deliver lectures every other Saturday, "the topics to be selected after consultation with the minister." Although there was sentiment in the congregation that "the lecturer ought to be a theologian," De Cordova's tenure extended from 1856 through 1864. When Merzbacher's successor, Dr. Samuel Adler, permitted the uncovering of the head during the English lecture that was delivered after the Sabbath service, the congregation decided to do away with wearing a hat at the service as well.[34]

Har Sinai and Emanu-El had been founded as Reform congregations, but more typical were those that began as traditional congregations and subsequently moved toward Reform, as was the case of Congregation

B'rith Kodesh in Rochester, New York. Founded in 1848 by German Jews, mainly from Bavaria, it remained fully traditional until 1862, when an organ and choir music were introduced. Family pews followed in 1869. A year later, some of the more radical members succeeded in having the minister of the Unitarian church lecture at the temple. In 1873, Unitarian lecturer Dr. N. M. Mann and Rabbi Max Landsberg brought their congregations together for a Union Thanksgiving Service.

In 1879, David Rosenberg was elected president on the promise that he would remove his hat at services when occupying his official seat. He did so, bringing "down upon his unprotected head a storm of indignation and abuse from the older members."[35] Nevertheless, during his administration the wearing of hats was abolished. In 1883, the temple introduced a new ritual that "practically excluded the use of Hebrew from the services, the English language being substituted. It was the first Jewish congregation in the United States, and probably in the world to take this step."[36] In the prayer book that Dr. Landsberg published two years later he notes that "he cannot find adequate terms to express my admiration to my dear friend Rev. N. M. Mann, Pastor of Unity Church, for the kind interest he has taken in the preparation of this Ritual, and the valuable services he has rendered in making the English more idiomatic and perfect." Dr. Landsberg also notes that "the desire for English prayers is growing everywhere, and will soon become universal in this country" and welcomes "the recent attempt to introduce an English Service for Friday night at the largest temple in Cincinnati."[37]

The Cincinnati temple was Isaac M. Wise's B'nai Jeshurun. Wise favored the use of Hebrew in public worship because "dispersed as the house of Israel is in all lands, we must have a vehicle to understand each other in the house of God, so that no brother be a stranger therein."[38] The prayer book he edited, *Minhag America,* read from right to left. It was an abridged, altered text of the liturgy, retaining the traditional order and rubrics, with either an English or German translation facing the Hebrew text. The main service of worship was held on Friday evening. Dr. David Einhorn produced his radical Reform *Olat Tamid* prayer book, a completely altered liturgy in German with Hebrew selections reading from left to right, for Sunday morning services. Comprising scriptural readings, prayers, and hymns in the vernacular, the service was conducted by the rabbi and featured the sermon. In 1894, when the official prayer book of the Reform movement, the *Union Prayerbook,* was published, it was modeled on the radical Reform *Olat Tamid* rather than the moderate Reform *Minhag America.* The Reform temple had become a religiously radical institution.

The service of worship was rabbi-centered, but governance and authority in the temple were in lay hands. Thus, at the annual meeting of the Chicago Sinai congregation on March 26, 1885, the president reported that questions on such matters as the rite of circumcision, the language of prayer, and the observance of a holiday on the Sunday nearest to it had been presented to the rabbi, Dr. Emil G. Hirsch, for his opinions, which were then circulated to the congregation. Thereupon the congregation decided through a vote what its policy would be. The rabbi had voiced his position, but the decision was in the hands of the laity.

The Reform temple served its congregants as a bond to Judaism and a portal to America. Beyond that, its leaders saw its purpose to be the creation of a new Judaism, suited to the new age and their new homeland. As the president of the Sinai congregation expressed it: "We have discarded many obsolete rites. . . . Our work will not be completed until we have removed every unnecessary vestige, until we have built on the old foundation a new structure, in keeping with the modern style of religious architecture. . . . [For] the observance of certain obsolete customs is inconsistent with true religion. . . . When darkness gives way to light, Sinai congregation will have the proud satisfaction of having served in the front ranks among the founders of a religion, broad enough for all humanity to stand on."[39]

The Reform temple was the product of the confrontation of the immigrant German Jews already undergoing cultural assimilation with an America that welcomed such integration and valued religious institutionalization, denominationalism, and experimentation.

THE ORTHODOX *SHUL*

In the last decades of the nineteenth century, when the great majority of American synagogues were turning to Reform Judaism, a new kind of congregation appeared on the American scene, the east European Orthodox *shul* (synagogue). The first "Russian-American Jewish Congregation" (as its chronicler J. D. Eisenstein called it) was organized on June 4, 1852, by east European immigrants and "several non-Russian Jews who were dissatisfied with the reform movement of their congregations."[40] It took the name Beth Hamedrash. A growing membership caused it to move to larger quarters twice in the first year of its existence. Among the organizers was Abraham Joseph Ash, who served as its rabbi. In 1856 it dedicated the former Welsh Chapel on Allen Street as its synagogue. Three "Portuguese" Jews provided almost three-fourths of the down payment of $4,000, leaving a mortgage indebtedness of $3,500. Rabbi Ash, having succeeded in eliciting support from wealthy nonmembers, enlarged his field of solicitation through a letter in the *Occident*. The appeal is prefaced by a description of the congregation: "Its founders were few . . . [but] one by one, daily, men of Israel united with them . . . and now it is supported by about eighty men. . . . Our members are poor in money . . . they labor hard for their daily bread, yet set aside from their limited means a portion for the holy offering."[41]

Ash also describes its activities: daily services, morning and evening; open all day for study; every evening "a portion of the law is expounded publicly . . . and there are persons who study the law for themselves, either in pairs or singly"; on Sabbaths and festivals "the house is full to overflowing"; "it is filled with all sorts of holy books, several sets of Babylonian and Jerusalem Talmuds, the Turim, Rambam, Rif, Schulchan Aruch, Rabbinical Opinions, Bibles, commentaries, Midrashim, Kab-balah." The rabbi sounds the challenging note that marked east European American Orthodoxy: "It is the only institution in the land, that is oth-erwise a waste, as regards religious knowledge, which laughs to scorn every scorner, him who goes astray. . . . It bids defiance to every unbe-liever and infidel . . . devoid of knowledge and devoid of faith . . . [who] makes lighter the yoke of the service of the Lord and his commandments . . . in the eyes of the blinded Hebrews . . . in order that they may be snared and caught in the net of the times."[42]

According to Leeser in his introduction to the Ash letter, the func-tion of the Orthodox shul was to promote "Talmudical knowledge and meetings for prayer"; in Ash's view, it was to wage the battle of the Lord for the true faith, against the infidel shepherds who were leading God's flock astray. Its more immediate and mundane mandate was to serve the needs of its immigrant congregants. This was no easy task, for their needs went beyond religious ministrations to like-minded communi-cants. Coming from different sections of the European continent, they brought with them diverse customs, and, feeling the need for the famil-iar, they felt impelled to transplant religious usage as they had known it in the Old World. It was not until later, however, that mass immigration permitted such diversification and that Jews coming from Russia, Po-land, Romania, Hungary, Lithuania, Galicia, and Bohemia would form their own *landsmanshaft* (common geographic area of migration) con-gregations.

The diversity of ethnic origin of the congregants made synagogue membership volatile. It was the usual and the accepted thing for congre-gations to splinter, sometimes in vying for power or even out of personal pique. Thus, after the dedication of the new synagogue of the Beth Hamidrash, a conflict between Rabbi Ash and the congregational presi-dent over the question of official authority and "honor" led to synagogue disturbances, contested elections, a court suit, and a split in the congre-gation. In 1858, a group led by Rabbi Ash formed a new congregation, the Beth Hamidrash Hagadol. Three years later, a split took place in the new congregation, this time over liturgical rite when a "musical cantor" was engaged for the High Holidays.

With the rapid increase in immigration, synagogues on New York's

Lower East Side proliferated, and the competition between them became keen. It expressed itself in ever "grander" synagogues and ever more costly imported "star hazzanim," climaxed by the importation of the world-renowned cantor Pinchos Minkowsky from Odessa at "the enormous salary of $5,000 per annum." The strain imposed on the resources of the congregations, Eisenstein reports, soon brought the inevitable crisis, and this expensive luxury had to be discontinued.[43]

Moshe Weinberger, in his *Jews and Judaism in New York,* estimates that there were 130 Orthodox congregations on the Lower East Side in 1887. Their function was "to gather twice daily, or on the Sabbath to worship together, to visit the sick, to provide a proper and honorable burial for the dead, and to help a brother member in time of need. But the highest ambition [was] to build an imposing synagogue edifice."[44]

It is, of course, not surprising that an immigrant community would transplant the institutions that had served its needs in the "old country." Oscar Handlin notes this about Christian immigrants to America. "The immigrants thought it important to bring their churches to the United States, to reconstitute in their new homes the old forms of worship."[45] The east European Jewish immigrant transplanting his synagogue, his *hevra* (mutual interest society)-congregation, to America, was engaging in an American immigrant experience. What role and function it served him in his life we can discern from a glimpse at some congregational constitutions and from a study of the minute books of the early years of one such congregation. The constitution and bylaws of the Beth Hamidrash Hagadol, New York, adopted in 1887, provide that the Ritual of the Congregation shall be conducted in accordance with the *Shulchan Aruch* (the Code of Jewish Law), that *Nussach Ashkenaz* be the only prayer book used for services, and that the Beth Hamidrash shall be open morning and evening for the holding of services and the study of Jewish texts. One who openly violates the Sabbath is ineligible for membership, as is one who is married "otherwise than in accordance with the law of Moses and Israel." If taken ill, the member will be visited daily by two brother members; if deathly ill, a person will be sent "to watch at the death bed, and to perform the religious rites." If a member, his wife, or children should die, the congregation will not only defray all funeral expenses, but will provide ten members to accompany the funeral to the cemetery, four of whom shall perform the burial ceremonies and rites; it will send a *minyan* (a quorum of ten men necessary for public worship) to the house of mourning, and a committee of five will "call and tender the sympathy of themselves and in behalf of the congregation."[46] Absent the extended family, the greatest benefits the congregation could provide were concern and brotherly care in case of sickness or death. The minutes of the congregation record a resolution that extends to a member the benefit of paying only one-half the pledge he publicly made at the reading of the Torah—no small inducement for membership to an immigrant for whom the best way to attain status would be through a display of generosity.

Although the salaried officers listed are "Rabbi, Chazan, Sexton and Secretary," only the duties of the latter three are described. The rabbi was considered a communal, not a congregational, functionary, in accordance with the usage in European communities. The governance of the congregation was American: president, vice-president, treasurer, and trustees. The title "president" was already a product of Americanization, the earlier incumbents in the 1850s and 1860s having borne the title *Parnas.* The Orthodox shul was further Americanized by incorporating the rabbi as a congregational functionary in recognition of the American practice of making the congregation, not the community, the functional corporate body. Thus the constitution of sister congregation Kahal Adas Jeshurun, adopted in 1913, devotes article 12 to the rabbi or *maggid* (preacher). "No Rabbi or *Maggid* can be accepted by this Congregation, who is not in possession of bona fide certificates *(smichot)* of at least three celebrated authorities on theology of Russia and Poland."[47] The benefits provided are similar to those of the Beth Hamidrash, as is the case in other congregational constitutions. The constitution of the Anshei Sefarad Synagogue of Manchester, New Hampshire, before listing benefits, states: "All brothers must keep the synagogue holy. It is forbidden to talk or to walk about during services. It is forbidden to smoke in the synagogue. One must wear clean clothes and clean shoes . . . and to refrain from spitting on the floor."[48]

The history, form, and function of one Orthodox shul, Beth Israel, Rochester, New York, is typical.[49] From 1848 to 1870 Congregation Berith Kodesh had served the entire Rochester Jewish community, "German, Englishmen and Poles, all acting in harmony."[50] In the late 1860s it began veering toward Reform Judaism, and the east European Jews, mainly of Lithuanian origin, formed congregations of their own, one in 1870 and another in 1873. A year later these joined together to form Beth Israel, which in all aspects was an Old World institution transplanted on new soil.

The time from the founding of the new congregation in 1874 to the building of its synagogue in 1886 was marked by congregational growth and division, by the acquisition of improved synagogal facilities, and by the professionalization of religious functionaries. Determined to retain its primacy in the face of growing competition from the new congregations produced by dramatically increasing immigration, it undertook the building of a grand synagogue. The cornerstone was laid with appropriate pomp and ceremony on June 27, 1886, and three months later the local press was able to report: "Yesterday was a memorable day to members of the Beth Israel Congregation. Shortly after 3 o'clock they moved from their old church on Chatham street, in which they had worshipped for years, into their new synagogue on Leopold street."[51]

The congregation was run by four officers—a president, vice-president, secretary, and treasurer—and four trustees. The one prerequisite for the presidential office was the ability to sign one's name. The first salaried functionary of the congregation was a shamash—collector responsible for maintaining the facilities and ritual objects, for arranging the burials in the congregational cemetery, and for directing (though not leading) the services. The first hazzan, Kalman Bardin, was a shohet, in keeping with the European tradition. He had the scholarly competence to serve as hazzan, but apparently lacked the voice, and from 1879 on the congregation was served by a succession of professional cantors. Tension between lay leaders and professionals was generally high, and tenure was precarious.

Time and again the question was raised whether a congregation needed a rabbi. East European Jewry knew a communal, not a congregational, rabbi. The west European and American Reform practice of using congregational rabbis as preachers, leaders of worship, and ambassadors to the world outside was strange to them. When in 1895 a conflict with a rabbi developed into a public scandal, the congregational president offered this defense in the public press: "A rabbi is not a minister. He does not belong to one congregation, but to the city."[52]

Now and again congregational schools were organized and then dissolved. In the European community, education was a private or communal concern, not a province of congregational responsibility. Parents sent their sons to a *heder* (private school for religious instruction) or engaged a tutor. The community maintained a school for the children of the poor. For Beth Israel to have an educational program was an accommodation to the "American way," an accommodation it was ready to make only when forced to do so by the demands of the congregants. In the first decade of the twentieth century, the congregation took the lead in organizing and supporting a communal Talmud Torah and, in response to the demands of younger members, conducted a weekday school for the sons of members and a Sunday school for their daughters.

The congregation served as an arena for acting out interpersonal relationships and provided members with a safe place in which to release their hostility. Strong words could be exchanged, charges brought, fines levied, sanctions imposed—and then reconciliations arranged, fines rescinded, peace restored. For the German Jewish immigrant, his temple served as a portal to America. For the east European immigrant, his shul served as a sanctuary and haven—a sanctuary in an America that threatened his faith, a haven to which one could return to join cronies in worship or fellowship.

Among the chief characteristics of the Orthodox shul retained in the twentieth century were the use of Yiddish, the landsmanshaft composition of its membership, and the centrality of the cantor.

In many congregations Yiddish was constitutionally mandated as the language of "all transactions." But with time and acculturation, English was grudgingly permitted to intrude. The constitution of two of the newer Rochester congregations, Agudas Achim (1911)[53] and Vaad Hakolel (1913),[54] mandated that all congregational business be conducted in Yiddish only. Beth Israel's constitution, adopted in 1906—when the congregation was already in its thirty-second year—retained Yiddish as its language but added that "speaking in the English language may be permitted."[55] In 1913, the long-established Kahal Adas Jeshurun of New York City, although retaining "Juedish-Deutsch," gave its members the "liberty to avail themselves of the English language during proceedings."[56] Congregation Reidfei Zedek Anshe Ritove, organized in 1885, adopted bilingualism only in 1930, accepting both the Yiddish and English languages.

Newark's Congregation Anshe Russia was its leading Orthodox synagogue. Similarly, congregations in many American cities bore the name of a European country, city, or town. The Warsaw and Bialystok synagogues of New York, for example, were composed of members who had come from these large cities, but small towns also gave congregations their names, as, for example, Anshe Janover, Anshe Balshovtza, Anshei Lebovner Wohliner.[57]

The star cantor continued to reign in the shul in the first decades of this century, which became known as the golden age of the American cantorate. The weal and woe of a congregation often depended on its ability to obtain and retain such a star. He could pack the synagogue and fill its coffers through the sale of tickets for High Holiday services.

All three of the characteristics described above came in for criticism. With English excluded from the services and governance, it was pointed out, the sons of immigrants could not participate in synagogal affairs and were discouraged from attending services. The landsmanshaft designation marked the shul as an Old World institution to a generation of young Jews seeking acceptance by the new. The centrality of the cantor shunted to the side gifted rabbis who might have made a more telling contribution to the solution of what Dr. Judah Magnes saw as the main problem of the synagogue "not so much an economic question or one of organization, as it is spiritual . . . the revival of religious enthusiasm."[58]

A solution was attempted by members of the second generation, the Young Israel movement. Organized in 1912 by a group of young men on the Lower East Side, its goal was to transform the shul into an Americanized synagogue that offered decorous services and a program of educational, cultural, and social activities using the English language but that remained fully Orthodox. The Young Israel Movement announced that the days of the transplanted east European shul were coming to an end and that America's Jews, even the Orthodox, were in need of a new type of synagogue that would serve traditional Jewish needs, but in a manner that would be attractive and meaningful to a generation undergoing rapid integration into the American scene.

THE SYNAGOGUE-CENTER: IN ITS URBAN SETTING

Mordecai M. Kaplan, who helped found Young Israel, viewed with alarm the condition of the synagogue in 1918. Noting that it owed its existence "more to the momentum of the past, than to any new forces created in this country," he warned that only the concentration of "all possible material and moral resources" might save "the synagogue from impending doom."[59] He proposed that a new type of synagogue be created, a Jewish center whose purpose would be to afford its users "pleasures of a social, intellectual, and spiritual character."[60] Such a synagogue-center, a *beth am* (house of the people) should provide "Jewish elementary school facilities; recreational facilities such as gymnasia, showers, bowling alleys, pool tables and game rooms; adult study and art groups; communal activities; religious services and festival pageants and plays; [and] informal meetings of friends and associates."[61] Kaplan saw social togetherness rather than religious worship as "the primary purpose of congregational organizations."[62] He was the founding rabbi of the Jewish Center (on Manhattan's West Side), which incorporated a synagogue, an assembly hall, a gymnasium, a swimming pool, meeting rooms, and classrooms.

The evolution of the synagogue from a worship-centered institution, as were both the Reform temple and the Orthodox shul, into a multifaceted entity serving the social, cultural, and spiritual needs of the community, as Kaplan advocated, began in the postwar years. The change was due in part to the new needs of a rapidly Americanizing community, in part to the response to a new conceptualization of America and the role of a minority culture within it, and in part to forces that had brought about a similar development in the American church. Henry Kalloch Rowe, in *The History of Religion in the United States,* notes that "up to 1890 most churches seemed to thrive . . . [then] conditions began to change. A shifting population drifted into the churches and out again." In the twentieth century, the change in conditions of life brought about the institutional church. "The principle on which it was organized was the obligation of the church to minister to all the highest needs of the human personality. . . . The institutional church opened its door every day. It equipped a gymnasium and baths. It provided a reading room and library. It organized classes for mental improvement. It provided wholesome recreation and the social opportunity of clubs."[63] The institutional church was created to retain the urban masses for Christianity; the synagogue-center had a similar purpose—to win the adherence to Judaism of the sons and daughters of the immigrant generation, a Judaism now more broadly defined as a civilization rather than a faith.[64]

The synagogue-center drew its ideological justification as an American institution from cultural pluralism, whose proponents argued that a minority group has both the right and the duty to retain and develop its culture. Indeed, such adherence and creativity were not only in the best interests of the individual and his group, but were a singular contribution to the strengthening of democracy and the flourishing of American civilization.[65] A synagogue so conceived and so fashioned had a great appeal for a generation of American Jews who were the children of east European immigrants and wanted to maintain their Jewish identity but who were also intent on becoming fully integrated into the American scene.

The Reform temples, Marshall Sklare states, "hesitated to expand their activities and to gain too many new adherents. . . . They were suspicious of too much nonreligious activity on synagogue premises," which would be an expression of "racial consciousness." They did not want to attract and serve "the unaffiliated," who were of a lower social and economic class.[66] The Orthodox shul viewed expansion as change and resisted it because any change, in its view, imperiled the faith.[67] The new expanded synagogue was the creation of the new emerging religious movement, Conservative Judaism, conforming to its definition of Judaism as an evolving religious civilization. In some instances, it was established by seceding members of an Orthodox synagogue; more often it resulted from the transformation of an existing synagogue from Orthodoxy to Conservatism.

Rochester's Beth Israel did not appoint an English-speaking "teacher and preacher" until the fourth decade of its existence. In 1911, Jewish Theological Seminary–ordained rabbi Paul Chertoff was elected "to deliver lectures and teach in daily school at a salary of $1,200, for one year trial." He was designated preacher or reverend, not rabbi; that title was reserved for the communal Orthodox *Rov.* The young preacher reorganized the weekday school for boys and the Sunday school for girls and organized Young Judea clubs for boys and girls and the Emma Lazarus Club for young ladies.[68] The synagogue building was alive with activity, but the congregation remained ambivalent about the role of a congregational rabbi and the scope and nature of congregational activities. In 1915, a group of younger members, apparently encouraged by Rabbi Chertoff, began to confront the issue. By the fall of the year they published their conclusion and solicited participation: "Recognizing that it is our duty as Jews to bear witness to the truths of our Faith in our days and generation as our Fathers did in theirs . . . we hereby constitute ourselves a Jewish congregation for the purpose of conserving Judaism."[69]

Their fathers had established an Orthodox shul; now, in response to their needs, they were organizing a Conservative synagogue, Beth El, which would have family pews for men and women; prayers in Hebrew and English; service conducted by the rabbi, cantor, and choir; congregational singing without an organ; the choir, composed of Jews; a congregation wearing hat and tallit; daily services; special services on Friday evening, Saturday morning, and holidays; and daily and Sunday school to be supported by the congregation.[70] The first three provisions separated them from the Orthodox movement, the next three from the Reform. Special emphasis was placed on education. The congregational constitution stipulated that the rabbi would "supervise the Sunday School and Hebrew School" and "establish . . . classes for adolescents and study circles of adults" in addition to attending all services and officiating at "all religious ceremonies." The rabbi was made the central congregational functionary, and the cantor was his associate and assistant. Within a year the group purchased and adopted for synagogue use the Park Avenue Baptist Church, and by 1922 it could boast of the largest congregational school in the city, with 270 pupils to Reform B'rith Kodesh's 175 and Orthodox Beth Israel's 100. In the 1920s and 1930s its Sisterhood, Men's Club, Junior Congregation, Boy Scout troop, youth clubs, and athletic teams made it "respected as an established coequal" of Temple B'rith Kodesh.[71]

Congregation Rodef Sholom, Johnstown, Pennsylvania, was established in 1885 as an Orthodox synagogue. In the 1930s, fearing that unless the synagogue was modernized the next generation would join the Reform temple, the board invited a Conservative rabbi, Ralph Simon, to "modernize" it. Rabbi Simon recalled:

> Very few changes [were made] in the Sabbath and holidays Synagogue service. It was only in Friday evening late service that changes could be made . . . sermons in English . . . decorum and interpretation of the liturgy. The major area of change was in the cultural and social programs. All the activities envisioned in the synagogue-center program of Dr. Kaplan were introduced. Adult education classes were organized. A good Hebrew school was conducted. There was an active Men's Club, Sisterhood and Youth Group. There were frequent programs of music, a new choir, dramatic presentations and guest speakers.[72]

Across the state in Scranton, Temple Israel was proud to report what a newly established synagogue could accomplish in but a year and a half:

1. *Education.* A Hebrew School . . . over 100 children attending daily. . . . The religious school meets every Sunday morning and the children are taught the elements of Jewish ethics, ceremonies and Jewish history.

2. *Social and Communal Activities.* Boy Scout Troop . . . second leading troop in the city. . . . Girl Scout Troop . . . carried away all the prizes for scout work.
3. *The Ham-Zam-Rim Society* . . . the musical glee club of the Junior congregation . . . only boys of musical and vocal talents are accepted.
4. *The Zadik-Zadik Club* of the Junior Auxiliary looks after the social programs.
5. *Junior Menorah Society* for high school boys and girls meets weekly for discussion . . . and papers are read by members.
6. *The Progress Club* consists of older sons and daughters of members.[73]

The emphasis of synagogal concern and activities was clearly on the youth. For the adult membership there were services, thrice daily, Sabbaths, and holidays; and "visiting speakers from New York were delighted to find such a large turn-out . . . at the late Friday night Services . . . considering the location of the Temple, being in the non-Jewish section of the city."[74]

Few congregations could have full programs of religious, cultural, social, and athletic activities. Most contented themselves with a synagogue center that served the religious and cultural needs of the majority of their congregants, its function being threefold: to act as a *beth hatefilah* (house of worship), a *beth hamidrash* (house of study), and a *beth hakenesseth* (house of assembly). Initially descriptive of the Conservative synagogues, this began to apply as well to a growing number of Orthodox and Reform congregations.

Orthodox Rabbi David de Sola Pool saw the synagogue-center as "one of the most promising features in American Jewish life. . . . The synagogue is tending to become once more a focus for Jewish needs and causes. In this lies a strong hope of a Jewish life once more integrated in and around the synagogue."[75] Others, however, felt some misgivings about the synagogue-center, as Reform Rabbi Abraham J. Feldman pointed out: "In actual practice, the Synagogue Center too often becomes a substitute for the Synagogue. . . . [Its] recreational and social attractions are primary, while the religious functions are little more than a concession to the proprieties. . . . Synagogue Centers have tended to detract from the centrality of religion in Jewish life."[76]

Conservative Rabbi Israel H. Levinthal, whose Brooklyn Jewish Center represented the synagogue-center at its best, was not unaware of its shortcomings, but nonetheless spoke of its potential contribution with satisfaction and optimism in 1936, when his congregation was at its height of activity and influence. "If the Synagogue as a *Beth Hatefilah* has lost its hold upon the masses, some institution would have to be cre-

ated that could and would attract the people so that the group consciousness of the Jew might be maintained. The name center seems to work
this magic with thousands who would not be attracted to the place if
we simply called it Synagogue or Temple. . . . The Center is a seven-day
synagogue. From early morning to late at night its doors should be open.
It is true that many will come for other purposes than to meet God. But
let them come."[77]

THE SYNAGOGUE-CENTER: IN SUBURBIA

In the years between the wars, the synagogue-center replaced the
classic Reform temple and the insular Orthodox shul as the prototypical
American synagogue. In post–World War II America, the synagogue became more than ever the central institution of the Jewish community.

During the 1920s and 1930s the synagogue had grown dramatically.
The Jewish population had increased by 40 percent, but the number of
synagogues had almost doubled, rising from 1,901 in 1916 to 3,118 in
1926 and to 3,738 in 1937.[78] What makes this growth all the more noteworthy is that the 1930s were the years of economic depression and a
time of difficulty for religious institutions, which were burdened with
heavy mortgage obligations inherited from the synagogue building boom
of the 1920s. The programs of expansion that had been undertaken in
the years of prosperity and optimism had to be curtailed and staffs pared.
Through it all, however, synagogues displayed a remarkable resilience.
All were hard-pressed and a few faltered, but almost none failed. In a
time of testing, American Jewry did not abandon its synagogues.

The war years witnessed an upsurge in the general influence of religion and the status of its institutions, which continued in postwar America. The postwar suburbanization of America greatly affected the country's Jewish population, which before 1945 had been concentrated in
urban areas. As Jews moved to the suburbs, the need to secure their status
led them to establish congregations and erect synagogues. The Jews became part of their new community through their religious institution,
which was accepted by the "natives" as part of the suburban landscape.

The *American Jewish Year Book* reported in 1954 that "the movement of the Jewish population to suburban areas continued to gain momentum" and "that the Conservative and Reform groups had been pio-
neers in establishing new synagogue centers in suburban areas."[79] It
noted further that the new synagogues being built "laid special stress on
original art forms" and had commissioned the work of leading artists.
All three religious movements were directing resources to the new suburban communities. The Union of Orthodox Jewish Congregations
launched a $300,000 campaign for a program to establish Orthodox con-
gregations in the suburbs. The New York Federation of Reform Syna-

gogues placed a pre–High Holidays ad in New York newspapers listing its congregations in the metropolitan area: there were thirty-three serving the 200,000 Jews in suburban Nassau and Westchester counties and fourteen serving the 1,345,000 Jews in the Bronx and Brooklyn. The architectural consultant for the Conservative United Synagogue claimed that, in 1954 to 1955 alone, 150 Conservative synagogues were being planned or constructed.[80]

Each movement claimed rapidly growing numbers of affiliated synagogues. All suburban synagogues boasted of increasing membership. The growth of synagogues and their status in the community were most pronounced in the area of education. Jewish school enrollment had risen from 231,028 in 1946 to 488,432 in 1956; that is, it more than doubled in the first decade after the war. Of that number, over 85 percent were in schools under congregational auspices.[81] In 1959, the *New York Times* reported that since the war fifty-seven Reform, sixty-eight Conservative, and thirty-five Orthodox congregations had been established in New York City's suburbs: "Congregations have sprung up in firehouses, banks and even Protestant churches. . . . The congregation in Harrison was organized as a Conservative temple, with an assist from a Protestant Episcopal minister."[82]

According to U.S. Bureau of Labor statistics, about 2,517 rabbis were serving congregations, and officials projected that "a sufficient supply of rabbis . . . is not likely to be available during the 1960 decade . . . to fill the openings which will be created by the formation of new congregations."[83] By the middle of the decade, however, it became obvious to observers of Jewish life that the bureau's projection had been too optimistic. Morris N. Kertzer noted that 1962–1963 "was the year of consolidation rather than expansion for the American synagogue,"[84] and Sefton D. Temkin wrote two years later that the same was true for the years 1964 and 1965. He noted that although there had been "no decline in Jewish religious life . . . the force of the upsurge, which characterized the American Jewish community immediately after World War II, has abated."[85]

The "upsurge" of Jewish religious life made the synagogue "suburbia's nuclear and most important Jewish institution."[86] Like its neighboring Protestant church, it emphasized "the ethical, moral and social values associated with religion, and the needs of living people."[87] Albert I. Gordon, in his study *Jews in Suburbia,* attributed the preeminence of the synagogue in suburbia in the mid-1950s not so much to its religious function as to its having been "usually the first organized body to provide a physical structure in which Jews can meet as Jews within the community . . . [because] it provides for the formal Jewish education of the children . . . and [because it] helps Jews feel Jewish even when there is little Jewish symbolism in the home." He describes the process of founding a suburban synagogue as beginning with the need for fellowship and friendship felt by the young couples newly arrived in a suburb. "A Jewish community center does not suffice, for they also need a religious school for their children, so they quickly conclude that a synagogue center with a rabbi and teachers will provide what they seek," an institution that will provide for their children's religious needs as well as for their own social and fellowship interests.[88] They soon find that the rabbi is available to counsel about the many personal and family problems that dislocation from extended family and integration into a new community and way of life may bring. They also find that the same rabbi who has become their counselor and friend is the recognized leader of the Jewish community as its esteemed representative to the general community.

Why did people affiliate? "Reasons vary," states Gordon, "because people vary":

> We want to give our children some kind of Jewish education, and we wish to be part of the Jewish community.
> The temple represents us to the Gentile world. They know through it that there is such a thing as a Jewish community. . . . In that way the Temple helps me and my family live as respected people.
> I belong to the synagogue because I have friends there. . . . It is true that we could get along without any synagogue . . . but our own non Jewish neighbors cannot understand that . . . so we are building one which will be a source of pride to all Jews and the whole community.
> We joined the temple to try to live a fuller life as a Jewish family unit. We want our children to know and appreciate their heritage.[89]

The great majority (83 percent), reports Gordon, thought their congregations were "doing a good job," but only 1.8 percent had cited "I am religious" as the reason for affiliation. Although most congregants were satisfied with the role and program of the postwar synagogue, sharp criticism was voiced for synagogues in which religious services played an auxiliary role to fellowship functions. Rabbi Eugene Borowitz spoke the sentiments of many of his colleagues:

> The average synagogue member . . . comes . . . to join the synagogue because there are few if any socially acceptable alternatives to synagogue affiliation for one who wants to maintain his Jewish identity and wants his children to be Jewish, in some sense, after him. Though this is not the only motive or level of concern to be found within the synagogue today, the Jew who does not rise above such folk-feeling unquestionably and increasingly represents the synagogue's majority mood. More than that, however, it must be said that he also represents the synagogue's greatest threat. . . . No one wishes to lose Jews for Judaism, but the time

has come when the synagogue must be saved for the religious Jew . . . [from] the indifferent and the apathetic who control it for their own non-religious purposes.[90]

Rabbi Gordon came to the defense of suburbia's synagogues: "The synagogue is not now and never was *only* a house of worship. It is also a center of fellowship for young and old. It provides leisure-time and recreational activities, as well as Jewish educational facilities, for young and old. It is the primary means by which identification as a Jew is currently achieved. Suburban synagogues are, in fact, synagogue-centers. They offer each Jew the opportunity to come to know his own rich heritage and to live his life as an American Jew."[91]

American Jews in the postwar decades chose to live a largely secular life, free of religious discipline, but at the same time demanded that American Jewry maintain a communal religious identity. For them this was the American way of life—to esteem established religion and its institutions, but to live free of its restraints. The synagogue-center was the institution that served well in this choice. To the world outside, it was a synagogue, a religious institution. For American Jews it was a center for Jewish fellowship; even the religious services and the cultural and educational activities served that function for the great majority of synagogue members.

In the postwar years, America accepted Will Herberg's image of America as the land of the three great faiths—Protestant, Catholic, and Jewish. That is to say, American Jewry was no longer considered one of many minority groups, but had risen to a prominent position among the leading religious and cultural groups of the nation. The tripartite status was expressed symbolically in a whole network of interfaith activities: joint church-synagogue visitations, teams of minister-priest-rabbi who made joint platform appearances at civic functions and college campuses and offered prayers at state occasions—activities that accorded Judaism parity and the Jew equal status. Because the synagogue was the vehicle through which this was accomplished, it established itself as the unchallenged central institution in American Jewish life.

The status of the synagogue was elevated in the 1950s and early 1960s through its participation with the church in spearheading the civil rights movement. The nation approved of organized religion fulfilling its mandate for social justice and none more so than America's Jews. For them, the synagogue was acting in the best prophetic tradition by helping to unfold the American dream. Through the synagogue, American Israel had entered the mainstream of progressive American enterprise. It seemed wise and rewarding for American Jewry to maintain a religious posture in a country in which religion was esteemed and its influence growing, as a Gallup poll conducted in 1957 indicated. Only 14 percent thought that the influence of religion was decreasing, whereas 69 percent believed that it was increasing.

THE CONTEMPORARY SYNAGOGUE: IN SERVICE OF THE INDIVIDUAL

The change in the cultural climate and the status of organized religion that took place in the late 1960s was as precipitous as it was dramatic. Americans turned their attention and concern from social betterment to personal satisfaction. The church as savior of society gave way to churches as servants of their communicants. The mainline Protestant denominations that had been in the forefront of civil rights activities suffered a loss of membership and influence. Fundamentalist groups, with their disdain for formalism, staid dignity, and impersonal authority and their emphasis on emotional expression, community, and charismatic leadership, grew in numbers. The privatization of religion eroded its influence. In 1970 a Gallup poll asked the same question as it had in 1957: "At the present time do you think religion as a whole is increasing its influence on American life or losing its influence?" Fourteen percent responded "increasing," whereas 75 percent stated "losing"!

The synagogue, which had benefitted from its association with the church in the "glory days" of American organized religion immediately after World War II, now was affected by the decline in status and influence of mainline Protestantism. However, to a degree unmatched by the major church denominations, the synagogues were able to retain their membership by becoming service synagogues ready to provide, as called upon, specific, discrete services: education; life passage rites for birth and Bar and Bat Mitzvah; wedding ceremony and celebrations; burial, mourning, and *yahrzeit* (anniversary of death) services; and various ministrations in the realm of spiritual social work.

The synagogue of the 1970s and 1980s, the "decades of the ethnics," has maintained its primacy because it continues to provide a spiritual and cultural nourishment that can be termed both religious and ethnic, and American Jews continue to prefer to live ethnically under a religious identity. Moreover, the synagogue has remained willing to adopt and adapt. In this era of pluralism and diversity, the synagogue has diversified itself into a mosaic of distinct and differing congregations, and individual congregations have effected inner diversification. A wide variety of synagogues serve a widely varied constituency. They range from a Hassidic *shtibl* in Brooklyn's Williamsburg or Borough Park, a prayer room presided over by a dynastic rebbe, to the Stephen S. Wise Temple across the continent in Los Angeles, with its staff of rabbis, cantors, educators, social workers, and executives administrating day care centers, schools, social service bureaus, and a fleet of buses.

Congregations grown large in the 1960s are attempting to answer the needs of the 1990s for the humanization and personalization of the synagogue. The *havurah* (fellowship), a product of the Jewish students' counterculture movement, has been embraced by a large number of synagogues. In 1973, Rabbi Harold M. Schulweis, who pioneered with *havurot* in his Congregation Valley Beth Shalom, Encino, California, shared his philosophy and experiences with his colleagues of the Rabbinical Assembly:

> We are challenged to decentralize the synagogue and deprofessionalize Jewish living so that the individual Jew is brought back into the circle of shared Jewish experience. . . . In our congregation, a havurah is comprised of a minyan of families who have agreed to meet together at least once a month to learn together, to celebrate together and hopefully to form some surrogate for the eroded extended family. . . . Cerebration must not eclipse celebration. . . . I know what it means for children to see ten Jewish males with hammers and saws helping to build a sukkah. . . . The havurot plan their own *Sedarim* (Passover home ritual meals). . . . They wrestle with the Haggadah and the decision to add and delete. . . . There was a death in the havurah. The widow had few members of the family around her. . . . I saw who was at the funeral, who took care of the children during the black week of the *shivah* (mourning period). . . . The havurah offers the synagogue member a community small enough to enable personal relationships to develop. It enables families to express their Jewishness. . . . Hopefully the synagogue itself will gradually be transformed into . . . a Jewish assembly [of] havurot. . . . My grandfather came to the synagogue because he was a Jew. His grandchildren come to the synagogue to become Jewish.[92]

Orthodox Judaism, especially the Young Israel movement, is meeting the challenge that suburbanization poses to the Orthodox way of life by making synagogues the hubs about which a Jewish community will be built. It views the synagogue as one of the quintessential Jewish communal institutions, the central institution that will give coherence and coordination to the rest. Advertisements in the *Young Israel Viewpoint*, inviting young families to move to the community served by a Young Israel synagogue, list these other institutions and services:

A Young Growing Orthodox Community
Young Israel of New Rochelle
Day Schools; New Completed Community Eruv; Yeshiva High School; Community Mikvah; Kosher Take-out Butchers; Kosher Bakeries; Good Access to Parkways; Easy Commute—25 minutes from Manhattan, Queens, N.J.[93]

The Young Israel of East Northport, New York, "near Nassau line in booming Suffolk county," where "the Accent is always on Torah education for all," promises "6 classes a week for adults," a day school "under the direction of Yeshivah Chofetz Chaim musmachim," and "luxurious, suburban living in modern, spacious homes."[94]

The American synagogue, coextensive with the entire historic experience of the Jews in America, has been remarkably sensitive to the changing needs of America's Jews and has responded by reordering its priorities and programs to meet these needs. It continues to retain its resilience and adaptability, but the problems besetting it are substantial. The power of the local Jewish community federations has grown, as vast sums from campaigns for overseas needs are now placed in their hands to allocate. More than half these sums are apportioned for national and local needs, and, as a general rule, federations choose the Jewish community centers to be their institutional counterparts in the community and allocate increasing subsidies to them. In the 1970s and 1980s, when synagogue building had all but ceased, multimillion-dollar centers continued to rise. Their new facilities and communal subventions enabled them to compete successfully with the synagogues in cultural and fellowship activities—activities generally of lesser Jewish content than those provided by the synagogues. With the federations and centers attracting the more affluent and able lay leaders, the financial burdens of the synagogues are becoming all the more difficult to bear. Adding to these problems is the changing nature and the high mobility of the Jewish community. As fewer Jews enter business and more become salaried professionals, the burden of maintaining the synagogues built by the businessmen—as a rule, generous and enterprising—will fall on the shoulders of professionals, who tend to be more conservative in giving and more timid in venture. The increasing mobility of American Jewry, making for a generation of consumers rather than supporters of institutional services, the diminishing status of synagogue and rabbi both within and outside Jewish communities, and its effect on the quality of future staffs are causes of concern to the synagogue.

Although the synagogue is experiencing some decline in membership and influence, it continues to be the preeminent institution in American Jewish life and bids well to retain its centrality in the foreseeable future. There is wide agreement with the view of Mordecai M. Kaplan, expressed in 1917: "In this country, as well as in all other countries where the Jews have been emancipated, the synagogue is the principal means of keeping alive the Jewish consciousness. . . . [It] is the only institution which can define our aims to a world that would otherwise be at a loss to understand why we persist in retaining our corporate individuality."[95]

2 The Americanization of Congregation Beth Israel, Rochester

On Sunday, June 28, 1874, seven representatives each of Hevra Sheves Ahim and Hevra B'nai Shalom met as a joint committee for the purpose of consolidation. David Solomon Caminsky of Sheves Ahim was elected president, and Joseph Minsky of B'nai Shalom was chosen vice-president. A secretary, treasurer, and four trustees completed the roster of officers. A *gabbai* (lay overseer) for the cemetery was also elected.

Kalman Bardin suggested that the new hevra be called Beth Israel, and "all happily agreed." Committees to prepare a constitution and by-laws, to set the books in order, and to go to a lawyer to make over all documents and deeds to Beth Israel, were appointed. It was decided that the whole membership of both *hevrot* (congregations) meet on Wednesday, July 1, to bring the Scroll of the Torah and the other ritual objects into the Sheves Ahim Synagogue. An expenditure of "up to $5.00" was authorized for the move.[1] Thus is recorded the birth of the Beth Israel Congregation of Rochester, New York, the first and for forty years the leading Orthodox congregation of that city.

The earliest Jewish settlers arrived in Rochester in the 1840s.[2] They came mainly from Germany, some having spent time in England and in New York and other American cities. In 1855, the *Occident* reported, "The congregation consists of Germans, Englishmen and Poles, who all are acting in harmony. Some, indeed, would have liked to have a mode of worship similar to the Emanuel Temple at New York; but they will not desire to introduce any reform which might lead to disunion."[3]

The congregation, Berith Kodesh, thus served west and east European Jews. The latter were few in number and of traditional bent. So long as the congregation did not turn Reform and east European Jews were few, one congregation served all Rochester Jewry.

In the 1860s Berith Kodesh began veering toward Reform, and a small but steady influx of Jews from eastern Europe began. The records of the Mt. Hope Cemetery Association, August 4, 1870, disclose that Sheves

Ahim purchased a lot to use as its burial ground. A year later another hevra, Bene Sholom, was ready to purchase its cemetery. Three years later, Beth Israel was founded.

The first forty years of Beth Israel provide a case study of the evolution of an east European hevra into an American congregation. This period may be divided into three eras: (1) 1874–1886, an east European hevra; (2) 1887–1899, from hevra to congregation; and (3) 1900–1912, the making of an American congregation.

AN EAST EUROPEAN IMMIGRANT HEVRA (1874–1886)

Beginnings

The dozen-year history of Beth Israel from 1874 to 1886 was marked by congregational growth and division, by the acquisition of improved synagogal facilities, and by the professionalization of religious functionaries.

Its first home was the prayer room *shul* (synagogue) of Sheves Ahim. The enlarged congregation needed expanded facilities, and the first order of business after amalgamation was the appointment of a committee "to seek a hall to serve as a synagogue."[4]

A hall was rented for $250 per annum, and a committee was appointed to "fix the hall . . . as needed."[5] On August 17, 1874, the congregation moved into its quarters and began preparations for the High Holy Days.

Disagreements that marked the early life of the congregation began at its birth. Two members were charged with rearranging the synagogue as it had been set up by the committee and trustees, placing the Ark and *bimah* (platform) where *they* felt they should stand. The beginning of confrontations between "traditionalists" and "progressives" can be found in the vote regarding where the hazzan (cantor) should stand. A motion was made that the hazzan always stand on the central bimah, as was the traditional mode. An amendment was offered that during the year he officiate from the bimah but on the High Holy Days from in front of the Ark. The amendment was defeated. The "traditionalists" gained another victory in voting that a curtain be hung between the synagogue and the *ezrat nashim* (women's section).[6]

Preparations for the first High Holy Day services went forth. Kalman Bardin, a shohet and a leader in the congregation, was elected as hazzan. Thus the European usage of shohet-hazzan was carried on by the hevra. The minutes of August 16, 1874, report that Mr. S. "sent in a petition . . . that he would *daven shaharit* (lead the morning prayers) on Rosh Hashanah and Yom Kippur for $25." Another aspirant offered to do it free of charge. By a secret ballot ("a vote with tickets") it was decided to engage Mr. Shencup and pay him the requested $25.

Fees for seats for the services were adopted. Those seats nearer to the east wall would be three dollars, and no seat should be sold for less than two dollars to a head of a family. Seats for unmarried men should begin at one dollar and go higher "as the trustees will decide." It was also passed that "the brother-in-law of Cohen the tailor should not receive a seat for less than three dollars" and that "a policeman should be hired for Rosh Hashanah and Yom Kippur to stand on the steps and not permit the boys to run around, and to keep out of the synagogue anyone who does not have a ticket, or anyone with a small child."[7] Two weeks later it was agreed "that no seat should be sold to Cohen the tailor at no price, because many members have heard him abuse the hevra with disgraceful talk." A day later the president called a special meeting "because he was abused with disgraceful talk in the synagogue by Mr. M . . . and Mr. L." It was voted that each be fined two dollars and that they ask forgiveness of the president. Both asked forgiveness, and it was granted. The minutes disclose that fines were rescinded almost as often as fines were imposed. America was the frontier of European Jewry, and these frontiersmen were men of bold, volatile spirit. But they were, above all, Jews, fellow Jews, sons of Abraham, "advocate of compassion," and disciples of Aaron, "pursuer of peace." As men of the frontier they were of short temper, quick of tongue. As Jews, immigrant Jews in need of the security of community, they were ever ready to forgive and forget.

A Synagogue of One's Own

What is a congregation without a synagogue of its own? Twice in less than a decade the men of Beth Israel fashioned synagogues. On February 7, 1878, it was reported that a house on Chatham Street was for sale for $1,650. It was moved that the congregation buy the house and fix it for a synagogue.

A month later the house was bought with a down payment of $700 and a mortgage of $950, and a seven-plank plan was unanimously adopted by the congregation prescribing that:

1. The congregation elect a standing committee of seven to make plans for a synagogue and *mikvah* (ritual bath).
2. The Committee elect its own secretary and treasurer.
3. Each member is to be taxed $10, to be paid within six months.
4. These monies are to be held by the treasurer for a synagogue and mikvah, and may not be used for any other purpose.
5. The Committee of Seven appoint a committee to solicit and collect contributions for the building fund.
6. A special committee be appointed to approach non-members for contributions.
7. The Committee order tin boxes to be marked "Women's Contri-

bution" *(nidrat nashim)*. These boxes are to be placed in homes. Monthly collections are to be made and a record kept with name and amount.[8]

Later the $10 assessment was hotly debated, sustained, and then cancelled, but the planning and work went on.

Mr. Harris Levi announced that he planned to build a mikvah and that he would charge not more than fifty cents.[9] An agreement was signed with Mr. Levi, and it was ordered that it be announced in the synagogue on the Sabbath that Mr. Levi's mikvah "is *kosher k'din u'k'das*" (in full accordance with the ritual law). Five months later Mr. Levi complained that the members had encouraged him to build a mikvah and that he spent a great deal of money to do so, but now their wives used the mikvah of "the goy." He demands justice![10] In response, he was asked to list the wives of members who use the "goy's mikvah" and then the hevra would take action.[11]

The minutes indicate internal dissension on many matters, heightened by a disagreement on whether to renovate the house or build a new synagogue. Matters were held in abeyance until February 1879, when a committee was appointed to see a cabinetmaker to get estimates of the cost of renovating the house into a synagogue. After two months of study the committee recommended that a new synagogue be built.[12] But only a week of further study convinced them that this was beyond the congregation's financial ability. The earlier recommendation was withdrawn, and plans for renovation of the house at a cost of $700 were proposed and accepted. Each member was to contribute five dollars at once.

Work proceeded apace and the collection of funds as well. Nathan Goldwater, David Caminsky, and P. Unterberg were appointed to solicit contributions from the "German Jews," and Messrs. Greenstein, Posner, and Slomianski were to do the same from "the Polish Jews."[13]

In August a special meeting of the congregation was convoked to arrange for the moving into the new synagogue. A committee was appointed to arrange for gas fixtures, carpeting for the bimah, and a reader's table, and another committee was authorized to engage a music band to accompany the Torah procession at a cost of $10. A guest cantor from Buffalo was invited to officiate on the Sabbath of Dedication.

The day of dedication was a day of joyous celebration for the Rochester east European Jewish community. Three years earlier their wealthy German brethren had built a temple; now, after years in a rented hall, they were to have their own synagogue. The entire Jewish community was invited to the celebration. Dr. Max Landsberg, rabbi of Berith Kodesh, a radical reformer, to be sure, but a neighbor and head of the sister congregation, gave the dedicatory address in German and English. A band played. Leaders of the congregation marched in the Torah procession, which honors they had bought at auction for prices ranging from eighty-seven cents to two dollars. At last the immigrants from White Russia and Lithuania were at home in the new world, in a synagogue they could call their own.

New facilities demanded new arrangements and activities. Amendments to the bylaws were adopted: "Each member must purchase a pew. Seats are to be sold to members at auction to highest bidder. The seat is then the property of the purchaser so long as he pays the annual seat tax. The seats at the East Wall begin at $30; the others at $20."[14] Within two weeks fifty seats were sold at auction at prices ranging from $20 to $91, with a total collected of $1,596.50.[15]

The congregation, with an eye to the future, decided to undertake an educational program. As early as July 4, 1875, it was reported at a meeting that "many members stated that they want a *melamed* (teacher)." A committee of three was appointed to take the names of those who wanted a school, how many children they would send, and how much they were willing to pay.[16] But nothing came of this early attempt. Now, four years later, with a new building and a growing congregation, the attempt was made again. On August 3, 1879, it was moved and passed that the hevra would engage a hazzan-reader-teacher at a salary of $500. To make this possible the annual dues were raised to a minimum of $12.[17]

On October 26, 1879, Moshe Weiss was elected hazzan-reader-teacher at a salary of $400 if he furnished the heder, $350 if the congregation did so. Tuition was set at $3 per annum, and a board of education of eight members was appointed. A day later, on October 27, a joint meeting was held of the board of trustees and the board of education to make the necessary arrangements.

The Expanding Congregation

With the synagogue renovated, a school established, and a cantor-teacher engaged, the congregation, at its quarterly membership meeting of March 14, 1880, affirmed previous trustees' amendments and added new ones to the constitution:

> The purpose of the hevra is to maintain a synagogue and a Cantor-Teacher.
> Dues are to be no less than 75 cents a month.
> There are to be no more than three Trustees.
> Each member is to purchase a permanent pew.
> *Aharon Hazak* (the final Torah honor at the conclusion of a book of the Torah) is not to be sold.
> Each member and seat-holder is to pay the annual seat tax before Rosh Hashanah, as well as the payment on the principal as stipulated in his

seat agreement. The price of a permanent pew to a member is a minimum of $30, 25% to be paid immediately, the balance in annual payments with interest for a period of five years.

A member does not have to pay for a seat for a child under 13. He is responsible for the behavior of the child. If the child misbehaves, the father is liable for a fine.

The price of $5.00 for a wedding is now to be $6.00, to include $1.00 for the *shamash* (sexton). If a member or his wife die, the hevra is to supply two carriages for the officers of the congregation, at the congregation's expense. A widow of a member, so long as she does not remarry, is entitled to a grave, as is a child under the age of 14.

The congregation was expanding. At a special meeting on March 29, seven new seat-holders paid between $30 and $54 for their pews. At the same meeting a congregational Hevra Kadisha (Holy Burial Society) was organized with an initial membership of twenty. The board of education notified the assembled members that no child above the age of thirteen would be admitted to the school.

While all was going well for the congregation, its hazzan-teacher was having his problems. Hazzan Weiss petitioned to be reelected at the same salary for another year, but by a vote of twenty-six to fifteen, his tenure was extended for only six months.[18] The hazzan soon received notice that he would not be reengaged, and it was decided to advertise for a new hazzan-reader at a salary of $600 to $700. Many candidates applied for the position. The incumbent's offer to accept a salary of $350 was turned down, and Mr. Ticktin was elected hazzan-reader-teacher at a salary of $600. A new tuition schedule of fifty cents a month was announced.[19]

But the congregation seemed to be losing interest in the school. A motion to have the school meet on the more desirable second floor of the synagogue building was defeated.[20] On July 3, the board of education was discharged, and a special committee of six was ordered to investigate whether the hazzan was attending to his teaching duties properly. The committee was also to tell the hazzan-teacher that he should teach only *ivri* (Hebrew rote reading) and not *Humash* (the Pentateuch).

The new hazzan was having even greater problems than his predecessor. Accusations were brought against him. At first the congregation attempted to protect him, adopting a motion that anyone slandering the hazzan might be fined by the president up to two dollars.[21] A month later formal charges were brought against the hazzan at a special meeting. Called before the meeting, he was accused of misbehavior, which he admitted, and he asked for mercy. He was found guilty, his contract was terminated, and he was invited to leave the city, being promised $25 extra when he did so.[22]

With his departure the school came to an end. In electing his successor, Hazzan Harris Louis, the congregation had the choice to elect him hazzan-reader-teacher for $500 or hazzan-reader for $400. By a vote of twenty-nine to nine, it chose the latter.

The congregation continued to grow. Immigration from eastern Europe sharply increased, and the situation in czarist Russia pointed to ever greater growth. The synagogue now seemed inadequate. Early in 1882 a committee of seven was appointed to make plans for a new building.[23] But internal problems continued to plague the congregation. Although Aaron Nusbaum, defeated a year earlier, was now elected president by a large majority, his authority was constantly challenged.

Harris Newyorker was ordered by the president *not* to chant the Hallel service from the pulpit. He did not obey the order, and a disturbance ensued. Mr. Newyorker then sued the president for one thousand dollars in damages. At a special meeting it was voted that the president have Mr. Newyorker arrested for having caused a disturbance, and he was authorized to carry on litigation at the congregation's expense. Ten days later, when the president convened a special meeting to bar Mr. Newyorker from the synagogue, the president was defeated by a vote of fifteen to sixteen.

The issue that led to a split in the congregation was the building of a fence for the congregation's cemetery. President Nusbaum was determined to build the fence and would brook no opposition. His opponents, to whom a new synagogue building was top priority, were equally set on directing the congregation's resources toward that end. When the president arranged to have the fence built, the vice-president convened a special meeting, stating that he did so in response to a signed petition of thirteen members. By a vote of twenty to nothing, with five abstentions, the contractor was ordered *not* to begin building the fence for six months.[24]

The opposition faction, now a majority, voted an amendment to the constitution that a president could not succeed himself. It also curtailed the power of the president by voting that he could not fine a member for being out of order unless he had previously called him to order, and the maximum fine for being out of order was set at twenty-five cents.

Outnumbered and outvoted, Aaron Nusbaum resigned from the congregation. His two brothers joined him. Together with some friends, they organized a new congregation, B'nai Aviezer (Sons of Aviezer), named for their father. The name was later changed to Beth Haknesses Hachodosh, but it was commonly called the Nusbaum Minyan.[25] That this new congregation constituted a threat to Beth Israel is attested by an amendment adopted on July 10, 1884: "It is forbidden for a member to attend the Nusbaum Minyan. If a member attends either weekdays or Sabbaths, he is to be fined 50 cents for the first violation and one dollar for the second. A third offense would bring expulsion."[26]

It may very well be that this controversy was an aspect of the differences between the "traditionalists" and the "progressives," which had existed in the congregation from its inception. Traditionalism led to emphasis on the cemetery, symbolic of reverence for the past. Commitment to progress led to interest and labors for a new synagogue, incorporating a school, that would point to and prepare for the future.

This division can be glimpsed in a controversy about the printing of the constitution and bylaws. After agreement had been reached that they be printed in both English and Yiddish, it was found that it would be too expensive to do so in both languages. The trustees, sensing the passions that this issue would arouse, voted not to print.[27] Three weeks later a vote to print the bylaws in only Yiddish provoked such an argument that the president could not bring the meeting to order. Five days later the vote for only Yiddish won, twenty-one to nineteen.[28] But so determined was the "progressive" opposition that the bylaws were not printed at all.

A Rabbi Comes to Town

Moshe Weinberger, reporting on the religious situation in New York City in 1886, wrote:

> Established rabbis, capable of giving rabbinic decision on Jewish law in this city of 100,000 Jews and 130 Orthodox congregations, number not more than three or four. Even these were not called to their rabbinic posts with honor but came here like other immigrants in search of a livelihood. After much hardship and labor they found a post. The congregations do not support them adequately—really so inadequately that it is shameful to report it in a book. They support themselves from meagre congregational and individual contributions which do not provide even minimal necessities.[29]

Small wonder, then, that Rochester did not boast an Orthodox rabbi until 1883. In the west European congregation of America, the rabbi was central. In the east European hevra, he was at best peripheral. The immigrant from western Europe knew a congregation where preaching was expected and a rabbi-preacher a necessity. For the east European the synagogue was a place for prayer, which could be led by a layman and, if by a professional, a hazzan. The Rov of eastern Europe was a communal rather than congregational functionary. The first east European rabbi invited to America, Rabbi Jacob Joseph, was brought here by an organization of congregations that looked on itself as a communal body.[30] Other *Rabbonim* (rabbis, especially east European rabbis) came to America and sought out their rabbinic positions as communal, rather than congregational, functionaries.

In June 1883, Rabbi Abba Hayim b. Yitzhak Isaac Levinson sent a petition to the Beth Israel Congregation informing it that he would like to serve as the community rabbi. By a one-vote majority, seventeen to sixteen, it was voted that a rabbi be engaged, and a committee of five was appointed to determine how funds might be obtained to pay the rabbi.

A month later, the matter was brought before the congregation. It was moved that the rabbi be paid $100 per annum. An amendment was proposed that the salary be $600. An amendment to the amendment suggested $150. The petition of Rabbi Levinson was then read and a secret ballot vote taken, and he was elected rabbi for one year by a vote of seventeen to thirteen at a salary of $150. The duties of the rabbi were not spelled out, but we may assume that they were nominal. Those who suggested a salary of $600 no doubt thought him a congregational rabbi, giving full time to Beth Israel. The majority of the membership apparently viewed him as a communal functionary, to be supported among others by the Beth Israel Congregation. That year, the shamash-collector for his part-time labors was receiving a salary of $150, equal to that of the rabbi. The cantor's salary was $400.

A decade later Jacob Rosenbloom, president of the congregation, expressed in the public press the congregation's view of the status and functions of a rabbi. "A rabbi is not a minister. His duties, only to a very small extent, resemble the duties of a Christian minister. He is an interpreter of the divine law, not a spiritual adviser. His duty is chiefly to interpret the law as it is written and apply it to particular cases as they are brought to him for decision."[31]

The first extra salary income for the rabbi was from the congregation itself. He offered to chant the *Shaharit* services of the High Holy Days at a price set by the congregation. It was voted to grant his request, add the sounding of the Shofar and Neilah to his duties, and pay him $40.[32]

Supervision of *kashrut* (dietary laws) in the community was his chief rabbinic duty. In fulfillment of this he ordered the *shohatim* (ritual slaughterers) of the community to come before him for examination. Kalman Bardin and Jacob Lipsky came before him and were examined and declared fit. Abraham Rosenthal came three days late, did not pass muster, and was ordered to return for a reexamination. This he refused to do. The rabbi's authority was thus challenged. At a special meeting called to deal with the matter the congregation voted to stand behind the rabbi in his supervision of kashrut.[33]

Controversy must have arisen in the city, for action had to be taken at the trustees' meeting a week later to protect the rabbi. It was voted that any nonmember who abused the rabbi would not be permitted to worship in the synagogue and that no "outside preachers" would be permitted to preach. Both of the above motions were passed only through the president's tie-breaking vote.[34]

The rabbi remained vulnerable. On July 7, 1884, a special trustees' meeting addressed itself to the report that "Mr. Eliezer Levin spoke disgraceful words against the rabbi of the congregation." A Beth Din (court of law) was convened and presided over by Rabbi Reb Binyamin (of whom no other mention in the minutes). Mr. Levin was called and asked to substantiate his charges. It was found that "whatever was asked him, he was unable to answer." The Beth Din then issued the verdict that Mr. Levin's mikvah be put under *herem* (ban) until Mr. Levin did the penance requested of him, and the ban was to be announced in the synagogue.[35] Three days later the rabbi was reelected unanimously at the same salary and an advertisement was placed in the Yiddish newspapers announcing Rabbi Levinson's reelection.

When the renewal of the contract came up the following year, a request was made that a vote be taken regarding whether the congregation needed a rabbi. The president refused to permit a vote. The rabbi's opponents then pointed out that the rabbi had not sent in a petition as the law required. "A great debate ensued." The president had to yield, and the shamash was sent to the rabbi and returned with the required document. By a vote of nineteen to six, Rabbi Levinson was reelected again at the same salary of $150. A month later Cantor Mirsky was given a two-year contract at an annual salary of $500.[36]

The Leopold Street shul

Moshe Weinberger, in the above-cited description of Jewish religious life in New York City, wrote:

> The purpose of most of the Orthodox congregations is to assemble twice daily, or on Sabbaths, for worship, to visit the sick and help them, to bury the dead and pay them last respects, and to help a fellow member in time of need.
>
> But the highest purpose is to build a synagogue—grand and beautiful. The congregation that succeeds in doing so—there is no measure to its joy, and the members feel that thereby they have fulfilled their obligations to the Faith of Moses and Israel.[37]

In this matter Beth Israel was not to be outdone. A good number of the first wave of immigrants, unloosed by the "May Laws" (harsh anti-Jewish laws enacted by the Russian government, May 31, 1882), came to Rochester, attracted by the men's clothing manufacturing industry, which was almost wholly in Jewish hands. Strengthened by those who came and emboldened by the promise of more to come, the congregation began to talk of building a synagogue. Only three years after moving into the house that it had renovated into a "house of prayer," the congregation voted to appoint a committee of seven to make plans for the building of a new synagogue.[38]

Internal difficulties resulting from a factionalism that eventually caused the defection of a number of members intervened and postponed plans and even discussion. Two years later, by a three to two vote of the trustees, a committee was appointed to begin planning the erection of a synagogue.[39]

Two weeks later the committee reported that it had placed plans for the new building before a contractor who gave a bid of $8,500. The committee was instructed to take other bids and not begin building before the following spring.[40] The vote was close, twenty-six to twenty-one. Opposition continued. A fight in the synagogue that caused damage to the bimah was apparently touched off by this issue.[41]

The way was cleared for the building of the synagogue by the resignation of a number of members led by Aaron Nusbaum, who had apparently led the opposition. But now another obstacle appeared. There was apparently an economic recession in the spring of 1885, for the secretary reported on March 22 that "many members claim that they are unable to make payments on their seats." Payments were postponed until after *Pesah* (Passover). The Nusbaum group founded their own congregation, and the growing number of immigrants led to the formation of other new congregations that offered competition to Beth Israel.

The new congregations were accepted as challenges, strengthening the determination of Beth Israel's leaders and membership. On February 6, 1886, the trustees asked the chairman of the building committee to ascertain the following: (1) the possibility of building without cash, through a mortgage only, (2) how much would a mortgage cost and what security would be necessary, and (3) how much would the desired building cost?

A month later a congregational meeting considered: "Shall the Committee be ordered to bring in plans and specifications?" The president then challenged the members present to declare their intentions to contribute for the proposed new building. Those present were called by name, and eighteen pledged to give. The president, secretary, and treasurer were constituted as a committee to call on the other members of the congregation.[42]

New impetus was given to the project in early spring. A sister congregation, B'ani Israel, requested to become part of Beth Israel, resulting in nineteen new members. At the special meeting called to welcome them it was voted to appoint a committee to consider the purchase of a lot on Leopold Street as the site for the new building. The trustees were authorized to sell the old building for a house or a synagogue. If it was to be used as a house, the asking price was to be $2,000; if for a synagogue, $3,000.[43] They apparently sensed that the Nusbaum group might want to purchase the synagogue. Old hurts still rankled, and they were not about to be of help to a dissident faction who had abandoned them.

Things now moved apace. The aim was to have a new synagogue for the High Holy Days. The minutes record:

> April 11, 1886:
>
> A committee is appointed to bring in plans, as soon as possible, for a new synagogue on the Leopold Street site. The synagogue is to be 75′ × 45′.
>
> May 16, 1886:
>
> A low bid of $10,717 for building and furnishings is reported. The members are obligated to sign the mortgage.
>
> May 22, 1886:
>
> The old synagogue is sold to Nathan Goldwater for $1,920. A bid of $2,200 by Aaron Nusbaum is rejected.

On June 27 the cornerstone was laid with all pomp and ceremony, as the *Rochester Democrat and Chronicle* reported:

> WITH TROWEL AND MORTAR
>
> Laying the Cornerstone of the New Beth Israel Temple
>
> WORK OF THREE PRESIDENTS
>
> The First Ceremony of the Kind in 25 Years Performed in the Presence of A Large Assemblage with Addresses by Rev. Landsberg and Others.
>
> Yesterday will be a memorable one in the Hebrew history of Rochester and is especially entered in the records of the Congregation Beth Israel.
> . . .
>
> The Congregation Beth Israel was organized June 27, 1874, in the Jardin block on East Main Street. Its membership was then thirty-five. February 17, 1878, the people purchased a lot in Chatham Street, and a synagogue was erected. In March of the present year commenced the movement which terminated in the purchase of the Leopold Street property and the commencement of the present edifice.[44]

On August 8, 1886, it was enacted that:

1. Each member must purchase a seat in the new synagogue.
2. The price of the seats should be in accordance with location. Seats 1–80, $175–$125. Seats beyond 80, $100.
3. On the day of purchase, 15% of the purchase price is to be paid.
4. The amounts paid on the seats in the old synagogue will be credited for the new seats.

On August 29, 1886, a committee was appointed to make arrangements "to move with a parade" and was empowered to "spend what will be necessary."

The "move with a parade" was duly reported in the local press:

IN THEIR NEW CHURCH

An Important Event for the Beth Israel Congregation

Yesterday was a memorable day to members of the Beth Israel Congregation. Shortly after 3 o'clock in the afternoon they moved from their old church on Chatham street, in which they had worshipped for years, into their new synagogue on Leopold street.

The members of the congregation and quite a large number of spectators gathered at the old synagogue at 2 o'clock in the afternoon. The exercises were opened by the pastor, Rabbi Levenson, who in a short address in German [sic] congratulated the members of his congregation upon the fact that their numbers had grown so large that a new synagogue was required and that the building had been supplied. When he had finished, the privilege of carrying the scrolls of the law and parchments to the new synagogue was disposed of at auction, book by book and parchment by parchment. This privilege is regarded very highly, and the bidding was quite brisk, much eagerness for the honor being manifested by the ladies as well as the gentlemen. The privilege sold for from 25 cents to $3 and $4. When the books had all been disposed of, the procession formed for its march to the new synagogue, led by the Lincoln Cornet Band, and headed by Rabbi Isaac Yoffe, of St. Louis, Rev. Dr. Rodden, of Elmira, Rabbis Ursky and Levenson, Rev. Erlich, of this city, and J. Lipsky, president of the society, after whom came representative members of the church, bearing the parchments, followed by the congregation. Arriving at the synagogue, the door was unlocked by President Lipsky, and the procession entered. In a very short time the building was completely filled.

The band took seats in the rear gallery and from time to time dispersed very good music. Rev. Ursky sang in German, and short addresses in the same language were delivered by Rabbis Yoffe, Rodden and Erlich. Then came the next feature of the exercises, the selling at auction of the privileges of placing the books and parchments in the Ark of the Holy Scriptures, in the rear of the pulpit. The sales were as lively as those at the old synagogue, and the prices realized were about the same. After these privileges had all been disposed of, the festivities began, cake and wine being passed through the audience. The time until 9 o'clock in the evening was spent in social intercourse.

The new synagogue is a plain but good looking building in size 45 × 85 feet. The interior is without decoration, but presents a neat appearance. Galleries extend along the sides and across the rear. The synagogue will seat about 800 people. Its erection was begun last June, and when finished, which will be in about two weeks, will cost, together with the site, $15,000. The synagogue has a basement comfortably and neatly fitted up, in which a Hebrew day school will be held. Prayer meetings will also be held there every morning and evening. The first regular services will be held at the synagogue next Saturday.[45]

We can imagine the pride with which the members entered the new and beautiful synagogue building. Their house of worship now took its place with the other religious edifices of the city, churches and Temple Berith Kodesh as well. Only a dozen years earlier they were a small struggling hevra furnishing a rented hall for Sabbath services, holding the daily minyan in prayer rooms. Seven years ago they thought it a heroic achievement to renovate a house into a synagogue of their own. Now they would be worshipping in a brick building of eight hundred seats.

The Hevra Congregation

Congregation Beth Israel (the term *hevra* was replaced by *congregation* in 1882) was not just a body of like believers joined for public worship. It was primarily a group of Jews, recent immigrants all, coming together to fashion a fellowship-community. The congregation provided not only a place for worship but also the organizational structure, the experiences of relationship, and the opportunities for status gratification and security assurance that a true community provides.

In answer to the congregants' religious needs, it provided both the place and the personnel requisite for public worship daily and on Sabbaths and holidays. Consecrated ground for burial and the interment preparations and services were available to congregants and their families. In sickness there would be visits by committee in formal obligation and by fellow congregants in friendship. And when the need for final parting came, the last days and hours were eased by the knowledge that the bereaved family would be consoled by visitations and aided by mandated contributions.

The congregation provided the individual immigrant Jew, cut off from home, a new and extended surrogate family in a community large enough to give him a feeling of security, yet small enough to provide him with the sense of worth born of being needed by it.

Beth Israel, as it moved into its new home, was providing its membership not only a place of worship but also a staff of religious functionaries: rabbi, cantor, shamash, and, whenever possible, a Hebrew teacher for its sons (its daughters had to wait for almost a quarter of a century). Its seemingly insufficient—certainly inept—attempts at establishing a congregationally sponsored and financed school was due not so much to a lack of appreciation for religious study as to an uncertainty as to where the responsibility lay for children's education.

In the east European community education was a private or communal concern, not a province of congregational responsibility. Parents engaged a teacher for their son or sent him to a privately run heder or a communally sponsored Talmud Torah (available for the children of the poor). Beth Israel in its early years was a transplanted European institution. If education there was to be, parents or community had to provide it. That the members of Beth Israel turned to the congregation for it is an indication that the congregation was to them their community; that the leaders of Beth Israel once and again attempted to provide it was an early accommodation to the "ways of America" that they were ready to make, but only if it was clearly in service of their institutional interest—rote reading for participation in worship and preparation for Bar Mitzvah. On March 29, 1880, hazzan-teacher Moshe Weiss was instructed not to accept pupils over the age of thirteen; on July 3, 1881, the board of education was instructed to order the hazzan-teacher to limit his curriculum to "ivri"—i.e., rote Hebrew reading. But pressure from parents caused an unending attempt to establish a school for their sons and later for their daughters as well. At all times it was not a question whether religious education should be provided but rather who should provide it, congregation or community.

Congregation as Community

The minutes are replete with accusations made, committees of inquiry established, and punishment meted out. Thus on January 20, 1877, a committee was appointed to investigate charges that Aaron Nusbaum slandered Abraham Shencup, "slandering" him by declaring that he lacked the piety that one who chants the service should have. On December 1, 1878, a special meeting was called to consider an accusation of slander by Kalman Bardin against Peretz Unterberg and Hayim Avner. Both were declared guilty. The punishment of Mr. Unterberg was that he might never hold an office, and Mr. Avner was fined ten dollars. More often than not, peace established, the fines were forgiven.

Elections were always hotly contested. Symbols of status were few in the immigrant society, so the presidency was coveted. Generally the victor acted magnanimously, and the loser accepted defeat in good grace, but not always. At the election held October 10, 1881, Aaron Nusbaum and Kalman Bardin each received nineteen votes. They were respective leaders of the two factions that existed until the Nusbaum family withdrew to form its own congregation. At this meeting neither faction was ready to give in. Arguments ensued. Many fines were levied, leading to even greater arguments, and the president was forced to adjourn the meeting. When the meeting was reconvened the next day, Bardin emerged victorious, and congregational life returned to its normal flow. No matter how violent an argument, neighbors remained friends. An immigrant community felt beset by all manner of foe, so it had to retain an inner solidarity that a settled community could afford to strain. The meeting to consider whether the bylaws should be printed in English as well as Yiddish had to be adjourned because order could not be maintained. But four days later the matter was settled by a vote, and the life of the congregation continued. One gets the impression that the meetings served a function beyond the obvious. Necessary business was enacted, but the meetings also provided an opportunity for the powerful to exert power, for the orators to orate, for elected officials to rule, and for all to rid themselves of the pent-up hostilities and frustrations that immigrant life provided in full measure.

The "fraternal lodge" aspect of the congregation was expressed in the pomp and ceremony attending the installation of officers and the voting for new members, which was by secret ballot. Five blackballs would keep a prospect out of the congregation. When this happened, and it did, it was generally changed at a subsequent meeting. Point made, it was deemed wise to strengthen the congregation by another dues payer.

The immigrant congregants were not a docile or genteel lot. The meek do not venture forth into a new world. When a Siyum celebration (at the conclusion of a course of study) was planned, the hevra voted to assume responsibility for any damage caused to the house in which the celebration would take place. A committee of seven was appointed to guard against damage.

In the European Jewish community a court system existed, and all matters of dispute were adjudicated internally. In the absence of organized Jewish communal structure in America, the east European immigrants turned to their hevra-congregation for this communal function.

On June 20, 1875, a special meeting was held for just such a purpose. Two members of the congregation, Joseph Minsky and Hillel Pashimanski, came before the assembled hevra, said that they had differences between themselves, and asked that a court be established to examine their claims, render its decision, and make a settlement between them. It was "moved, seconded and passed" that the hevra accept their request. The meeting was then organized as a "court of justice." A trial was held, and a decision was rendered to the satisfaction of both parties.

As a community, the hevra extended a helping hand to its members. On November 22, 1875, a special meeting was called by a petition of twelve members. Peretz Unterberg was in financial need, and he had applied for assistance. It was voted to lend him $25, with individual members assuming personal obligations of $1 to $5 if the loan would not be repaid to the congregation. On February 5, 1882, it was reported that

Harris Fisher was ill and needed help. Twenty-five members signed for him, accepting responsibility for a $20 grant from the congregation until such time as the congregation would be able to vote on it, which it did at its next meeting. Free cemetery land for the indigent, postponement of monetary obligations where indicated, and direct aid when requested were common. This was a community of friends and neighbors—rubbing one against the other as friends are wont to do and on occasions irritating each other as neighbors sometimes do, but at all times concerned about each other and helping one another.

The sense of security and status that a community provides was granted to its members by the Beth Israel congregation. It was in structure a congregation but in function a mini-community. As such it was a European institution transplanted to American soil. In the congregation's first dozen years of existence, America made hardly an impress on it. As a matter of fact, it may very well have insulated itself against American influences so that it might remain the hevra the immigrant knew in his native town. America presented so many unfamiliar challenges that the hevra provided the security of the known and the habitual. Beth Israel was the secure haven to which one could return for religious services and fellowship after peddling in the countryside or laboring in the city.

FROM HEVRA TOWARD CONGREGATION (1887–1899)

First Year in a New Building

All energies and enterprise had been invested in the planning and building of the synagogue on Leopold Street. The celebration of dedication over, the congregation turned its attention to the problems and responsibilities that now faced them.

The first order of business was to secure the building. A debt was owed, so a mortgage was sought. The builder offered to give the needed mortgage, but a bank offered better terms. At the December 8, 1886, meeting of the trustees a resolution inscribed in English by Jacob Rosenbloom was adopted: "Resolved, that the president and Sec. of this congregation be and they are hereby authorized to sign application to the supreme court to get permission to borrow 7500 of the monroe county savings bank on the lot #126 of the Sherman track situated on Leopold St. and on the building erected thereon for religious worship and to give a second mortgage to J. N. Smith for the balance due him on contract price."[46]

The cost of the building, including the inside, came to $13,592. The mortgage indebtedness, over 80 percent of the total at 5 percent interest, was a formidable debt to be carried by a small group of economically struggling immigrants. The interest payments alone totaled more than the combined salaries of the rabbi and the cantor, and they cast a heavy financial burden on the congregation for years to come. But in the fall of 1886, spirits were buoyant, and the mood was generous. The beautiful synagogue building served not only the religious needs of the immigrant community but also the psychological as well. To the larger community the edifice announced that immigrants had struck roots in America; haven had become home. To the German Jews it issued a challenge of equality, if not yet in affluence or influence, at least in communal enterprise. The imposing new building on Leopold Street stood as an expression of determination to carry on the old faith in the New World.

The Hevra Mishnayes

The leaders and members had erected a synagogue building; Rabbi Levinson seized the opportunity of infusing "a soul within the body" by organizing a Hevra Mishnayes (Mishnah text study group), on October 31, 1886, just a month after the dedication of the building.[47] Its rules and regulations describe its purpose:

> I. The purpose of the society is to study as a group one chapter of Mishnah without fail each day, with the exception of the eve of the Sabbath and holidays, when most people are so busy that they cannot meet for the regular study session. . . .
> II. The time for study is immediately after the evening service, summer as well as winter.

The initial initiation fee was set at one dollar, but those joining later would have to pay three. What is of interest, because it informs about communal and interpersonal tensions, is Section V:

> V. One or two members do not have the power to keep out one who wants to join the hevra, if the majority do not agree with them. This obtains if they wish to keep him out for reasons that do not pertain to the hevra, as for example, personal enmity or strife. If, however, their reason pertains to the welfare of the organization, as for example, the prospective member spoke ill of the hevra or if they have information which would indicate that the prospect is unworthy of membership in the hevra, then they are to bring their charges before a general meeting. The hevra is then to judge "according to the sight of their eyes," whether that person is to be admitted.

Membership in a religious organization in the immigrant community was an indication of acceptance and approval. In a long-established community, social sanctions are "natural," i.e., they are embodied in the web of intrasocietal relationships. Family lineage, scholarship, personal integrity, and piety are factors that determine communal approbation in an established society. In a community coming into being such approbation becomes the function of institutions and organizations. Membership applications in immigrant congregations were fully, sometimes heatedly, discussed, and provisions were made for blackballing. This was true also of the Hevra Mishnayes. A prospect "unworthy of membership" could be kept out and apparently by "one or two members." Institutions and organizations in young communities are frail entities, and thus exists the high sensitivity to "slandering" or "speaking ill" of the hevra or congregation.

The purpose and function of the Hevra Mishnayes was not only cultural-educational but fraternal-pastoral as well: "VI. If a member is in mourning or has taken ill, it is the duty of each member to visit him at least once during the period of mourning or weekly during his illness. He who does more is deemed praiseworthy."

The hevra functioned as an expanded, surrogate family in the immigrant community in which there were many single people and nuclear families in need of familial associations. It even provided service to its members beyond life: "XII. If a member dies, all members of the Hevra are to accompany the body to the cemetery, and during the week of mourning, the hevra is to meet in the house of mourning to conduct there their accustomed study." Nor were social needs neglected: "XIV. At each Siyum a repast is to be served to the members. The repast is to be served on the day of the conclusion of the study of an Order and may not be postponed."

For Rabbi Levinson the Hevra Mishnayes served another function. It brought him into daily contact with the twenty or so most scholarly members of Beth Israel, a coterie of friends whom he could turn to in times of need. He knew the precariousness of religious office in the immigrant community. The most stable, the most pious, and the most scholarly in the east European community rarely left for America. Few were those among the immigrants who really appreciated the scholar, but most would understand and reward usefulness. To come to the synagogue and see a rabbi surrounded by a group whom he was teaching would strengthen his position and justify his support. As for the rabbi, it did one thing more. It lifted him above the chore of slaughter inspector and kashrut supervisor to the role of teacher of the Torah, for which he had been trained and ordained and in service of which he had directed his life.

The Cantor

The new building did not serve the incumbent cantor well. Being the most visible of the clergy, he was the most vulnerable. A cantor adequate for a converted house-synagogue was not good enough for the new spacious brick edifice. On May 1, 1887, it was unanimously agreed to "instruct the secretary to inform the cantor that his contract expires on the 19th of July and that his services will no longer be needed."

The search for a "good cantor" was the central activity in the summer and fall of 1887. Aspirants came, "showed their wares," and departed. None were the "good cantor" sought, for at the special meeting called to discuss the matter of a hazzan, it was voted that a cantor be hired only for the High Holy Days, a decision that was soon reversed. Cantor Kertzner, elected overwhelmingly over Mirsky and Binkowitz, was asked to come officiate at the Selihos service, which he declined to do. Time was now of the essence. A telegram was dispatched to "Rabinowitz in Baltimore that he immediately send Cantor Moshe Wilinsky who had wanted to come 'on trial.' " Cantor Wilinsky did not come, but a formerly rejected candidate, Cantor Zundel Binkowitz, reappeared, offering to serve as cantor for an annual salary of $300, provided he would be permitted to "teach children in the meeting room." Mr. Binkowitz may not have been the "good cantor" they were seeking, but the High Holy Days were at hand and the price was right, so Zundel Binkowitz was elected cantor on September 10.

Only a month later Cantor Zundel Binkowitz was again on the congregational agenda. At the special meeting to install the new officers, the assembled were informed that their cantor "sent a communication asking the hevra to do with him as they think best, for he cannot make a living from his salary and no children had come for instruction." The congregation thought it best to dispense with his services and offered to pay him $150 for services rendered, which after some negotiation he accepted, and the enterprise of seeking "a good cantor" was temporarily suspended.

The minutes convey the feverish activity of the endeavor. Candidates are invited, telegrams dispatched, meetings called, opinions expressed, negotiations conducted, votes taken. One can only imagine the long and no doubt heated discussions, and one can surmise the satisfaction afforded leaders and members alike by the opportunity to express "expert opinion" and by the power to make decisions on a matter so central in the life of the congregation and the gossip of the community.

Even as the new synagogue edifice mandated a new "good cantor," so it demanded a higher order of decorum than was tolerated in the old. The *Jewish Tidings*, ever alert to point out the uncouth ways of the east European Orthodox community, regaled its readers with a report of what happened at the Rosh Hashanah service at Beth Israel.[48]

A Scene in Church
During services at Leopold Street Synagogue last Tuesday morning, an attendant at worship was ordered by one of the trustees of the congre-

gation to remove his son, who persisted in giving vent to a series of unearthly yells. It seems that the father used no unseemly haste in obeying this mandate and the aforesaid trustee placed his tender clutches on the lad and ejected him into the corridor. This done, he attempted to throw the child from the entrance to the ground below. Fortunately, the father arrived in time to thwart this design, which might have ended in the boy's death. The irate father and the maddened trustee engaged in a fight, which might have resulted disastrously for the combatants, but for timely interference.[49]

Two weeks later a letter to the editor written by the spokesman for Beth Israel, its secretary Jacob Rosenbloom, did not deny the incident but argued that the printed report "places the blame for the trouble where it does not properly belong. Censure should be given to the father of the child instead of the trustee."[50] A week later, another letter, signed merely "Beth Israel," defended the original article, stating: "I am willing to affirm . . . that the trustee did treat the child cruelly, and that he had no cause therefor. Still I do not blame Secretary Rosenbloom for trying to relieve an officer of his church of reproach and censure."[51]

No echo of the incident is found in the minutes of the congregation. The new building was meant no doubt to purchase respectability for a much maligned group of immigrants. The less said about untoward behavior, the better. The same issue carrying the last letter announced the election of Jacob Rosenbloom to the presidency of Beth Israel, a post he was to occupy seven times in the next nine years. Mr. Rosenbloom and his fellow officers could take satisfaction that the *Rochester Union-Advertiser* took note of their election and listed them by name and office in its issue of October 10, 1887.

To Secure the Future: A School

Cantor Binkowitz had hoped to augment his income by conducting a school in the Beth Israel meeting hall. He must have based his projection on the number of boys of school age in the community. He soon found that he attracted no students to his proposed school. The reasons for this failure we can only surmise. He had to contend with the European experience that a Talmud Torah (a publicly sponsored religious school) was for the children of the poor. The Beth Israel membership was of the upper economic rung of the east European community, which would be reluctant to send its boys to a school that had the appearance of public sponsorship and support. An imported prejudice against "public" education apparently thwarted the American practice of congregationally sponsored education.

Beth Israel's new president, Jacob Rosenbloom, among the most Americanized members,[52] was convinced that an American congregation needed a religious school. Even as the search for a "good cantor" was revived in the spring of 1888, plans were under way for the establishment of a congregational school. A special meeting on May 27 authorized the appointment of a committee of five "to ascertain how many members would send their children to a school conducted by the cantor of the congregation, and if they would pay tuition monthly with their dues." A week later Jacob Lipsky reported for the committee that thirty-three children of members were ready to attend and pay tuition of 25 cents per week. Thereupon the resolution that was passed to advertise for a hazzan was amended to "a hazzan and a teacher" and carried by a vote of twenty to two. A motion that "a member should be charged no less than 25 cents a week per child," amended to "a yearly charge of $15," carried. The more conservative element, fearing too modern a school, pushed through a motion that "members may send only boys to study and only till their Bar-Mitzvah." It was further agreed that a cantor-teacher should be paid up to $800 per annum and that he was to teach up to twenty-five students. Cantor Jospe was thereupon elected "Cantor, Reader and Teacher" for two years at an annual stipend of $800.[53]

The resolutions were confirmed at the quarterly membership meeting of June 17. A week later a board of education was appointed, and it was voted to stipulate in the cantor-teacher's contract that he should "teach the students in accordance with the instructions of the Education Committee."

At a special meeting a month later, Jacob Lipsky, chairman of the board of education, reported an enrollment of twenty-two students, and the president stated that he had ordered a floor made for the room in which the school would meet and asked the Education Committee to purchase school benches. The room was apparently in the basement, for among the improvements made to accommodate the school was "a box for the coal in the furnace room" and the fixing of the pipes "that water should not enter the basement." It was also voted that if the enrollment should pass twenty-five another teacher would be added. Soon thereafter, when the enrollment numbered twenty-five boys in four classes, an assistant teacher was hired for five dollars a week on a trial basis.

A special meeting concerning the school met on October 28 and heard that twenty-six boys were now enrolled and that the assistant teacher, Jaffe, was doing well and should be retained. The president reported, however, that the income of the school could not support a second teacher and suggested that children of nonmembers be accepted. Fearing that to accept children of nonmembers would destroy the congregational character of the school, nine members signed a petition obligating themselves to raise $500 a year for the school, $400 of which was to be used for an assistant teacher. Tuition was raised to $20 a year, and it was voted not to accept children of nonmembers. Mr. Jaffe was continued as assistant teacher at a salary of $400 per annum.[54]

Indication that the school was having problems is found in the report of the secretary at the spring 1889 quarterly membership meeting relating that a number of members who had withdrawn their children from the school refused to pay the tuition owed. A month later, the congregation was forced to beat a retreat. The president reported that he had accepted four children of nonmembers because there was not a sufficient enrollment of members' children; that the $1.25 monthly fee was reinstituted; and that children of nonmembers "fit for the classes" would continue to be admitted.[55] The enrollment continued to decline. The remedy suggested was that the board of education instruct the cantor to teach Hebrew reading and not Bible in the time allotted for instruction.

The cantor realized that the experiment had failed. He asked to be released from teaching, offering to take $100 reduction in pay. The request was granted, for all now realized that a congregational school was beyond Beth Israel's capability.[56] The process of acculturation of the members and the Americanization of the congregation had still a long way to go before a congregational school would become a matter of highest priority.

Jacob Lipsky, the chief proponent of Jewish education in the Beth Israel community, was among the first to yield to the frustrations encountered in the attempt to maintain a congregational school. Early in 1889 he resigned his chairmanship of the board of education and began to direct his energies to the establishment of a communal Hebrew school. By the summer there was already strong sentiment in and outside of the congregation for such an institution. We can thus understand the apparently weak endeavors of the congregation to maintain its school and the calm manner in which its demise was accepted.

The last act of the administration that attempted the congregational school was to act on the vote of the congregation to appoint a committee of five, the president to be among them, to meet with representatives of other congregations in the city to discuss matters touching on the welfare of Judaism in the city and report back to the congregation. What the minutes veil in generalities an article in the *Jewish Tidings* reports in detail.

A WORTHY OBJECT

Movement For a School For Poor Polish Children

A committee of five members from each of the three Polish congregations[57] in this city was appointed a week ago Sunday who are to have charge of the arrangement for the establishment of a school for poor Polish children. The committee met last Sunday evening and effected a temporary organization by choosing A. Nusbaum[58] President and J. Lipsky Secretary.

A general meeting of the three congregations will be held in the new temple on Chatham[59] on Sunday morning; effort will be made to raise funds and to put the movement under way immediately. It is a worthy object and deserves hearty support. There is no doubt to its success as the men interested are working energetically.[60]

It is significant to note that this intercongregational endeavor that joined in common enterprise leaders of competing congregations came only a half year after congregational strife on the issue of kashrut supervision, which arrayed the community into an "armed camp." What the issue of kashrut had rent asunder, the need for education of a rising generation now brought together.

The school was a classic Talmud Torah "for the poor children." It took the name Hebrew Free School, met in the building of the Beth Haknesses Hachodosh, and continued a precarious existence until 1895. The wealthier families continued to hire private tutors for their children.

Beth Israel, as the oldest and largest congregation, one that pioneered in such endeavor, felt a special obligation to support the school. In May 1891, it granted "full power to the president to sign a contract with the teacher of the Talmud Torah to bind the hevra for $300 a year [on the stipulation that the Beth Haknesses Hachodosh will sign], and to appoint a committee of seven to control the Talmud Torah."[61]

When the Talmud Torah closed its doors in 1895, a new effort was made in Beth Israel to reestablish a congregational school. In September of that year, a special meeting was called to consider a petition signed by twelve members that they be allowed to use the "downstairs" of the synagogue for a Hebrew school for children of members. There was reluctance to grant the request, for a committee of five was appointed "to search for rooms in another place and report to the president. If they cannot find space elsewhere, the president will call a meeting of members." Three weeks later, under a new administration headed by Jacob Rosenbloom, permission was granted to the school to meet for one week in the *Beth Medrash* (chapel).[62] The school seems never to have established itself, for nothing more is heard of it.

Failing in their efforts within the congregation, those needing or desiring a school took the leadership in founding a new communal school, the Rochester Hebrew School, soon thereafter.[63] Although the school met elsewhere, it had especially close ties with Beth Israel. Thus, on September 14, 1897, a special meeting was called at the request of the officers of the Rochester Hebrew School to consider engaging jointly a cantor-teacher. The congregation would then have an "inexpensive" cantor and the school would have a "cheap" teacher. The "communication" was accepted, but apparently a desirable candidate could not be found, for the congregation went through the year with visiting and temporary cantors. What may have prevented acceptance of this arrangement was a growing sentiment in the congregation for a *preacher.* If a dual functionary was to be sought, why not a cantor-preacher? Indeed, a Mr. Zadikow had acted in that capacity in the summer months of 1897.

At the winter 1898 quarterly meeting, a committee from the Rochester Hebrew School appeared, pleading that "they are hard up financially, and since it was established by members of the Beth Israel congregation, they request that the hevra help them." A committee appointed to consider the matter reported that, after due consideration, "the only thing that can be done is to lend the Rochester Hebrew School a Sefer Torah, so that they might have their own minyan till Pesah, and benefit from the 'shnodder' money" (pledges made for Torah honors granted). The congregation was not about to set up another competitor, so the suggestion was rejected, and thus the matter ended.

As the century was coming to an end, Beth Israel seemed to be waning as well, plagued by financial troubles and internal strife. Caught between the conflicting press of congregational and communal loyalties, challenged by old congregations growing stronger and new ones coming into being, it needed an enterprise that would retain the active support of its old members and, even more important, attract new ones. The new administration that was to lead it into the new century charged a special committee to draw up a plan for congregational renewal and revival. After due deliberation the committee recommended: "Congregation Beth Israel should engage a teacher-preacher, so that the children will be educated in Judaism. A school should be established and hold its sessions in the meeting room. In the congregational school only children of members are to be admitted. One day a week girls should be taught, as well as those who cannot attend the regular school."[64]

It was to be years before a viable congregational school was established. By the end of the century, however, after a quarter of a century of existence, the acculturation of the membership and the Americanization of the congregation had progressed to the point where there were the strongest sentiments not only for a congregational school but for a one-day-a-week school (Sunday school) for girls and others, as well, under the tutelage of a teacher who could also serve as the congregation's preacher.

Congregational Rabbi/Communal Rov

Three rabbis served Beth Israel in the nineteenth century, and their existence was a difficult one, economically precarious and spiritually unsatisfying. Rabbis Abba Hayim Levinson, Abraham Rosen, and David Ginsberg were scholarly products of Lithuanian *yeshivot* (schools of higher learning). In Rochester they became mere functionaries supervising kosher slaughtering and the butcher shops. Each year they had to petition in writing for reelection by the congregation and the meager congregational stipend. Each one was involved in one or more battles with the butchers on whom his livelihood depended.

Rabbi Levinson, who began his tenure in 1883, received an annual salary of $150. From time to time the congregation would give him small sums for special services rendered, such as sounding the shofar, but his chief source of income was payments of $50 per annum from each of the four kosher butchers to whom he gave certification.[65]

The minutes contain little information on the role and function of the rabbi. He called himself "rabbi of Congregation Beth Israel," and his chief congregational duties seem to have been to teach the Hevra Mishnayes daily, to be available to answer ritual questions, and to undertake some liturgical functions during the High Holy Days. Most of the references to the rabbi concern his reelection or touch on problems he was having. Thus, for example, a special meeting was called on August 3, 1890, at the request of a number of members because "the rabbi cannot make a living because the butchers have stopped paying him." Asked that they continue their payments, all the butchers save one refused to do so. A collection was thereupon taken, and twenty-two members contributed $119 in sums ranging from $3 to $25.

This crisis was the result of long-standing problems that Rabbi Levinson had with some butchers. The *Jewish Tidings,* happy to report on strife in the Orthodox Jewish community, published a story on December 28, 1888, with the following headline: "A Rabbi's Edict: It Causes Bickering in the Polish Quarter." The story read in part: "The Polish districts are again in the throes of a civil war. . . . It appears that Rabbi Levison [sic] of the Leopold Street Congregation has found the salary accruing from his pastoral services insufficient to meet his wants, and it is alleged that he has taken four butchers under his protecting wing for the consideration of $50 each per annum, and declare from his pulpit that the meat sold by these four butchers was strictly kosher, but that the meat of all other butchers was trefe."

The *Rochester Democrat and Chronicle* could not pass up so titillating a story and sent a reporter who found that "in the dispute the congregation of Beth Avezer [sic] took sides with Mr. Amdoursky (a butcher who was not given certification) and the president M. Nusbaum called a meeting last night, at which it was decided to become entirely independent of congregation Beth Israel. Rev. Leeser Anixter of Chicago was elected rabbi for the next two years at an annual salary of $600."[66]

Rabbi Levinson was caught in the vise of intercongregational conflict between his own Beth Israel and the break-away B'nai Aviezer. When he became rabbi of Beth Israel the only competing congregation was Hevra Tillim. It was smaller, and its members were Polish Jews. Rabbi Levinson was accepted as the rabbi of the community because Polish Jews would accept the scholarly authority of a Lithuanian rabbi. B'nai Aviezer, in order to establish itself, decided to do so through engaging a rabbi of greater scholarly reputation than the resident rabbi. Rabbi Anixter's scholarly credentials moved the butchers who were Rabbi Levinson's mainstay into his camp, and hence the crisis of 1890. At the next quarterly meeting on March 8, 1891, Rabbi Levinson tendered his resignation, asking that $200 be granted him for expenses to move from Rochester. Both the resignation and the request were approved unanimously.

Less than a month later, the *Jewish Tidings* carried the news from Baltimore that "a number of the Russo-Polish congregations have contributed to a fund to support a chief rabbi who has just arrived from Rochester, Chief Rabbi Abraham Chaim Levinson." The *Tidings* could not resist the temptation to editorialize: "Rabbi Levinson was minister of the Leopold Street Temple. For his services he received the princely sum of $3 per week. It has remained for Baltimore to discover and appreciate his remarkable Talmudical learning."[67]

After a year without a rabbi, Beth Israel found a most desirable candidate for the congregation and the community. At first he was referred to merely as the rabbi "from Syracuse." On July 13, 1892, it was reported that other congregations were interested; some even pledged money. Beth Israel obligated itself to pay $200 toward the salary of Rabbi Abraham Abba Rosen. On July 31, the president reported to the trustees of Beth Israel that the committee to collect the salary of the rabbi had close to $300 in pledges. The minutes record that at a mass meeting of "the entire city," Rabbi Abraham Abba Rosen was elected city rabbi at a salary of $500 per annum.[68]

The rabbi, a native of the town of Wilki near Kovno, was thirty-six years old. He had been the rabbi of Tsaritsin but, because of the residence restrictions imposed against Jews in inner Russia, had been forced to leave, coming to America in 1890 and settling in Rochester two years later.

Rabbi Rosen's three-year tenure began with a lawsuit, was plagued by economic problems, and ended in community strife and division. The very plan for the payment of salary boded ill for his economic security and his spiritual authority. Individual congregations assumed annual obligations, and he was beholden to the butchers for a good part of his livelihood. Since he had no specific congregational duties, a congregation could withdraw support with equanimity. His dependence on the butch-

ers caused him his first problem. The established butchers used the
rabbi's religious authority of certification to stifle competition, as an article in the September 30, 1892, issue of the *Jewish Tidings* discloses.

AGAINST A RABBI

Rabbi Rosen and seven other Jews of Polish extraction were examined
before Justice Gorham in Brighton Wednesday on information lodged by
Morris Abramson and Max Amdoursky, who alleged that the rabbi has
conspired with several others to ruin the [kosher meat] business of the
complainants. They purchased a meat market on 178 St. Joseph street
of Thomas Page. The trade of the market is confined almost wholly to
Jews of the Polish nationality. . . . The meat must be killed by licensed
butchers who must pass an examination before the rabbi. . . . There are
six of these "schechters" in Rochester. The complainants allege that
the "schechters" and rabbi conspired to ruin their business. . . . [The
schechters refused to slaughter for them and] the rabbi refused to license
anyone else to do it.

To be hauled into court just two months after having been declared rabbi
of the community was not an auspicious way to begin one's spiritual
leadership, but the real troubles were yet to come.

In June of the following year there was again a mass meeting "to
make a plan how to obtain the money to pay the rabbi." Some congregations were reluctant to participate. But after a month of rancorous negotiations all congregations agreed to the reelection of Rabbi Rosen for two
years at a salary of $600. Hevra Tehillim pledged $100, Beth Haknesses
Hachodosh $150, Hevra Hesed Shel Emes $50, and "the Polish Hevra"
$25. The minutes of July 16, 1893, record: "Therefore $275 is still
needed, so it was moved and seconded that Congregation Beth Israel
should 'be good' for the balance, $275. Carried."

The monies to pay the rabbi did not come out of congregational funds
but were collected for that purpose from those who wished to contribute.
No central organization existed to support the rabbinic office. Ad hoc
committees called mass meetings; congregational committees collected
funds. Not only the incumbent but also the office was wholly dependent
on the ongoing good will of an unorganized constituency. Whatever good
will there was seems to have evaporated during the year, for in July 1894,
it was reported that the rabbi did not have enough for a livelihood and
that a special committee had to be appointed "to go out to collect for
the Rabbi."[69] A special meeting to deal with the problem was attended
only by Beth Israel, Hevra B'nai David, and the "Polish Shul." Although
the rabbi had been elected for two years, little could be done to assure
the payments pledged by the congregations. Since their collecting committees were having little success, a new plan for financing the office of

the rabbi was voted by Beth Israel. Instead of paying three cents for the kosher slaughtering of a chicken, buyers would be charged five cents, two cents to go for the support of the rabbi.[70] But the other congregations rejected the plan, calling it "karobke," the hated tax imposed by the czar's government on kosher meat.

By the end of 1894, all other congregations had withdrawn support; only Beth Israel continued paying $16 a month. When the president reported to the winter quarterly meeting that the rabbi was destitute, a committee was appointed to approach the other synagogues to urge them to "try to do their best." But when the rabbi requested to be permitted to preach in the synagogue to augment his income, it was reluctantly granted by a vote of twelve to eleven. His position was clearly untenable, and by the spring of 1895 even Beth Israel had decided to dispense with his services. On March 3, it was moved to pay the rabbi what was owed him to the termination of his contract on July 16. A motion to table was defeated, but a committee was appointed to call on him to urge him not to mention shohatim or butchers in any sermons or "abuse" any members of the congregation.

On July 15, the day before the termination of the rabbi's contract, a special trustees meeting was called because disturbances were anticipated. Precautions were taken. The synagogue was ordered closed till Minha (afternoon prayer) time. It was voted to have a policeman in attendance to prevent a "gathering around the synagogue." The shamash was to deliver to the rabbi his tallit and *tefillin* (phylacteries), together with a notice from the secretary that he was not to come to the shul anymore. These steps were felt necessary because, as it was reported at the meeting, "the Rochester papers are filled with reports that there will be disturbances when Rabbi Rosen is led from Leopold Street to Hanover Street."[71]

This was no exaggeration. As early as April 2, 1895, the *Rochester Union-Advertiser* carried the story:

RABBI RETIRED
Trouble in the Beth Israel Congregation Causes Hard Words
At a recent meeting of the congregation of Beth Israel, on Leopold Street, Rabbi Rosen, who has had charge of the church for some time, was retired.
The trouble is said to have arisen from the opening of a Jewish meat market by the Friendly Brothers, concerning which a dispute arose in which the rabbi offended some of the congregation, one of whom said in regard to the affair:
"We are displeased with the man and therefore after July 1st he will cease to officiate in our congregation. We have found him backward in his duties, such as keeping his flock in harmony and looking after the

spiritual development of the minds of the children. The meat market matter is really the smallest affair, but like the proverbial straw, has broken the camel's back."

Rabbi Rosen stated:

"The whole trouble is caused by one individual whom I will not name, as he has lately appeared before the public in a very unpleasant light, and who aspires to lead our people not only in matters religious, but in politics as well. He takes delight in stirring up strife, and having practically nothing else to do, spends his time in intriguing and scheming. My predecessor, Rabbi Levinson, who is a man of profound erudition, a grand Talmudic scholar and a model of piety and virtue, was also reviled through this man's machinations."

It is probable that the rabbi's friends will soon call a mass meeting and try and arrange for him to remain in Rochester.[72]

The individual blamed by the rabbi for his troubles was Jacob Rosenbloom. During the 1890s he was the "strong man" in the Beth Israel Congregation. He had leadership pretensions in the wider community and some political ambitions as well. A man of some education, he was possessed of a strong character, was more feared than loved or respected, and bore the nickname *Shwartzer Zelig*, "Black Selig." The rabbi's friends did call a mass meeting on his behalf as announced in an article two days later.

RABBI ROSEN'S FRIENDS

They Will Meet and Protest Against This Removal

The trouble in the Hebrew congregation of Beth Israel, which was supposed ended with the removal of Rabbi Rosen, bids fair to live for some time to come. The friends of the deposed rabbi have issued a call for a mass meeting to be held in Goldstein's Hall, corner of Chatham and Kelly Streets, on Tuesday evening, April 9th, for the purpose of protesting against the removal of the rabbi and devising some way to secure his reinstatement.

The friends of the rabbi contend that his removal was unjust. Until a short time ago, they say, he commanded the respect of all the orthodox Jews of Rochester, and was beloved and looked upon by all as a good authority on religious questions.[73]

From April 2 to July 17, the Rochester daily press published eight lengthy feature articles on the Rabbi Rosen affair, reporting the mass meetings called by friends and foes of the rabbi and interviews with supporters and opponents.

Jacob Rosenbloom felt impelled to unburden himself to a *Rochester*

Union-Advertiser reporter. Of particular interest is his account of the trials and tribulations of attempting to maintain a rabbi and his delineation of the role of a rabbi.

BETH ISRAEL
Statement of the Trouble in the Congregation
President Rosenbloom Gives the Reasons for the Discharge of Rabbi Rosen
Duties of Rabbi Defined
President J. Rosenbloom of the Congregation Beth Israel of orthodox Jews was interviewed by a Union reporter this morning over the trouble which is alleged to exist over the removal of Rabbi Rosen.

Said Mr. Rosenbloom: "I wish to correct the distorted report which has several times appeared in Rochester papers with regard to the Congregation Beth Israel, of which I have the honor of being president. I had thought not to notice what appeared mere irresponsible gossip, but the frequent repetition of the misstatements has induced me to put a stop to them by the true statement of facts.

"An uninformed reader would draw the conclusion from the reports above referred to that the members of the Congregation Beth Israel are at knives' points with regard to the recent discharge by the congregation of Rabbi Rosen; that there are divisions and quarrelings and all sorts of unmanly conduct between the partisans of the rabbi and his opponents, and also that I myself am the chief instigator of this little brotherly war.

"In the first place Rabbi Rosen was no more our rabbi than he was the rabbi of all the other orthodox congregations of the city. He is an interpreter of the divine law, not a spiritual adviser. His duty is chiefly to interpret the law as it is written and apply it to particular cases as they are brought to him for decision. Moreover, the feeling which animates all orthodox Jews of obligation to preserve the knowledge of the law and to support students of the law simply as students, is their principal motive in keeping a rabbi. Thus you will see that it is entirely wrong to represent the discharge of a rabbi as analogous to the discharge of a minister.

"Three years ago four congregations of Rochester pledged themselves to contribute to the support of Rabbi Rosen in proportion to the size of their membership. Ours, as the largest, paid the largest share. Last year all the other congregations, for reasons which it would not interest the general public to know, withdrew their contributions. Our congregation strove to maintain the rabbi single-handed, and to that end tried to rally public opinion among the orthodox Jews of Rochester to his support. But we received scant response. There was no alternative for us then but to give up the struggle, and accordingly, on March 3d, the Congregation

Beth Israel, by a vote to which there were only two dissenting voices, resolved to notify the rabbi that they would be unable to maintain him in his position any longer."[74]

The last of the dozen articles appeared in the *Rochester Democrat and Chronicle,* July 17, 1895.

RABBI ROSEN INSTALLED

He Finds a Synagogue to Give Him Shelter

Despite all apprehensions to the contrary, the transfer of Rabbi A. Rosen from the synagogue Beth Israel, on Leopold street, to the synagogue Benai David, on Hanover street, was accomplished last evening without friction of any kind between the two factions, although the hostile feeling is intense. In accordance with a request made to the authorities by the friends of the rabbi, Lieutenant Samuel Schwartz was present at the scene last evening and he had with him for possible emergencies Officers Alt, Shepard, Sheehan and Scholl. . . .

The rabbi's friends assembled at the synagogue Benai David, on Hanover street, where they were marshaled into line by Nathan Greenberg, to the number of about sixty, and proceeded thence, accompanied by a part of the police detail and several hundred of whooping and yelling children, aged from 4 years to 14, to the residence of the rabbi, at No. 104 Kelly street. Several cheers were given for Rabbi Rosen, when the procession arrived at the residence, and a deputation of venerable appearing and gray whiskered Jewish elders entered the residence and soon reappeared on the street, with the rabbi in their midst. He was escorted about the streets of the neighborhood for a short time, but the procession, very sensibly, avoided the vicinity of the Leopold street synagogue, where services were in progress, and returned to the Hanover street edifice where Jewish services were held, consisting mainly of the offering up of prayers by the newly installed rabbi.

Nathan Greenberg, who is one of the leaders of the friends of Rabbi Rosen, stated that the congregation of Beth Israel, or its leaders, had insisted that the rabbi should interpret the Jewish law only as they desired it to be interpreted. When he had declined to do this they had discharged him. The present movement was for the purpose of restoring the rabbi to his religious liberty, so that he would not be under obligations to anyone. He stated further, that an organization was effected last May, soon after the congregation of Beth Israel notified the rabbi that his time would expire on July 16th.

It did not take long for Beth Israel to find and engage a new rabbi. The congregation's committee on kashrut reported to the meeting on August 4, 1895, that it had met with the representatives of the other congregations and that all "concluded that they could not enact ordinances for the regulation of kashrut without a rabbi." They also reported that "they think that a rabbi can be hired without cost to the congregation" and had a candidate to recommend, Rabbi David Ginsberg. It was voted that when the intercongregational committee would have a "foundation" from which to pay a rabbi, they might engage him and Beth Israel would recognize him as the "Rabbi for the City." A limitation was set however; the rabbi could not be elected for more than one year.

The background of the new rabbi, David, the son of Rabbi Isaac Ginsberg, was similar to that of his predecessor. He too was born in the Kovno environs and received his ordination from Rabbi Isaac Elchanan Spektor. His first position in America was in Rochester, which he served for fourteen years.

Rabbi Ginsberg's tenure was longer and less stormy than that of his predecessor, but it was not without its problems and incidents. After his first year, he was reelected for two years at a salary from Beth Israel of $150. Financial arrangements continued to be precarious, for, as earlier, the salary did not come from congregational funds but had to be collected from "subscribers." The instructions to the Committee for Solicitation that it "be done with dignity" suggests that it was not always done so.[75]

In September of his second year, he joined with Rabbi Rosen (who remained in Rochester until 1901) to ban the meat of shohtim who had interests in butcher shops. This led to a dispute in the city, as the president reported to Beth Israel: "There is excitement in the city concerning the shohtim and the butchers. Rabbis were brought to decide the matter, and they recommended a meeting of representatives of all the congregations to reach agreement on the matter of kashrut. I appointed such a committee and it met with the other committees, but they could not agree. Our committee sees no need to make the enactments concerning the shohtim which the other committees demand." It was voted that "our synagogue should not participate with the butchers in their designs, for their motives are not to benefit Judaism; they only want to take revenge on the butchers who are also shohtim. [Two long-time leaders of Beth Israel fit that description, Kalman Bardin and Jacob Lipsky.] It is the duty of our congregation to protect our butchers when they follow the law, as determined by our rabbi, Rabbi David Ginsberg."[76]

Two leading members of Beth Israel were affected by the attempted ban. Their congregation rose to their defense and apparently attempted to force the hand of their rabbi while publicly proclaiming his authority. The position of the rabbi was a difficult one, but he succeeded in maintaining his integrity and retaining his position.

He had left his family in Europe and now needed a leave to go get them. But he was owed half his yearly salary and was in debt. The matter was aired at a special meeting in November where it was voted to pay him $50 then and $50 when his family arrived. He did not leave until the spring, waiting until his contract was renewed on May 16, 1897. On the back of the contract permission was granted for a two-month leave to fetch his family from Europe. On September 14, the congregation heard the good news that Rabbi Ginsberg was already on the ship and was due to arrive with his family in a week. It was voted that as soon as the definite time of arrival was ascertained, members were to be notified so that they could go to the depot to greet the rabbi and family. On the renewal of his contract in 1898, he was voted a raise to $250, and there was a suggestion that it be $300. He had weathered the storm that threatened his tenure and grew in influence and affection as time went on.

The Cantor of the Congregation

The reporter of the *Rochester Democrat and Chronicle* perceived it well and stated it accurately in 1895: "A rabbi does not necessarily occupy the same position in the orthodox Jewish church that a priest or minister does in the Christian churches. . . . The leader of the services in the synagogue . . . the official of the Jewish synagogue which most closely approaches to the Christian minister is called a cantor."

The chief synagogal functionary of the Beth Israel congregation was its cantor. Upon him depended the quality and attractiveness of the services and, in great measure, the popularity of the synagogue itself. We have seen that the search for "a good cantor" was the main order of business of the congregation when it occupied its new edifice. The presence of a "star" cantor, Hayim Weinshel, made it easier to dispense with the presence and services of Rabbi Levinson. The report on the departure of Rabbi Rosen in the *Rochester Democrat and Chronicle* notes that the position of cantor "is occupied in the Beth Israel Synagogue by Samuel Cantor, who has held the place for three years and will remain undisturbed."[77]

The importance of the cantor to the synagogue is indicated by the compensation he received. While Rabbi Rosen was receiving a total of $500 in salary from the entire community ($200 from Beth Israel) in 1893–95, Beth Israel was paying Cantor Samuel Cantor $900. It is no wonder then that the minutes disclose that more discussion was devoted at meetings to the office, search, election, compensation, tenure, and critique of the cantor than to all other functionaries combined.

In 1890, the popular Cantor Jospe announced his resignation because, as it was reported to a congregational meeting, "he was elected in New York for much more money,"[78] and it took a full year to find an acceptable replacement. The departure of a tenured officiant had its rewards as well. Quality departs, but variety has its charms and provides excitement. Visiting cantors come, perform, leave. Self-declared experts deliver themselves of opinions, critics analyze, partisans debate. During that entire year the synagogue was at the center of communal interest and discussion.

The minutes record the audition visits of half a dozen candidates before Hayim Weinshel was elected hazzan for two years at a salary of $800 per annum. An extra $100 was voted for a choir; he was given $25 for expenses, and when he signed the contract he received $50 to bring his family.[79]

Cantor Weinshel was not only a cantor of note but a pioneer of Hebrew poetry in America as well. Just before coming to Rochester he had published *Nitai Naamanim (Luxuriant Plantings,* New York, 1891), a one-hundred page volume of twenty poems and six letters. The noted biblical scholar Arnold B. Ehrlich wrote a laudatory introduction, hoping that others would take a lesson from him and write in Hebrew rather than Yiddish "so that our holy tongue will prosper in this land in which we live." Of particular interest is the poem *Shir Sipuri (A Narrative Poem)* subtitled "The vision which I saw in America," a poem of fifty-nine quatrains descriptive of Jewish religious life in America. He describes his visits to three cities as a guest cantor and gently satirizes the cantors, rabbis, and synagogue officials he met. Cantor Weinshel was born in Minsk and had lived in Suwalk, so he came from the same area as the leaders of Beth Israel. The congregation could now boast of a published poet as well as a star cantor. By 1891 there were in Rochester a group of Hebraists who would boast of it.

By the spring, however, he was having financial problems. He asked the congregation for a grant above his salary because he needed a new suit for Pesah but could not afford it. Instead of money the trustees granted him permission to sell tickets for Passover services. To ease his financial plight, he was also given a leave of three weeks to lead prayer as a visiting cantor. But problems mounted. A special meeting was called on July 31, 1892, to decide whether to give the cantor his salary in advance because there were rumors that he was planning to leave. Nevertheless, his popularity was such that he was granted the requested advance. But try as it might the congregation could not retain its star cantor. The trustees met hurriedly on August 13 to hear the president report that the cantor was told not to be away "this Sabbath," but he did not obey. A special emergency congregational meeting was called the next day to be informed that the cantor was away from his pulpit without permission to try out for a position in another city. It was regretfully voted to declare his contract null and void.[80]

Hazzan Weinshel left, and once again a string of candidates came during the entire year,[81] among others Cantors Fine, Feinberg, Sholom Diamond, and Judah Oberman. Finally, on May 28, 1893, Cantor Samuel

Joseph Cantor was elected for a period of two years at an annual salary of $900, but he was to provide a choir. Even as the congregation was assuming the obligation of a $900 expenditure for cantor and choir, arrangements were being made for a mass communal meeting to discuss where and how money might be obtained to pay Rabbi Rosen his $500 salary obligated to him by the entire community. Two years later the cantor was reelected unanimously at the same salary and was granted the request that it be stipulated in his contract that he need not share fees received for a wedding or *brit* (circumcision) with the rabbi.

When there was no money to pay the rabbis, committees were formed to go out and solicit contributions. But when the treasury was short and the cantor's salary was due, it was voted to "borrow money on a note" so as to be able to pay him on time.[82] A few months later, the congregation undertook to guarantee a loan of $75 for the cantor. Despite this obviously fine treatment by the congregation, Samuel Cantor decided to leave the cantorate. The spring 1896 quarterly meeting heard the president report that their hazzan was planning to open a liquor business in Syracuse. Called to the meeting he verified the report, and it was thereupon voted to void the contract, but he agreed to remain through the High Holy Days and be paid $600.

One cannot help but note how differently Cantors Weinshel and Cantor were treated in comparison to Rabbis Levinson and Rosen. The rabbis were in a precarious economic situation during their tenure, were abruptly dismissed, and left in an atmosphere of ill will and recriminations. The cantors were paid their salaries, given gifts and loans, and treated with respect and generosity when they left. The rabbis were communal functionaries without a communal organization charged with the responsibility for their livelihood and without an organized constituency to whom they could turn. One senses that the leader of the congregations viewed them as a necessary but unwelcome burden that a community had to bear. They were of little practical worth to the congregation, adding neither to its status nor to its strength. The cantor was a congregation's most cherished possession, chief contributor to its standing and popularity. His utility was constantly visible to all members of the congregation. For some he provided aesthetic pleasure, to others spiritual uplift or a combination of both. Beyond that, he provided the community with a subject for critique and conversation and had his coterie of devotees who were jealous in protecting in word and deed this object of their affection. Visibility, to be sure, could make for vulnerability; critique could turn to criticism and conversation to cavil, but he had the supreme virtue of usefulness. He was, as the reporter observed, "the leader of the services in the synagogue," and in the American community the services were at the heart of the synagogue and the synagogue in the very center of the community.

During the last years of the century, the cantorate of Beth Israel was in decline, as was the congregation. A cantor-teacher was proposed to be shared with the Rochester Hebrew School. The salaries paid Cantors Weinshel and Cantor were not equaled until well into the twentieth century, but in difficult times as in times of well-being the cantor remained until the end of the century the central functionary in the east European Orthodox congregation.

Relationship with Other Congregations

In the years 1886–1900, the relationship with other congregations in the Orthodox community progressed from competition to cooperation. Initially it was forbidden for members of Beth Israel to attend services at the competing congregations Hevra Tillim and the Beth Haknesses Hachodosh. But mutual interests and common problems led to cooperative efforts and joint enterprises. The areas of cooperation were in kashrut, education, burial, and security. The supervision of kashrut necessitated a rabbi. When Beth Israel engaged Rabbi Levinson, congregation and community were synonymous. As he became identified with Beth Israel alone, another rabbi was engaged by its sister congregation Beth Haknesses Hachodosh. But congregational rabbis were not in the tradition of east European religious life; in time traditionalism and financial prudence brought the congregations together to establish a communal rabbi and call Rabbi Rosen to the office and, after him, Rabbi Ginsberg. Rabbi Levinson called himself "Rabbi of Congregation Beth Israel"; Rabbi Ginsberg was the "Rabbi of the Rochester Community." Both were correct in describing their office.

Beth Israel's abortive attempts at a congregational school soon led it to take the initiative in establishing first the Talmud Torah and then the Rochester Hebrew School. These were not intercongregational enterprises, but the fact that leaders of Beth Israel could give leadership and support to a school meeting in the building of Beth Haknesses Hachodosh is an indication of trans-congregational cooperation. Similarly, the Jewish Benevolent Society at the Beth Israel Synagogue had members of Beth Haknesses Hachodosh among its officers.

"The abuses and outrages to which the newly immigrated Jews are frequently subjected" united the east European community in a mass meeting at Blumberg's Hall on July 18, 1890. Kalman Bardin opened the meeting; Jacob Rosenbloom presided. Both were leaders of Beth Israel, but this did not prevent Aaron Nusbaum of Beth Haknesses Hachodosh from speaking and being the first signatory on the resolution passed.[83] An ongoing joint enterprise with Beth Haknesses Hachodosh was the purchase of adjoining cemetery lands and their development as a burial place for the community.

The congregations joined in establishing a semiautonomous "authority" to be in charge of the cemetery lands. It was a device that permitted cooperative effort yet preserved the individuality and permitted the fullest independence of the two congregations. Had a similar organization been fashioned to be in charge of kashrut supervision and the city rabbi, it might have prevented the intercongregational disputes that marred communal life just at that time. It seems that in the matter of cemetery the congregations were ready to delegate authority to a trans-congregational entity—death leveled parochial identity—but in the matter of kashrut and the rabbi, they would not yield power or share control. The reason may have been ideological, the reluctance to permit compromise of what was the central religious communal enterprise and issue— the supervision of kashrut. More likely it was sociological, congregations differing ethnically (i.e., in place of origin of members) remaining suspicious of the religious integrity of those with whom they lived in proximity but with whom they as yet had not become fully integrated. Old World prejudices, for example, of the Lithuanian Jew disparaging the scholarship of the Galician, and the latter suspecting the piety of the former, must have persisted in the immigrant community. This may also account for the fact that the two "Lithuanian" congregations, Beth Israel and Beth Haknesses Hachodosh, had a closer relationship and cooperated in communal endeavors with each other more than with any other congregation when we might have expected that since they were competing for members from the same ethnic pool, competition would have prevented cooperation. The immigrant community apparently maintained a continuity of imported attitudes as well as of institutionalism.

The continuity of both caused Beth Israel and Beth Haknesses Hachodosh to join together a month after the cemetery venture to urge the retention of the European institution of community rabbi. They chose as the worthy incumbent a product of Lithuanian yeshivot, Rabbi David Ginsberg, who had been ordained by the dean of the Lithuanian rabbinate, Rabbi Isaac Elchanan Spektor.

Events and Incidents

A study of the ledger containing the signed indentures of the purchase of seats in the new synagogue building in 1886 discloses that of the forty-four seat holders, twenty-five signed their names in English and two in Hebrew, while seventeen made only a mark.[84]

In the early years of Beth Israel, disputes, "abuses," strife, and litigation were not uncommon. A reading of the minutes discloses that greater harmony was established with the passing of time and that the individual members exerted greater self-discipline. Yet sufficient incidents of disagreements and abuses are recorded.

Boycott was used as a means of enforcing congregational/communal discipline. "It is right," it was suggested at the November 14, 1886, meeting, "that no member buy groceries from Untenberg, because he insulted our synagogues and its members, with disgraceful talk." Soon after, Mr. Untenberg left the congregation to become a leading member of Beth Haknesses Hachodosh.

Jacob Cohen pleaded to have a $1.75 fine forgiven. In March 1888 his plea was refused, but a month later it received a favorable vote. A month later it was reported that Eliezer Rosenberg did not obey orders of the hevra and that he "abused the Trustees." It was voted that he receive notice not to attend services at the synagogue. The warning was then extrapolated into a law that a "stranger" who does not obey orders may not rent a seat, receive an honor, or recite kaddish.

From time to time the congregation interceded to make peace among members. On May 14, 1893, "Mr. Shevah Simon claimed that he was fined a dollar unjustly, and that Abraham Levy abused him without cause." It was voted that a committee of five be appointed to "straighten out between the two."[85] A week later the committee reported that the antagonists "were not yet ready to make peace." The president granted the committee more time, and time seems to have brought conciliation.

A year later, on April 18, 1894, a committee of three was appointed to investigate charges brought against Nathan Reicher by the president, Abraham Blum, "for abusing him in the synagogue." Two months later Fishel ben Yitzhak was warned that if he brought his small child who disturbed services to shul again, he would be fined $2 "and he will have to pay it." The next week the president ordered that the fines levied against Blumberg and Levy be canceled. Accusations of abuse, some disputes, some fines—generally forgiven. The synagogue had become a disciplining force on the east European Jewish urban frontier but one with overriding compassion.

The decline of the synagogue as a social center is noted. The minutes record the occasional serving of a repast after a meeting, the Hevra Kadisha was treated by the congregation to an annual dinner, but in the years 1886–1900, there is a record of only one major social event. On October 20, 1889, a committee of three was appointed to secure a hall for a Purim Ball. Four months later, on March 6, 1890, the *Rochester Union-Advertiser* reported:

A PURIM BALL

The congregation of Beth Israel gave a masquerade Purim ball last night at Germania Hall, to raise funds to decorate their synagogue on Leopold Street. A prize was given to the one that sold the highest number of tickets. The contest was between I. Hershberg, D. Seraski, and E. Kominski. The former sold the highest number—683. After a grand march J. Rosenbloom, the president, called the three named and thanked them in behalf of the congregation for the good work they had done and presented a gold medal to I. Hershberg.

At the spring 1890 quarterly meeting a report was given on the great social event. The president announced that the committees of the Purim Ball and decoration of the synagogue "had attended to their duties in the best manner." More important, a "clear profit" of $506.40 was made.

The minutes do not indicate that it was a masquerade ball. A ball of such nature represented such a departure from traditional celebration, such a yielding to American ways, that the secretary was loath to include it in the official records of this Orthodox congregation.[86]

More appropriate entertainments for an Orthodox congregation were Hanukkah concerts presented by the cantor. On October 24, 1894, permission was granted to Hazzan Samuel Cantor to charge admission to such a concert and keep the profits, providing the hevra "should not lose thereby." Similar permission was granted a year later.

Wedding services and celebration were generally held in the home of the bride. The more affluent would have the service in the synagogue and celebration in one of the neighborhood halls or in a hotel ballroom. To encourage the use of the synagogue, a *huppah* (wedding canopy) costing $60 was ordered, and the minutes record a number of weddings solemnized in the new synagogue.

There is a more precise account of deaths within the congregation and burials in the congregational cemetery. Since permission had to be given for such burials, special meetings were called for the purpose, and the name of the deceased and the charges made were recorded. From 1874 through 1886, when twenty deaths are listed, twelve were of children or stillborn infants. Sixty-seven burials are noted for the period 1887–1900; of these twenty-eight were children, and nine were stillborn infants.

The incidence of deaths of children—well over 50 percent—not only reflects the high infant mortality rate among the immigrants but also indicates that it was a community of young married couples producing many children. A high birth rate might suggest optimism about the future. The minutes indicate that even in darkest times, there were no counsels of despair.

Optimism about the future was marred by uncertainty about the children, a generation growing up in the environment of the public school under the influence of the American street, speaking a strange new language. There was closeness between parents and children but estrangement as well. To an institution like a synagogue, which, as a religious institution, is conservative in nature, this presented particular problems. Shall we encourage the participation of the young in congregational matters? Shall we invite their organizations to use our facilities?

A "communication" was brought before a membership meeting on April 30, 1893, stating that "sons of members had organized a club and ask permission of the congregation to meet in the meeting room." A committee of three was appointed to determine whether it was "fit for our congregation to permit them to meet in our meeting room, and if permission be granted should they pay for the room which they would use." The congregation was concerned about expenditure that might be incurred, but one senses an even greater fear as to what might happen at such a meeting, whether it might compromise the congregation. Clearly the conduct of the "sons of members" was suspect.

Two years later the Hebrew Young Men's Historical Society asked to use the meeting room. They offered to pay all expenses, and authorization was voted to the trustees to make the necessary arrangements. Time and experience may have altered attitudes and allayed suspicions, or it may have been that greater trust was put in a cultural rather than a social club.

The real testing came the next year. A committee from the Judean Club, a cultural and literary club of teenage boys, appeared before a special congregational meeting and received permission to meet at the Beth Israel building. The only payment requested was one dollar a month to the shamash for cleaning. After only a half year, on January 10, 1897, it was voted "to notify the Judean Club that it should look for another place to meet." No reason is given. Among reasons later recalled was that someone had found the name Jesus Christ in a book being used for the study of Jewish history, that young ladies had been invited to the meetings, and that there was social dancing.[87] Beth Israel had recognized the need to attract the youth into the orbit of the congregation, but it was not ready to accept the acculturation and Americanization of their children. The end-of-century synagogue served as a sanctuary for the old generation; it lacked the capability (and often the will) to make it a spiritual, cultural, and social center for the new.

The minutes of the last years of the century present a picture of a congregation enjoying greater equanimity and living in greater concord than in its first two decades. The average age of the congregant was now higher, so that youthful exuberance, often erupting in contention and strife, was now muted. There now were a number of congregations of differing ethnic composition and religious mores, permitting the deviationist to leave for a hevra more congenial to his religious habits and liturgical taste. It made for greater homogeneity of the Beth Israel membership. With the proliferation of organizations in the immigrant community, there were more openings for leadership positions, thus curtailing the competition for honors in the congregation. As the congregation and its members became more integrated into the American scene, and more open to public interest and scrutiny of neighbors and press, the members exercised greater self-discipline in concern for the reputation of the congregation and their own good names.

At Century's End

The income of the congregation remained constant in the last years of the century. For the quarter ending June 1896, it was $446.22; for the same quarter of 1899 it was $420.97. Expenditures, however, were down to $377.42 from $468.42. In a growing population, which the Rochester Jewish community was (five thousand in 1890; seven thousand a decade later),[88] a level income was a sign of congregational torpor. Debts were incurred, and money was borrowed from one bank to pay another.

The deteriorating financial condition forced the congregation to vote a reconsideration of the election of the rabbi and cantor, and a motion to send notice of dismissal to both was not defeated but postponed because of great arguments. Two weeks later it was carried, and it was further decided that no cantor or rabbi be elected for a two-year period until August 1901. The secretary was notified to send notice to both incumbents informing them of the reconsideration of their election because of lack of funds. Cantor Lieberman asked to be released at once. After arguments that lasted all summer, Rabbi Ginsberg was reelected for a one-year term at a salary of $150, with the proviso that if he would obtain a new position during the year his salary would be prorated—a clear suggestion that he do so. Clearly something had to be done to stem the downward sag of the congregation. A special committee charged to suggest a course of action for the "betterment of the situation" recommended that a teacher-preacher be engaged. This was not acted on for a half-dozen years. Beth Israel continued its stubborn struggle to maintain its status not only as the pioneer but also as the premier congregation in the Rochester Orthodox community.

One can only surmise the reasons for the lack of success of Beth Israel at the turn of the century. A constancy of leadership was maintained over a period of a quarter of a century. It may be argued that this was a sign of stability, but it can also be an indication of stagnation. Younger men of ambition and ability were apparently not readily welcomed, so they exercised their leadership in the new congregations springing up. For the sons of the first members, almost all American born or American reared, the congregation's religious conservatism and its self-insulation against the language and influences of America had little appeal. They might on occasion, or often, as did young Louis Lipsky,[89] attend the synagogue to hear a maggid, but to become involved in its management would hardly occur to them. The immigrants of the decade 1890–1900 were mainly from Poland and Russia and would not likely join a congregation made up largely of Lithuanian Jews. The members of Beth Israel, now "long-time" residents, men of the middle class, attempted to maintain the position of being the aristocrats of the community. It is doubtful that they would have made a recent immigrant worker feel welcome in their synagogue. So the newcomers joined the more hospitable hevrot or formed their own, the *Vaad Hakolel* congregation in 1895, the *Chevra Chyateem,* the Tailors' Congregation in 1896, and a half dozen others.

One senses that religious considerations were factors as well. The suggestion officially recorded at the end of 1899, to engage a preacher-teacher, must have been a topic of serious discussion among Beth Israel's members for months, if not years. The suggestion held intimations of "Reform" tendencies, a word that was anathema in the immigrant community and a way that it feared would lead to total assimilation, even apostasy. The Rochester Jewish community was polarized religiously as it was socially and economically. The German Jewish congregation B'rith Kodesh had been led to an extreme radical Reform by its rabbi, Dr. Max Landsberg. The specter of a B'rith Kodesh Judaism thwarted any attempts at religious moderation. There seemed no middle course between isolated, insulated Orthodoxy and radical Reform. "A teacher-preacher is a Prediger (preacher), like Dr. Landsberg," an immigrant community, uneasy in its present and fearful for its future, could reason. Such extrapolation of fear might well have been the cause that the recommendation of the "Committee for Betterment" was not acted on. But the recommendation and its implications kept the zealous or fearful away from the doors of the Leopold Street Shul, as the congregation came to be called at century's end.

THE MAKING OF AN AMERICAN CONGREGATION: 1900–1912

The Committee for the Betterment of the Congregation recommended a twofold program of strategy and tactics. The long-range strategy called for the reshaping of the congregation into an American synagogue whose chief activity would be educational, providing a school for the children and lectures for the adults. The central functionary would be an English-speaking preacher-teacher. With the usual wariness against recording departures from tradition, the minutes speak only of a school and a teacher-preacher. The tactics called for enhancing the image of the congregation at services, beginning with the removal of the president and vice-president from the pulpit and appointing six ushers to aid the trustees in maintaining the decorum that would mark an Americanized congregation.

Strategy demands planning, an investment of resources, and a step-by-step implementation. In the first years of the new century, the congregation had neither the resources nor the will to carry out the program suggested by its own "betterment committee." The friends of

Rabbi Ginsberg opposed engaging a preacher-teacher who would vie with the resident rabbi for religious authority. The rabbi not only represented authority demanding strict religious conformity; he also symbolized the traditional, the known, the habitual, and the comfortable. There were too many things in the life of the immigrant that forced change on him—change of location, change of occupation, change of language. The synagogue in its traditionalism afforded him the security of sameness and continuity in a world where everything else was new and different. A congregational school that made provision for the education of girls destroyed traditional patterns. A preacher speaking the language of the world outside would permit that world to intrude into the synagogue sanctuary. Whether the immigrant Jew hewed to traditionalism because of piety or in response to psychological needs, he kept his synagogue traditional long after he had surrendered to untraditional ways. Those recommending change came up against the determination, almost obsession, of Jews, even those no longer traditional in personal life, adamant in retaining the old ways in the synagogues.

The situation of the congregation, which had caused the committee to be appointed, did not permit for its recommendations to be totally ignored. If the strategy was ahead of its time, the tactics could be undertaken now. The minutes permit us to reconstruct a game of "movable chairs" engaged in by the "traditionalists" and the progressives. At first it was suggested that the president and vice-president remain in their pulpit chairs until the coming of a preacher. The progressive forces defeated that proposed retreat. At the winter quarterly meeting a new attempt to return the officers to the pulpit seats was narrowly defeated. At the spring quarterly meeting, it was again moved for reconsideration and was defeated by only one vote. To give permanence to the decision the trustees voted four days later to take the pulpit chairs from the sides of the ark and place them in the meeting room. A year and a half later, when it became obvious that a preacher was not in the congregation's foreseeable future, it was voted to return the chairs to the pulpit, a dramatic way of announcing the defeat of proposed strategy for change.[90]

Ideological ambivalence and financial insecurity continued into the new century. On June 17, 1900, representatives of the Young American Zionist Club asked that it be permitted to use the meeting room for a library and headquarters from which to carry on Zionist work. The sentiment of the rabbi and congregation being strongly pro-Zionist, it was voted to grant the request. The trustees' meeting four days later voted to table the request until the quarterly meeting, and the summer congregational meeting voted to do the same.[91] A decision was not made because Beth Israel did not want to take any action that might be construed as anti-Zion, but discomfort with the young and their activities prevented positive action.

The preacher-teacher project had long since been laid aside. It now went beyond cantor-teacher, advertising for a multi-purpose functionary: hazzan, teacher, mohel, reader.[92] The motivation was "money-saving," for the congregation was in continued financial distress. Its mortgage payments, amounting to half the budget and twice the salaries, were constantly in arrears. Speaking to the bank president, outlining the financial plight of the hevra, but pointing to the accounts receivable from the members, was of little avail. Mr. Simon, the treasurer, came to the rescue, taking a note for $150. Meeting after meeting heard the same old plaint: members are in arrears, bills are coming due, there is no money in the treasury. On May 5, a former president pleaded for a loan of $35 to bring his family from Chicago. It is to the credit of the members that, although there was no money in the treasury, it was voted to give him a note for that amount and to wipe out all his debts to the congregation. At the same meeting, both the president and the treasurer tendered their resignations. But the program of the congregation went on. The rabbi was reelected, a cantor was engaged for the High Holy Days, and some housekeeping improvements were planned.

In 1902 the congregation reached its nadir. The winter quarterly meeting could not be held for lack of quorum. The number of meetings diminished; none were held between January and June. The only hope lay in the cemetery, and a committee was appointed to look into buying land in the desirable Mt. Hope Cemetery. In August it was reported that some of the leading members were twelve months in arrears. Only $150 was allotted for a cantor for the High Holy Days, and it was enacted that no expenses would be paid him, and he was not to have a choir. The shamash could take it no longer and resigned.[93] A special meeting called to elect a *baal shaharis* (precentor of first section of the service) had no attendance. The income for the year was $2,255.19, and the expenditures were $4,187.64, of which $2,093.82 was for payment on debts. The main topic of conversation at the recorded meeting was the cemetery. It seemed to sustain the life of the congregation.

The next two years witnessed dramatic improvement. The whole community seems to have come out of the doldrums, and Beth Israel with it. It began with a reorganization of the communal educational system. The initiative for the organization of a new Talmud Torah now came from some of the younger congregations. The Beth Israel minutes merely record that it was passed that the new Talmud Torah that had been organized was recognized by the congregation and no more.

It no longer was in a position to initiate; it could now only recognize. The recognition of its present status spurred the congregation into action. Five applied for membership in January 1903. Membership in Beth Israel was again becoming desirable. Other congregations initiated the founding of the new Talmud Torah, but by the spring of 1903, Beth Israel was taking leadership in the project. A special meeting on April 26 was told that Beth Israel member "Joffe [Abraham D.] told some members that he is ready to give the house at 164 Chatham St. to the community for a Talmud Torah, providing that the community will assume the responsibility to maintain the school, and pay the $2,000 mortgage indebtedness on the house." By unanimous agreement a committee of five was appointed to meet with similar committees of other congregations, to get Mr. Joffe's offer in writing, to draw up plans, and to report back to a special meeting.[94]

The activity revived congregational life. At the summer quarterly meeting, the rabbi was reelected, the officers were empowered to borrow money to pay the interest on the mortgage, and it was voted to speak to Beth Haknesses Hachodosh about erecting a joint "house" on the new cemetery. A month later the president and secretary were authorized to make needed repairs in the synagogue. Five new members joined on August 30, and seven were added on October 8.

By the spring of 1904, Beth Israel was well on the way to full recovery. It voted unanimously to purchase a set of the new edition of *Talmud Yerushalmi* (Palestinian Talmud) that Rabbi Jacob David Willowsky, known by his acronym, the *Ridbaz*, had published and had come to America to promote. It also voted to seek a hazzan who was also a shohet, for as it was explained to the spring quarterly meeting, "a shohet is needed here." There is thus a return to the traditional dual-functioning hazzan-shohet after experimentation with a hazzan-teacher. Education was now firmly in the hands of the communal Talmud Torah; the shohtim who had been leaders in Beth Israel were getting on in years; the community was growing, and a hazzan-shohet seemed to fill the need. The congregation had not yet returned to its former well-being—support of a full-time cantor.

By the summer, the congregation was engaged in a number of projects: negotiations with Beth Haknesses Hachodosh about the cemetery house, planning to make improvements in the synagogue building—painting, electrifying, adding two windows in the gallery—and setting up an organization to accept the proffered Talmud Torah building and administer the school.[95]

The request from the Council of Zion that a Jewish National Fund four-cent stamp be placed on the High Holy Day tickets was granted. The expenditure of $1,200 was authorized for synagogue improvements. What is more impressive is that the Merchants Bank was ready to lend the money and that members were ready to endorse notes. The annual financial report showed a balance of $1,078.10 and $389 in the fund for fixing the synagogue. Most impressive of all was that twenty-five new members joined in a single week.

The September 26, 1904, minutes read: "The young Cantor Rogoff sent an application that he wants to be Cantor and Reader at a salary of $400 a year. It was voted to engage Cantor Rogoff, on condition that he not be given a contract until a committee report on his character." His youth urged caution. There was still the feeling that the young ought to be suspect until proven worthy. The committee reported, and a contract was granted later. Cantor Rogoff served the congregation with devotion and distinction for many years.

To further dignify the services of this pioneer congregation, it was voted that the officers come to synagogue on Sabbath and holidays dressed in a manner appropriate to the status of Beth Israel, wearing stovepipe hats. The move was meant to add dignity, but it aroused controversy. A trustee who refused to wear a top hat was deposed from office. He took exception and spoke out at a trustees meeting, was fined once and again, and finally left in a huff. But at a subsequent meeting, with apology made, fines were forgiven.[96]

Progress continued. On July 9, nine new members were welcomed, the rabbi was given a three-year contract at a salary of $250, and a similar sum was allocated to reintroduce the choir. Six new members joined the congregation in September and October. Income continued to rise. The sale of nine seats brought in $1,779.

Beth Israel had made a remarkable recovery. It was now in a healthy financial condition. New members were swelling in ranks. Its present secure, it could now, with confidence, look to the future.

An English Preacher-Teacher

The recommendation was first made by the Committee for the Betterment of the Congregation on October 1, 1899. Now six years later the plan was revived. The earlier suggestion was for "a teacher and a preacher, so that our children be educated in Judaism." The new recommendation was specific in its emphasis. "The greatest improvement for our synagogue would be an English preacher for Friday evenings, who would also be a teacher for our children." Preaching now had highest priority, and it was to be in English and on Friday evening for young and old. All three elements—regular preaching, in the English language, on Friday evenings—were American innovations. Beth Israel had moved all the way from a transplanted European hevra to an American congregation.

The earlier recommendation had remained just that. There is no evidence of any attempt at implementation. The weak state of the congregation had made innovation hazardous. In sister cities east and west, Syracuse and Buffalo, there were Orthodox congregations that had become far more Americanized by the end of the century. Buffalo's Beth El, that city's pioneer synagogue, had as early as 1877 sought a minister who could preach in both English and German.[97] The one English ser-

mon preached in the nineteenth century in Rochester's Beth Israel Synagogue was by the Reverend Dr. S. S. Kohn, late of the Buffalo congregation (where he had served for but six months). In 1894 Adath Yeshurun
in Syracuse had called to its pulpit the Jewish Theological Seminary's
first graduate, Rabbi Joseph Herman Hertz (who later served as chief
rabbi of United Hebrew Congregations of the British Commonwealth). It
may well be that in the view of most of Beth Israel's members, both of
the neighboring congregations had departed too far from traditions, and
there was fear that a preacher—even if teaching was his primary obligation—might do the same to their synagogue.

The reluctance to hazard the enterprise may also have come from
the lack of suitable candidates for such a position. In 1900, the Jewish
Theological Seminary, the only school in America training such religious functionaries, had come on hard times. It was ordaining few rabbis,
and these would hardly desire a position that was primarily that of
teacher.

With the reorganization of the seminary under Dr. Solomon Schechter
in 1902, religious functionaries suitable to an established Orthodox synagogue in the process of Americanization were being trained and ordained
in larger numbers. It was to the seminary and its head, Dr. Schechter,
that Beth Israel turned for its "English preacher-teacher."

The congregation had been strengthened by the influx of new
younger members who had children of school age. Some had already undergone a process of acculturation; all were living in the era when Americanization had become the highest priority in immigrant life. These new
members gave the leadership the encouragement to proceed at once with
the project. The meeting that heard the new recommendation voted to
appoint two trustees to canvass the membership to see whether it would
"pay extra" in order to engage the desired functionary. At the following
meeting, the two reported that they had not as yet seen all the members
but that $850 per annum had already been pledged. The enthusiasm was
such that two more were appointed to the committee. The search for a
preacher-teacher was accompanied by a general sense of optimism about
the future of Beth Israel. The winter quarterly meeting authorized the
purchase of more cemetery land for $3,000; voted to exceed the recom-
mendation of the trustees for the reelection of Cantor Rogoff at a gross
salary of $650 ($450 salary plus $200 for choir) by $100, to a total of
$750; and heard the committee on the preacher-teacher report that over
$1,100 had been pledged and that "they expect much more."

At the first meeting of 1906, the trustees instructed the secretary to
"send notice to all those who signed pledges to pay for a preacher to come
to a meeting, Wednesday evening January 31, where each would be asked
what he would expect of a preacher, and all would decide whether the
preacher should conduct a school."[98] All emphasis is on a *preacher*. It

was apparently not at all certain that he would have teaching duties. There must have been strong sentiment that a school that would compete with the communal Talmud Torah should not be established, and there must have been those who felt that the prospects for the engaging of a desirable preacher would be better if teaching were not part of the job.

At a special meeting "of the members who signed to pay for a preacher," after animated discussion on job definition it was voted unanimously that the secretary record: "It is the sentiment of the meeting that the congregation engage a preacher and teacher, to deliver lectures and give lessons in religion to the young people and to the children of the congregation."[99] The minutes note that the motion was adopted by a "standing vote." The meeting was followed by a special congregational meeting on the question: "Is it the 'consent' of the members to engage a preacher and teacher for the young children of the members?" A debate ensued with Abraham Joffe speaking in favor and Joseph Simon against. "Many others joined in the discussion," which concluded in secret ballot vote, forty-four to thirteen, that "the congregation engage an Orthodox preacher and teacher to teach the children and deliver lectures, in accordance with the wishes of the congregation."

At the same meeting that accepted the added financial obligation of a preacher, a communication was received from Rabbi Ginsberg stating that his income was not what it used to be and asking to "please help." A committee of two was appointed to go out to solicit for the rabbi. The transfer of interest and allegiance from community rabbi to congregational preacher was already evident even before the new post had been filled.

President Jacob Lipsky, who had been given expenses to go to New York and "see Prof. Schechter about a preacher" reported that Professor Schechter recommended a young man named Dobrin, who was invited for "Passover for a trial." Dobrin came and was paid $50 for officiating. He sent in application to serve as preacher and teacher at a salary of $1,250 but then withdrew it. The congregation, not to be outdone, wrote to Dr. Schechter that Dobrin "is not really right for our synagogue, and if he has another candidate to so inform us."

The seminary was not the only source for prospects. A member was dispatched to Buffalo to interview a prospect; and a committee of three was to go to Elmira to "see what kind of teacher Dr. Marcus is." If he was judged a good teacher, then he was to be invited as guest preacher for a Sabbath. There was apparently strong sentiment on the part of the "subscribing" members for a preacher who would also teach, but the more practical leaders of the congregation knew that teaching would have to be the higher priority or that there would be difficulty in justifying the post and collecting the salary.

The more desirable candidates were those ordained by the seminary. A meeting of trustees and search committee heard a letter from Nathan Blechman offering to come preach and was informed that Margolis of Cleveland might consider an invitation. Both were seminary trained. Rabbi Margolis was not interested, but Blechman came, applied, and was elected by a thirty-four to two vote as "preacher and teacher" for one year at a salary of $1,200 "to preach Friday evenings, Saturday mornings and holidays, and teach Hebrew school." The president called a meeting of "the younger members, especially those who subscribed payment for a teacher and preacher, that they should organize themselves to plan a Hebrew School and for other matters."[100]

Blechman is referred to as *Mr.*, not rabbi. His ordination from the Jewish Theological Seminary conferred on him the title of "Rabbi, Teacher and Preacher in Israel"; Beth Israel was ready to accept only the last two. Its rabbi was still "der Rov," David Ginsberg; his younger colleague was called "der Prediger." The status and duties of Rabbi Ginsberg were a continuum of the European way; the role and function of Mr. Blechman were in answer to American needs.

The "subscribers" held their own meeting to make the necessary "arrangements for the preacher and teacher." It voted that each subscriber pay 20 percent of his pledge at once and that "a committee of twelve be appointed to deal with all matters pertaining to the preacher." They were becoming a congregation within the congregation, seeking a sizable "board of trustees," as it were, of their own. The president of Beth Israel, aware of the dangers of giving too distinctive an identity to the group, postponed its appointment and, when pressured, named only five. The next half dozen years were marked by the challenge of maintaining a congregation that would satisfy the needs of those who were comfortable only in an east European hevra and the desires of those who for themselves and their children demanded an "American congregation."

With the coming of the preacher-teacher the special needs of the school became the central concern of the congregation. Adequate facilities for a school were lacking, so a church on Oregon Street that was for sale was examined as a possible site. At a meeting of the trustees and the Education Committee, the preacher "explained the need for various text books." It was voted not only to order the books but to pay for them from the treasury, to recommend to the congregation that a man be engaged to help the preacher "with the children and be the collector for the school," and that only children of members be admitted.

In the minutes of the fall quarterly meeting, the preacher is called "our Rev. Dr. Blechman." The "Rev. Dr." designation was at that time the title used for American clergy. Its use was not only an indication of the further Americanization of the congregation but also an intimation that an unstated but nevertheless valued function of the preacher was to further this Americanization in a controlled manner. The congregation remained formally Orthodox in every way. The late Friday evening gatherings addressed by the preacher were just that—gatherings. The Sabbath eve services continued to be held at the traditional sunset hour, and no changes were made in the liturgy and ritual. The educational program, however, permitted innovations. A Sunday school for girls was organized to complement the afternoon Hebrew school, which began to be conducted along more modern lines, as the preacher's introduction of "text books" indicates.

The late Friday evening gatherings attracted people who could not or would not attend the regular services, and it became for them *their synagogue experience* by whatever name it was called. It also opened the door to the introduction of a late Sabbath eve service—an American innovation.

Rabbi Nathan Blechman (we may call him so, even if the congregation did not) introduced into Rochester the role and function of the modern traditional rabbi. Meticulous in his personal religious life, yet active in communal and civic enterprises and causes, he even became friendly with Dr. Rush Rhees, a Baptist minister serving as president of the University of Rochester.[101] For the younger generation he served the role model of a Jew at home both in the tradition and in America. We may assume that this important contribution did not escape the notice and appreciation of the parents. Nor did the leaders of the congregation fail to realize the attraction the "Rev. Dr." and his school had for potential members.

The Education Committee, in its quasi-independent status, was interested in increasing the size and hence the faculty and the quality of the school and voted to open the school to children of nonmembers and to set a uniform tuition of $25 a year for the weekday school. But the trustees voted not to accept the recommendation, an action affirmed by the congregation at its spring quarterly meeting. The announcement at the meeting that Beth Israel membership had grown to 142 no doubt pointed out to many the practical wisdom of limiting attendance to the children of the congregation.

The experiment with a preacher-teacher had succeeded. The congregation grew. Activities increased. The mood was optimistic. Yet, after a year of service, Rabbi Blechman left. Beth Israel was not yet prepared to accord him the title and status conferred by his ordination. The congregation had attracted younger members, but the majority had grown old along with the congregation. A motion that the office of preacher-teacher be continued was carried by a vote of only twenty-five to eighteen. The prudent felt that the sizable salary was too great a congregational burden. The devotees of Rabbi Ginsberg were unhappy with a young "Rev. Dr." replacing the resident rabbi in the religious life of segments of the congregation. They must have particularly resented the congregational ordinance of March 16, 1907, that the preacher must officiate at all weddings in the synagogue. There were those who no doubt felt that a preacher, and the changes he introduced, foreshadowed serious departures from tradition—danger to the faith, potential if not at the moment imminent. Certainly there were those to whom the Rochester Hebrew School was dear, who considered the congregational school and the preacher who brought it into being and fostered it destructive of the communal system of education.

Rabbi Ginsberg continued officially to be the Rov of the congregation, but functionally the rabbinic office as defined by the American experience and the Reverend Dr. Nathan Blechman's incumbency was being fulfilled more and more by the preacher. He might be called "Rev. Dr.," "Prediger," or "Reverend," but in function he was the religious teacher and cultural guide of the congregation, looked on by Jew and neighbor alike as the Jewish clergyman, the rabbi.

No sooner had the determination been made to continue the office of preacher than the search began. The secretary was instructed to communicate with institutions and "private people." To solidify the position of the preacher and to "modernize" congregation usage, it was voted to eliminate "schnodder money" (publicly announced monetary gifts). This had been a source of income for the rabbi, cantor, and shamash on which Rabbi Ginsberg depended for part of his livelihood. To eliminate it was a subtle but forceful way to begin to veer Beth Israel away from its close association with the communal rabbi. His supporters forced a special meeting that became so heated that the president, unable to keep order, closed the session. Reopened by the vice-president, it postponed the "evil decree" until after the High Holy Days. But the point had been made.

Attention was now returned to the main order of congregational business, the election of a preacher. At a joint meeting of the trustees and the Education Committee, it was voted to recommend the election of Dr. Lauterbach as preacher and teacher. The teaching was by now auxiliary, for the recommendation stipulated that the salary be $1,000 as preacher and supervisor of the Sunday school; $200 would be added if he also conducted a Hebrew school. The partisans of the Talmud Torah had sufficient influence to have him elected initially as preacher and Sunday school supervisor only. The minutes are careful to note that at the meeting at which the designated candidate spoke, he did so "in English."[102] The Sunday school was opened to children of nonmembers, and a weekday Hebrew school was established. This was done at the "recommendation of Dr. Lauterbach who appeared at the meeting and graciously explained that this would be good."

Jacob Zallel Lauterbach (1873–1942) was born in Galicia, studied at the Universities of Berlin and Goettingen[103] and received rabbinic ordination at the "Rabbiner Seminar für das Orthodox Judenthum" (Hildesheimer Seminary) in Berlin. In 1903, he emigrated to the United States and served on the staff of the *Jewish Encyclopedia*, writing most of the articles on rabbinic Judaism that appear in volumes eight through twelve. He then served a congregation in Peoria, Illinois, prior to coming to Rochester at age thirty-four. By that time there were a sufficient number of *maskilim* (intelligentsia) in the congregation to take pride in their preacher's having participated in American Jewry's greatest scholarly accomplishment, the *Jewish Encyclopedia*.[104] The fact that he had already served an American congregation gave him the authority of expertise. He is referred to in the minutes as "Dr. Lauterbach," and so he was called by all. What attracted this scientific scholar of liberal religious tendencies to this Orthodox congregation, other than the need of a job, is difficult to divine.

Its budget having risen to over $5,000 in 1908, the congregation engaged in stabilizing and "rationalizing" its operations. Heretofore, the collection of dues was done at meetings or by a collector. In times of shortages special committees went out to solicit contributions. A "foundation" was now established to bring order to the collection and distribution of monies for ongoing operations and special projects. More significant was the appointment of a committee to "join with Dr. Lauterbach" in soliciting and accepting new members—an indication that it was expected that Dr. Lauterbach would attract new members and that he had the expertise to take leadership in this crucial congregational endeavor. The founders and early leaders of the hevra had been so jealous of their prerogatives that the religious functionaries were kept from all decision making. The professional expertise that this preacher brought forced the lay leaders to accept a sharing of power. Slowly, but inexorably, the congregation was moving in the direction of the professionalization that marked American religious life.

The chairman of the board of education[105] (now called) proposed that a Sunday and Hebrew school be maintained to be conducted by the preacher and an assistant. He argued that a registration of forty in the Hebrew school would cover almost all costs. To do so, a tuition of $20 per annum was enacted. Dr. Lauterbach was reelected thirty-four to twelve at a salary of $1,300 to deliver English lectures Friday evenings and to teach and supervise in the Hebrew school and Sunday school. Rabbi Ginsberg did not fare as well. In response to his request for a raise in salary, twenty-two voted for a salary of $400, while thirty voted to retain the old salary of $250—a minority favoring the retention of the centrality of the communal rabbi, the majority urging ever greater congregational intensification through a transfer of rabbinic function to the preacher. Having been denied a raise, Rabbi Ginsberg was extended the right to have contributions to him announced at the Torah Reading. The resolution specifically stated that "shnodder" may be announced only for the rabbi, not for the cantor or the shamash, "because he does not receive enough. His salary is so small that he is unable to make a living." What increase these contributions made to his income we do not know, but we may safely conclude that to be singled out for the charitable good-will of the congregants added little to the dignity of his person and further weakened the authority of his office.

The congregation had its usual quota of problems with finances (as always), with personnel, and with governance. Professionalization carries its problems with it as well as its rewards. Professionals know they must succeed in that which is most crucial to their calling, the preacher in his preaching and the cantor in his singing, so the preacher would rather not teach and the cantor would rather not be the Torah reader. The cantor was warned that he would read or be fined, and as long as there were students to be taught the preacher continued to teach. The *gabbaim* (lay leaders) of the Hevra Kadisha grew tired of their demanding tasks. So, resignation and replacement resulted.[106] The presidential candidate, running unopposed, had thirty-three blank ballots cast against him to fifty-one for him. No one accepted the nomination for vice-president at first. Rabbi Ginsberg was ill and needed help, so $50 was voted from the treasury. The daily Hebrew school diminished to fifteen pupils; the Sunday school numbered sixty. Apparently the Talmud Torah more than held its own as the vehicle for education of boys of the community. There was a problem with the venue of the daily school, the trustees demanding that the preacher move to the meeting room rather than teach upstairs. The preacher responded by claiming that he could not teach in the meeting room because "the air is bad" and availed himself of the opportunity to dispense with his teaching duties. The trustees agreed, and he accepted a reduced salary of $1,000 "to preach and teach Sunday School."[107]

The emphasis on preaching and Sunday school is reflected in the new contract of the cantor. Added to his duties were attendance at "the late Friday evening services when the preacher lectures, and to assist in the Sunday School by teaching songs." The membership continued to grow and the income with it. When an opening for shamash occurred, there were no less than nine applicants.

Despite the surface appearance of well-being, the basic problem of the congregation persisted. It was a problem inherent in the very nature of the congregation, an east European immigrant congregation in a community undergoing rapid Americanization. Beth Israel was affected far more than its sister Orthodox congregations. Because it was the oldest, its members the most Americanized, it moved with greater urgency to respond to the wishes of the more acculturated and younger members. This in turn met with more stubborn resistance on the part of the older and more traditional. Hence, deeper division and more intense confrontation. The struggle was symbolized in the reelection of rabbi-and-preacher in the summer of 1909.

On June 20, at the summer quarterly meeting, Dr. Lauterbach was reelected forty-two to twenty-eight, with a raise in pay of $100. In his acceptance remarks, he thanked the congregation for his reelection and the increase and pledged to "try to make progress in the year ahead, as this was made this year." He urged the election of a good board of education to improve the Sunday school and made a plea for increased attendance on Friday evenings, "men and *also women*."[108] Rabbi Ginsberg petitioned to be reelected, asking that his salary be increased because he "can't make a living." A special meeting called to consider his request rejected by a vote of thirty-five to twenty-eight the motion to reelect the rabbi. When the president declared the motion lost and that a rabbi would not be elected, such commotion erupted that the president, unable to restore order, closed the meeting. An even more heated meeting was held the next day, fines were levied, and threats to split the congregation were voiced. The strife finally subsided when it was realized that to dismiss the rabbi would cause harm to the congregation. Reappointment was arranged, but his duties were limited "to teach *mishnayot* (ancient Jewish legal code) daily, to answer ritual questions, to preach when invited" at the same salary of $20.83 per month.[109] The preacher was reelected in dignity with an increase in salary; the rabbi was kept on for the same pittance after bitter strife.

The direction in which the congregation was moving was now clear. It was attempting to unburden itself of its rabbi, committed as it was to a preacher-oriented synagogue. The direction may have struck a responsive chord in the community, for in October twelve new members were welcomed.

Rabbi Ginsberg recognized that his days at Beth Israel were limited. In anticipation of dismissal, he sent a letter of resignation. The letter read and accepted, the trustees voted: "Our congregation should not engage a rabbi for our congregation alone." No sooner was the action taken than a committee of Beth Haknesses Hachodosh appeared, urging that all synagogues join in appointing a rabbi for the whole community and inviting Beth Israel's participation. The trustees voted acceptance of the invitation.

The decision to encourage the resignation of Rabbi Ginsberg was directed not so much against him as against the nature of his office. Although he styled himself as "Rabbi of the Community of Rochester," he was never accepted as such by all the congregations. Until 1901, Rabbi Abraham Rosen remained in Rochester serving congregations Vaad Hakolel and B'nai David. From 1902, Rabbi Isaac Caplan served in his place. Rabbi Ginsberg was identified with Beth Israel as its rabbi. So long as Rabbi Ginsberg remained, Beth Israel could not engage a *congregational rabbi.* It had progressed from the teacher-preacher to preacher-teacher to preacher. The next step was to bring to its pulpit one who would fill the roles the ordination from the Jewish Theological Seminary conferred on its graduates: "Rabbi, Teacher and Preacher." The congregation, remaining Orthodox, readily accepted the need for a communal rabbi to deal with matters of ritual in general and kashrut in particular. Such an office accepted by *all* congregations would not, however, prevent Beth Israel from taking the next step toward its full Americanization—the engagement of an English-speaking congregational rabbi.

The opportunity to do so was presented by the decision of Dr. Lauterbach to leave Rochester. Both its preacher and its rabbi were leaving Beth Israel. Both went on to distinguished careers: Dr. Lauterbach served for many years as professor of Talmud at Hebrew Union College; Rabbi Ginsberg rose to national leadership in the American Orthodox rabbinate. Beth Israel was now ready for the final act in its transformation from an east European hevra to an American congregation.

A Rov for the City/A Rabbi for the Congregation

The search for a Rov for the community and a rabbi for the congregation went on simultaneously.[110] The Committee on Communal Rov, consisting of founding member Isaac Lipsky and young leader Abraham D. Joffe, reported to a special meeting on May 10, 1910, that the committees representing the congregations had decided that each synagogue contribute four dollars a week for the support of the Rov. Abraham Joffe, who had upheld the need for a preacher-teacher when that issue was debated, spoke in favor of a *Rav Hakolel*—a head rabbi for a united community. His position was not contradictory, but consistent. One Rov for the whole community, not identified with any single congregation, would make it even more necessary for Beth Israel to have its own rabbinic functionary. Unlike the earlier financing systems in which Beth Israel had assumed a larger obligation than the others, now all would share equally.

Approval for Beth Israel's participation in the support of a Rov was passed by a narrow margin, twenty-eight to twenty-five. The opposition may have been to the whole concept of a Rov or to Beth Israel's participation in a project that in the past had caused it grief, or it may have been a protest vote by friends of Rabbi Ginsberg, still smarting from his unceremonious departure.

At the same meeting a step was taken in preparation for the forthcoming rabbi-preacher. Cantor Rogoff was reengaged at a salary of $750, a $100 raise. Fully $300 was voted for a choir. The choir was to join the cantor on the High Holy Days and festivals, as well as on Friday evenings, when the preacher lectured, to sing appropriate Sabbath hymns and "to entertain the assembled." Note the emphasis given the late Friday evening gatherings at which the preacher and his lecture played a central role. It should be noted, too, that while the expenditure of $200 a year for the Rov had barely won, the cantor and choir were approved forty-one to one. Clearly the first loyalty of Beth Israel's members was to the congregation rather than community, another indication of how far the men of Beth Israel had moved from the European to American perceptions of Jewish corporate identity.

On July 30, 1910, the trustees voted to recommend to the congregation that it engage a "teacher and preacher who can also serve as rabbi at a salary of $1,500 a year." The recommendation barely squeaked through the congregational meeting, twenty-one to twenty, but the president ordered the committee to proceed with the search. Whether it was the innate conservatism of Beth Israel that caused opposition to a congregational rabbi or whether the salary loomed as too great a burden, we cannot know, but the report a week later that "there is no money to pay salaries" would suggest that cause for opposition was financial.

Despite the bleak financial report, the search for a communal Rov and a congregational preacher proceeded. A "preacher named Minkin from Brooklyn, N.Y."[111] was invited to preach, and three members were appointed to greet him at the train and arrange his accommodations.

Rabbi Solomon Sadowsky of Albany was elected Rov at a salary of $1,000, toward which Beth Israel undertook an obligation of $400 a year, on condition that the Rov teach Mishnayot daily at the synagogue. The "Preacher Minkin of Brooklyn" did not fare well. He came and preached and then was interviewed and rejected. The preacher recommended by Rabbi (Mordecai M.) Kaplan[112] said he would come if invited, but when the secretary stipulated that he must know English well, the candidate withdrew. The congregation was now sufficiently Americanized to be concerned about the public image of their rabbi. But even more it feared that its English-speaking children would react negatively to a preacher deficient in the language. Rabbi Sadowsky made so favorable an impact that the earlier enthusiasm for a rabbi-preacher seems to have waned. With so able and popular a communal rabbi, some must have argued, do we really need to undertake the heavy financial burden of a congregational rabbi? The older job definition of teacher-preacher was revived, but prior to engaging one, it was decided to seek an appropriate place for a weekday Hebrew school. Once again, the attempt would be made to finance a preacher through the income from his labors as a teacher. For the next half year, negotiations, long and complicated, continued for the purchase of a house owned by Jacob Present to be used for a school.[113] During this time there was no action taken in the search for a preacher.

Rabbi Solomon Sadowsky was a fine scholar, a gifted speaker, and an able organizer. As soon as he came to Rochester he perceived that his tenure would be secure only if there was to be a communal organization composed of congregational representatives. The congregations would support such a body, but it would have an identity of its own and the legal power to sustain its independence. Within a year the communal Rov had been able to organize the community, give it organizational structure as a *Kehillah* (community), with a board of education and committees on religion and charity, and win the participation of congregational leaders in its committees. The recently established Kehillah of New York[114] no doubt provided the example and gave the project both big-city and "American" legitimization. Accordingly, the trustees of Beth Israel voted six to one to reelect the Rov for a two-year term, affirmed by a congregational meeting, forty-five to twenty. The duties of the Rov were spelled out in a written report presented to the meeting by Mr. Joffe. Among them is the significant provision: "Once a week let him deliver a lecture for the young men and women, so that the young may learn something of Judaism. If it is possible for him to lecture in English it will be most desirable."[115]

The pro-preacher forces were not dormant. It was more than preaching that they desired. It was a congregational rabbinic functionary, English-speaking, American-trained, who alone could give the service and leadership that would assure the future of the congregation and its next generation. Seminary graduate Rabbi Eugene Kohn, rabbi of Adath Yeshurun of Syracuse, was brought to lecture and no doubt to demonstrate the kind of rabbi Beth Israel should be seeking.

By the end of the summer, two factors had forced the hand of the congregation. On May 28, 1911, the cornerstone was laid for what was to be the $90,000 edifice of the Beth Hamedrash Hagadol.[116] The building would outstrip in size and grandeur all other synagogues. Clearly Rochester's pioneer Orthodox synagogue needed to do something to retain its vaunted status. A preacher-teacher would give Beth Israel something that her sister congregations did not have—an American distinctiveness. A school building was ready, and by August 17 twenty-one students had registered and a teacher was needed. Three days later a special congregational meeting elected the Reverend Paul Chertoff, ordained by the Jewish Theological Seminary, as preacher "to deliver lectures and teach in daily school and Sunday School at a salary of $1,200, for one-year trial" by a vote of thirty-five to sixteen. But such was the popularity of Rabbi Sadowsky that only eleven days later the trustees voted to pay him $400 a year to teach mishnayot daily and deliver sermons on Sabbaths and holidays.

The preaching duties were divided between Rov and preacher. "The Preacher will lecture the first day of Rosh Hashanah and after Musaf on Yom Kippur in English. Rabbi Sadowsky will deliver a sermon on the second day of Rosh Hashanah and Shabbat Shuva in Yiddish." (Note: lecture by preacher; sermon by Rov.)

Rabbi Paul Chertoff, a respected scholar who later served on the faculty of the Jewish Theological Seminary, is referred to in the minutes as "reverend" or "preacher," never as "rabbi." A board of education of ten was appointed to help him in his program. An extant record book of the Hebrew and Sunday schools kept by Rabbi Chertoff indicates that he had superior organizational abilities.[117] Rabbi Paul Chertoff is listed as "Rabbi and Principal of School," assisted by Joshua Egelson. The three Sunday school teachers were Miss Raye Kirszenbaum, Miss Eva Harrison, and Miss Frieda Frankel. Abe Ginsburger was the Hebrew teacher. Thirty students were registered in the Hebrew school, twenty-seven boys and three girls, and the same number registered for religious school (i.e., Sunday school), of whom four were boys. A page was allotted to each pupil, giving date entered, age, teacher, and subjects studied. Most students entered in October and early November of 1911. Rabbi Chertoff taught the more advanced students. Among the subjects were "Hebrew Translation and Writing," "Abbreviated Humash," "Jewish Biblical History and Religion," and, of course, "Elementary Reading."

Rabbi Chertoff was enthusiastically accepted by the congregation. Soon after his arrival, congregational disenchantment with Rabbi Sadowsky's "United Congregations" (the Kehillah) set in. The minutes of November 12, 1911, read: "The secretary reported that Rabbi Sadowsky sent a letter in which he requests that a committee be sent. The president does not permit the reading of the letter. Many members demand that the letter be read. . . . A standing vote was called and all stood up in favor of reading the letter. . . . The vice-president Max Cohen read the letter in which the Rov urges the congregation not to withdraw from so important a matter, and send a committee to the *Board of Kashrus* as it did the previous year."[118]

The meeting voted thereupon to send representatives, but the reluctance of the leadership of the congregation to have Beth Israel participate in the Kehillah continued. Special representatives for the Kehillah came to the meeting of March 24, 1912, to urge the congregation's continued participation. It was voted to send delegates, but it reads like a pro forma act and no more.

At the June 13, 1912, meeting the majority of the trustees expressed the sentiment that the congregation needed a preacher and teacher but that the synagogue did not have the funds to pay his salary. It was suggested that the board of education seek subscribers whose pledges would be "charged to their dues," and Rabbi Chertoff was reelected, by the narrow margin of twenty-nine to twenty-three, to "preach and teach" at a salary of $1,300. At the same meeting a letter from Rabbi Sadowsky urging help in building a new mikvah was peremptorily referred to the Committee on Religion. The president brought charges against three leading members of the congregation for causing disturbances in the synagogue. The secretary challenged the president, arguing that the president was doing so without legal basis. An undercurrent of unease and contention in the congregation was palpable.

The last meeting recorded in the minute books is the annual meeting and election of officers for the year 5673 (1912–1913). The financial situation was a difficult one. The operating deficit was over $2,000, some 25 percent of the budget. At the elections, many were nominated, but all declined except those finally elected. The final order of business:

> The shamash Mr. Gordon sent his resignation. He can no longer serve as shamash and collector for he isn't feeling well. His resignation was accepted, and it was ordered that the president should announce from the pulpit on *Sh'mini Atzeret* (the eighth day of the Sukkot Festival) that applicants for the position should send their applications to the secretary. The meeting was closed.
> J. Rosenbloom, Secretary[119]

The congregation itself was ailing and its decline was hastened by two events, one external, the other internal.

For almost forty years Beth Israel had been the leading congregation in Rochester's east European Jewish community. As the first and, therefore, most aristocratic, it assumed leadership in all communal matters. Its strength lay in its self-perception of preeminence, a status widely acknowledged as justly earned. In times of congregational prosperity as, for example, the decade 1886–1895, it was in the forefront of communal endeavor and drew further strength from its position of leadership. In times of difficulty as in the decade 1896–1905, its memory of past glory gave it hope for future resurgence. At all times its assumed or presumed image sustained it.

The Jews of Rochester, by Isaac A. Wile and Isaac M. Brickner, was published in 1912. An illustrated volume giving the history of the leading institutions and organizations and biographies of the leading citizens, it became the "Blue Book" of Rochester Jewry. Inclusion conferred status. As would be expected, the bulk of the historical section is devoted to the German Jewish community, its Temple B'rith Kodesh, its organizations, and its leading citizens. The biographies of a few east European Jews are included, and their Associated Hebrew Charities is described. There is only passing mention of the Beth Israel synagogue, but two and one-half pages are devoted to a description of the cornerstone laying and the dedication of the Beth Hamedrash Hagadol. As soon as its building went up, it became the dominant synagogue in the Orthodox community. It had the most imposing building and soon had the largest membership and widest program of activity. The "star" cantors sang from its bimah; the most eminent guest rabbis preached in its sanctuary. Beth Israel lost its greatest source of strength—its prestige.

Three years later, it lost even more. In 1915, a group of leading younger members left Beth Israel to organize a conservative congregation, which they called Beth El. They issued a call to like-minded persons to join them, offering "family pews, prayers in Hebrew and English conducted by Rabbi and Cantor; a daily and Sunday congregational school," and more. The three preachers of Beth Israel had prepared them for this step, none more so than Rabbi Chertoff. Personally pious, he nevertheless urged and instituted a program of activities of broad Jewish cultural interests and helped the young find their way into Jewish organizational life by forming clubs and stimulating activity. Institutionally he turned the congregation to the influence of the Jewish Theological Seminary and the organization of Conservative congregations, the United Synagogue of America. In the *Report of the Second Annual Meeting of the United Synagogue,* Rabbi Paul Chertoff is listed as representing "Rochester New York. Cong. Beth Israel."[120] The best young leaders of Beth Israel gone, Rabbi Chertoff left in 1916. Beth Israel remained an Orthodox congregation until 1974, when it amalgamated with the relocated Beth Hamedrash Hagadol, which had earlier turned to Conservative Judaism.

There was one more factor that led to the decline of Beth Israel, a factor over which it had no control—geography. The children of the congregation's leading families, and some of the more affluent members themselves as well, were moving to the second area of Jewish residence in Rochester, the Park-Oxford neighborhood. It is where its daughter congregation, Beth El, made its home.

In the eyes of many Orthodox Jews, Beth Israel had begun to veer too far from strict traditionalism. Those who welcomed its progressive steps were moving away. The Beth Hamedrash Hagadol had taken its position of preeminence; Beth El had taken its best younger members. What remained was an Orthodox congregation, one among others, meeting for worship, for study, and for occasional cultural and social events, with fading memories of pioneering accomplishments that had made it possible for a community of immigrant Jews to maintain its faith in a new and strange land—a land of growing economic well-being and continuing spiritual challenge.

PART TWO

The American Rabbinate

In his *Discourse Delivered at the Consecration of the Synagogue Shearith Israel in the City of New York* on April 17, 1818, Mordecai M. Noah remarked that "a congregation without a pastor is like a flock without a shepherd." He reminded his audience that "my great grandfather [David Mendes Machado] who officiated as pastor of this congregation, seventy years ago occupied the same spot on which I now stand."[1] The rabbinic presence in America goes back even further. In 1710, Abraham De Lucena, who described himself as the "minister of the Jewish Nation Residing in the City of New York," sent a "humble petition" to "His Excellency, Robert Hunter, Esq., Captain General and Governor in Chief of the Province of New York," asking that the courtesies extended to the clergy be extended to him "as have formerly been granted to my predecessors."[2] The rabbinic office (lay ministers, to be sure) goes back to the earliest years of Jewish presence on this continent.

A century and a half after Noah's *Discourse,* Charles S. Liebman described the role of the rabbi in the post–World War II American Jewish Community: "The rabbi is the most important figure in American Jewish life today. . . . All Jewish leaders, to a greater or lesser extent, depend upon the rabbi to mobilize the Jewish community in support of the goals and programs they seek to achieve. The rabbi is the only figure in Jewish life who can command leadership, deference, even awe, by virtue of an ascribed title."[3]

The central task of the American rabbi was succinctly described in a bilingual broadside that greeted Rabbi Jacob Joseph when he arrived in New York in 1888 to take up the position of chief rabbi: "He is to be the leader in the battle which must be waged in order to keep the next generation faithful to Judaism."[4]

3 Expanding the Parameters of the Rabbinate: Isaac Leeser of Philadelphia

At the ordination exercises of the Jewish Theological Seminary of America in 1945, Judge Simon H. Rifkind observed that, whereas in Europe the rabbi was the product of the community, in America a community was the product of its rabbis. Even a cursory glance at the early history of any American Jewish community discloses the overarching influence of its pioneer spiritual leaders—none more so than Philadelphia's Isaac Leeser.

"There is probably no name so familiar to American Israelites, as that of Isaac Leeser; and none will ever say that the fame acquired was not justly earned," Henry S. Morais wrote in 1879. "The present advanced condition of Hebrews in this land of freedom must chiefly be attributed to his ceaseless exertions for their moral and spiritual welfare. In fact, the history of American Judaism and that of Isaac Leeser are one and the same."[1]

Eulogistic hyperbole[2] aside, the evaluation stands. With the possible exception of Isaac Mayer Wise, no American Jew was more widely known; certainly none had made a more lasting contribution to the spiritual, cultural, and communal life of the American Jewry. The forty years of Leeser's residency in Philadelphia, 1829–1868, may be properly called the *Leeser Era* in the American Jewish historic experience.

In 1829, at the age of twenty-three, Leeser came to Philadelphia to assume the post of hazzan-reader of Congregation Mikveh Israel, at that time one of the two leading synagogues in America. Strange quirks of fate—such as only a frontier community engenders—brought the German-born and German-educated young immigrant, slated for a mercantile career, to the spiritual leadership of a *Sephardi* (descendants of Spanish and Portuguese Jews) congregation whose leaders were native born or acculturated Americans.

Born in Neunkirchen, Westphalia, Prussia, on December 12, 1806,

Leeser was orphaned at an early age. He received his religious education from Rabbis Benjamin Cohen and Abraham Sutro of that city.[3] The reaction that set in after the Congress of Vienna of 1815 stripped Jews in German states of civil rights and economic opportunities and brought on an emigration that began in the 1830s and sent some 150,000 Jews to America in the half-century that followed. Among these was Isaac Leeser, who at the age of eighteen joined his uncle Zalma Rehine in Richmond, Virginia. The scholarly young man was sent to school on his arrival, but when the school folded some ten weeks later, young Isaac went to work in his uncle's store. He continued his scholarly interests while learning the intricacies of a mercantile establishment and put his scholarly attainments to use by assisting the local religious functionary, the Reverend Isaac B. Seixas, in his school and, on occasion, by leading the religious services.

Leeser's acculturation to America, both its form and spirit, was rapid and remarkable. Within five years he had so mastered the English language as to be able to write a masterly work on Judaism "whilst I was engaged in pursuits quite uncongenial to literature."[4] The atmosphere of freedom and equality urged on him a public defense of Judaism in the *Richmond Whig*. Leeser, who signed himself "A Native of Germany," describes it: "Sometime last fall [1828] a gentleman of this city showed me an article in the *London Quarterly Review*, in which our nation [the Jews] were very much abused. . . . The article in question was republished in a New York newspaper. . . . I verily believed that its circulating without a reply would be extremely injurious to the interests of my brethren in this country. I therefore undertook . . . the task of refuting the accusations it contained. . . . I had soon the satisfaction of discovering that my feeble efforts had met with favourable notice."[5]

Among those who took favorable notice of Leeser's essays were some leaders of Philadelphia's Mikveh Israel congregation, who, on learning also that Leeser had teaching skills and experience in leading a Sephardic service of worship, elected him to its pulpit. Leeser arrived in Philadelphia in 1829 possessed of a fine background in Jewish and general studies, a good knowledge of the English language, and a zealous desire to make Judaism—"the excellence . . . of our laws and ceremonies"—known to the American Jew and his neighbors. For the next half-century he did so through the spoken word in sermons and lectures and, for the audience beyond the confines of his congregation, through textbooks, a journal, religious tracts and translations, and educational and philanthropic organizations that he founded or inspired.[6]

When Leeser came to Philadelphia, the Jewish population of the United States numbered six or seven thousand, served by a dozen or so congregations. It had no textbooks, no periodicals, and no ordained rabbis. A few charitable institutions and organizations served its communal needs. But the prospect and promise of a growing immigration from central Europe indicated that there soon would be need for institutions, publications, and spiritual leaders. Philadelphia itself was a growing metropolis, a city of culture, mindful of the heritage of Benjamin Franklin, Dr. Benjamin Rush and colleagues, and the liberal Quaker tradition. The Gratz family leadership of the Jewish community, exercised by Michael and Barnard in the late eighteenth century, was continued by Hyman and Rebecca in the nineteenth. Later the Moss, Hart, Hackenburg, Sulzberger, and Solis-Cohen families put their talents and wherewithal in service of Jewish cultural and communal enterprises. Philadelphia was a good city, a good community for a gifted, serious, devoted young man burning with ambition to serve. In 1836 Leeser wrote to Chief Rabbi Hirschel of England: "Knowing my own want of proper qualification, I would never have consented to serve, if others more fitting in point of standing, information or other qualities had been here, but this not being the case . . . I consented to serve."[7]

Throughout his career Leeser was conscious of, and often confessed, his "want of proper qualification." It served him not as an excuse for failure to act but as a spur to try all the harder, a mandate for selfless dedication of time and energies. So abundant were his enterprises, so varied and great his contributions, that they can only be understood as those of a man driven to rise above his self-perceived and acknowledged inadequacies. Let us look now, all too briefly, at five areas of his endeavors: literary, religious, educational, institutional, and communal.

LITERARY ENDEAVORS

Leeser brought with him to Philadelphia his translation of J. Johlson's *Instruction in the Mosaic Religion* and had it published in 1830. It is appropriately dedicated to his uncle Zalma Rehine. It is a catechism prepared by a teacher "of an Israelitish School at Frankfurt am Main," translated and adapted by Leeser for "the instruction of the younger part of Israelites of both sexes, who have previously acquired some knowledge of the fundamental part . . . of their religion." Leeser urges "its introduction into schools . . . or to be used as a book of instruction in families."[8] He undertook its publication because "it is universally acknowledged, that there is a great scarcity of elementary books of this kind amongst us; and this is, therefore, the first in a series, which is attempted to remedy this defect."[9] All of his publications can be viewed as textbooks, whether they be a lesson book of the Hebrew language or a new translation of the Bible into English. "Having been appointed . . . a labourer in the vineyard of the Lord," Leeser felt it his bounden duty to prepare the texts for the instruction of "that part of the vineyard entrusted in my care." He was the reader of a congregation in Philadelphia, but his ministry, he felt, extended to all of American Israel. All he wrote, all he published, and, indeed, all he did was for the "part of the vineyard entrusted" to his care, the growing Jewish community of the New World.

In 1834 he published *The Jews and Mosaic Law*, a defense of the Revelation of the Pentateuch and of the Jews "for their adherence to same." Its twenty-six chapters show a wide reading in general of contemporary religious literature. Leeser knew that just as he was reading works on religion written by Christians, so were many other young Jews. What was needed was a work of defense of the mother faith against those espousing a betrothal to the new, a polemic arguing for loyalty to the ancestral faith and adherence to its ways.

His sermons, titled *Discourses, Argumentative and Devotional on the Subject of the Jewish Religion* (1837), were, as the title page reports, "delivered at the Synagogue Mikveh Israel, in Philadelphia, in the years 5590–5597" (1830–1837). Its 590 pages show these to be not only sermons in the usual sense but also scholarly essays on such themes as God, the Holidays, and, in seven lectures, "The Messiah." An address on behalf of "The Female Hebrew Benevolent Society" of Philadelphia emphasizes his espousal of women's participation in communal enterprises, and an address delivered at the Shearith Israel Synagogue in New York, on behalf of "The Society for the Education of Poor Children," points to Leeser's growing national reputation.

The year 1838 saw the completion of a major enterprise, a truly monumental achievement, the publication of a six-volume edition of *The Form of Prayers According to the Custom of the Spanish and Portuguese Jews.* Of the magnitude of the task, Leeser writes: "The truth is, there was not a single prayer book, the text of which I could implicitly follow . . . there being no persons here acquainted with Hebrew composition. . . . To my own lot, a considerable share of labour has fallen."[10] It was published with the Hebrew and English on facing pages and was an achievement not only for its corrected text and improved translation but also for the quality of its typography and book craft. All this was accomplished by Leeser's thirtieth year.

A half-dozen years later, in April 1843, Leeser launched the most important and most influential of his literary enterprises, the monthly journal *The Occident and American Jewish Advocate*, devoted to the "spread of whatever can advance the cause of (the Jewish) religion, and of promoting the true interest of that people which has made this religion its profession."[11] It was very much the creature of its editor, whose broad Jewish interests and activities the journal expressed. There was such remarkable consistency in both form and content that the very first issue can serve as a prototype for the 391 issues that followed.

Volume 1, number 1, Nissan 5603, April 1843, of the *Occident*, described on the title page as "A Monthly Periodical devoted to the diffu sion of knowledge on Jewish literature and religion, under the editorial supervision of Isaac Leeser," opens with introductory remarks by the editor, which lay out as projected contents:

> articles which elucidate our peculiar opinions . . . one sermon by one of the modern Jewish preachers . . . reviews of such new books as concern our people . . . controversial articles, if written temperately and candidly . . . accounts of public religious meetings. . . .
>
> We also request the respective presidents and secretaries of our American congregations to send us a condensed account of their first establishment and of anything of interest connected with them. Such a regular series would serve as the best history of the American Jews, who have always been hitherto in too small numbers, and have happily been always unmolested, to fill any large space in the history of the country independently of its other inhabitants.

There follows a sermon "On Miracles," again by Leeser; translated excerpts of a French work, *Les Matinées du Samedi*; news items ("chiefly from the latest European papers") touching on Jewish life in the United States; a juvenile department; and notices. Of more than passing interest is an article by Julius Stern of Philadelphia advocating "The Establishment of a Jewish Colony in the United States"; a report on the "fifth anniversary examination" of the Sunday School of Religious Instruction of Israelites of Philadelphia, and a report on the missionary society "The American Society for Meliorating the Condition of the Jews, and Its Organ, The Jewish Chronicle." The last page lists agents for the journal in twelve American cities as well as in Montreal, Canada; St. Thomas, Barbados, and Kingston, Jamaica, in the West Indies; and London and Liverpool, England.

Leeser's literary activity did not slacken during his entire life. An edition of the Pentateuch in five volumes "edited, and with former translations diligently compared and revised by Isaac Leeser" came out in 1845; an edition of *The Book of Daily Prayers for Every Day in the Year According to the Custom of the German and Polish Jews,* edited by Leeser, appeared in 1848; and his magnum opus, *The Twenty-four Books of the Holy Scriptures: Carefully Translated According to the Massoretic Text, On the Basis of the English Version, After the Best Jewish Authorities; and Supplied with Short Explanatory Notes* by Isaac Leeser, was published in quarto-size edition in 1853. The product of seventeen years of work, it was the first translation of the Bible into English by a Jew to be published. Until the edition by the Jewish Publication Society in 1917, a collaborative effort of editors and scholars, it served as the authoritative translation, reprinted again and again. The notes are copious, comprising about one-sixth of the volume, and bear evidence of a sound knowledge of medieval Hebrew and nineteenth-century German Jewish biblical commentaries. Of the entire enterprise Leeser writes in the preface: "The whole work has been undertaken at the sole responsibility, both mercantile and literary, of the translator. No individual has been questioned respecting the meaning of a single sentence; and not an English book has been consulted, except Bagster's Bible."

Two years later, in the preface to an octavo edition of the work, Leeser expresses his disappointment that it has not "a reception as would have gratified his ambition" but takes heart in the hope that his labors will be instrumental "in diffusing a taste for Scripture-reading among the community of Israelites, and be the means of a better appreciation of the great Treasures of revelation to many who never have had the opportunity of knowing what the Hebrews have done for mankind."[12]

Defense of the Jewish faith against detractors continued throughout his life. The first volume of the *Occident* began a serialization of Benjamin Dias Fernandes's polemical *A Series of Letters on the Evidences of Christianity,* which Leeser subsequently published in book form in 1853 and again in 1859, explaining, "We owe it to ourselves to defend our religion; and it would be a shame if, with a free press at our command, we do not scatter light all over the land, and 'teach the sons of Judah to wield the bow,' the arrows of which slay unbelief and exterminate erroneous teaching."[13]

Some "sons of Judah" were ready to wield more than a figurative bow in defense of their faith and the dignity of its institutions, as an open letter of Leeser "To the American Tract Society" discloses:

> An agent of your honorable body . . . visited our place of worship on last Sabbath (Jan. 30, 1836), and after the conclusion of the service, he posted himself at the entrance, and as the congregation was leaving the Synagogue he handed copies of a tract . . . contravening the tenets which we profess, to ladies, gentlemen and even children. . . . I think it my duty to warn you against a repetition of a similar kindness; for as we are naturally jealous of our religious rights, being unwilling to allow anyone to interfere in our conscientious scruples, and totally averse to listening to doctrines which we believe erroneous, another visit of your agent . . . may be received rather unkindly; and much as we might deprecate violence . . . we cannot answer for the forebearance of the ones amongst us, who might perhaps be induced in their honest indignation, to eject an impertinent intermeddler, mildly if they can, forcibly if they must.[14]

As a Jew, Leeser was indignant; as an American, he felt free to speak out forcefully; as a writer, he turned to the national press to express his indignation and issue a warning.

On the thirtieth anniversary of the publication of his *Discourses, Ar-*

gumentative and Devotional, Leeser published his collected sermons and essays in ten volumes, titled *Discourses on the Jewish Religion.*[15] In the preface he writes: "Since the date of the first appearance of my public addresses the number of Israelites has increased immensely in this country, and a new generation has sprung up to whom I would gladly leave these volumes as my religious legacy. . . . I hope they will be useful to some, conscious that they cannot be injurious to any of our people."[16]

RELIGIOUS ENDEAVORS

"Since the first edition was issued," Leeser writes in the above-noted preface, "many changes in our religious affairs have taken place among us; but in my own mind the old faith has not been supplanted by the new ideas which have found so many adherents and many advocates among men claiming superior learning."[17] He remained a staunch Traditionalist, resisting, confronting, battling the rising Reform movement. He recognized that a community of Jews integrated into the life of the larger community, its culture and way of life, would need to effect changes in its synagogal mode and ritual. But he would accept only "cosmetic" improvements, such as led to greater decorum, a more aesthetic service of worship, a sermon in the vernacular. He was staunchly opposed to reforms that would make "inroads on the principles of faith and practice." And he argued: "Orthodoxy is not that unbending, unyielding, bigoted opposition to improvement which our opponents represent it: it understands perfectly well what the spirit of the age requires; but it can yield nothing to public clamor, nor to the demands which seekers of innovations may make to render Judaism a thing to accommodate itself to every phase of history. Such a religion would be none at all."[18]

It was Leeser who made the sermon, a sermon in the English language, an accepted part of the service of the American synagogue.[19] Dissatisfied with the ignorance of his fellow believers, Mayer Sulzberger reports, "He introduced the system of delivering English discourses at stated periods, and pronounced his first address in June 2, 1830."[20] It was not until thirteen years later that the board of the congregation formally authorized preaching in their synagogue.

The middle decades of the nineteenth century saw a growing religious division in the American Jewish community between the Traditionalist and the Reform forces. Leeser was spokesman for the former; Isaac Mayer Wise was champion of the latter. Early friends who became strong antagonists, they put aside their differences in service of communal unity to participate in a conference met to forge an American Israel in Cleveland, Ohio, in October 1855. Leeser's contribution was his attendance, thus giving recognition to rabbis of the Reform school. Wise's offering on the altar of unity was acceptance of the proposition: "The

Talmud contains the traditional, legal and logical exposition of the biblical laws."[21] The conference and both its principals and principles drew opposition from elements in both camps to such a degree that the breach between the two widened and grew even more pronounced. Leeser became an implacable opponent of the Reform movement, opening the pages of the *Occident* to its opponents and to attacks on its leadership. Wise, in his *American Israelite* (founded in 1854), made Leeser the chief target in his denunciation and ridicule of Orthodox Judaism.

Leeser's Judaism was rooted in *halakhah* (Jewish law) but open to broad cultural influences and some modest change. It was a Judaism aimed at keeping its adherents devout in their ancestral faith but not separated from the larger community of which they were part.

EDUCATIONAL ENDEAVORS

Textbooks were the first need, hence *Instruction in the Mosaic Religion* in 1830 and in 1838 *The Hebrew Reader,* which begins with *The Spelling Book;* and a year later came the *Catechism for Jewish Children.*[22] The *Reader,* initially prepared for a newly established Sunday school in Philadelphia, was (in the words of Leeser) "used over a large surface as a first book of instruction in Hebrew,"[23] attaining a seventh edition in 1873. Of the *Catechism* Leeser wrote: "If any event in my life can afford me some degree of satisfaction, it is the consciousness of having added one contribution . . . to satisfy the demand for information in the ways of the law of God. And it will be to me a far greater gratification than any public applause, could I be convinced that the thoughts offered in this guide to the young Israelites has led a few as sincere worshippers to the house of our God."[24]

The *Catechism* is dedicated to "Miss Rebecca Gratz, Superintendent of the Sunday-School for Religious Instruction of Israelites in Philadelphia." Leeser credits the founding of the school to Miss Gratz, grande dame of Philadelphia Jewry and American Israel of the time. It was he himself who was no doubt the instigator of the enterprise, for while yet in Richmond he had, together with the Reverend Isaac B. Seixas, founded such a school, which met "with but partial success."[25] As early as 1835, Leeser urged the establishment of a Jewish all-day school,[26] and in 1848 the Hebrew Education Society of Philadelphia was founded, whose "object and design (was) the establishment of a school or schools within . . . Philadelphia, in which are to be taught the elementary branches of education, together with the sciences, and modern and ancient languages, always in combination with instruction in Hebrew language, literature and religion."[27]

The charter also granted the right "to establish . . . a superior seminary of learning . . . the faculty of which . . . shall have power to furnish to graduates and others the usual degrees of Bachelor of Arts, Master of Arts and Doctor of Law and Divinity."[28] The lead article of the August 1867 issue of the *Occident* was titled "A Hebrew College." Leeser writes: "In our last we briefly announced that the Trustees chosen jointly by the Board of Delegates and the Education Society of Philadelphia, had elected a number of gentlemen as professors of the new institution, which by-the-way has been styled Maimonides College."[29]

It was the culmination of four years of labor on the part of Isaac Leeser—the first Jewish theological seminary in America. "This idea has been urged for several years past in the Education Society's meetings," Leeser writes. "The plan was nearly realized already, when the late unfortunate civil war broke out."[30] On 1 July 1867 the college was established "under the charter granted to (the Hebrew Education Society) by the Legislature of Pennsylvania."[31] Criticism was raised, mainly in New York, that there was not sufficient consultation or sufficient planning; that the faculty was lacking in distinction, et cetera. Leeser wrote in defense: "New York has immense wealth which is lavishly spent upon all manners of objects; if, now, the Philadelphia movement does not suit the fault-finders, why have they not taken a course of their own years ago? There has been no want of schemes, but a sad absence of co-operation; the only method of succeeding is not to talk, but to work."[32]

New York had the numbers, the wealth, the prospective faculty; Philadelphia had Leeser. It was not until two decades after the founding of Maimonides College that New York established a seminary of its own, the Jewish Theological Seminary, and in its establishment, Philadelphians, disciples and colleagues of Isaac Leeser, played a central role. One of these, Mayer Sulzberger, wrote of Leeser and Maimonides College: "When the College was to be pushed forward, his voice was heard, his exertions were felt. His personal influence procured considerable subscriptions. . . . When the institution was opened, as a just tribute to his eminent abilities . . . and the honorable dignity of being the oldest Jewish minister in the country, he was elected Provost, or President of the faculty, his principal branch of instruction being homiletics and belles-lettres."[33] The college survived Leeser by but four years, closing its doors in 1873.

Leeser's commitment to popular education about Judaism for Jews and non-Jews alike was carried out through the printed page and on lecture platforms. Leeser traveled extensively to dedicate synagogues, to address schools and participate in school examinations, to preach, to lecture, and to help organize. Reports of his travels and descriptions of the religious and communal life of cities visited make the pages of the *Occident* the richest source for Jewish life in mid-nineteenth-century America.

On December 10, 1845, as corresponding secretary of the American

Jewish Publication Society,[34] he issued a circular "To the Friends of Jewish Literature," announcing the formation of a society to publish "books illustrative of our blessed religion . . . elementary works, which a parent could with safety place in the hands of his children."[35] The fourteen little volumes that the society published are not books for children but works of popular appeal for young and old: Hyman Hurwitz's *Hebrew Tales*, the *Memoirs of Moses Mendelssohn*, an abridgement of the Holy Scriptures "for the use of the Youth of our Nation," *The Path of Israel*, Grace Aguilar's *The Spirit of Judaism* and *The Perez Family*, and the like. The books were well received, but a warehouse fire that consumed the stock put an end to the enterprise.

Leeser carried on a voluminous correspondence across the American continent, reaching across the Atlantic to European countries and extending to Palestine. He encouraged and aided others to publish their works. He introduced the works of Grace Aguilar to an American audience, translated and arranged for the publication of Yehoseph Schwarz's *A Descriptive Geography . . . of Palestine*,[36] and edited textbooks and anthologies prepared by others. The pages of the *Occident* were open to America's rabbis for works both scholarly and polemical and to creative writers and poets. The first published American Hebrew writings in prose and poetry were on the pages of the *Occident*, which also contained substantive works in English translation, such as Moses Mendelssohn's *Jerusalem* and Giovanni De Rossi's *Dictionary of Hebrew Authors*.

INSTITUTIONAL ENDEAVORS

Leeser's primary contributions were to literature and education. Significant too was his advocacy of philanthropic organizations and charitable institutions; generally, in matters communal, what Leeser proposed, Philadelphia's Jews undertook. He urged consolidation of fundraising, and the Hebrew Charitable Fund of Philadelphia "in aid of the Funds of the Hebrew Education and Fuel Societies" came into being in 1853. He early advocated the establishment of a home for widows and orphans. Charitable ladies of the community created (and administered with motherly concern, committees of three paying daily visits) the Jewish Foster Home in 1856. The Jewish Hospital of Philadelphia, which opened its doors in 1867, was proposed by Leeser more than a dozen years earlier. In antebellum America, Philadelphia's Jewish community set the standards for cultural life, for educational and charitable institutions, and for a view to the necessity of a united American Jewry that was organized to face up to its problems at home and to assume its obligations to brethren in need abroad. In all, the vision and leadership of Leeser was central. As Sulzberger sums up in 1868: "His far seeing vision, years and years ago, projected a Hebrew College, a Jewish Hospital, a Foster home, a Union of Charities, a Board of Delegates of American Israelites, an Education Society; an American Publication Society, and everything else that could promote the welfare of his fellows."[37]

With it all, Leeser served as the congregational rabbi (though, lacking ordination, he never used the title), designating himself hazzan or minister of Mikveh Israel from 1829 to 1850 and of Beth El Emeth from 1857 to 1868. He served his congregation well, conducting all services, preaching regularly, officiating at weddings and burials, supervising education, teaching and lecturing, and giving his attention to all manner of pastoral ministration. He gave leadership to Philadelphia Jewry, and his concerns and influence extended to all American Jewry. He saw its ills, recognized its shortcomings, and labored to alleviate both. He advocated and undertook the organization of America's Jews in a national body that would assume responsibility for the quality of Jewish institutional and spiritual life and forge the vehicles for its improvement.

COMMUNAL ENDEAVORS

In July 1841 seven leaders of the Philadelphia Jewish community sent a circular letter to the dozen or so congregations in the United States. The letter was an invitation to form a "general union" of the Jews in America, the first attempt to organize American Jewry. In an article for a volume on religious denominations in the United States, Leeser describes American Jewry at that time:

> We have no ecclesiastical authorities in America, other than the congregations themselves. Each congregation makes its own rules for its government, and elects its own minister who is appointed without any ordination, induction in office being made through his election, which is made for a term of years or during good behaviour. . . . As yet we have no colleges or public schools of any kind, with the exception of one in New York . . . one in Baltimore and another in Cincinnati, and Sunday Schools for Religious instruction in New York, Philadelphia, Richmond, Charleston, Columbia, S.C., Savannah and Cincinnati. There can be no doubt that something will be done for education, as soon as we become more numerous.[38]

It was to do something for the cultural and spiritual life of a community that he felt certain would become more numerous that he prepared a plan for the "general union" he advocated. It called for the establishment of a central religious council and the appointment of an ecclesiastical authority; its plans envisaged a network of all-day religious schools recognizing each community's responsibility for the education of its young; and it spelled out a table of organization that would encompass all elements of a diversified community.

Leeser, writing almost two decades later, reports: "The circular . . . was sent . . . but, in brief, the conference did not meet, no rabbinical authority was instituted, no school was erected, no union was established, and the incipient division and party strife were permitted to take what shape they pleased."[39] He blames the failure on New York's Shearith Israel's fears "that the Germans would obtain the whole or too great part of influence, owing to their being already a majority in the country, and would thus outvote the Portuguese."[40] Leeser concluded: "It was jealousy, littleness of conception, a false estimate of the present position, which prevented a union in 1841; and these evils will do so again, unless the men at the head of affairs will once and for ever lay aside all differences of sentiments arising from a variety of the places of birth and Minhagim."[41]

The issue of the *Occident* that carried Leeser's sad memories of the first attempt at union reported a new effort to unite the congregations of the United States, "which would enable us to act for the interests of Israelites all over the world." Leeser advised the nascent organization that took the name the Board of Delegates of American Israelites that "we would merely suggest, that for the present the plan to be proposed should leave 'all over the world' out of sight, and confine itself to laboring for the United States and the countries contiguous; when we have taken care of our religious interest thus far, and produced a little cohesion among the disjoined masses, it will then be time enough to look elsewhere for objects of our vigilance."[42]

Leeser became a vice-president of the board and immediately put forth a proposed program of activities for it. He urged the establishment of committees of arbitration to serve individuals and congregations; a board of three rabbis to extend Jewish law to American Jews; the promotion of Judaism through publications and schools; a fund to be used to send rabbis to small congregations; a school to train rabbis; a rabbinical conference; and a plan for the unification of charitable endeavors. These were largely extensions on a national scale of activities that Leeser had advocated and helped organize in Philadelphia. But what could be attempted in a local community was apparently impractical on a national scale. Opposition to the board of delegates was immediate and pronounced. That expressed by Reform congregation Emanuel in New York sums it up. For Jews to act in concert in social and political matters would mark them as an *imperium in imperio* in America; no outside body should interfere with religious matters (which should remain the province of the individual congregations); and the congregations themselves can dispense charity without the help of the board. The board then has neither utility nor validity. Leeser, zealous for unity, cooperation, and discipline, offered to travel the country to plead the cause, but the wiser heads in the leadership of the board dissuaded him, for they feared that his zeal for unity would alienate more than it would attract. The board limited itself to defending Jewish rights at home and abroad, and in that it recorded some accomplishments. After a quarter of a century it was subsumed as a committee of the Union of American Hebrew Congregations, whose program was remarkably similar to what Leeser had proposed for the board.

In the middle decades of the nineteenth century no American Jewish leader had a clearer concept of what American Jewry needed, and none framed more practical programs and launched more effective vehicles for their attainment than Leeser. He was the first successful architect builder of the American Jewish community, establishing in Philadelphia a local prototype for a national enterprise.

Moses A. Dropsie's evaluation of Leeser is laudatory but candid:

> Mr. Leeser's learning was not profound . . . but he possessed a great fund and variety of learning. There were few subjects in which he had not some information. . . . He saw at a glance, and from all sources, absorbed knowledge which became indelibly fixed in his wonderful memory.
>
> His traits of character were strongly marked; his idiosyncrasy unmistakenly distinguished him from his fellows; with an indomitable will, he had but few negative qualities. His industry was marvelous.
>
> His perseverance was untiring, his energy was inexhaustible, his determination was unfaltering. He regarded life as a period of obligations and duties; impressed by its stern realities, he rarely indulged in those amusements or enjoyments which lighten our burdens and invigorate mind and body.
>
> In his ardor for accomplishment of some good purpose . . . he sometimes forgot that all were not gifted with his quick perceptions, and, in urging them on, was impatient and impetuous, and at times he would wound tender sensibilities by his frank and outspoken manner. . . .
>
> Mr. Leeser dedicated his life to Judaism. . . . Not having the cares of a wife or family, he watched over it with the fond solicitude of a husband and parent.[43]

4 From Campus to Pulpit

Simon Tuska of Rochester

Simon Tuska of Rochester, New York, decided early in his student years at the university of that city that he would devote his life to "the Jewish ministry. . . . I will devote myself to the sacred cause of my religion, of humanity, of my country."[1] Why did a young man living in mid-nineteenth-century America plan for the rabbinate, and how was he to realize his plan?

Simon Tuska was the son of the Reverend Mordecai Tuska, "Rabbi, Reader . . . Shohet . . . Mohel" of the Rochester Jewish community, who was called there in 1849 shortly after his arrival from Hungary.[2] The elder Tuska had been preceded to America by four sons. Fifteen-year-old, Hungarian-born Simon, the youngest, came with his father. Only two years later, the *Rochester Daily Democrat* announced that "the Board of Education after a very patient examination of some fourteen candidates, selected Thomas Dransfield, Ephraim Gates and Simon Tuska for admission to the Rochester University."[3] The *Rochester Daily Advertiser* added the pertinent information that these young men were admitted for "gratuitous education." The young Tuska, after only two years of American schooling, had been awarded one of the first scholarships to the recently founded University of Rochester.

At the university, Tuska specialized in Greek and Latin and graduated with the class of 1856.[4] Dr. Martin B. Anderson, president of the university, took a personal interest in the promising student, whom he later characterized as one of the best scholars the university had graduated.[5] At his request, Tuska wrote an essay on the Hebrew idea of the immortality of the soul, which was published in a denominational journal at Andover, Massachusetts.

Tuska's chief interest was Judaism, and he supplemented his university training with the study of rabbinical literature under his father's guidance. When Isaac M. Wise visited Rochester in 1854, he was delighted with the young man's deep interest in Jewish studies and encouraged him "to study for the ministry."[6]

While still a student, Tuska wrote a forty-page book called *The Stranger in the Synagogue; Or The Rites and Ceremonies of the Jewish Worship, Described and Detailed*,[7] which found a local publisher. In the introduction, he explains his purpose to be "to explain the rites and ceremonies observed on the Sabbath and other festivals of the Jews, to those who are led either by interest or curiosity to attend the synagogue on such days. Without such an explanation they will rarely be able to receive a clear idea of the services from mere sight, especially as these are wholly conducted in Hebrew. But to make this work interesting to readers in general, it has been thought fit to intersperse and affix several interesting Jewish usages."

The author then presents a concise description of the Jewish holidays and how they are observed in the synagogue. He also describes and explains the *tallit*, phylacteries, and the Jewish marriage ceremony. The appendix consists of the thirteen articles of faith of the medieval Jewish scholar and philosopher Maimonides. But Tuska goes beyond description; he is critical of certain customs and usages: "In many synagogues some unsocial customs ordered by the Rabbins are reformed, and the vain traditions of the Talmud rejected. . . . Most of the ceremonies prescribed in the *Talmud* are more interesting to Christians than they are approved of by the majority of the Jews."

The Jewish periodicals of the time noted the appearance of this small volume with varying reactions. The *Israelite*, edited by Isaac M. Wise of the Reform wing in Judaism, agreed with the author's presentation of Jewish rites and ceremonies, but the traditionalist Isaac Leeser did not. In a review he prepared for the *Occident* as its editor, he takes Tuska to task for "a sort of anti-Talmudic confession of a scriptural Judaism, in our opinion quite unnecessary to his subject." He recognizes the "laudable ambition" of the author, credits him with making moderately good use of his material, notes that he is "yet a mere youth" and that it would therefore "be absurd to expect any great profundity." Leeser holds forth the hope that Tuska "will study carefully all accessible sources of Jewish literature, and arrive thereby at a correct appreciation of the value of the rabbinical institutions and labors in behalf of Judaism, as it is not safe to be guided in this respect by what our opponents say of us."[8]

An unsigned letter to the editor of the *Occident* tells more about young Tuska and the reason for his undertaking the publication of *The Stranger in the Synagogue:*

In this city [Rochester] there are many distinguished American Christians, who are deeply interested in witnessing the services of the Synagogue; almost on every Sabbath and festival, some are led by curiosity, others by interest, to enter the Synagogue. Our acquaintance with these, however, is mostly owing to our Rabbi's son, whose good standing in the

University of this city has gained him the friendship of many educated Christians. To show the real character of a refined and educated American, we were told, in a conversation with Mr. Tuska [the son], that never, during the two years that he has now spent in the University did any professor or student desire to discuss the topic of religion. Mr. Tuska is a promising youth of seventeen or eighteen, and ere this greets the eye of your readers, will probably have given to the public a work entitled *The Stranger in the Synagogue.* This work he had undertaken at the request of many *Christians* who felt a deep interest in the rites and ceremonies of Jewish worship. The young author, however, in writing the book, did it with an eye to his brethren in faith also, and expressed his conviction that he endeavored to make his work of equal, if not of more utility to Jews.[9]

Tuska's pen did not remain idle. Both the *Occident* and the *Israelite* published his essays and translations, which bear witness to the intellectual courage, clear mind, and fine style of the young writer. From time to time he reported news of the Rochester Jewish community and displayed a mature understanding of Jewish communal structure and the problems attendant on an emerging Jewish community.

Isaac M. Wise, editor of the *Israelite,* published all that Tuska sent him and solicited more articles. Isaac Leeser, editor of the *Occident,* was also interested in him and sent him a letter in an attempt to lure him away from Wise and the *Israelite.* "Why do you write for Dr. Wise? His paper pretends to be everything without having anything of real value in it. He has the obduracy to claim for himself the first rank in Israel, with what justice you may determine yourself. It is not worth-while for any young man to see the public light through such a medium. I say this for your own good. I acknowledge having no good will for him; but it seems to me that I would say the same were he my most intimate friend."[10]

The young college student is thus caught up in the great Leeser-Wise Tradition-Reform controversy. Ideologically and practically, he chose Wise, and his commitment to Reform is already indicated in *The Stranger in the Synagogue.* Wise, the champion of Reform, became his guide and mentor. He understood that Tuska was more than a promising Jewish writer; he knew that his yearning was for the rabbinate.

Thus when Tuska sent Wise a sermon he had prepared, Wise hastened to reply: "I perused it with delight, and cannot depress the ardent hope to see you take hold on the Jewish ministry. As regards Hebrew learning, your father will instruct you so far, as to go on alone. I will give you a full plan to do so whenever you require it. If you would come to this city [Cincinnati], I would offer you every opportunity to finish your education in this capacity."[11]

Although Tuska turned to teaching on his graduation from the university, he never gave up his ambition to enter the rabbinate, and he enrolled as a special student in the Rochester Theological Seminary. Lest Dr. Wise be disturbed about the prospects of a prospective rabbi studying theology at a Christian seminary, Tuska reassured him in a letter dated August 11, 1856, that "I have become so fully convinced of the fundamental principles of our faith, that I do not fear to confront in personal debate the arguments of the most learned of Christian divines." He added that while attending lectures on systematic theology, he planned to "take out the cream, leaving the whey for others."[12]

Tuska's reasons for not attempting to find a pulpit upon his graduating cast light on Jewish congregational life in mid-nineteenth-century America. He felt he was too young for the rabbinate, being only twenty-one years of age. But his chief reservation seemed to be the recognition of a language barrier. Most congregations at the time conducted their services in Hebrew, with German as the language for congregational readings, preaching, and instruction. "If I am ever to accomplish some good by sermons," Tuska writes, "they must be delivered by me in English; and there are few congregations in this land, who can fully appreciate an *English* discourse. This will not cease to be the case until the rising American-born generation will have come to manhood. Then, no doubt, a fair field of labor will be spread before the *English* preacher. Till then it will be my task to instruct the *young*, hoping thereby to become one day enabled to instruct the *old*."[13]

"Till then," Tuska accepted an appointment to teach languages at the Collegiate Institute at Brockport. He assured Wise that he would continue during his leisure hours to devote his attention to the study of Jewish philosophy and religion. Wise responded to Tuska with a plea: "Forget us not!" He writes:

> We must inform our friend, that there are many congregations in this country who would gladly employ the service of a minister, who preaches but English. Besides this we know how extremely easy it would be to him, to acquaint himself sufficiently with the German, to enable him to preach in this language. Forget us not young man! The Synagogue is poor in this country, lacking talent and devotion. We have plenty of *Hazzanim* [readers of the service], *Shochtim* [ritual slaughterers], etc. also old fashioned Rabbinists, who have no idea of the learning and wants of our age; but we have not sufficient literary men. Forget us not![14]

Wise, who was deeply convinced that Jewish religious life in America needed Americanization, was, no doubt, greatly excited about the possibility of a graduate of an American university entering the rabbinate. Later in life he would establish a theological seminary for the training of American rabbis; now at least he wanted an American university graduate in a Jewish pulpit. This, to him, would represent the first step in the making of the American rabbi. So Wise continued to encourage Tuska in his Jewish studies and interests.

Tuska's academic pursuits placed him in Athens and Rome—but his heart was in Jerusalem. Though he longed for the pulpit, he knew what Wise would later express publicly: "None will have his son educated for the ministry when any clerk, bookkeeper, cutter or foreman, is paid better than the Rabbi or teacher of a congregation, and is more independent too."[15] Teaching was the more likely career for a young Jewish college graduate in mid-nineteenth-century America. But if teaching it had to be, Tuska wanted to teach subjects closer to his primary interests. So in the summer of 1857 he applied for and was appointed to teach Hebrew at the Union Theological Seminary of New York. He was to teach elementary Hebrew; exegetical Hebrew would be entrusted only to a Christian. But before the new instructor could begin to teach, circumstances forced him to resign his position. The Reverend Dr. Riggs announced his availability and willingness to take over the whole Hebrew Department "exegetical as well as elementary," whereupon Tuska tendered his resignation. The head of the seminary, the Reverend Dr. Robinson, wrote a letter in which he remarked that "in all his intercourse with me, the conduct of Mr. Tuska was that of a gentleman and a scholar."[16]

The young gentleman and scholar returned home to Rochester no doubt saddened, but not giving up the hope that he would qualify some day to occupy a pulpit. In Rochester he had the opportunity to preach, and did so, but he continued to aim at rabbinic training.

Wise's continued interest and urging finally bore fruit. Late in 1857, Tuska decided to go abroad to prepare himself for the rabbinate. Wise was delighted to announce this in the January 8, 1858, issue of his *Israelite:*

> Our young friend Tuska of Rochester, has now decided definitely, to go to Breslau, in Prussia, and study Hebrew theology. He is the first American Israelite who goes to Germany for the purpose of studying Hebrew theology; and we wish not only, that he may succeed well, but also that other young men may soon follow his example. It is a sad truth, that we suffer a perceptible want of thorough theologians, and, therefore, any body who has brass enough in his face, styles himself a reverend or a rabbi, so that many of our ministers excel the Methodist preachers in ignorance and misconceived piety. It is but a few hours ago, that we saw the signature of a man, who styles himself a rabbi preacher, in one of the Atlantic cities, of whom we are morally certain, that he can not read a page of either the Talmud or the *Moreh Nebuchim;* still he coined himself a Rabbi in Israel.
>
> Also, this is a sad fact, that many of our learned men are not suffici-

ently acquainted with the vernacular of the country, the field in which they are expected to toil, the religious wants of the community, and position of Israel in this country and its relations to other religious sects, and, therefore, are unable to do as much good as if those deficiencies would not exist.

Wise later reported that "his funds being insufficient to carry out this object, he delivered public lectures on the doctrine of immortality among the ancient Hebrews, contra Bishop Washington. These lectures were delivered in June, 1858, in Cincinnati and Louisville, and not only replenished his purse but also established his reputation as a fine English scholar and a rational theologian."[17]

At the end of June, the purse partly filled, Tuska returned to Rochester. The Jewish community was aware of the distinction that Tuska's going to Breslau conferred on it. Rochester was to be the first Jewish community in the United States to give a son to the study for the rabbinate. The young man who had brought distinction and fame to the community was invited to deliver a farewell sermon to the congregation. On the following Monday, the leaders of Rochester Jewry expressed the wish of the community that Tuska return to Rochester to serve as rabbi of his home community and presented him with a sealed letter containing "a substantial token of their best wishes and regards." That evening the young honoree assured his townspeople: "Should it be my lot hereafter to cultivate the field of Judaism on the soil of Berith Kodesh in the Flour city of this State, I trust that with the psalmist, I shall be able to say, [Hebrew] my lines have fallen unto me in pleasant places."[18]

Armed with letters of introduction and charged with a sense of mission, Tuska set out for Europe. Writing from Hamburg on July 16, 1858, he announced his purpose "to gather the material requisite for rearing and upholding the noble edifice of Judaism on American soil."[19]

Neither Rochester nor American Jewry would forget Tuska during his two years in Europe. He wrote twenty-three letters of great interest and importance to the *Israelite* between the summer of 1858 and the spring of 1860. Through them American Jewry learned a good deal about Jewish religious life and practices in Hungary, Prussia, and Austria; the condition of the Jews in those countries; and Tuska's view of the conflict between Orthodoxy and Reform. Unfortunately, he said little about the Breslau seminary, its course of study, its famed faculty, or its student body. Wise states that Tuska "wrote on almost any subject except the Breslau seminary" because "he did not like it there."[20]

The Jewish Theological Seminary in Breslau was the leading institution of its kind in the world. It was founded and headed by Dr. Zacharias Frankel, a noted scholar and expounder of the positive historical school of Judaism. On its faculty were some of the world's leading authorities in Jewish theology, literature, law, and history. Tuska was deeply impressed with and very fond of his professors, particularly Frankel and Heinrich Graetz, the great Jewish historian. "But" Wise confides, "[he] heartily disliked everything else." "A professor to be again a student under seminary discipline and a liberal-minded American to submit to all those forms of orthodoxy is a difficult task," Wise explains.[21]

In his first interview with Dr. Frankel, Tuska was asked about Jewish life in America. Tuska reports:

> I, of course, told him of the lack of English preachers among us—which most persuaded me to prepare for the Ministry, in which I might make myself more useful to my American brethren than in anything else. Dr. F[rankel] congratulated me on being the first American youth who crossed the ocean for so holy a purpose; and having noticed from my remarks during the course of the conversation that I desired to be prepared as soon as possible to mount the Jewish pulpit, the Doctor thereupon said to me: "Be not in haste; it will be far easier for you to officiate as Rabbi, and you will find the rabbinical functions by far less burdensome, after having spent a year *more* rather than one year less in the preparations requisite for a Jewish minister." I replied that with the help of Providence I hope that my zeal to supply a great desideratum in America will so spur me on in my studies as that I shall be able to go forth the sooner with the necessary ministerial utensils.[22]

Tuska reports that Dr. Frankel informed him that the course of study at Breslau was for three years, although it was possible to conclude it in two years or even one. The seminary had two departments, "one for training of Rabbins, and the other for that of teachers." Of the forty students studying in 1859, the only non-European was Tuska.[23]

While at Breslau, Tuska became friendly with Benjamin Szold, who was called to Baltimore and to a distinguished career in the American rabbinate in the spring of 1859. Earlier, Tuska had written about him admiringly, as a young rabbi who "preferred to decline the honorable post [Stockholm] he might otherwise have so easily obtained because the congregation had made it a condition, that he should introduce the prayer book in the Swedish language. . . . But as the service would in this way have utterly lost its Jewish type and color, Mr. S[zold] could not conscientiously submit to that condition."[24]

Tuska's education for the rabbinate extended beyond the walls of the seminary at Breslau. He visited some of the leading temples and rabbis in central Europe. The Hamburg Temple, a famed early stronghold of Reform, impressed him greatly, though he notes that it is not "so thoroughly reformed [as Temple Emanuel in New York], for there is still an extra gallery for the ladies, and the Sexton still continues to run to and fro during the reading of the Torah, notifying the several persons to be called up to the law." He does approve of the greater congregational participation in the Hamburg Temple. While in Hamburg he called on the venerable Dr. Gotthold Solomon of the temple, a retired octogenarian. His successor, the Reverend Dr. Naftali Frankfurter, commends Tuska on his undertaking. "We know too well what sort of people you have in America, considering the mixed character of the people who emigrate thither from Europe. It is well, therefore, that young men acquainted with the circumstances and the language of the Jews in America, take hold of the Jewish ministry, since they alone are fitted for the task."[25]

During Tuska's visits to synagogues, he observed their services, considered the innovations instituted, and stored up practical knowledge about synagogue procedure. He found Orthodox services quite distasteful, but was greatly impressed by Dr. Abraham Geiger's temple and by Geiger himself, a founder of Reform in Germany. A long and highly laudatory description of Geiger's service and sermon was sent to America. Tuska had left America committed to Reform Judaism; his European experience deepened his conviction and strengthened his commitment.

In Vienna, Tuska heard and met Salomon Sulzer, the distinguished cantor and musicologist of his day, and discussed the Jews in America with Vienna's great preachers, Isaac Noah Mannheimer and Adolf Jellinek. In Prague, he visited the celebrated Rabbi Solomon Judah Rapoport. Tuska's coming to study in Europe was a revelation to Rapoport. "Why, I am most agreeably surprised that there is still a sense for Jewish learning among your practical countrymen. I always thought that Judaism was on the decline in America."[26]

Tuska remained in communication with Wise during his stay in Breslau, and the latter continued to guide him. In a letter sent April 21, 1858, Wise offered some good advice: "I would advise you to write some exposition on a literary or scientific theme occasionally. You have the best chance for it in Breslau, it will do you good here." He added that "a thorough course of natural science and history would benefit you decidedly." This was a far cry from the scope of competence traditionally expected of a rabbi. And Wise does not forget that the prospects of a position are always alluring. He informs Tuska: "Louisville is waiting for you, and I can manage it that they wait till you return."[27]

Louisville was not a sufficient lure for Tuska to return, but Temple Emanuel in New York apparently was. The rabbi of the congregation was Dr. Samuel Adler, a respected scholar and spiritual leader, whose native language was German. The day Tuska looked to, "when the rising American-born generation will have come to manhood"—those who could appreciate an *English* discourse—was now at hand. The congregation needed a rabbi who could preach in English because, to the sons and daughters of the German-speaking immigrants who founded Temple

Emanuel, English was the native tongue. In 1860, when the congregation advertised for an English lecturer, Tuska returned to New York City to preach a probationary sermon. Anxious for the Emanuel pulpit, he left Breslau without ordination. Wise recalls that "he failed in giving satisfaction to that community, more probably by his feeble voice and small stature than by any other cause."[28]

Tuska's own account is somewhat different. The rumor was apparently current in Rochester that Tuska had become the English lecturer at Emanuel, for he wrote from Memphis, Tennessee, to Dr. Martin B. Anderson, his friend and former teacher, on July 19, 1860: "You will observe from the date above that I am *not* English lecturer of the 12th St. Temple in New York. My voice for the present not yet fully developed cannot, without too much exertion, fill every part of that lofty and spacious edifice. I, therefore, did not apply as Candidate for that place at all—though my trial-lecture pleased those *who heard* it—but resolved to wait for some favorable opportunity in a smaller locality."[29]

Rochester itself was such a smaller locality. But as Simon Hays, a leading member of Congregation Berith Kodesh, disclosed after the death of Simon Tuska: "When he returned [from Europe] it was expected that the Flour City would be his abiding place. But it is said great men do not have honor at home. Some little prejudice prevented his staying here."[30] The "little prejudice" apparently was that Tuska's religious views were too radical for the congregation.

Memphis, Tennessee, proved to be the "smaller locality." After preaching both an English and a German sermon, Tuska was unanimously elected for three years as regular preacher in the synagogue and instructor in its religious school.

Tuska's election to the pulpit of the Memphis congregation is an important landmark in the history of Jewish religious life in America. He was the first graduate of an American university to serve as a rabbi and the first to go from America to Europe to study for the rabbinate. Many followed his example even after America established its own rabbinical seminaries.

Tuska preached every Sabbath in English or German, alternately. He set as his goal the cultivation of his voice "so as to be soon able to speak with sufficient loudness and distinctiveness in much larger halls."[31]

Tuska's ambition to speak "in much larger halls" was never realized. He was destined to spend the remainder of his all-too-brief life in Memphis. He led his congregation through the very difficult Civil War years and through the equally trying period of Reconstruction. In the latter sixties the congregation so flourished so that Isaac M. Wise called it "one of the best organized and most peaceful Reform Congregations of our country."[32]

It was the sad duty of Isaac M. Wise, Tuska's friend and mentor, to report in 1871: "Simon Tuska is no more among the earthly pilgrims. The lips which so often and so earnestly pronounced the words of God are closed forever. . . . Friday evening last, he conducted the divine service in the Temple as usual, preached a sermon and returned home to his family. A few hours afterwards, he was a corpse, a disease of the heart having suddenly cut short his earthly career."[33] Tuska was mourned by the whole Memphis community; clergymen, lawyers, judges of courts, county and city officials, journalists, and leading merchants attended the funeral service.

He was only thirty-six when death claimed him. Yet during his brief life, and very brief ministry, which lasted but little more than a decade, he was able to make a number of significant contributions. One of America's pioneer rabbis, he set the pattern for American rabbinic training—university degree plus theological seminary studies. He recognized the need for English-speaking, American-trained rabbis for the rapidly growing American Jewish community; among the manuscripts he left were guidelines for a seminary for Reformed Judaism in America.[34]

5 American Rabbis for America

Solomon Schechter Comes to the Seminary

A century has passed since American Jewry's leaders in intellect and wealth joined forces to bring Professor Solomon Schechter to these shores. Philadelphia provided the intellectual leadership in the persons of Dr. Cyrus Adler, Judge Mayer Sulzberger, and Dr. Solomon Solis-Cohen. New York's contribution was the philanthropic generosity of Jacob H. Schiff, the Lewisohns, and the Guggenheims. The former provided the persuasion and the latter the possibility of plucking from Cambridge University its reader in rabbinics and placing him at the head of a reorganized and endowed Jewish Theological Seminary of America.

As the nineteenth century gave way to the twentieth, the men who felt responsibility for the future of Jew and Judaism in America recognized that the ever-increasing immigration from eastern Europe was rapidly reshaping the American Jewish community. They feared for the future of the American Jew and the quality of his moral and spiritual life. Danger provided a challenge; a problem could be turned into a project. What was now needed was a plan and the personnel to execute it. A seminary for the training of English-speaking rabbis who were traditionalist promised salvation; Solomon Schechter was the man to give it leadership and direction.

Cyrus Adler, reminiscing about the coming of Solomon Schechter, remarked: "I believe that eight cities claim the honor of being the birthplace of Homer. I cannot recall how many people claim the honor of having been instrumental in bring Doctor Schechter to the United States."[1] Dr. Solomon Solis-Cohen reported that "in the year 1890, I had the privilege of bearing a message from Sabato Morais and his colleagues of the Jewish Theological Seminary, then recently established in New York, asking Schechter to consider the possibility of joining the teaching staff of that institution."[2]

For a dozen years thereafter, intermittent but ongoing negotiations continued between Schechter and those eager that he make the New World his arena for scholarly creativity and spiritual influence and leadership. Schechter himself was eager that the matter remain current. Thus he writes to Alexander Kohut, rabbi, scholar, and professor of Talmud at the seminary, in November 1893: "What is your College doing? America must be a place of Torah, because the future of Judaism is across the seas. You must make something great out of your institution if the Torah and wisdom are to remain among us. Everything is at a standstill in Germany; England has too few Jews to exercise any real influence. What will happen to Jewish learning if America remains indifferent?"[3]

Although the seminary was located in New York, Philadelphia's Jewry felt it had at least an equal share in its founding and maintenance and, therefore, its direction. The founder and first president was Sabato Morais, the rabbi of Philadelphia's Mikveh Israel. It maintained a strong and active seminary association. Among the most influential lay leaders were the aforementioned Dr. Solis-Cohen as well as Dr. Cyrus Adler and Judge Mayer Sulzberger. During the latter half of the nineteenth century, Philadelphia was blessed with remarkable Jewish lay leadership—men of established and esteemed families, scholars in secular and Jewish studies, traditional in observance and conservative in religious outlook. They saw in Schechter a kindred soul who would establish in America a sound base for Jewish scholarship and who would make traditional Judaism intellectually viable.

In the early 1890s both Dr. Adler and Judge Sulzberger visited Schechter in England and came away impressed with the man and convinced that America must be his field of activity. An opportunity for American Jewry to meet Schechter and for Schechter to see America soon presented itself. Congregation Mikveh Israel was the beneficiary of a trust estate created by Hyman Gratz "for the establishment and support of a College for the education of Jews residing in the city and county of Philadelphia."[4] Dr. Solis-Cohen was appointed chairman of a congregational committee to concern itself with this matter. The $6,000 per annum income from the trust was deemed insufficient to maintain a school of learning, so "at a meeting of the committee held November 29, 1894, it was resolved that a series of lectures be given during the year 1894–95, and that Mr. S. Schechter, Reader in Rabbinics in the University of Cambridge, England, be invited to deliver a number of lectures in this series."[5]

The resolution was preceded by negotiations and carried on by Dr. Solis-Cohen and Schechter. In reply to a letter of inquiry, Schechter wrote on June 14, 1894: "I think I could see my way to falling in with your convenient proposal: matters of this nature, as you say, are better discussed by word of mouth than by correspondence."[6]

The word-of-mouth discussion was with Dr. Adler, who visited England a few weeks later. At year's end, in a letter dated December 19,

1894, Schechter informs Adler of his acceptance of the invitation, thanks him for his kind efforts, and exclaims: "What a joy in heaven it will be to see old friends again."[7]

The reader in rabbinics who arrived in America for the first time in February 1895 was already a well-known figure in Jewish scholarly circles. A product of Romanian and Galician yeshivot, he had continued his studies in Vienna and Berlin. The West added scientific order and method to the knowledge he had amassed in the East. Added to scholarly acumen was a lively and exciting personality. His was the happy combination of imagination and intellectual daring coupled with sound and solid scholarship.

The young Claude G. Montefiore met him in Berlin and persuaded him to continue his journey westward to England to act as the young man's tutor. After he was "inducted into the mysteries of the English language" Schechter became a leading figure in Anglo-Jewish intellectual life. Joseph Jacobs writes: "It is impossible to convey any adequate idea of the genial radiance and élan of Schechter's personality at this period. At the height of his physical and mental vigor, appreciated for the first time at his true value, surrounded by an ever-increasing circle of admiring friends, he burst upon us as a blazing comet in the intellectual sky."[8]

A position was obtained at the University of Cambridge where he continued his scholarly output and developed a masterly style that won the admiration of skilled writers for whom English was the native tongue. He put his knowledge and style to use in scholarly popularizations of various aspects of Jewish life and thought and gained ever wider fame. The university expressed its esteem by awarding him the degree of master of arts *honoris causa* in 1892.

This then was the man who was being brought to America to see and be seen. Schechter's coming was announced in Cincinnati's *American Israelite*,[9] and heralded in New York's *American Hebrew.*

> The gentlemen who constitute the Trustees of the Gratz Fund . . . have manifested a wise and liberal-minded conception of their duty by prevailing upon Mr. Schechter . . . to visit this country and deliver a course of lectures. . . .
>
> The Jews of America will certainly delight in according to Mr. Schechter a welcome that will well repay him for the trip; that will manifest to him that whatever may be at fault with Judaism as it is constituted in this country, we still have an ardent appreciation for ripe scholarship and warm sympathy with the studious temperament.[10]

Philip Cowen of the *American Hebrew* wanted Schechter to like the American Jewish community and wanted American Jewry to appreciate

Schechter. "Mr. Schechter, indeed, deserves a great deal of credit. Now that the public has grown up to draw from the well of Hebrew learning transferred into the English tongue, he has given a wonderful impulse to the movement for creating this Anglo-Jewish literature, and he has indelibly impressed this movement with his scholarly character. It is to him that we owe in a great degree the fact that this Neo-Jewish literature shall be Jewish and scholarly."[11] A plea was put forth that Schechter be invited to repeat his lectures in New York, but the metropolis was apparently not yet ready for him.

The lectures, six in number, which were delivered in the Academy of the Fine Arts from February 11 through 28, were widely quoted in the American Jewish press and served to introduce Schechter to an ever-wider audience. His own reaction is typical of him: "I gave my first lecture yesterday. The hall was crowded, and I hope that at least a minyan understood my English, and that I shall be saved for the sake of the ten."[12] This he wrote to Dr. Adler from the home of Judge Sulzberger. His friendship with both men, who became lifelong coworkers, deepened and ripened during Schechter's sojourn here. Later they were to be most instrumental in bringing him back to these shores.

Schechter returned to his scholarly work in Cambridge. His unearthing of the Cairo Genizah and his discovery of a Hebrew text of the Book of Ecclesiasticus not only increased his scholarly stature but won him international repute. To the popular mind here was a scholar-adventurer, combining all the best features of a questing mind and a courageous heart, braving the heat of Cairo and the dust of centuries in his search for truth. It is no wonder then that when Sabato Morais, president of the Jewish Theological Seminary, breathed his last, the quest for his successor turned to a scholar sorting and deciphering manuscript leaves and fragments in Cambridge.

His name had been kept current and his fame celebrated by the two Jewish periodicals that represented his conservative Judaism point of view, the *Jewish Exponent* of Philadelphia and the *American Hebrew*, thus preparing the ground for his acceptance as head of the Conservative seminary. On May 9, 1897, Schechter wrote to his friend and confidant, Judge Sulzberger:

I was lately approached from New York with the question whether I should care to come to New York to take charge of the Chancellorship of the Jewish Theological Seminary. I do not care to mention the name of my correspondent as the matter is confidential. Besides you know probably by now who it is. I have not answered him yet; but I am going to refer him to you. I hardly need to tell you that America has certain attractions for me. But I am anxious to be there quite independent as well as sure of doing there some good by founding there a school on a scientific basis. You probably know what I want or rather what I ought to want better than myself. Hence the best thing is that you decide for me in this respect.[13]

Judge Sulzberger urged patience, as did Dr. Adler, as the latter attests: "Some of his more impetuous friends urged him to join the Seminary at once, but I was very solicitous and in this Judge Sulzberger joined, that he should delay until we had a sufficient foundation to make him secure here."[14] Schechter grew more anxious. He yearned for America. He unburdened his soul in a number of interesting and instructive letters to Judge Sulzberger: "New York offers nothing fresh as I see; but I gather from the *JC [Jewish Chronicle]* that the Gratz College was reorganized on a new basis, etc. I cannot deny that I hope better things from it, both for the College and perhaps for me. However, one disappointment more in the life of a Jewish student is not of much consequence and I am grown quite accustomed to it now."[15]

Sulzberger apparently urged Schechter to be content with his lot, for Schechter writes: "I have very little hope from anywhere but if I tell you that after years of killing work I have not the least hope that they will increase my salary with six pence, whilst on the other hand, education is very expensive here so that I have not the means to bring up my children in the way they ought to be brought up—you will perhaps see my reasons for not being quite content."[16] What a poignant plaint of a scholar-father, who gives his life and health to the advancement of knowledge but is not rewarded with the means to enable him to provide an education for his children!

Matters take a turn for the better, for now Schechter discloses to the judge: "The New York news are so far satisfactory and I thank you for all that you have said and you have done."[17] Negotiations continue apace. The seminary is again represented by Dr. Solis-Cohen. Schechter leans heavily on the advice of Judge Sulzberger. He asks his advice on certain expense stipulations and on the question of the proper title. As Schechter explains: "The question of title is also of some importance as I could undertake no reform in the place without the proper authority for doing so."[18] Schechter has obviously given considerable thought to his plans for the seminary. No doubt he feels that matters are coming to a head.

While negotiations are going on, the name and stature of Schechter continues to grow in America. Thus, when the *American Hebrew* conducts a symposium titled "A Synod—Shall We Have a General Assembly," Schechter is the only non-American whose opinion is solicited. His reply appears with those of Judge Sulzberger, Lewis N. Dembitz, Rev. Max Heller, and Rev. Meldola De Sola of Montreal.[19] An editorial note a month later states: "The full text of Professor Schechter's introductory lecture at University College will be awaited with great interest. . . . His intimation of the importance of the discovery of the original text of Ecclesiasticus in disproving certain assertations of Biblical critics are of the highest importance."[20]

In the spring of 1899, Henrietta Szold delivered an address before the New York Council of Jewish Women on "Catholic Israel." She quotes approvingly and at length from Dr. Schechter, attributing the phrase to him and expounding on its meaning. Her address is published in the *American Hebrew*.[21] Schechter hears of it and writes Sulzberger for a copy. He states, "I should very much like to read it." In the same letter he writes: "The *J[ewish] Chronicle* of today reproduces from *Jewish Exponent* a paragraph relating to my possible appointment in New York etc. Have you any fresh news from that place."[22]

The article Schechter refers to, titled "A Call For Professor Schechter," is the lead editorial in the October 6, 1899, issue:

> The Jewish Theological Seminary, after fourteen years of existence, has arrived at a turning point in its career. . . . There is one man whom the friends of the institution have long and earnestly hoped could be induced to accept its leadership. Above all others available for the office Professor S. Schechter of Cambridge University, is superbly endowed with scholarship, with the force and convictions of a great personality, with a magnetism and a world-wide reputation admirably qualified to lift the Seminary to an eminence toward which the eyes of the Jewish people, scholars, students and laity, will be hopefully and enthusiastically directed. We believe that Professor Schechter's opportunities in this country would be practically unlimited and that his coming here would be productive of great results both in the Seminary itself and throughout the American Jewish Community. The efforts that [they] are now making to induce him to accept the call of the Seminary should be presented with unremitting fervor until they are crowned with success in the near future. The Jewish people can be depended upon to second and support every effort in this direction.[23]

A week later the *American Hebrew* echoed the *Exponent*'s approval and appeal:

> The authorities of the Jewish Theological Seminary of New York are in want of funds to enable them to carry out their cherished project of placing their institution under the capable direction of the well-known Professor S. Schechter, now of Oxford [sic] University, England. If a ripe scholar of such world-wide reputation as Professor Schechter could be induced to settle and teach among us, who can doubt that there would be a brisker and higher cult of Judaism as a resultant?
>
> The Seminary, founded on tested lines, and aiming, *mutatis mutandis,*

at reproducing in this land the tried and trusted methods of the Old World, has a distinct claim for support and encouragement. Every Jew who loves his race and religion, whatever be his "doxy" must recognize the value to American Judaism of the transference of the influence and labor of Professor Schechter to this land.[24]

While the journals were espousing the cause, negotiations continued on. By the end of October, Schechter listed his rabbinic credentials for Sulzberger: "I have rabbinic ordination from I. H. Weiss . . . these last twenty years. It was given to me when I left the *Beth ha-Midrash ha-Gadol* in Vienna where Weiss was rabbi and lector . . . in the year 1879. I have also one from the late Dr. Frankel, Rabbi in Berlin. I can give *Morenu*-ordination to anybody I like. I never referred to this fact in the *JC [Jewish Chronicle]* or any other paper as I hate advertising and despise such foolishness."[25]

In November an official letter of invitation went from Mr. Blumenthal, president of the Jewish Theological Association. Schechter "held out hopes to him of acceptance but did not commit myself positively."[26] Once again Schechter left everything to Judge Sulzberger's discretion.

The judge was discreet and realistic. In a letter to Cyrus Adler he indicated the sacrifices that Schechter would be making, and he put forth terms: "If he is prepared to make the sacrifice of (1) scholarly implements, such as a library, and (2) social position, for which in this city a man without money cannot find even a proximity of an equivalent; if, further, he is prepared for a certain gratuitous hostility which could only be endured and not battled with, then I think that his usefulness here can be greater than anywhere else, and I have no objection to his accepting this offer."[27]

Judge Sulzberger knew, however, the precarious financial situation of the seminary. It had no endowment, and its entire income was dependent on annual contributions. As a friend and representative of Schechter, he therefore insisted on the provision that "the sum alluded to is pledged, either by deposit or responsible subscription or absolute payment, to Schechter over four years, without the power of the Seminary for any reason whatever, to abridge this period."[28]

As the year 1899 came to a close, the whole matter was still unresolved, Schechter yearned to come, and he encouraged Blumenthal to expect a favorable decision. What restrained him was the judge's insistence that a proper contract be drawn up before Schechter should sever his ties in England. Sulzberger considered the time right psychologically for the advent of one who "has scholarship, talent, and enthusiasm," but he was concerned with financial conditions in the country and positively unhappy with the composition of the seminary's board. "I have intimated to Dr. Solis-Cohen that unless the Board of Trustees is reorganized on the basis of secularity, I shall advise your declination."[29]

At the time the seminary was under the direction of a rabbinical board, which, as Sulzberger put it "may be properly orthodox in belief or expression, but they do not command the financial support of the only people to be relied upon to maintain the Institution in permanence."[30] The judge knew who to turn to. "I have discussed the matter with Schiff, who is *the* Yehudi of New York, and we have agreed that to render the place assured, a friend of mine, Louis Marshall, should be president. . . . With him at the head of us . . . things would be perfectly safe. Without him . . . I should feel equally unsafe."[31]

Schechter agreed and confessed: "I have always felt rather uneasy at seeing so many rabbis in the list of the trustees of the Seminary."[32] He told of the visit of Mr. [Leonard] Lewisohn and reassured the judge in a letter dated on the Ides of March: *"I shall not accept any offer from America which does not come from you."*[33] Schechter had learned caution from the judge to whom he wrote at the end of 1900: "Of New York I can only say the whole matter is wearisome. I had also some 12 days ago a letter from Mr. Lewisohn—the one I met in Germany. . . . I have full confidence in him; but I have answered him that I should like to view first the situation in New York myself."[34]

The *Jewish Exponent* had been carrying on an enthusiastic campaign in furtherance of the cause. It invited an article by Israel Zangwill, who was then in America. In the October 20, 1899, issue, Zangwill wrote of the competition going on between England and America for Schechter: "For Dr. Schechter is the greatest European scholar in Jewish Science . . . the ancient University of Cambridge, England rejoices in the possession of him. . . . Dr. Schechter is the most wonderful combination of learning, wit and spiritual magnetism that it has ever been my good fortune to encounter. . . . If America succeeds in obtaining Dr. Schechter . . . it will have done much to shift the center of gravity of Jewish thought to New York."[35] How could America not relish to gain the prize?

A week later an editorial plea was put forth: "Here . . . he has original materials to work upon . . . a great living, throbbing community destined to play a leading part in the determination of catholic Israel. Dr. Schechter will come where the need is greatest, and that greatest need is here. Across the mighty waters the sound of the call is heard and like a parent's heart, the answer is unhesitatingly and unquestionably I will come."[36]

The report in December of 1899 that Dr. Schechter had accepted the call brought forth warm response from all segments of American Israel. "An auspicious moment in the history of American Israel," the *Jewish Messenger* proclaimed.[37] Even the radical reformer Emil G. Hirsch hailed his coming: "The coming of this great scholar, facile princeps among modern students of rabbinical literature, will mark an epoch in the development of Jewish science in America."[38]

The editor of the *Exponent,* Charles I. Hoffman, soon recognized that the necessary ingredient to assure the coming of Dr. Schechter was adequate financial support. An editorial in early 1900 solicits generosity: "The wealthy Jew or Jews who would signally associate themselves with this would deserve and receive the immortality that comes to those who have aided in the establishment of a great and permanent undertaking."[39]

The wealthy Jew in this enterprise as in all major Jewish undertakings at the turn of the century had to be Jacob H. Schiff. In 1901, the death of Joseph Blumenthal made possible the reorganization of the seminary. Dr. Cyrus Adler, who played a central role in this endeavor, tells how it came about:

> In 1901, I . . . was invited to a man's party at the house of Mr. [Isidor] Straus. There was a small group standing together and they were speaking of Jewish affairs in New York and particularly of Jewish education. I said . . . that the Jewish community of New York, which was destined to be the largest community in the world, was allowing its only institution of higher Jewish learning to perish, and I told them something of the precarious situation of the Seminary. Mr. Schiff, who was a man of quick decisions, said to the men standing around, "Doctor Adler is right," and a few weeks later I received a letter from him, asking me when I was coming to New York next time, so that he might invite a few men to meet with us. Among the men, I remember, were Leonard Lewisohn and Mayer Sulzberger, joined the next day by Daniel and Simon Guggenheim. I shall not go into the steps that brought about the reorganization of the Seminary Board, with the powerful help of Louis Marshall, but suffice it to say, that within a few months an Endowment Fund of over one-half million dollars had been secured . . . which rendered it possible to invite Doctor Solomon Schechter . . . to come to America, as head of the Seminary.[40]

With an adequate endowment secured, Schechter's coming was now assured. Despite an increase in salary granted him by Cambridge University, Schechter was anxious to come to America. But even though both parties were eager that the ongoing flirtation be crowned with consummation, the road of love had its hazards. Thus, Schechter in a moment of high indignation wrote to Sulzberger in April, 1901: "Please do not bother about the New York affair, I am quite sick of it. If they ever come to you and to me with anything fair we will consider it; but I have really too much to do to spend a thought on the humours of Mr. Schiff and his brother magnates. . . . If I ever go to America I mean to be treated like a gentleman and a scholar and also to be paid accordingly. If they cannot see that I might do something for America . . . then let them be d——d." [41]

Sulzberger, who heretofore had been a reluctant intermediary, now became an eager proponent. In June, Schechter wrote to him: "What you tell me about New York is very satisfactory and I feel un-sicked. Everything is left to you, and when you will say the blessing, I will answer Amen!"[42] The blessing was said in the form of an invitation and contract, and Schechter said, "Amen." To his intimate friend Herbert Bentwich, he wrote on December 24, 1901: "I have to tell you that I have definitely accepted the New York offer. . . . It is with heavy heart that I have to take this step, but it had to be done for the sake of my family, and perhaps also for the sake of American Judaism with which the future rests."[43]

At the turn of the century Schechter was one of Jewry's leading scholars. He had captured the popular imagination with his Genizah and Ben Sirah explorations and discoveries. He was a zealous and observant Jew, but withal a man of the world, possessed of a magnetic personality that won him adoring friends and disciples. With all this he was possessed of a remarkable English prose style that made his essays models of scholarly popularizations. He was in training, experience, and commitment the perfect man to head an academic institution for the training of English-speaking rabbis.

There was also American "pioneer pride"—that pride that caused other men of wealth to bring to America Europe's finest art and rarest books—which moved Jewish men of substance to choose Schechter. Jacob H. Schiff put it in his own direct manner: "We in the United States, who are ever striving to secure the best, were not long in the discovery [of] Solomon Schechter."[44]

Why did Schechter come to America? Coming consists of departure and arrival. He was anxious to leave England because he lived in a non-Jewish environment and dreaded raising his children without adequate Jewish associations. He desired an education for his children, which his meager reader's salary would not provide. He confides to Bentwich: "I could not bear the idea of taking money from private individuals any longer."[45]

What rankled even more was that this money came largely from Claude G. Montefiore, who favored Sunday services[46] and who declared that he felt more worshipful, more prayerful, more drawn Godwards when he heard English than when he heard Hebrew, although he understood the latter.[47] As early as 1895, Schechter complained to Sulzberger about English Jewry: "I cannot help saying that there is a little too much *Meshumadim* cult in England; which is probably due to the influences of the D'Israelis, Herschel and other illustrious successful *Meshumadim* [apostates]. I will protest against it."[48] His protest appeared five years later in four letters to the *Jewish Chronicle* in which he is strongly critical of English Jewry's assimilationist tendencies, its "jingoism," its lack of spirituality, and its indifference to Jewish learning.

As an east European Jew he is particularly sensitive to the discrimination practiced against the immigrant Jew in England. He bridles at Jewish communal life being under the benevolent despotism of "our stock exchange chaplains" who were destroying the Jewish consciousness. In justifying his first letter, which Schechter confesses had a "horrifying effect," he writes to Sulzberger: "It was . . . highly time to tell them (the stock exchange chaplains) that millions do not compensate us for their ignorance and that they hadn't any claim of intellectual or spiritual superiority over their brethren abroad—particularly the Russian Jews whom they are always bullying."[49]

Although the atmosphere in Cambridge was congenial to scholarship, it was Jewishly unsatisfactory, and Schechter was above all a zealous, enthusiastic Jew. Life without Jews meant "spiritual death" to Schechter. True, he had more manuscripts to edit than even a hundred years of life would exhaust, but his ambitions were greater and higher. "In your country," he explained to Sulzberger, "I can hope to 'make school' and to leave students [who] may prove useful to the cause of Judaism as well as that of Jewish scholarship."[50] The "make school" that would provide scholarly, spiritual leadership for American Jewry and that would foster Jewish scholarship is what drew Schechter to America. In the letter just quoted he proclaims, "My hope for the future of Judaism and its literature is in America." The institution that would assure this future is the seminary, and Schechter longs to make it his life's work. "It would lengthen my life" Schechter writes to Sulzberger, "to be with you and [a] few other friends, together all active to establish a school of Torah in America where the future of Judaism is."[51]

Freedom, which Schechter craved, and the frontier, which his adventurous soul yearned for, drew him to the land, which he loved from the days of his first visit. Lincoln was an early spiritual hero, and he was utterly fascinated by the Civil War. Even while in England he badgered Sulzberger for more and more works on this conflict.[52] Zangwill reports Schechter's reaction to America: " 'A great people,' he cried to me enthusiastically on his return, 'great people.' "[53]

Schechter summed up his desire for America in a letter to Adler on the first day of 1900: "America has thus only *ideal* attractions for me, offering as it does a larger field of activity which may become a source of blessing to future generation[s]. I also feel that I shall be more happy living among Jews. I want my synagogue and my proper Yomim Tobim among my people. There is also the question of the children being brought up among Jews, which is the only guarantee for the acquiring of a real heartfelt Judaism. . . . I am prepared to give the Seminary all my faculties, even my very life."[54] Destiny marked Schechter for America, and the forces of history coalesced to fulfill this destiny.

Among the forces that "coalesced" were the Philadelphia group that provided American Jewry its intellectual leadership and the New York millionaires whose concern and generosity gave reality to the dreams and projects of the former. What promise did Dr. Solomon Solis-Cohen, Judge Mayer Sulzberger, and Dr. Cyrus Adler see in Schechter's coming to America? The first saw in him the needed leader to give direction to American Jewry, "striving vaguely, not knowing what they want, but knowing that they want something." Sulzberger, ever the scholar, thought the time propitious for laying the foundations for a knowledgeable Jewry. "He who has scholarship, talent and enthusiasm may be more appreciated for the first time in our history than he who leads a party." Adler was anxious for the future of the seminary and saw in the enterprise of acquiring Schechter an opportunity to enlist in the seminary's support the resources of Schiff and his friends. An observant Jew, he was deeply disturbed by the inroad that Reform had made and saw in Schechter the one possibility to establish an institution that would initially stay and eventually turn the tide.

The inroads of radical reform gave concern to a man like Schiff as well. What concerned him even more were religious indifference and political radicalism.

> Solomon Schechter . . . was the one man fitted to be placed at the head of the American Jewish Theological Seminary, . . . in which were to be reared a class of Jewish Rabbis who could be counted upon to maintain inviolate our faith in its ancient purity, and to assure through their ministrations and teaching adherence to Jewish forms and traditions amongst those, who both at the present time and in coming generations need form the bulwark against the inroads of indifference and irreligiousness in the life of at least a large portion of American Jewry.[55]

Schiff, the Lewisohns, the Guggenheims, and their group were much concerned about the children of the east European immigrant. The problem of the East Side agitated uptown Jewry. The plight of the immigrant population moved many to socialism and anarchism. The social flux, the breakdown of the family unit, and the bewildering difference in social patterns often led to crime. There is no question that the uptown Jews saw in the seminary-ordained rabbi and his teachings a force that would bring moderation, stability, and order to the community and higher standards to personal life. Dr. Mordecai Kaplan, coworker with Schechter as a member of the faculty of the seminary (never comfortable with the monied elite) considered the chief motive of the newly constituted board of trustees under the chairmanship of Louis Marshall "to establish a

training school for American trained rabbis who might stem the proliferation of gangsterism on the Jewish East Side. Graduates of the then
existing Hebrew Union College could not serve that purpose."[56]

Mrs. H. Pereira Mendes, wife of Shearith Israel's minister and chairman of the Committee on Religion of the National Council of Jewish
Women reported in June 1899: "I have urged a plan for the religious
betterment of our poorer brethren, by employing our English-speaking
Seminary graduates, who are so eminently qualified for that work."[57]
The *American Hebrew* editorially applauded this suggestion, pointing
out that "the young men and young women, English speaking children
of jargon-speaking immigrants, are entirely unchurched."[58] Concern for
those "unchurched" was a powerful motive in the reorganization and en-
dowing of the seminary that provided for Schechter's coming.

What the children of the immigrants needed was not only Judaiza-
tion but also Americanization. Here, too, it was felt an English-speaking,
seminary-trained rabbi could play an important role. In the *American
Hebrew*'s editorial obituary for Leonard Lewisohn, who gave "$50,000
toward the rehabilitation of the Theological Seminary," we find "most
recent of all was his interest in the Jewish Theological Seminary, as af-
fording the surest and safest means of handling the down-town problems
of Americanizing the foreign element by sending among them trained
and well-equipped Rabbinical teachers."[59] Even in the founding of a theological seminary, the strongest motive was the ongoing, inherent promise
that "the uptown mansion never forgets the downtown tenement in its
distress."

This attitude, that the reorganization of the seminary and the bringing of Schechter was primarily a philanthropic gesture, must have crept
into the negotiations with Schechter. He felt it three thousand miles
away. Ever the proud Jew, he shared his chagrin with Sulzberger: "I dearly
hope that the magnates of New York do not believe that they have to deal
with some Maggid who cannot possibly expect to be treated with the
same liberality as the Rabbi-Preacher."[60]

Schechter's coming, his leadership of the seminary, and the movement he founded did very much to bridge the gap between "uptown" and
"downtown." His arrival on April 17, 1902, was widely hailed as the beginning of a new era in American Jewish religious life and scholarship.
For once anticipations were not exaggerations. The *American Hebrew*'s
welcoming editorial spoke prophetically: "He was born a Romanian, was
educated in Germany, has been studying and teaching in England, but it
seems he will be especially at home in an American atmosphere, where
he will be a leader in our development."[61]

6 New York Chooses a Chief Rabbi

Jacob Joseph of Vilna

It is not surprising that the first effort toward a union by east European Orthodox Jewry of New York was for the purpose of electing a chief rabbi. Doctor Nathan Marcus Adler, chief rabbi of the British Empire, was their example. Accepted as spokesman for religious Jewry by rulers and subjects alike, yet unflinchingly Orthodox, author of responsa and novellae, he had shown that Orthodoxy and social status were not mutually exclusive.

To the Russian Jews who feared the effects of the American environment on their faith and felt their inferior standing in the eyes of the Americanized, a chief rabbi renowned for scholarship and spirituality could obviate both disabilities. He could exert a power and influence in American Israel similar to that of Rabbi Nathan Adler.

The term *chief rabbi* and the advocacy of a *spiritual chief* were not unknown to American Jewry. Isaac Leeser, hailing the election of Rabbi Nathan Marcus Adler in 1845, had editorialized: "Moreover, if Dr. Adler can show by his acts the usefulness of a spiritual chief, it will not be long before the American Israelites will also demand the election of a chief with several associates to preside over our worship and education. . . . We indeed candidly think that we require in this country some ecclesiastical authority over and above the independent ministers."[1]

This feeling was shared by the Reverend Abraham Rice of Baltimore, first ordained rabbi to officiate in the United States. He wrote to the editor of the *Occident:* "I, however, think it my duty to call your attention to a subject on which I have kept silent hitherto, from the sole motive that someone might believe me speaking from interested motives. It is to urge upon the Jews in the United States the great importance of selecting a spiritual chief."[2] The Reverend James K. Gutheim in 1846 reported the installation of "Dr. M. Lilienthal as Chief Rabbi of the three congregations of German Jews" (of New York) and stated: "Indeed, the appointment of a Chief Rabbi may be considered a new era in our religious concerns."[3] Twenty years later Leeser again urged the election of a chief rabbi of the United States.[4]

THE FIRST ATTEMPT

In 1852, the first Russian-American Jewish congregation, Beth Hamidrash Hagadol, was organized. For four decades it was the leading east European Orthodox Congregation. Abraham Joseph Ash served intermittently as its rabbi from 1860 on. In 1876, he took up the business of importing kosher wine from California,[5] and in the spring of 1877 he resigned his position. In the fall of 1879, he resumed his religious functions at a salary of $200.[6]

During the interregnum, the first attempt was made to import a chief rabbi. There had been dissatisfaction with the incumbent because he alternated between business and the rabbinate, and was inclined toward Hasidism. Many of the more learned members, particularly the shohatim and butchers, did not recognize his authority because of his meager scholarship.

After Ash had resigned, the choice for the proposed post of chief rabbi fell on Rabbi Meir Loeb ben Jehiel Michael Malbim, noted Talmud scholar and Bible commentator, whose battles against Reform had caused his imprisonment in Bucharest and expulsion from Romania. For similar reasons, he was ordered out of Moghilef and forced to leave Koenigsberg. The year 1879 saw him free to accept a call from a new community.[7] The *New York Herald* assigned a reporter to attend one of the earliest organization meetings, held at Beth Hamidrash Halchei Yousher [sic] 44 East Broadway, at which delegates from thirty-two congregations "were to appear to discuss the question of establishing a Chief Rabbi and Beth Din (religious court) for all the congregations in the United States who desire to join in the project." By four PM, twenty-eight people were present. The reporter learned that "Rabbi M. L. Malbini [sic] of Koenigsberg had been invited, and would come if accepted by a majority of the congregations."[8]

At the next meeting, held at the Deborah Nursery, 95 East Broadway, a permanent organization was effected, under the name of "Board of Delegates of United Hebrew Orthodox Congregations." J. P. Solomon was elected permanent chairman, and M. Cohn was chosen secretary. Twenty-six congregations pledged annual contributions totaling $2,800. The board decided that as soon as $5,000 was pledged a formal invitation would be sent to Rabbi Malbim.

A "Call to Israel"[9] was then circulated among the congregations, soliciting the cooperation of "those who are desirous of perpetuating the ancient faith and transmitting intact to their children that priceless inheritance." A leader "whose character will inspire respect, whose abilities will impart confidence, and whose erudition and reputation will silence all disaffection" will stem the "open and flagrant desecration of the Sabbath, the neglect of dietary laws and regulations, the formation of various shades and degrees of Orthodoxy and Reform." Such a leader "can be found in the eminent Rabbi, Dr. Mayer L. Malbim." The call boasted that twenty-four congregations were already in the fold, and twenty-five more were ready to cooperate.

The *Jewish Record* of Philadelphia, which reported the meeting and published the full text, was favorable to the idea but questioned the wisdom of choosing that candidate. It stated: "Rev. Dr. Malban [sic] is over seventy years of age, and it appears to us that no matter how learned or distinguished a rabbi he may be, it would be folly to select a man of his age, ignorant of the language and customs of this country, to fill so responsible a position. Surely, some learned English speaking rabbi in the prime of life might be secured if the matter were once settled upon."[10]

Critical of the idea was the New York correspondent of the *American Israelite*, Julian Werner. He reported that at the third meeting seventeen congregations agreed to subscribe $1,500 per annum and that among the speakers was "Dr. Horatio Gomez of the Nineteenth Street Synagogue [Shearith Israel], which shows that the movement is not confined to the numerous 'Houses of Learning' situated in Bayard Street, East Broadway, and the other localities where the Russian and Polish Israelites mostly dwell."[11]

Strong disapproval was voiced by Isaac Mayer Wise in an editorial that conceded that "as a man of rabbinical learning he [M. L. Malbim] is highly respectable [but] he appears not to have the slightest idea of the wants and demands of this age. . . . He would be played out in New York four weeks after his arrival, because he could not do anything very useful and startling for his Congregations."[12]

Rabbi Malbim, after his sad experiences in three European communities, favored the opportunity of migrating to the "Land of the Free." But when he was then called to the rabbinate of Krementchug he readily accepted. While on the way to his new position, the aged rabbi became ill, and he died in September 1879. The death of Rabbi Malbim and the reappointment of Rabbi Ash ended the first attempt to elect a chief rabbi. The Beth Hamidrash Hagadol was the leading congregation, without which nothing would be attempted. The idea, however, continued to challenge leaders and spokesmen in America and in Europe.

More than fifty thousand Jews immigrated to the United States from east European countries during 1881–1885.[13] The rabbis of the mother community were increasingly aware of the potential of the American Jewish community and the religious problems of the immigrants. In 1887 Jacob Halevi Lipschitz wrote from Kovno:

For some years now, many leading rabbis who are greatly concerned with the welfare of their people and the Torah have turned their attention to their brethren in America. Since the material and spiritual lives of American Israel are so intertwined with our brethren here, in matters of aid and support, in matters of family purity, marriage, and divorce, which are officiated over by improper men, in matters of kashrut. . . . [To deal with these problems] the leading rabbis held three conferences two years ago [1885] in Telsiai and in Ponevezh to seek ways and means of elevating Jewish religious life in America.[14]

Jacob Halevi Lipschitz was the capable and energetic secretary of Rabbi Isaac Elhanan Spektor, leading rabbi of east European Jewry. These conferences were probably called at his instigation. He subsequently played an important role in promoting the idea of a chief rabbi and his own candidate, son of Rabbi Isaac Elhanan. American Israel needed distinguished rabbinic leadership, to be obtained only if the east European congregations in New York would invite "an outstanding rabbinical leader." This is what Jacob Halevi Lipschitz urged as "the best advice of the European rabbis" when they learned of the passing of Rabbi Ash on May 6, 1887.[15]

According to an estimate of Rabbi Moses Weinberger, New York City in 1887 had a Jewish population of 100,000 to 120,000 families.[16] The majority were east European immigrants residing on the Lower East Side. For some 130 Orthodox congregations, there were only three or four Orthodox rabbis, largely ignored, officially and financially. Of unattached "itinerant preachers" and "marriage performers" there was an abundance. What each congregation wanted was an outstanding hazzan to enhance both its prestige and income.[17] There were many private *hadarim* (old-fashioned elementary schools), housed in cellars, stores, or in the apartment of the melamed, who was all too often incompetent and harassed. The two Talmud Torahs for poor children derived their precarious support from the "Uptown Jews."[18] Kashrut was big business, chaotic, unorganized, and unsupervised. The shohatim were a law unto themselves. An attempt of the more dedicated and scholarly to organize themselves into an association, Zovchei T'mimim [sic], did not endure. A growing group of radicals, socialists, and anarchists who were opposed to religion in principle found in them ready fuel for their fires of calumny and ridicule. The east European Jew, though scorned by his uptown brethren, nevertheless cast covetous eyes on their spiritual leadership, which possessed prestige and the interest of the general press. As already stated, the position of chief rabbi of Great Britain served as a continual example and challenge.

An attempt at uniting the Orthodox congregations in the mid-1880s under the name U.H.O.A. proved ineffective.[19] However, it kept the public aroused about the abuses in Orthodox religious life and kept alive the desire for congregational union. An important writer and communal figure proposed that a month-long congress be called to consider the problems and to propose solutions. He was heartened by the successful achievements of the Congress of the United States and the Jewish synods of the Middle Ages. A call was issued to the congregations to foster the idea of a united Orthodox community.[20] Rabbi Weinberger suggested as a solution a program consisting of four parts:

1. Amalgamation of the 130 small orthodox congregations into ten or twelve synagogues of size and substance.
2. These newly amalgamated congregations to unite into a congregational association.
3. Each congregation to appoint a worthy rabbi as spiritual leader.
4. A "Chief Rabbi" or a "Supreme Tribunal" to be established.[21]

Among leaders of the Beth Hamidrash Hagadol the desire for a chief rabbi continued to be voiced. The more scholarly wanted a man who would rank with the spiritual authorities of the communities whence they came. The "worldly" wanted a man who would have status in the Jewish community and in the general community.

ORGANIZING FOR THE SEARCH

In the spring of 1887, Rabbi Abraham Joseph Ash had died. Before the *sheloshim* (the mourning period of thirty days) had passed, official steps were taken to secure a chief rabbi, as stated in the minutes of a meeting of the Beth Hamidrash Hagadol on May 23. The suggestion was made: "It is the duty of our Synagogue to seek out ways and means of bringing a Chief Rabbi for New York. The president [Dramin Jones] comments on the suggestion favorably and orders the Secretary to send notices of letters to presidents of some sister congregations of New York, that the day after Shabuot, all presidents shall assemble for a meeting in this Synagogue to discuss the matter under what conditions and from where a chief rabbi should be invited."[22]

The response was heartening. A special committee to call on congregations was appointed on June 9. By June 12, a number of intercongregational meetings had been held and financial plans laid. A special meeting of the sponsoring congregation held that day voted that the Beth Hamidrash Hagadol obligate itself to contribute $500 per annum for five years toward the support of a chief rabbi. Appointed to represent the congregation were Moses Butkowsky, Meyer Freeman, and its president, Dramin Jones.[23]

By the end of the month $2,500 was pledged by the following congregations and individuals:

CONGREGATIONS

Beth Hamidrash Hagadol	$500
Kahal Adath Yeshurun	300
Mishkan Israel Anshe Suwalk	250
Hebra Kadisha Anshe Kalvarie	200
Kol Israel Anshe Polin	150
Mahzike Talmud Torah Mt. Sinai	150
Beth Hamidrash Anshe Ungarn	150
Mikra Kodesh	100
B'nai Emet Anshe Merimpol	75
Tiferet Israel Anshe Neustadt	50
Kenesset Israel Anshe Russia	50
Shaare Torah	50
Talmud Torah Anshe Augustov	50
Ahavat Sholom	30
Shaare Binah	25
Other congregations	120

INDIVIDUALS

Zvi Elhanan [Henry] Chuck	100
Joshua Rothstein	50
—— Storman	50
—— Richter	50

The participants organized themselves into the Association of American Orthodox Hebrew Congregations, with Dramin Jones as president, Nathan Levine as vice-president, Sender Jarmulowsky as treasurer, and Judah Buchhalter as secretary, who was charged with carrying on the affairs of the association. A board was established consisting of congregational representatives, determined by the amount the congregation was contributing. Thus the Beth Hamidrash Hagadol was entitled to ten representatives for its share of $500.[24]

THE SEARCH

No time was wasted in beginning the search. Announcements appeared in Russian Hebrew periodicals. The secretary was then instructed to write to eight leading rabbis for their recommendations. On July 24, the letters were dispatched with the hope that one of the correspondents would offer himself as a candidate.[25]

Those asked for their recommendations were Rabbi Isaac Elhanan Spektor of Kovno, a leading member of the east European rabbinate; Rabbi Hillel Lifshitz of Suwalki; Rabbi Elijah Hayyim Meisels of Lodz; Rabbi Jacob Joseph of Vilna; Rabbi Azriel Hildesheimer of Berlin; Rabbi

Elijah Levinson of Krottingen; Rabbi Joseph Duber Diskin of Brest-Li-
tovsk; and Rabbi Hayyim Berlin of Moscow. They were informed that

> Three months ago, Rabbi Abraham Joseph Ash, who was Rabbi of Beth
> Hamidrash Hagadol, of New York, passed away. To him all our brethren
> here turned for religious guidance and ritual decisions. After his death
> the members of the congregations met to decide whether to engage a
> successor or not. After due deliberation we decided that it is not advis-
> able that we choose a rabbi for ourselves alone and have each congrega-
> tion elect a rabbi to serve that congregation alone. This is not advisable
> nor beneficial, for a number of reasons. First, each congregation would
> be concerned with its own welfare and not that of Judaism. Second, and
> this is most important, many improvements must be undertaken to raise
> the standard of Judaism in our own country, and if the Orthodox con-
> gregations do not unite, then there is no hope for the preservation and
> upbuilding of Judaism in our city.[26]

The leaders of the association felt that the fragmentation of religious
organization into independent congregational units was sapping the
authority and the vitality of religious life. They either failed to recognize
or found undesirable and unacceptable that, unlike Europe, American
Jewry's religious unit was the congregation. To help effect unification
they sought a chief rabbi whose scholarship would be revered and whose
authority would be unchallenged. The letter continued:

> For this purpose there assembled members of the above mentioned Con-
> gregation and important individuals of other congregations to bring this
> matter to fruition. We unanimously decided to invite as our spiritual
> leader a rabbi noted for his scholarship and piety. His mission would be
> to remove the stumbling blocks from before our people and to unite the
> hearts of our brethren, the House of Israel, to serve God with one heart
> and soul, and to supervise with an open eye the shohatim and all other
> matters of holiness to the House of Israel, which to our deep sorrow are
> not observed nor respected, because there is no authority nor guide re-
> vered and accepted by the whole community, and each one is an author-
> ity unto himself.[27]

It is significant that from the earliest stages, the major project for the
chief rabbi was the supervision of kashrut. The abuses in this area were
apparent and their correction seemingly simple, i.e., stringent supervision by an acceptable authority. It was recognized that the chief inducement would have to be monetary. The promise was held out that "the
congregations, already participating, have pledged to offer a salary of
close to three thousand dollars per annum, and many other congregations

stand ready to join the Association. Each new congregation will add to the treasury and thus make it possible to offer the rabbi a generous salary as would befit the chief rabbi of so important a Jewish community as New York."[28]

But America was suspect in the eyes of the learned and pious European Jew. A rabbi of status and ability would not immigrate to a land where it was felt scholarship was not respected and religion was abused.[29] Discouraging reports depicting American Jewry as materialistic, boorish, and impious, respecting neither person nor position, had appeared in the Russian Hebrew periodicals. The framers of the letter felt the need to suggest that the rabbi accepting their call would do so out of concern for the religious welfare of a growing Jewish community and in a spirit of sacrificial dedication. They wrote:

> We are not unaware, that the person we would invite is respected in his community, and there is no reason that would urge him to leave his home and travel across the seas. Yet our faith is in God, that there have not ceased among our people those who are deeply concerned with the preservation of our holy faith. The rabbi who heeds our call will do so for the sake of the Jewish community across the sea, to save many souls of our brethren who have emigrated and wandered to this land, and infuse in them the spirit of knowledge and the fear of God.[30]

The answers were cautious—asking more than answering. Rabbi Isaac Elhanan Spektor congratulated the association on its decision. He saw the rabbi as a unifying force, and he considered unity essential. However, he asked for more time to consider their request.[31]

Short and to the point was the reply of Rabbi Hillel Lifshitz.

1. Which are the groups and the congregations which have already joined and who stand ready to affiliate?
2. Will the position of chief rabbi be recognized by the Government as an official permanent position?[32]

The same question was asked by Rabbi Elijah Hayyim Meisels. A chief rabbinate such as that of Great Britain attracted them, and they were desirous of learning whether the American counterpart would have similar official recognition. Rabbi Meisels pointed to the difficulties of establishing the office. The rabbi would have to win acceptance not only for himself but also for the position. He must therefore be not only a scholar but an administrator and diplomat as well.[33]

Somewhat apprehensive was Rabbi Hayyim Berlin. He, too, offered his commendation on the unification of the congregations. The position required an accomplished man, and that was not easy to find. He also required more details and more signatories and asked for two months in which to consult with other rabbis.[34]

Rabbi Jacob Joseph, rabbi and communal preacher of Vilna, was interested. He suggested that there were individuals in America who could offer opinions as to proper candidates, and he would then be happy to comment on their choices. He assumed that the association's letters solicited volunteers as well as recommendations. Surmising that his services would be sought by the association as well as his advice, he suggested that his ears were attuned to the sound of a call.[35]

THE LEADING CANDIDATES

In control of the association were wealthy Orthodox businessmen, "worldly" in outlook, who wanted a scholarly chief rabbi to be accepted by the larger Jewish community and the non-Jewish world. To be a master of Talmud was important, but equally important were general culture and knowledge of the tongue of the Americanized element of the community. Dramin Jones, president of the association, was their spokesman, strongly supported by Henry Chuck and Asher Salwen. Their choice was Rabbi Hillel Lifshitz, noted both for his Talmudic scholarship and his wide general culture, including a command of the German tongue.

The secretary was instructed to issue the invitation. A letter was dispatched on September 18, indicating that his attainments made him the ideal person for the position. It stated that a state charter had already been granted and that the heads of the congregations had committed themselves in writing and paid their initial obligations. Actually the charter was notarized on December 2 and filed on December 6 of that year, and congregational presidents did not sign contracts, nor did congregations advance funds until after the first of the following year.[36]

The choice of Rabbi Lifshitz was far from unanimous. His partisans felt obliged to warn him to exercise care in regard to letters he might receive and that he should pay heed only to those with signatures of the president and the secretary of the association. They had received formal notice of a different candidate, in a letter from Jacob Halevi Lipschitz, secretary to Rabbi Isaac Elhanan Spektor. In commanding terms Lipschitz notified the association that the leading rabbis of Europe had been meeting for some time concerning a chief rabbi for New York and that they had decided that the proper person was Zvi Hirsch, son of Rabbi Isaac Elhanan. All that had to be now determined were the conditions of employment. He also informed the association that a proper salary should be offered and that a letter be sent at once to Rabbi Isaac Elhanan, requesting that he grant his son permission to accept. He even suggested the text of the letter and offered his services as intermediary.

Lipschitz correctly surmised that a letter might not be sufficient.

New York Orthodox leaders were less awed by the authority of Isaac El-hanan and by the decisions of his office than their east European coun-terparts. A twofold program was therefore instituted. Meyer Freeman, a learned leader of the Beth Hamidrash Hagadol, rallied the "scholarly ele-ment" to urge the election of Rabbi Zvi Hirsch. Leading European rabbis were urged to write favoring the election of Rabbi Isaac Elhanan's son. They were also informed that he was the association's choice and that any other dealings with the New York group would be considered inter-ference. At the same time Lipschitz had leading rabbis write to Rabbi Isaac Elhanan urging him to second his son's candidacy. Among these were Rabbis Joseph Duber Diskin, Mordecai Gimpel, Alexander Moses Lapidutsohn, Hayyim Judah Ticktinsky, Judah Leib Rief, Solomon Shapiro, and Hillel Lifshitz, the association's choice.

Rabbi Isaac Elhanan then sent a lengthy letter, stating his approval and commendation of the association's project. Many rabbis, he informed them, had written, urging him to permit the candidacy of his son, and though it pained him greatly to see his son depart, he felt he must bow to the decision of his colleagues in a matter touching on the preservation and strengthening of the faith. The letter was sent on September 8, 1887. Recipients of the original letters were prevailed on to write the president urging the election of Rabbi Zvi Hirsch. Rabbis Elijah Levinson, Hayyim Berlin, Azriel Hildesheimer, and Jacob Joseph did so.

The plan was bold in formulation and execution. All possible candi-dates were induced to rule themselves out. Strong support was organized in New York and a special emissary sent to promote the candidacy. The candidate himself was young in years but already a recognized scholar. As to experience with governmental authorities, he had undertaken a mission to St. Petersburg during the difficult days of the 1880s.

No European community could have withstood all this influence and pressure. What had not been anticipated was the independence of the leaders of an American Jewish community. They apparently resented be-ing dictated to. That their chosen candidate had been forced to withdraw added stubbornness to their resentment. They did not want Zvi Hirsch. Then they discovered that Zvi Hirsch had suffered business reverses and was unable to pay his creditors. He had changed his patronymic from Spektor to Rabinovich. His wife had become insane, and he had separated from her in a manner that left wide room for criticism.

Judah Buchhalter stated these as reasons for rejection in a letter to Rabbi Hayyim Berlin, asking him to propose another candidate. Rabbi Berlin, however, never replied. The only putative candidate who had not disqualified himself was Rabbi Elijah Hayyim Meisels of Lodz. An invi-tation was issued to him. He was asked to state his conditions and was promised that immediately on receipt of his acceptance a contract would be sent him. Rabbi Meisels was slow in replying. When his answer finally arrived it proved a medley of interest, suspicion, and apprehension. He was interested, but he would not discuss terms through letters. He suggested that he meet with two representatives in Hamburg so that they might determine whether he was the proper candidate and so that he might become better acquainted with the duties, problems, and prerogatives of the position. Lest he be accused of trespassing on the interests of a powerfully backed colleague, he added that he had met Rabbi Zvi Hirsch, who was ready to accept the position, and urged that the association engage him. The delay in answering and the conditions set turned the leaders from Meisels to the one man still interested. On the eve of Sukkot, 1887, the association dispatched a letter to Rabbi Jacob Joseph, communal preacher of Vilna, inviting him to become its chief rabbi.

The leaders were disturbed by their lack of success, by the attempt to foist a candidate on them, and by the waning enthusiasm of the congregations. Their letter to Rabbi Jacob Joseph had an urgent, even desperate, tone. Are you ready to accept the position? If so, let us know immediately. We will then call a meeting to elect you and send you the contract. Rabbi Jacob Joseph did not keep them waiting. Within the month he informed them of his willingness to accept, stating that leading rabbis had urged this action. He suggested that his salary be such as would befit the office and permit its incumbent to live in comfort and dignity. He also demanded a six-year contract.[37] Seemingly as an afterthought he mentioned that he would need a substantial advance before he could leave Vilna.

The association acted quickly. A state charter was notarized on December 2 and filed with the secretary of state on the sixth of the month. The incorporators were Dramin Jones, president; Nathan Levin, vice-president; Sender Jarmulowsky, treasurer; Meyer Freeman, and Moses L. Abrams. The stated purpose was

> to encourage, foster and promote the observances of the Orthodox Jewish religion, to spread and disseminate the doctrines and learning of the said religion, to improve and elevate the moral, social and spiritual condition of the Jewish people, to designate, support and maintain a Chief Rabbi and such other officers as may be deemed necessary or advisable, and to do, perform and effect all other charitable and benevolent acts and purposes, as may be specified in the Constitution and By-Laws.[38]

Armed with a charter, the association held a meeting on December 7 at which Rabbi Jacob Joseph was elected chief rabbi for a period of six years. His salary was to be $2,500 per annum, and an apartment suited to the position was stipulated as well. In the letter informing him of his election, the association also undertook to provide traveling expenses for himself and family and to grant him the advance requested. The individual congregations were asked to obligate themselves for six years and to sign a contract of obligation to the association.[39]

The Reform Jews of America were informed of the election by the *American Israelite*'s New York correspondent, Mi Yodea: "At a meeting of the delegates of the Orthodox Congregations held Wednesday in the Beth Hammidrash Haggadol [sic], it was unanimously resolved to engage the well known Gaon of Wilna, Reb Yankele Charif, as Rab ha-Kolel."[40] The *Jüdisches Tageblatt* joyfully announced in its January 23 issue that Rabbi Jacob Joseph had accepted the association's invitation. His letter was greeted with great joy by the delegates, who, at a meeting on January 18, a few days before, had decided to urge him to come as soon as possible, preferably before Passover. It was not until February 24 that the subscribers of the *American Hebrew* learned that "a number of prominent downtown orthodox congregations have selected Rabbi Jacob Charif as *Rav Ha-Kolale,* or Rabbi of the United Congregations."[41]

THE VICTOR

Rabbi Jacob Joseph was at that time the *maggid mesharim* (communal preacher) and *moreh zedek* (religious judge) in Vilna, known as "the Jerusalem of Lithuania." It had not had a communal rabbi for over a century and a half; Rabbi Joseph was one of its spiritual leaders. Prior to coming to Vilna in 1883, he had served as rabbi in Vilon, Jurburg, and Novy Zhagare. He had studied in the famed yeshivah of Volozhin under the renowned scholar Rabbi Hirsch Leib Berlin and later under the celebrated Israel Salanter.[42] As an outstanding student, he was accorded the title *harif* (possessor of a keen mind), which he carried throughout his life. Although he was a recognized scholar, it was his preaching that had brought him to Vilna and spread his fame to the New World. His published book of sermons[43] reveals him as a man possessed of an orderly mind and liberal outlook. The sermons are clear, well constructed, and ethical in emphasis.

When the call came, he was a popular and respected figure in Vilna. The love and esteem in which he was held in Vilna is expressed in a letter from Michael Bairack of Vilna to his nephew Abraham Cahan in New York:

> He is very dear to us. He is both brilliant and unusually pious. It pains us deeply that we had to bid him farewell. We did not want to lose such a precious possession. See to it that New York Jewry knows that they took from us a rare jewel. See to it that he is properly appreciated. I know that you do not go to the synagogue, but you do have a Jewish heart. Therefore, won't you tell everyone that Vilna gloried in him and that New York must recognize that it now wears a precious crown.[44]

Rabbi Joseph, however, was heavily in debt. Though reluctant to leave Vilna, he saw the position in America and the monetary inducements his only chance of settling his difficulties. Immediately on election he informed the association that he must have five thousand rubles. The request came as no surprise, but the sum threw the association into confusion. They had never contemplated so great an amount. Public solicitation would have to be undertaken. The leaders of the association feared public reaction. The election had not met with great enthusiasm initially, for many felt he had been chosen not so much for his abilities as for his availability. Rabbi Joseph was informed that great embarrassment would result from making the amount of his debts public. They suggested that he accept 2,500 rubles immediately, which could be collected privately and without publicity, and promised him another 2,500 on his arrival.

This was unacceptable to Rabbi Joseph. He feared lest his creditors would appeal to the government to prevent his departure. The leaders of the association were at a loss. They had gone so far, and they feared that the entire project would collapse if they now withdrew their invitation. Public solicitation to pay the rabbi's debts would shake whatever confidence they had won, undermine the prestige of the association, and create serious doubt as to the rabbi's integrity. Already news had leaked out, and aspersions on the honesty and prudence of the rabbi's family were being bruited about. The reaction of the New York correspondent of the *American Israelite* was typical: "Is it possible that the holy man, like holy Russia, has debts? I give it up."[45]

The association decided that it must sink or swim with Rabbi Joseph. At a meeting held at the end of January, $1,000 was pledged by a small group and sent to Vilna. The proponents of the chief rabbi, believing the matter at an end, began to make preparations for his arrival in time for the Passover holidays. They hoped he would free them of their embarrassment and difficulties just as Moses had liberated their ancestors from Egyptian bondage. Meetings were arranged at various synagogues to collect money for the travel expenses of the rabbi and his family.[46] A vigorous campaign was undertaken to cover fare, rent, house furnishings, and other expenses. Representatives of seventeen congregations met on Sunday, March 11, at Pythagoras Hall to repledge their annual commitments. The Reverend Doctor H. Pereira Mendes, minister of the Spanish and Portuguese Congregation Shearith Israel, and Rabbi Bernard Drachman addressed the gathering. But even the elements frowned on the project, for the blizzard of 1888, which paralyzed New York, blew up a few hours after the meeting.[47] It not only prevented carrying out the plans but also dampened the enthusiasm of many heretofore warm supporters, who saw in this occurrence the warning finger of God. Nevertheless, the leaders carried on doggedly. A call dated April 1888 was issued in English and

Hebrew to all Orthodox congregations to join the Association of the American Orthodox Hebrew Congregations.

The call reminded the Orthodox Jews that in this land of liberty the observance of their religion required strengthening and that certain congregations had united "to create an intelligent orthodoxy" and to prove that also in America proper observance of religious duty could be combined with honor and culture. To keep the next generation faithful to Judaism, Rabbi Jacob Joseph of Vilna had been chosen to lead them. A Beth Din under his leadership would be formed to meet the religious and judicial needs of the Jewish community. An appeal was made for proper support, and organizations and congregations were summoned to organize, to contribute financially, and to "show the world that Orthodox Judaism has zealous followers."[48]

The call reveals that the leaders of the association were fully aware of the problems confronting Orthodox Judaism in America. They recognized that the corrosion that was weakening Orthodoxy was caused not only by the environment of the New World but also by the abuses and malpractices present in Orthodox religious life. A chief rabbi of stature, vested with authority, could cope with the former and correct the latter. It was, however, a statement that should have been issued when the movement was first initiated. Now it bore an air of desperation.

CONSTITUTION FOR THE ASSOCIATION

Should the chief rabbinate be the instrument of an organized community, or would union come to Orthodoxy through the enthusiasms engendered and the influence exerted by the incumbent? Those who looked to the chief rabbinate and to the person of the rabbi as a source of prestige and acceptance spent their energies in selecting the proper man and in exalting the office. Others, who saw the election as a means toward the consolidation of Orthodoxy and the office of the chief rabbi as an effective way to deal with the abuses that plagued the Orthodox Jewish community, contended that greater concern and labor be devoted to strengthening the organization and establishing its effectiveness through committees and boards.

The leaders, Henry Chuck and Dramin Jones, chose to concentrate on the rabbi. But as the candidate's needs and demands caused such widespread embarrassment, the group that placed emphasis on organization began to exert greater influence. In April, a committee of five was appointed to draw up a constitution and bylaws. J. D. Eisenstein was named chairman, and among the five was the influential Sender Jarmulowsky, treasurer of the association. The constitution itself, published and circulated prior to consideration by the association, reflected the views of those who saw the chief rabbi merely as a functionary of an organized

Orthodox Jewish community that would be able to exist and function without the office.[49]

The object of the association, as stated in the "Fundamental Principle and Object" of the constitution, was "to unite and harmonize Jewish Orthodox Congregations in matters concerning Jews and Judaism." "Chief rabbi" is not even mentioned in Article II, which proclaims the association's object and purpose. The chief rabbi, however, was its main functionary, and about his position the program of the association revolved.

The classes of membership and their dues, as well as their privileges and limitations, were dealt with in Article III. No congregation was entitled to more than ten delegates. Provision was made for noncongregational members. The elected officers were a president, vice-president, and treasurer. The secretary was to be appointed by the president, with the consent of the board of twenty-one trustees.

Of particular interest is the list of standing committees proposed, for it discloses the interests and functions of the association. They are:

1. Committee on congregational matters.
2. Committee having charge of the maintenance of the chief rabbi and *dayyanim* (religious judges).
3. Committee to have under its care and management *shehitah* (slaughtering) and matters pertaining to kashrut. This appointment must have the consent of the chief rabbi.
4. Committee on Hebrew schools and institutions.
5. Committee on membership.
6. Committee on finances.

Article VII dealt with the office and powers of the chief rabbi and with their limitations. The rabbi was to "be chosen by a vote of at least two-thirds of the delegates of the congregations, for a term to be agreed upon by a majority of the delegates."[50] The right to vote for the chief rabbi was limited to the delegates of the congregations only. The document also guarded against the possibility of a single congregation or group capturing the office.

The chief rabbi was expected to appoint dayyanim to assist him in his work, but they had to be approved by the board of trustees. His prerogative to grant ordination or to issue religious licenses and permits was subjected to the approval of the board. Only if appointed by both parties as arbitrator in a civil dispute was the rabbi permitted to render a decision. The board had to grant its consent before he could issue a divorce. Nor was the rabbi permitted to accept fees for *haskamot*[51] or *heksherim.*[52]

On the other hand, the congregations could not appoint a congregational rabbi "without authority from the Chief Rabbi," nor could a congregation recognize any heksherim "without authority from the Chief Rabbi." The control and management of shehitah were in the hands of the board of trustees, and it had the power "to charge a fixed fee for haskamot and heksherim, that the Chief Rabbi may issue." All funds derived from the supervision of kashrut "shall be added to the funds of the Association."[53]

The proposed constitution placed the constituent congregations in the power of the chief rabbi, and he in turn was subject to the control of the board of trustees of the association. Not only did he owe his election to it, but he could not carry on his normal duties without its constant approval.

The powers and prerogatives of the rabbi of a European community were also limited. Virtually every contract included limitations, largely as to money matters. In matters of ritual law the rabbi was the final authority. The constitution of the association limited the chief rabbi's powers in ritual matters that involved finances. He could not grant heksherim, although the decision whether a butcher shop or slaughter house was kosher was his prerogative, for the granting or withholding a heksher was fraught with economic consequences. The kashrut business provided a ready source of income. The leaders of the association not only recognized that fact, but the constitution discloses that they planned to utilize it. The charge, that it was employing the office of the chief rabbi not so much to bring order and integrity into kashrut as to bring money into its own coffers, had some degree of justification. That this income was used for worthy purposes was not sufficient to rebut the criticism that the association would compel buyers of kosher meat to foot the bill for the office of chief rabbi.

THE CHIEF RABBI ARRIVES

The readers of the *Tageblatt* learned the good news on the morning of July 1, 1888. "Now It Is Certain," the headline proclaimed. The chief rabbi would arrive in ten days. Mr. Jarmulowsky, the treasurer, had cabled that Rabbi Jacob Joseph had boarded the ship *Aller* at Bremen and was already on his way.[54] The article also warned against previous conjectures and announcements. Some had asserted that Rabbi Jacob Joseph would never reach the New World. M. N. Swartzberg, Boston correspondent of the *Ha-Zefirah,* declared that the *Hebrew Standard* had disclosed that Rabbi Joseph had wired to the head of the association saying he would not leave Europe unless a six-year contract were sent him, while the *New Yorker Zeitung* announced the rabbi's arrival in two weeks. "Whom shall we believe?" he asked.[55] By July 1 the editor of *Ha-Zefirah* had added a footnote that the rabbi was already on his way. Preparations to welcome the great man were begun. An apartment was rented and furnished. The press was alerted. The leader of the association spent a busy week of frenzied activity. Among those preparing for the advent was the "Hebrew Ritail Butcher Union" [sic]. An invitation was issued for "only those butchers who sell Kosher meat" to attend a meeting, Monday, July 2, at 125 Rivington Street. Matters pertaining to Judaism in general and "the Union and butchers in particular" were on the agenda. Prominent speakers were promised.[56]

On early Saturday morning, July 7, the ship *Aller* reached its American port, Hoboken, New Jersey. The rabbi spent the Sabbath aboard ship, and his congregation counted the hours to sundown when they might cross the river to welcome their leader. Sundown, and Rabbi Jacob Joseph debarked. After evening services were over, "delegates of the United Congregations went over the ferry for the purpose of giving their rabbi a reception at Meyer's Hotel."[57]

Dramin Jones headed the delegation. He welcomed Rabbi Joseph, offered him bread and salt, and recited the traditional benediction on seeing a great scholar: "Blessed art Thou, O Lord our God, King of the universe, who hast imparted of Thy wisdom to those who revere Thee" and added "Blessed art Thou, O Lord our God, King of the universe, who hast given us life and sustained us and privileged us to reach this day."[58] He then introduced the rabbi to the large crowd that had come to greet him. The chief rabbi responded in a brief address calling for unity and cooperation to carry on the holy work. The procession set out from Hoboken to the rabbi's residence.[59] When it reached the house at Henry and Jefferson Streets, thousands upon thousands of Jews milled about. Police had been called earlier. There were some curiosity seekers, but the crowd was composed almost entirely of east European immigrant Jews who felt that the arrival of Rabbi Joseph marked the beginning of a spiritual revival for American Jewry and a new deal for the disregarded and despised Russian Jew.

It was with great pride that the Jews of the Lower East Side learned of the article on the chief rabbi's arrival that appeared in the *New York Herald* of July 8. "The only such dignitary in this country," this important American newspaper called him, further disclosing that "he was till recently in charge of the largest synagogue in Wilna."

The Anglo-Jewish press, which had heretofore presented the uptown Jew's view of his east European coreligionist as the uncouth product of a barbaric state and, at best, displayed an air of benevolent tolerance, now spoke of these Jews and their rabbi with respect. The conservative *American Hebrew* editorialized: "He has been accorded a welcome commensurate with the high position he now occupies and the grave responsibilities with which he is confronted. His future will be watched with more than mere curiosity by all who have the weal of Judaism in America at heart. The possibilities of his career are tremendous, not so much for himself as for Israel in America."[60]

"The rabbi will find his uptown brethren eager to welcome him and to cooperate with him," the *Jewish Messenger* commented editorially, but added: "providing he remembers that with all our freedom the law of the land is supreme over rabbinical interpretations, that in marriages and divorces the courts of the State must be sought for redress, not the rabbinical court that he is reported to favor."[61] A warning was sounded, too, by the *Jewish Exponent* of Philadelphia: "Our fellow believers who have elected him ought to know that their interests are the same as those of the whole community of Israel, and they should not endeavor to arouse dissension and division in our camp."[62]

The long-awaited chief rabbi was here, and the Jewish world now looked on with anticipation and interest. Feelings varied. Some invoked God's aid in what they considered the beginnings of a religious revival in American Israel, while others viewed the rabbi and the religious institutions he represented as a deterrent to progress and a blight on civilization. None were indifferent to the significant experiment whether east European Orthodox Judaism could survive and flourish in the free atmosphere of the New World in an organized and disciplined manner.

"WHAT IS HE TO DO?"

The editors of the *New York Herald*, sensing that there was divergence of opinion about the office of chief rabbi in the Jewish community, assigned a reporter to solicit the views of leading rabbis and Jewish laymen. Criticism had begun with the promulgation of the plan and was becoming more intense. As mentioned above, Doctor Isaac M. Wise had sharply questioned both the office and the candidate during the 1879 attempt to invite Rabbi M. J. Malbim. The maskilim, for whom both institutionalized Orthodoxy and Jewish life in America were objects of scorn, found a spokesman in Shalom Joseph Silverstein even before Rabbi Jacob Joseph's arrival. His article in *Ha-Meliz* had touched off an argument that was for some time waged in the Hebrew press in Russia. He rightly questioned the wisdom of not inviting any of the New York Orthodox rabbis to the plenary sessions of the association. Neither had their opinion been solicited. He felt that seed for discontent had been sown. He then described the state of Judaism in America and the chaotic conditions obtaining in Jewish religious institutions. A chief rabbinate, he conceded, was an idea with great merit, but what were to be the rabbi's functions in New York? What was expected of him, and in all candor what could he accomplish? He advised Rabbi Jacob Joseph to remain in Vilna and suggested that only a man of liberal outlook, speaking the language of the country, should be considered.[63] An answer to Mr. Silverstein and an attack on his views appeared in *Ha-Zefirah*, and the association felt compelled to despatch a letter to the rabbi-elect to disregard the author's advice.

"What is the Chief Rabbi to do?" had already been asked in December 1887 by the perceptive New York correspondent of the *American Israelite*, Mi Yodea. He stated that even those "most eager for the creation of this new office" did not quite know what its functions were to be. The correspondent for the leading journal of Reform Judaism then advised his Orthodox brethren that "a man who can speak neither German nor English, and whose vernacular is an unintelligible jargon, cannot be a fitting representative of Orthodox Judaism to the world at large." To render ritual decisions he was not needed, nor were preachers a scarce commodity; and it seemed highly unlikely that the congregations would import a chief rabbi just to sit and study day and night.[64]

An uptown periodical, the *Jewish Messenger*, was critical of the entire undertaking. If downtown Jewry had thousands of dollars to import rabbis, why, questioned the *Messenger*, did they not support the charitable institutions such as hospitals and homes that their population used? "What do we need of an immigrant and prejudiced rabbi?" asked the Reform periodical *Jewish Tidings*. "He should go back to the land that gave him birth."[65] In a later issue the argument was carried further: "Rabbi Joseph is unfamiliar with the language of this country and is therefore unfitted to exercise authority or influence over American Jews. The Jews of this country do not need a Grand Rabbi and one from a foreign country; one who is reared among the prejudices and bigotries of the Eastern countries will certainly prove an obstacle to the people over whom he is expected to exercise control."[66]

Doctor H. Pereira Mendes, minister of the Shearith Israel Congregation and a founder of the conservative Jewish Theological Seminary of America, was also disturbed by the diversion of funds to the project. The seminary was then an insecure infant, and the founders had counted for support and interest on the more enlightened and scholarly east European Orthodox Jews. Now, Doctor Mendes and his cofounders discovered that the proposed chief rabbinate had garnered both the interest and the financial resources of the community. He, thereupon, issued a circular criticizing downtown Jewry for not supporting the newly established seminary. He argued that the money spent in importing rabbis was largely wasted, for only graduates of an American seminary speaking the language of the land would be able to appeal to the younger generation. Doctor Mendes even carried this message to a meeting of the association, called to collect funds to advance to Rabbi Joseph. He still felt that the project was draining resources needed for the seminary. The coming of the chief rabbi would spell the doom of the theological institution that he had helped found and that he believed held forth the only promise for a vital and creative traditional Jewry in America. "Will he be able to take up the fight against the encroaching steps of Reform in America?" he challenged. "Do not give way to false hopes. Those who come after you will be Americans, full-blooded Americans like your brethren in faith uptown."[67]

In view of the imminent danger to the seminary, it is not surprising that the answer of Doctor Sabato Morais, president of the seminary, to the enquiring reporter of the *New York Herald* proved so vitriolic: "I never before heard of Rabbi Joseph. I am familiar with the manner in which the Hebrews in the place whence he comes are educated, and I know he is not a cultured man. He does not possess the knowledge nor the literary attainments which a rabbi should possess."[68] Quite a positive statement for one who had "never before heard" of the rabbi.

Doctor Mendes, now mellowed, told the *Herald* reporter that "the introduction of the office of Chief Rabbi is a very good move in the right direction." He apparently recognized that the chief antagonist of traditional Judaism was Reform, for he quickly added: "Most of the uptown Jews themselves who may object to it are a bad lot, except in a charitable way, and are hardly Jews at all."[69]

Adolph L. Sawyer, an officer of Temple Emanuel and ex-president of the board of aldermen, saw a civic good deriving from the office of chief rabbi. "If he is a wise man," he stated, "and acts properly, he can remedy many abuses which today bring the Hebrews of the East Side into disrepute, especially in regard to the sanitary laws of the city which are being violated continually." Both Mr. Sawyer and Doctor Morais pointed out that "the office of Chief Rabbi . . . is not officially recognized in Judaism." "Judaism in America is without a head," declared Doctor Morais. "Each congregation has its own rabbi," he added.[70]

The most bitter opponents were the Jewish radicals, socialists, and anarchists. Religion to them was the "opiate of the masses." The institutions fostering Orthodoxy were creations of the exploiters, designed to keep the suffering masses inattentive to social gospel and inert to social action. The chief rabbinate became the symbol of what they despised. The *Jüdische Volkszeitung* and *Der Volksadvokat* carried on a continuous stream of caustic attacks on the office and the person of the chief rabbi. The latter, "published every Friday, Professor G. Selikovitch, Chief Editor," knew no limits in its acrimonious and satirical attacks.

The criticism of this group was not confined to the Yiddish press. A lengthy article appeared in the *New York Sun*, headlined "Opposed to the New Rabbi." It extolled the Americanization of immigrants accomplished by the radical societies and labeled Orthodoxy an anti-intellectual force hindering the progress of Americanization. "A dense cloud of superstition follows us from Russia in the shape of a rabbi's ignorance of any knowledge save that contained in the Talmud and Midrash," the article quoted from a Yiddish newspaper, "and thus the immigrant after crossing the great ocean sinks into a mire of prejudice, bigotry, and illiteracy."[71]

What was purportedly an article on the chief rabbi, a newsworthy figure that week, turned into an attack on Orthodoxy and its institutions and a protestation that the Jewish radicals were the most loyal Americans. They had jumped into the melting pot and were stirring the fires to accelerate the process, while their Orthodox coreligionists had kept far from the pot and thrown sand on the flame.

One of Rabbi Joseph's most insistent demands was a six-year contract. But no contract could be sent him, for the issuance of such a document would violate the law. A contract for employment of labor could not be dispatched across the sea. That a minister of religion was subject to the provisions of this law had been established by Judge Wallace's decision in the case of a Reverend Warren who had been sent a contract by a New York Episcopal Church. The action was declared illegal and the church fined $1,000. Thus the *New York Herald* in its article on the arrival of Rabbi Joseph was careful to state that he had come to this country without contract, to avoid the question of imported labor.

The first order of business after the rabbi had been given a chance to stretch his sea legs was the writing of the rabbinic contract. Judah Buchhalter claimed credit for its composition and sent a copy to *Ha-Zefirah*, where it was published.[72] It read as follows:

We the representatives of the Congregations united as the Association of the American Hebrew Orthodox Congregations, unanimously decided at a meeting held on Wednesday, the tenth day of the month of Ab [July 18, 1888] to invite as our guide and rabbi the great Gaon and complete sage, the pride of Judaism, world renowned for his keen minded knowledge of the whole Torah, the Honorable Rabbi Jacob Joseph, may the Lord guard him and keep him in life, to serve as Chief Rabbi for the Congregations already united and those which will yet come under our banner; to teach us and to judge us in all matters pertaining to the laws of our holy Torah, to show us the road to follow and the thing to do; to his voice shall we give heed, and from his word we shall not depart either to the right or to the left in every matter touching upon our faith. We have obligated ourselves to pay the Chief Rabbi $3,000 per year,[73] and also to provide for a fine dwelling place and furnishings which are to cost no less than $1,000 per year; his will also be the income from weddings, circumcisions, holiday gifts and the like. Excluded as sources of income are divorces, heksherim and licensing of shohatim, from which it is herewith stipulated that he may not derive any income. These will be under the supervision of the Association as far as their fees are concerned. The Rabbinic Court will have the jurisdiction to arrange the *get* [bill of divorcement] or grant the heksher, and to license a shohet, all subject to the authority of the Chief Rabbi. We have accepted the above obligations subject to the following conditions:

A. The arrangement of *gittin* [bills of divorcement] under the supervision of the Board, and they may only permit the granting of a get which does not violate the law of the land.

B. The Rabbinic Court is to be chosen by a two-third vote of the congregational representatives, and may be chosen only with the approval of the Chief Rabbi.

C. The Chief Rabbi has the right to dispose of any member of the Rabbinic Court if he so desires.

D. The Chief Rabbi may not grant a heksher to a butcher or wine merchant, until the applicant brings a certificate from the Committee appointed for this task, stating that he is a trustworthy person and may be relied on in matters of kashrut.

E. Any person who officiates at a marriage ceremony for members of the Association must have received authorization to do so from the Chief Rabbi.

F. The Association obligates itself to pay in equal monthly installments on the basis of $3,000 per annum salary.[74]

Signed this fourth day of the week, ten days in the month of Ab in the year 5648 [1888], here in New York.[75]

The contract between the association and Rabbi Jacob Joseph was similar to like documents granted rabbis in other communities. The conditions and stipulations promised no more and withheld no less. It is important to note, however, that the association retained financial control over kashrut, the licensing of shohatim, and divorces.

The salary of $2,500 per annum was a fantastic sum to the Jew of the Lower East Side who had heretofore considered $400 an adequate rabbinic salary.[76] It was further exaggerated by the press. A headline in the *New York Sun* read: "A $10,000 Rabbi from Russia on his way to this City."[77] The *Jewish Messenger* spoke of a "chief rabbi who receives over ten thousand dollars as a guarantee, and a salary of five thousand dollars a year and perquisities."[78]

The feelings of the congregants toward the rabbi's salary were ambivalent. On the one hand, there must have been considerable resentment. But then again, who would not be proud to be a communicant of a rabbi worth so high a salary equaling that of the rabbis of the uptown Jews? Actually in comparison with the income of some uptown colleagues, the stipend was quite modest. The Reverend Doctor Gustav Gottheil of Temple Emanu-El was granted a five-year contract in January 1888 at an annual salary of $10,000, and a young man, Joseph Silverman, was brought in to assist him at a stipend of $5,000. The latter also was the remuneration of the Reverend Doctor H. Pereira Mendes of the Shearith Israel Congregation. The salary was the cause of much grief for the rabbi and the association, for it aroused the envy of other Orthodox rabbis and the taunts of the rabbi's enemies. Many were the complaints that the rabbi lived in luxury through the sweat of the workingman.

FIRST SERMON

The Beth Hamidrash Hagadol was packed beyond capacity. A vast overflow crowd had gathered at the synagogue's entrance on Norfolk Street. Even when they realized that they could not enter the synagogue, they wanted to get near enough to see the chief rabbi enter. The police found that the crowd was beyond their expectations, and reinforcements were sent for.

Soon a vanguard of four policemen cleared a narrow path, and the rabbi, accompanied by four leaders of the association, made his way from his home to the synagogue. Only the threats of force by the police and their fulfillment now and then kept the crowds at bay.[79] In the synagogue the heat of the bodies added to the heat of the day, but no one left. This was the hour the leaders of the association had worked for and that all the East Side had awaited. A dignified advertisement had appeared in the *Tageblatt* on Friday, July 20:

The Chief Rabbi,
The Gaon Rabbi Jacob Joseph
Will, tomorrow Sabbath Nahamu at 4PM,
Deliver his first Sermon
Beth Hamidrash Hagadol
52–56 Norfolk Street
The Synagogue will open at 3.00 PM
Admission free—to everyone.

The announcement was hardly necessary, for everyone knew that the first sermon would appropriately be delivered on the "Sabbath of Consolation" and where but at the Beth Hamidrash Hagadol, the oldest, largest, and most influential east European congregation? And when does a rabbi speak but on Sabbath afternoon?[80] "Comfort ye, comfort ye, my people" that Sabbath were no longer the words of God through Isaiah to the exiles in Babylonia but the message of the Lord to the Jews of America. American Israel had "received of the Lord's hand double for all the sins." The Lord had now sent a shepherd who would "gather the lambs in his arms, and carry them in his bosom, and gently lead those that give suck." A thousand eyes looked to the man on the pulpit, as he began: "A book is always provided with a title page whereon its subject is inscribed, and with an introduction in which the author explains the guiding principles and method in handling his subject. The present address, too, in inaugurating a new movement in Judaism in the United States, should be regarded as a title-page and introduction to the record we intend to make in the book of life." The address continued for forty-five minutes. "During the delivery of the sermon he did not use any gestures, and spoke his sentences in a clear and distinct manner. He gave the text in Hebrew, which he translated into German. The sermon was listened to with the most intense interest."[81] It was not a war cry against the infidels but a reasoned plea for loving kindness and understanding among his adherents. "Our principal efforts," he proclaimed, "shall be to gain recognition and to attract the adherence of others to laws of grace and truth, by virtue . . . of our moral living and our deeds of liberality and kindness."[82]

The first public appearance of the chief rabbi was widely acclaimed. Judah Buchhalter, secretary of the association, and the rabbi dispatched an account to Europe the next day, proclaiming, "Yesterday was a joyous holiday for us,"[83] and the veteran *American Hebrew* writer, Mordecai Jalomstein, allowed that the first sermon had surpassed everyone's expectations.[84] "The contents of his lecture surprised me agreeably," the New York correspondent for the *American Israelite* reported. "The favorable impression which he made on me at our first interview, I now find strengthened after his first discourse."[85] The *Tageblatt,* a strong supporter of the rabbi, proudly announced that all now agreed that the right man had been brought over. An English translation was published in the general press, the *Sun* of New York devoting a column and a half to it.[86] Doctor Felix Adler, highly respected by the Jewish community, was sent a copy, and he replied: "I have read the address with interest and profound satisfaction. If such is to be the tenor of the new rabbi's teachings, we must all, no matter what our opinions, welcome his advent to this country and congratulate the congregations over which he presides upon the admirable choice they have made."[87]

The personality, character, and manner of Rabbi Jacob Joseph won over even his most severe critics. "Ish Yemini," author at the end of May of a vitriolic letter against the idea of a chief rabbi, now esteemed the man but felt that the rabbi made a grave mistake in leaving "a place where he was respected and understood by both officers and laymen. Here, on the contrary, while his talmudic learning is not comprehended by the officers, his preaching of morality is rejected by both."[88] The New York correspondent of the *Jewish Exponent,* Alcyphron, in its issue of September 5, 1888, felt that "Rabbi Jacob Joseph . . . is a conundrum. . . . [His] orthodoxy is genuine and sincere; [he] just came from the very hot bed of Jewish learning and piety; and yet he makes the impression of a broadly tolerant and liberal-minded gentleman." The chief rabbi had dispelled Alcyphron's preconceived stereotype of an Orthodox rabbi, leaving him pleasantly surprised but still somewhat incredulous.

Only the editors of the *Jewish Messenger*, who often referred to east European Jews as coming from the "semi-barbarous parts of Russia" were unimpressed. They did not like the sermon, nor the man, nor the behavior of the crowd. But even they grudgingly admitted that "his supporters are sanguine that he will prove a success."[89]

An editorial in the sympathetic *American Hebrew* best describes the initial impact made on New York Jewry by Rabbi Joseph:

> AN AGREEABLE SURPRISE
> When it was first announced that Rabbi Jacob Joseph had consented to come to America, most of the representative spokesmen of this [Reform Jewish] element adopted a sneering, patronizing tone. . . . "They who came to scoff, remained to praise," is a proper paraphrase expressive of the disappointment awaiting those who were to disparage and ridicule the Grand Rabbi. Everyone who has heard him or who has conversed with him, and who has published the impressions made by him, testifies to his great abilities, to his strength of mind, and most particularly to the breadth of view and liberality of thought that characterizes him.[90]

CHIEF RABBI JACOB JOSEPH

Rabbi Jacob Joseph was beginning to fulfill the hopes of those who had looked to a chief rabbi to raise the status of the Russian Jew in the eyes of the Jewish and general community. The incumbent was accepted by the leaders and spokesmen of uptown Jewry. His activities were considered newsworthy by the general and Anglo-Jewish press. Only the radicals continued their criticism, and they were personae non gratae to the "respectable" elements of the Jewish community. Pride and joy welled up in the hearts of the leaders when the Reverend Doctor H. Pereira Mendes, minister of Congregation Shearith Israel, and Judge Philip J. Joachimsen called on the chief rabbi to accompany them on a tour of inspection of the Hebrew Orphan Asylum. Heretofore the Russian Jews had been looked down on and at best tolerated; now their rabbi was accorded respect and equal status by the spiritual leader of New York's oldest and most aristocratic congregation and by one of New York Jewry's most prominent communal and civic leaders.

Guided by the association's energetic and ambitious secretary, Judah Buchhalter, Rabbi Jacob Joseph acted the role of a chief rabbi. His appearance at the funeral of victims of a fire on the Bowery that had roused the entire Jewish community and his vigorous appeal on behalf of the families left widowed and orphaned were acclaimed as acts of a public-spirited individual who matched authority with responsibility. On the day before Rosh Hashanah he "personally applied to the Commissioners of Charity and Correction with the request that Jewish prisoners be permitted to rest from labor on the ensuing holidays. He was very courteously received and promised that his request would be complied with."[91] Before election day the chief rabbi, at the request of the Political Reform Club, issued a proclamation to his constituents: "The laws of the country must be obeyed even as religious laws. Hence it is our duty to admonish all our brethren who are not legally entitled to vote, to keep away from the voting places."[92]

Buchhalter overlooked no opportunity to place the rabbi's name and words in the public press. The maiden sermon was read by thousands of New Yorkers in their newspapers. The term *chief rabbi* appeared so often that Doctor Kaufmann Kohler of Temple Beth-El felt constrained to send a letter to the *Evening Post* protesting: "As regards the title of chief rabbi, it is simply a matter of option with the congregation. It implies no jurisdiction over other rabbis beyond his congregation or congregations."[93]

Jews were no doubt highly elated that a rabbi of a German congregation and a leading spokesman for Reform had been moved to publish a letter so defensive in tone. Doctor Kohler's letter had little effect, for in February of the next year the *Jewish Messenger* repeated the protest: "It may be timely to remind the general press that Rabbi Jacob Joseph is not by any means the 'chief rabbi of New York.' "[94]

The association elected new officers on Tuesday, August 7. Henry Chuck, assiduous worker and generous patron, was chosen president, and Moritz Alexander was elected vice-president.[95] The president was a native of Berlin, who had come to America in 1848 and prospered in business. Despite his German birth, he associated with Russian Jews and was a leading member of the Beth Hamidrash Hagadol. Had it not been for his generosity, the association would not have found it possible to bring Rabbi Joseph to New York. Mr. Chuck threw himself into the work with all the energy and ability at his command. Almost nightly he would come down to the Lower East Side from his home on 61st Street to conduct the affairs of the association. To the day of his death, May 13, 1890, Henry Chuck was its unchallenged leader.[96] With so able a spiritual leader as Rabbi Joseph and so energetic a lay leader as Henry Chuck, the association now turned to fulfill its promise of bringing order to the organized religious life of East Side Jewry.

KASHRUT: PROBLEMS AND PITFALLS

The area that the chief rabbi undertook to organize and supervise was the kosher meat business. Time and again the Jewish community of New York had witnessed intramural squabbles among the butchers, accusations and counter-accusations among the shohatim, and abuse of the rabbis who had tried to impose some system of supervision. Rabbi Abraham Joseph Ash had suffered during his incumbency from butchers who flouted his authority and attacked his person. Fistfights were not uncommon, and disregard for Jewish law and Board of Health ordinances was rampant. Some even informed on their competitors—an act that had for centuries been considered a most heinous crime. To inform against a fellow Jew brought shame to the community and to the God of Israel.

The energetic steps that the chief rabbi and the association took toward the eradication of evil in dietary observances would have been applauded by all under ordinary circumstances. But the leaders of the association saw in the supervision of kosher meat a source of income for the organization. They argued that proper supervision cost money, and those who benefitted from it should pay for it. The chief rabbi, however, was opposed to any direct charge for the supervision of kashrut. He maintained that it was in the interest of the entire community that order and harmony exist in this industry and that the costs of administering it be borne by the communal religious agency, the Association of American Orthodox Hebrew Congregations. But he had to surrender to the superior wisdom and experience of the "American business men" who had brought him to this country. He was able, however, to exact the compromise that the tax for supervision be placed not on meat but on poultry because it was believed that poultry was for the most part bought by the wealthier Jew. Meat was the staple of the poor, chickens of the rich, and if a tax must be levied let it at least fall on those who could best afford it.

The matter having been decided and agreed on, it was formally announced through a circular in Yiddish, followed by an English version, distributed in downtown New York.

Announcement from the Chief Rabbi

Herewith I make known to all our brethren, the children of Israel, who tremble at the word of the Lord, that inspectors have already been appointed in the poultry slaughter houses to test the knives and to have supervision of everything in their care. From this day forward every bird slaughtered in the abattoir under our supervision will be stamped with a *plumbe* (lead seal). On the plumbe will be the words (Rab ha-Kolel R. Jacob Joseph) and we make it known to you that if you find any butcher's chicken not so stamped, that it was not killed under our supervision and we cannot guarantee it to be kosher. May those who hearken [to our words] prosper and share in the heavenly blessing. On the third day of the *Sidra Ha-Berakhah,* 5649 [September 18, 1888].

—Saith: Jacob Joseph, Chief Rabbi of New York[97]

One cent was to be charged for the metal tag attached to the leg of the chicken to certify its kashrut. In the English announcement that followed, a footnote was added: "The fowl bearing seals should not be sold for any higher price than others, except one cent on each fowl for the seal." The attack against the plumbe and the charge began before the office of the chief rabbi issued the circular. With the appearance of the announcement on the streets and the lead seals on the chickens, it mounted in intensity. Housewives protested the extra charge. The butchers resented any control, and the other Orthodox rabbis saw a source of income taken from them. The radical press was now able to defend the poor housewives against price gouging and to attack organized religion at the same time. However, they found ready allies among the butchers, some shohatim, and some rabbis. It was a heaven-sent opportunity, and one did not have to believe in heaven to take advantage of the opportunity.

Karobka became the battle cry. Karobka was a tax imposed by the Russian government on kosher meat. The Russian Jew knew its meaning well, and the very mention of the word conjured up all the disabilities and persecutions suffered in the land of the czars. They knew, too, that income from the tax, leveled on a Jewish ritual requirement, was used for anti-Jewish purposes. Thus an annual sum of 15,000 rubles was appropriated from the proceeds of the tax for special night police to rout out of Kiev Jewish visitors who had overstayed their time. Many had read Mendele Mocher Seforim's *Die Taxe*, in which the hated tax was attacked, and the leaders of the Jewish community who helped the government collect it were held up to ridicule and scorn. Karobka represented everything evil in czarist Russia. What was the chief rabbi's poultry tax but karobka? Were the heads of the association any better than the Jewish tax farmers who were lackeys to the czar and enemies of their people? A successful catchphrase is often far more effective than the most reasoned argument. Karobka was such a word. It evoked deep emotion; there was no arguing its evil, and it could so aptly describe the newly imposed tax.

Professor Getzel Selikovitch, a gifted satirist, jumped to the forefront of the anti-karobka forces. He was then chief editor of the weekly newspaper *Der Volksadvokat*. His readers had chuckled at his lampoon of the association's "Call to the Congregations." The United Chinese Orthodox Laundries were importing the town preacher of Peking, and the association would levy taxes on laundry goods, even as the Jewish "Board of Ritual Slaughter" had imposed a tax on the orthodox chickens on whom they hung lead medals.[98] Not satisfied with his prose efforts, Selikovitch wooed the muse. Page one of the following week's issue featured a poem in bold type titled *"Karobka":*

Dance, orthodox chickens;
Make merry, have no fear

For the Rabbi an order has issued
Shiny lead medals you'll wear.
You'll wear them after your slaughter
That the Chief Rabbi may live;
They flay the skin off the worker
—A fat salary the Great One to give.[99]

The poem was followed by others in Hebrew and Yiddish. Feuilletons echoed every complaint and criticism leveled against the chief rabbi.

More formidable opposition made its appearance on Sunday, September 23. The butchers who opposed supervision, the rabbis who resented the power and were envious of the salary of Rabbi Jacob Joseph, and an assortment of malcontents, including a "Reverend"[100] and a prominent "intellectual," gathered to discuss the problem. The butchers organized the Hebrew Poultry Butchers Association. The same group had met prior to the rabbi's coming and were awaiting the opportune moment to announce their opposition. Morris Levy, elected president, complained that the rabbi had been imported by the association, which had then foisted him on the butchers, who were now forced to support him. This the butchers would never do, he vowed, as he called for a revolt against the plumbe.

The Hebrew writer Shalom Joseph Silverstein was introduced as a noted Talmudist, and he decided that the action of Rabbi Joseph was against Jewish law. As a newcomer to the community, he maintained, the chief rabbi had no right to make enactments without consulting the established rabbis. He then suggested that it was not yet too late to call on the resident rabbis to decide on the legality of the plumbe. The meeting was expertly staged. Mr. Silverstein's suggestion was a cue, for the rabbis referred to were promptly produced and their opinion solicited. They were Rabbi J. Segal, the "Sherpser Rav," Rabbi H. Lass, the "Yezner Rav," and Rabbi S. Weiss, the "Vizaner Rav." All three spoke out against the poultry tax and the plumbe. Rabbi Segal stated that the plumbe had been instituted to pay the chief rabbi's salary, and Rabbi Lass declared that as a result of the poultry tax more *trefah* (nonkosher) meat was consumed in New York than at any time in the past twenty years. They all pledged their support to the Butchers Association and announced their willingness to wage battle against the plumbe.

The oration of the day was delivered by the Reverend H. Brodsky, "marriage performer, mohel, and preacher," who argued that Rabbi Jacob Joseph had no right to the title of chief rabbi since he had been elected by a handful of small congregations that were not even interested in Judaism. He called on the assemblage to expose Rabbi Joseph as a tool of men who were making a business of him and his office. The assemblage then voted that the only shohatim they would use were those approved by the three aforementioned rabbis. A committee was appointed to carry on the fight against the incursion of the association into the kosher meat business, and dues of $2 per butcher were decided on.[101] The perennial gadfly, the *Jewish Messenger*, labeled the anti–chief rabbi forces "an anti-tag movement" and wrote with relish of his discomfiture.

The Hebrew Poultry Butchers Association held its second meeting a week later, on Sunday, September 30. Five rabbis inimical to Rabbi Joseph were now present, and listed as guests of honor were Professor G. Selikovitch, editor of *Der Volksadvokat*, and Mr. Wagman of *Die Volkszeitung*. Both men and their papers had little use for Orthodoxy, but the butchers did not discriminate in their choice of allies. The Reverend Doctor Leopold Zinsler delivered an impassioned oratorical exercise in which he deposed Rabbi Jacob Joseph from leadership because he did not know the language of the land. Why had he begun with kashrut, he questioned, and neglected other pressing needs, such as a downtown hospital? The Reverend Brodsky spoke of the rabbi's large salary, as an onlooker observed, "with obvious envy."

An anti-karobka resolution was passed with enthusiasm. It stated:

> The karobka plumbe on chickens which evil men wish to import from the old country to the New World is an insult to Judaism and an affront to Mosaic law, because these men mean only to flay the skin off our backs through this despicable tax and put us to shame in our city, New York. Therefore at this assemblage in the presence of three rabbis, we declare as terefah all meats sold by the butchers who have made common cause with the charlatans who impose the karobka. All this we do and ordain with the permission and under the supervision of the Beth Din Zedek (Righteous Court) which consists of three rabbis. Down with the shameful karobka![102]

The leaders of the association felt the threat posed by this movement. A group led by Dramin Jones attended the meeting to protect their interests and protest against any inaccuracies. When Mr. Jones did raise objection to the scurrilous attack against Rabbi Joseph by the Reverend Brodsky, he and his group were ejected from the hall.

The same issue of *Der Volksadvokat* that carried the account of the meeting also contained a paid advertisement: "Important Announcement from the Beth Din Zedek: We, the Great Court, have set qualified ritual slaughterers in the slaughterhouse, and appointed two supervisors who serve without pay." There followed a list of thirty-one butchers under the supervision of this anti–chief rabbi rabbinic court. Thereafter a weekly list of butchers under the supervision of this group appeared in *Der Volksadvokat*. The Butchers Association continued to hold meetings to bolster their own morale and to regird themselves for the battle.

The twofold attack took a heavy toll on the position and authority of the chief rabbi. The butt of sharp humor, widely bandied, he could hardly retain the aloof dignity and universal respect necessary for his exalted office. Both lines of attack were effective because the action of the association had rendered the chief rabbi vulnerable. Even some of his staunchest supporters began seriously to question the wisdom, and even the right, of the association to become part of the complex and unsavory kosher meat business. Now, only a defensive rear guard action could be undertaken, and to this unpleasant and unrewarding activity, the chief rabbi had to direct his energies.

MISMANAGEMENT

Rabbi Joseph answered vituperation and rebellion with understanding and forgiveness. In a letter to the association about the regulations governing shehitah, he spoke thus of his opponents: "Those who oppose my regulations are nonetheless to be treated with humane consideration. It is a question of business with them, a question of gaining a livelihood. . . . I would beg of you, my brethren, not to interfere with them in the practical walks of life. Believe me, I have not the least sense of resentment in my heart for all the evil they speak and publish against me."[103]

On Thursday, October 11, the meat butchers who had responded to the association's call met and pledged to place their shops under the supervision of the chief rabbi. Each was to contribute his share for the cost of supervisors, but no tax was placed on meat.[104] The disastrous experiment with the plumbe was still bedeviling the association. Beginning with the November 20 issue of the *Tageblatt*, and appearing in each subsequent one, was a list of butchers, under supervision of the chief rabbi, who had a right to display signs in their window thus attesting that they were under the chief rabbi's supervision. The list contained sixty-five names. By February 26, the number had grown to eighty-six.

Rabbi Joseph carried on a full schedule of preaching. He alternated among the congregations with the association and often spoke on the morning and the afternoon of the Sabbath. The sermons were in the traditional, pilpulistic, halakhic manner, but they also contained practical application to the affairs of the day. To judge from the three sermons that he published, his chief interest was his attempt to institute reforms in kashrut.[105]

Before the congregation of the Beth Hamidrash Hagadol Anshe Ungarn on Saturday, November 24, he called on those in a position to help the reorganization of kashrut supervision not to stand aloof. "I have found here," Rabbi Jacob Joseph admonished, "pious individuals who observe the commandments with all their hearts, but who are not at all concerned about their brethren, and lift not a finger to help. Let them consider to whom they will have to render a final accounting." One may be tempted, the rabbi warned, to be lenient in his judgment of pious men and scholars who concern themselves only with their piety, and one may forgive them their inactivity, thinking they are unaware of how serious and important a duty it is for a Jew to be concerned about his brother. But it should not be forgotten that the rabbis taught that the more learned the man, the more accountable is he for his deeds or lack of deeds. Certainly one who considers himself a scholar cannot claim ignorance of the law as an excuse. The learned man, Rabbi Joseph hinted, knows that he is duty bound to care for his brother, and if he does not it is not because of ignorance of the law but because of his indifference to its preservation.[106]

On the next Sabbath, the chief rabbi preached at the Congregation Shaarai Torah. Those who permitted the cent tax on chickens to stand between them and proper observance of kashrut were the subject of his criticism. The matter of kashrut is in the hands of the women, the rabbi stated. If they choose, they can demand truly kosher meat, or if they choose they can buy whatever is offered them, little concerned whether it is really kosher or not. Few, far too few, he complained, bother to demand certified kosher meat. The others buy without proper concern, not because of ignorance or spite but because of the extra penny that is charged them. "May God make them all rich. Then they will all return to the observance of kashrut. The penny for which they now permit themselves to eat trefah meat will then not be a factor, so they will not only attain wealth but piety as well."[107]

These are obviously the words of a man whom the community's lack of support was beginning to embitter. The housewife was unwilling to make a minute monetary sacrifice for kashrut, and the pious scholars had withdrawn from the field, leaving Rabbi Joseph to wage this battle. He had two powerful allies in this battle, the rabbis of uptown Orthodox congregations, Doctor H. Pereira Mendes and Doctor Bernard Drachman. Both appreciated and applauded his efforts. The *American Hebrew* as early as October hinted editorially: "It would have been well if the Grand Rabbi had first consulted some of his rabbinical colleagues in the upper part of the city in regard to the matter [the supervision of Jewish butchers]."[108]

Now Rabbi Joseph turned to them for help. Their aid was effective. Representatives of the wholesale butchers, among them those who had declared defiance of Rabbi Joseph, now met with the three rabbis and accepted their authority to supervise kashrut. The rabbis then constituted themselves into a Shehitah Board, with sixty-five butchers under its jurisdiction. Each butcher shop was to contribute $5.50, for which it was given a display sign certifying its kashrut. The actual supervision was in the hands of Rabbi Joseph. His colleagues had merely lent their names to strengthen his hand. This experiment in partnership was apparently short-lived, for criticism against this latest project was directed solely at the chief rabbi.

One area of kashrut supervision led to another, and in early December the office of the chief rabbi issued a circular and placed announcements in the Yiddish press inviting flour merchants who planned to sell flour for the baking of *matzot* (unleavened bread) to submit to the supervision and receive the approval of the chief rabbi. These actions again loosened a tide of criticism. Silverstein, with new targets, found new ammunition and jumped merrily into the fray. The editors of the *Jewish Messenger* were quick to publish a critical letter, signed "A Friend." The friend, who re-echoed this periodical's attitude, roundly berated the chief rabbi for having taken businessmen as counselors instead of rabbis. The various charges for kashrut supervision, one cent per chicken, $4 per month per meat butcher, and $1 per barrel of Passover flour, were enumerated.[109] Grave objection was raised against them and against their author. Even the *American Hebrew* now spoke in warning tones:

> From the very first announcement of the fact that it was intended to secure a Chief Rabbi for the United Orthodox Hebrew Congregations we have been extremely interested in the project. . . .
>
> We trust that his further usefulness will not be hampered, as there seems danger of its being hindered by the officious intervention of men who would like to enact the role of power behind the throne. All the good results of his beneficent influence can be blighted by using him as a tool for monetary ends. The United Orthodox Congregations must seek other means of supporting the organization they maintain than by using the grand rabbi's name as a means of extracting money. . . .
>
> No decent intelligent Israelite will here in America tolerate the elevation of a man to an exalted position in Israel simply for the purpose of using him as a means to develop the pecuniary prosperity of individual congregations.[110]

This was strong language for a heretofore friendly periodical. But when months passed and the plea went unheeded, they published a lead editorial that declared their disappointment and disillusionment. "Mismanagement," the headline stated, and the editors declared: "The first and greatest mistake was to use him as a source of revenue. This was a profanation, a sacrilege. . . . Such a shameless outrage as bringing here a learned man to act as Grand Rabbi and then setting him to collecting money for them."[111]

"Very true it is," they admitted, "that some phases of his duty would be the oversight of the Shechita and Kasherith [sic]." "It is true also," they allowed, "that these might be made to contribute to revenue of the

Associated Congregations. It is, however, most decidedly and emphatically not true that his revenue system is the only duty he has to perform."[112] The editors rightly concluded that this emphasis on kashrut supervision and its income was not the chief rabbi's idea nor doing. He was a captive of the association. Kashrut needed organization and supervision, and supervisors had to be paid. The financial structure of the association was now hopelessly inadequate. Money had been advanced to the rabbi to pay his debts in Vilna; promised as a gift, it was really an advance on salary.[113] True, he had a six-year contract, but how would he collect if the party of the second part disappeared? So, Jacob Joseph, "Chief Rabbi of New York and Environs,"[114] now limited his authority to "Chief Rabbi of the Association of the American Orthodox Hebrew Congregations" and carried out to the best of his ability the required duties as overseer of kashrut among the butchers who accepted his authority.

PROJECTS, PROSPECTS, AND RIVALS

The chief rabbi did not intend to ignore the duties other than kashrut he felt the office demanded. The state of Jewish education on the Lower East Side was most deplorable. The small independent heder, which taught little more than mechanical reading, was the accepted educational institution. The teachers were inept; the students disinterested. The standard tuition fee in 1887 was ten cents a week. Competition was keen among melamdim, not to improve the quality of instruction, but to increase the number of students. Two Talmud Torahs provided adequate instruction to a small percentage of Orthodox Jewish boys. The Hebrew Free School, supported by uptown Jews, introduced a large number of children to their faith. For those interested in an intensive education the newly established Yeshivat Etz Hayyim held forth great promise.[115]

One of Rabbi Joseph's first official acts was to visit Etz Hayyim on Tuesday, July 25.[116] He became an enthusiastic supporter of this yeshivah and often appealed to his congregants to give it generous support.[117] Had he been able to devote as much time to the problem of Jewish education as to kashrut, his would have been a major contribution to the strengthening of Jewish cultural and religious life in America.

The practice of men and women sitting together in the synagogue, a problem still vexing Orthodoxy today, received the attention of the chief rabbi. No one in the member congregations of the association would have advocated mixed seating, as practiced in Reform congregations. But during weddings solemnized in the synagogue, the men and women permitted themselves to sit together. The rabbi saw this not only as a violation of Jewish law but also as the beginnings of what might develop into advocacy of the same during services. To put an end to this violation, the chief rabbi issued the ordinance that in the future, at a wedding in a house of worship, all women and girls, except the bride and the nearest relatives, must sit in the place assigned their sex—the women's gallery.

To acquaint the Jewish community with the chief rabbi and the activities of the association, a periodical was launched in January 1889. It bore the title *Sefer Toledot Ya'akob Yosef be-New York* (The Book of the History of Jacob Joseph in New York). The title page contained the explanatory legend: "History? These are the words which I preached and the things which I did, with the help of God, to strengthen Judaism and our faith, and the response which I issued in response to legal questions put to me, while I was here in New York." In the introduction the chief rabbi stated: "Here before you, dear reader, is a pamphlet, which I have begun to publish, concerning communal matters in which I am engaged, and that which I preached on matters current and relevant to the time and place in which we live."

The reader is invited to subscribe to the periodical, planned as either a monthly or semimonthly. He is also asked not to question the purpose of the publication since "I cannot give you a proper answer." Information about the association would appear in the periodical, it was promised. The member congregations would be listed together with the names of the presidents, as well as the leaders of the association and the *Va'ad Ha-Kashrut* (Kashrut Committee). If any congregations throughout America wished to report their activities they were invited to submit the information. No advertisements would be accepted.

In the first and only issue of the periodical the performance does not live up to the promise. Its twenty-two pages contain portions of three sermons delivered by the chief rabbi, a responsum on a question of kashrut received from Scranton, Pennsylvania, and some comments occasioned by the conclusion of the public reading of the book of Genesis in the synagogue. Wholly lacking is the promised information about the projects of the association and the names and officers of the constituent congregations.

From the genesis of the movement, the chief rabbi was envisaged as head of a staff of religious functionaries. The association's "Call to the Congregations" of April 1888 had promised: "Assistant Rabbis will be chosen to form with him [the chief rabbi] a [Beth Din], thus to give proper attention to religious and judicial requirements of a Jewish community."[118]

"A Beth-din will be established," the *American Hebrew* informed its readers in the article that announced Rabbi Jacob Joseph's election.[119] The proposed constitution made provision for dayyanim to serve under the rabbi.[120] The *New York Herald*, in reporting the chief rabbi's arrival, had added, "He will organize a court of arbitration shortly, to consist of five rabbis."[121] The *Jewish Exponent* informed its readers that "a court of four ministers is to be shortly established, which will expound Mosaic law twice a week under the direction of Rabbi Charif."[122]

The association set out to fulfill the promise made in its "Call." In June 1888, Rabbi Joshua Segal, known as the Sherpser Rav, was offered the position of *Ab Bet Din* (head of the judicial court of the chief rabbi).[123] Rabbi Segal, who was a scholar of repute and had been in New York since 1875, feeling it beneath his dignity to be subservient to a newcomer, declined the invitation. It is likely that the leaders of the association attempted through this move to gain the participation of the *hasidim*[124] and Galician Jews, among whom Rabbi Segal had a considerable following and who were beginning to murmur that the association was run by and for Lithuanian Jews. Most of the downtown synagogues were landsmanshaft congregations, and there existed considerable animus between the Galician and Lithuanian Jews. The former questioned the piety of the latter, and the Lithuanians mocked the lack of learning of the Galicians, many of whom were hasidim and valued piety above scholarship. Each group would have felt their position strengthened and prestige heightened by election of a chief rabbi from their section of the Old World. When the association turned for guidance to Lithuanian rabbis, the Hungarian and Galician congregations voiced their dissatisfaction. And when the choice fell on a rabbi serving the community of Vilna, the spiritual center of Lithuanian Jewry, their disapproval took more concrete form. As early as July it was common knowledge that some Hungarian and Galician congregations were seriously considering the importation of a chief rabbi of their own.[125] Rabbi Segal knew of this and decided to bide his time.

Rabbi Israel Kaplan[126] came to America to serve as dayyan of the chief rabbi not long after Rabbi Joseph's arrival. With ordination from the leading rabbis of eastern Europe, he was a person of scholarly attainments and independence of character. After some two years of service, he resigned his position, highly critical of the leaders of the association, yet retaining his respect for Rabbi Joseph. In 1892, his position was assumed by Rabbi Osher Noah Rapeport.[127]

What was a rumor in July became a reality in October. Rabbi Segal was declared chief rabbi of some twenty congregations. A circular was sent to the other downtown congregations inviting them to accept the authority of this new chief. "Congregations of Israel, Men of Poland and Austria," the name of the new association, indicates that this federation was comprised of congregations of Galician Jews. The major activity of the new chief rabbi (who assumed the title "Chief Rabbi of Congregations of Israel of New York") was also in the field of kashrut, and the competition became keen and lively. It was to his advantage that the majority of butchers were Galician Jews, and he soon had a good number of kosher butcher shops under his supervision.[128]

Chief Rabbi Jacob Joseph had established a rabbinic court, so the opposition followed suit. Late in October, three rabbis who led the opposition constituted themselves the *Beth Din Hagadol* (The Great Court). This was done at the urging of the Butchers Association. On November 2, 1888, *Der Volksadvokat* carried announcements about the formation of the Beth Din. The rabbis would sit as a court each day in the Sarayer Synagogue at 41 Hester Street, and all were cordially invited to turn to it for all matters pertaining to the Jewish religion. The members attacked Rabbi Joseph continually. They placed an announcement in the *Volksadvokat* that they had found plumbes of the chief rabbi on choked and putrid chickens.[129] Emboldened by rabbinic backing, the butchers who refused to accept the chief rabbi's supervision visited the district attorney to ascertain whether Rabbi Joseph's organized supervision constituted restraint of trade.[130]

The attacks from the radical element continued apace. To criticism by pen and mouth was added defiance and ridicule by deed. Organized flagrant violations of the Sabbath were carried on in the streets of the Lower East Side to mock the authority of the rabbi. Wagons were rented, and young men and young women smoking cigarettes (some for the first time in their lives) paraded past the synagogues of downtown New York on the Sabbath. Tempers grew hot, and fists, bricks, and sticks flew in this new "religious war." The derision was climaxed by the first "Yom Kippur Ball," arranged by the anarchist youth organization Pioneer of Freedom. While father and mother walked solemnly to shul to recite the *Kol Nidre,* son and daughter marched mockingly to the dance hall to dance and feast.

Here and there a ray of hope broke through the darkness. In early October, the chief rabbi was informed that a group of members of the uptown congregation, Beth Israel Bikkur Holim, had left the synagogue when it introduced mixed pews and planned to consolidate with other small uptown congregations, build a house of worship, and maintain an Orthodox service under the guidance of Rabbi Joseph.[131] At the conclusion of the Sukkot festival the rabbi received gifts in honor of the holiday from a number of his constituent congregations.[132] The money was very welcome, for the rabbi was still in debt, but more welcome still was the expression of confidence and goodwill these gifts bespoke.

Under the pressure of organized opposition and in face of a threatened rebellion, the chief rabbi ordered that new signs certifying his supervision be given free of charge to those butchers who would accept his authority. More important than the revenue now was his authority; and Rabbi Joseph canceled the charge to preserve it.

New sources of revenue were needed. The approaching Passover holiday provided the answer. In the same "Important Announcement" that proclaimed the end of fees for kosher signs for the butchers, the rabbi urged his people to buy matzot and wine bearing the seal of his approval.[133] Earlier he had invited flour merchants to accept his supervision and approval of the flour to be used for baking matzot.

DECLINE AND DISSOLUTION

The Pesah flour incident caused the final dissipation of the authority of the chief rabbi. It brought to an end the hopes that Rabbi Joseph would bring order out of chaos in Jewish religious life on the Lower East Side, raise the prestige of Orthodoxy, and act as an effective deterrent to the spread of Reform. To many this act was evidence enough that the chief rabbi was only a tool in the hands of ambitious men who were interested only in the aggrandizement of their names and the welfare of their pocketbooks.

Henry Chuck, president of the association, invested $6,000 in flour for the baking of matzot. The customer was charged twenty-five cents per barrel for supervision, the income of which went to the association. Even though this "tax" amounted to about one-eighth of a cent per pound of matzot, a hue and cry went up that the leaders of the association were commercializing the Jewish religion for their own financial benefit. The leaders of the association and their spiritual head were labeled pious frauds, concerned more with money than with kashrut at the expense of the poor and needy whom they burdened with the despised karobka and new taxes that even the depraved czar would not have imposed.

These accusations were as unjust as they were indecent. It cost the association far more than a penny a chicken to supervise its kashrut properly. The shohet had to be examined and approved. The actual shehitah had to be supervised, the chicken labeled as kosher, and the butcher shops watched to protect the buyer from error or dishonesty.

To accuse Henry Chuck of profiting was foolish, knavish, or both. He spent upward of $10,000 in support of the association and its attempt to bring some order to a chaotic and hardly reputable business. In an attempt to silence the opposition, Joshua Rothstein, a leader of the association, sent letters to the leading rabbis of eastern Europe enclosing printed accusations distributed against Rabbi Jacob Joseph by his New York opponents. Letters came back expressing sympathy for the plight of the chief rabbi and anger against the assailants. Rabbi Simon Strashun of Vilna wrote: "To my grief I received your letter and the enclosed announcement. It is not possible for me to set upon paper the depth of my sorrow and grief on the pain and suffering of the great rabbi, renowned for his learning and piety. We never would have believed that this could happen to him, after the honor and glory which was his in this community."[134]

Other rabbis poured out their wrath, pledged their support, and urged Rabbi Joseph to take courage and wage the "battle of the Lord." But it was all to no avail. The opposition defied Rabbi Joseph's defenders as they had defied him. The association began to totter. Congregations began to skip payments and gradually withdrew their support entirely. Henry Chuck was growing weary of accepting the responsibility for a growing budgetary deficit. An agreement was reached with a number of leading butchers to assume the salary of the chief rabbi and the other rabbis who would oversee the supervision of kashrut. Rabbi Joseph was to receive annually $2,500, and a like sum was to be paid the others. This arrangement brought to a final end the "noble experiment." The chief rabbi and his staff were now to all practical purposes the employees of the butchers whom they were to supervise.

Rabbi Joseph could do naught else but accept. It is to his credit that he was still able to maintain his dignity and integrity and continue his labors. "The office [of the Chief Rabbi]," a visitor recalls, "was always bustling with rabbis, authors and various religious officials. Some visitors are anxious to be ordained as rabbis. Others were eager to receive the rabbi's *haskamah* (endorsement) for their manuscripts and perhaps for him to write an introduction to their works; still others were eager to receive *kabbalah* (a certificate that enables one to act as a shohet)."[135]

He examined young rabbis and added his authorization to previously received ordination. One such authorization reads (in translation from the Hebrew):

> With the help of God:
> To the young man, Rabbi Simon Burstein, this is given to testify that he is deeply learned and skilled. This is given furthermore to testify that he has the right to decide cases of ritual law and I am sure that he will not commit any errors. May God be with him.
> Signed this day, the 2nd of May, 1894 [5654], Jacob Joseph, Chief Rabbi of New York.[136]

The association continued to exist—largely on paper. The minutes of the Beth Hamidrash Hagadol reflect its status and fortunes:

> January 25, 1893:
> It is passed at a general meeting to appoint a delegate to the Association of Congregations, to find out and to report to us, its income and expenditures.[137]
> May 7, 1893:
> A motion is made and passed to appoint ten delegates to the Associa-

tion of Congregations, that they may bring us an accurate report on its income and expenditures. The delegates have no right to assume any financial responsibilities for the Beth Hamidrash Hagadol. Such financial matters must be brought back to be discussed and decided at a general or special meeting.[138]

January 10, 1894:

It is passed to call a special meeting on Sunday, January 14th. Since the contract with the Association of Congregations with regards to the Chief Rabbi ends this month, the brothers should discuss and decide what and how the Beth Hamidrash should do for the future.[139]

January 14, 1894 (Special Meeting):

A motion is made and carried that since the contract with the Association of Congregations with regard to the Chief Rabbi ended on January 10th, it is decided that the Beth Hamidrash Hagadol should remain a member of the Association for another year, and that it pay $100.00 dues for the year. An amendment is proposed that the contract be signed for one year, but that no sum be stipulated. Thirty-five votes are cast,[140] fourteen for the motion and twenty-one for the amendment. It is therefore passed that a one year contract be entered into with the Association at no specified monetary obligation. It is also decided that a letter be written to the President of the Association asking him to call a meeting of the presidents of the congregations which belong to the Association, to examine the finances of the organization, and that our President call a special meeting at which the members will vote a specific sum to pay to the Association.[141]

An effort to revive the association was obviously being attempted by members of the congregation that had given birth to the idea of a chief rabbi and provided leadership and support. The Beth Hamidrash Hagadol had fulfilled its entire obligation to the association, but it was far too late to attempt to revive it.

Rabbi Joseph retained the title of chief rabbi and played the role of leader of Orthodox Judaism, but he knew and the community knew that it was one thing to be the head of an association of congregations and quite another to derive one's livelihood from payments for butchers' *hashgahah* (supervision). Conditions took a serious turn for the worse in the spring of 1895. The retail butchers banded together and rejected Rabbi Joseph's authority and dispensed with his supervision. A contemporary records: "The Rabbi was left without any income and is in dire straits, and there is nothing that can be done with him now. He and his whole family are in very serious difficulties, yet he refuses to accept any remuneration for matters which come from outside the city."[142]

In early spring of that year the economic situation of the chief rabbi became so serious that he had to ask for the resignation of his dayyan.

Rabbi Rapeport was then forced to visit various communities in the United States to seek financial help.[143] After three years of labor for the association as dayyan for the chief rabbi, he found it impossible to eke out a living in New York and had to resort to soliciting financial aid from charitable persons outside the city. The association was no more than a shadow organization, and when the butchers withdrew financial support it collapsed so completely as to force a devoted employee to seek help in other communities.

To Rabbi Joseph's financial distress was added physical illness. He was confined to his bed, an invalid the rest of his life. The community that had once hailed him now completely neglected him. Forgotten was all he had done to elevate the position of the east European Jew and to establish dignity and integrity in the religious institutions that served him. All but forgotten, he lay on his bed of pain, remembering what had been and musing no doubt on what could have been.

At the end of July 1902, the chief rabbi once again became the topic of discussion. On the twenty-eighth of the month he breathed his last, and headlines announced his demise the next day. He died at age sixty-two after a five-year confinement to his bed because of paralysis. An incident far more shameful than any that had transpired during his life took place on his death. Congregations that had rejected and neglected him now vied for the honor of having the rabbi's earthly remains interred in their cemetery. The rabbi's body had commercial value, for it was correctly surmised by the leaders of the competing congregations that the presence of his body in the cemetery would increase the value of the neighboring plots. So the bidding was brisk. As in all matters pertaining to the chief rabbi, the Beth Hamidrash Hagadol exceeded all others. The rabbi's widow was promised $1,500 in cash and $15 per month for life in return for permission to have its cemetery designated as his final resting place. The money was paid and the transaction completed. It proved a wise financial move for the congregation, for the Sarasohn family immediately bought the plots adjoining Rabbi Joseph's grave for $1,500. The section of the cemetery was named after the chief rabbi, and grave sites there brought premium prices. Even in death the rabbi could not escape being used by unprincipled men for commercial purposes.

The obituaries spoke with respect for the man, though some were critical of his associates in the association, and others assailed his opponents. The then militantly antireligious *Jewish Daily Forward* called Rabbi Joseph a fine and honest man but declared that "the socialists and freethinkers may with pure hearts throw in the face of the hypocrites this story of a man who lived and died in America as a sacrificial offering to business Judaism."[144] The *Jewish Gazette,* reflecting the view of Orthodoxy, editorialized: "In spite of all that was said against the Rabbi during his lifetime, we all loved him, because of his estimable qualities and the blameless life he led. Against the man himself, even his most bitter opponents never dared breathe a word, though it must be admitted, and with deep regret, that many of his unscrupulous opponents linked his name, unjustifiably and without the slightest reason, with the scandals that arose from time to time in the kosher meat affairs."[145]

As if in atonement for the abuse and neglect of Rabbi Joseph during his lifetime, downtown Jewry turned out a hundred thousand strong to pay him final respect. The funeral was the largest the East Side had ever witnessed, and the mourning was genuine. Mourned was not only the man but also an idea that had great promise and a movement that had raised the hopes of so many an east European Jew in this "golden land."

It was not the rabbi's fate that this final tribute be unmarked by unpleasantness and strife. When the funeral procession passed the building of the R. H. Hoe and Company, manufacturers of printing presses, workmen bombarded the mourners with refuse, stones, and pieces of metal. A riot ensued, in which the police seemed to confuse attackers with victims, and as many Jews fell victim to police clubs as to the flying missiles. Wide political repercussions followed the riot, and it brought to an end heretofore tolerated anti-Semitism on the part of many members of the police force. The press of the country rose in anger not only against the rioters but also against conditions that had made such an anti-Jewish riot possible. There was wide approval that the attacked Jews had fought back, and the press voiced the belief that henceforth such riots would be neither attempted nor tolerated. "When it is learned that our Russians (Jews) are capable of being their own police," the *Brooklyn Eagle* editorialized, "their rights will be respected."[146] The *Standard Union* of Brooklyn hoped that "this riot may result in better treatment of the Jews. If it does the suffering and loss will not have been in vain."[147]

The death of Rabbi Jacob Joseph ended a significant chapter in the history of the American Jew. It was the first self-conscious attempt by east European Jewry at communal unity and united enterprise. Though it failed in its objective, it nevertheless unleashed forces and harnessed energies that were to play a vital role in the shaping of the New York Jewish community.

SUMMARY AND EVALUATION

Why did an endeavor so devoutly desired, so enthusiastically promoted, and so zealously pursued end in such quick and total failure? An adequate answer must give proper consideration to the organization of religious life in the general and Jewish community in America; the composition and leadership of the association; the role envisaged for the chief rabbi; the method of election; the successful candidate's abilities and shortcomings; the task thrust on him; and the opposition to the person, the position, and the practices of the chief rabbi.

Is the religious climate of America hospitable to a "chief rabbi"? The Jewish community and its organizations and institutions are often a reflection of parallel institutions of the general community. A "chief rabbi" of a "united synagogue" could be expected and almost predicted in England. The Church of England is the established church, with an acknowledged religious head. A "chief rabbi" of a "united synagogue" would be its counterpart in the Jewish community. There is no established church in the United States, and therefore no ecclesiastic head. The independent congregational church is strong, and even the denominational church unit retains a great deal of independence.

The unit of religious organization in America is the congregation and not the community. This is obvious even to the most unversed observer of the American Jewish scene. It was unrealistic to expect to transplant the organizational form of religious life of the European community to American soil. There the rabbi was the spiritual head of a community; in America a rabbi's authority extended only to the congregation he was elected to serve. The leaders of the association who were European Jews either did not recognize this or refused to accept it.

The chief rabbi in England did not spring full-blown from a "united synagogue." Gradually and painstakingly the religious head of the leading Ashkenazi synagogue in London labored to establish the holder of this position as the ecclesiastical head of English Jewry. Rabbi Nathan Adler devoted a lifetime to it. The office was established as a result of a long and carefully nurtured development. A "chief rabbi" was not thrust on a community. The Rabbi of the Great Synagogue was indisputably the leading religious figure in English Jewry. He did not have colleagues of the calibre of Rabbis Kaufmann Kohler, Gustav Gottheil, Alexander Kohut, Aaron Wise, F. De Sola Mendes, and H. Pereira Mendes to question his right to the title.

The English Jewish community during the incumbency of Doctor Adler was Orthodox. The leading American congregations were in the Reform camp. Ashkenazic Jewry had already supplanted Sephardic in mid-nineteenth-century England. The east European Jew was still the object of ridicule or charity when Rabbi Jacob Joseph came to New York. It was therefore highly unrealistic to expect or even to hope that if England had a chief rabbi the same office could be established in America. It was more unrealistic still to expect that a rabbi of the type of Jacob Joseph, Talmudic scholar though he was, could play the role in America that a Nathan Adler did in England.

The goals of the chief rabbi as conceived by the leaders of the association were threefold:

1. To be the leader in the battle . . . to keep the next generation faithful to Judaism.[148]
2. To correct abuses which have appeared in the religious life of New York Orthodoxy.[149]
3. To unite Orthodox Jewry.

In each of these the chief rabbi was destined to fail, as indeed any one of his east European colleagues would have failed. The background and experience of a rabbi who had served an east European community were not at all the prerequisites for a rabbi who could accomplish the association's threefold program.

The Reverend Doctor H. Pereira Mendes voiced his skepticism concerning Rabbi Jacob Joseph's ability to "keep the next generation." It bespeaks his sincerity and courage that he did so at a meeting of the association. He asked:

> Will he be able to take up the fight against encroaching Reform in America? Has he the power and ability and education enough to enter the lists for Orthodoxy? Will he dare oppose the uptown ministers, some of whom maintain that God did not dictate the Torah word by word to Moses? Indeed, can he enter into a polemic with them in order thereby to lead the errant sheep back to the fold of our faith? Do you believe in the possibility that by virtue of the authority he possesses in the old country, he will be able to exert a salutary influence on the youth of America?[150]

Doctor Mendes was right, of course. To the son and daughter of the immigrant Jew, trying desperately to be fully accepted as Americans, the bearded, Yiddish-speaking Rabbi Joseph represented the Europe they were attempting to expunge from their experience. They certainly would not permit it to cross the sea and take up residence in America. It would not only impede Americanization of the new generation, but the existence of what he represented on these shores would raise questions as to the possibilities of the east European Jew's Americanization. Neither could a man of Rabbi Joseph's background and training take up the defense of Orthodoxy before "the next generation." He did not speak the language of that generation, literally and figuratively, and he lived in quite a different world. To cast on such an individual the responsibility of securing the new generation for Orthodoxy was to saddle him with failure from the start.

That abuses existed in the institutions serving Orthodoxy in New York no one could deny. That the correction of these abuses was a matter of gravest importance all agreed. Had Rabbi Joseph gained success in this area alone, the office of the chief rabbi would have been credited with a major accomplishment. To make kashrut his first and then only area of activity weakened his status. To make it a source of income to the association was to sound its knell. Long before Rabbi Joseph came, M. Jalomstein reasoned against kashrut as a source of income.[151] But his advice was ignored. Karobka was a terribly effective accusation, one that was not, and indeed could not, effectively be refuted.

That such an obviously disastrous step had to be taken was due to the precarious financial structure of the association. Monies sufficient to run the office of the chief rabbi were never pledged. Even his salary was not underwritten by financially responsible congregations. He was brought with the hope that once the office was established it would win approval and thus acquire the necessary support.

The rabbi could not effect orderly procedure in the supervision of kashrut since he, himself, was a recipient of its rewards, and his motives could therefore always be questioned. If he had not been forced to seek income from supervision, it is likely that he would have been able "to correct abuses." No one engaged in the business of kashrut could remain unsoiled. Shalom Silverstein suggested in an article in the *Volks-advokat*[152] that the greatest service a chief rabbi could perform was to unite the German and east European Jewish communities. The German Jews considered the Russian Jews "uncivilized," and to the Russians the Germans were not pious enough. A chief rabbi who could make the German Jews more observant and the Russian Jew more modern would really be performing a service.

The leaders of the association were less ambitious in their goals. If the chief rabbi could have united the east European Jewish community in New York, they would have been well pleased. But even here the association created obstacles. The established local rabbis were not consulted about the association's plans nor about the candidate. Each rabbi had some following, and even before Rabbi Joseph came an opposition had been created. The Galician Jews and the hasidim were not invited into the counsels of the association's leaders, and it was an obvious insult to consult no Galician or Hungarian rabbi about candidates.

That Rabbi Jacob Joseph was a "consolation prize" further weakened his position. He was chosen largely because he was available. J. D. Eisenstein, a leader of the association, stated this as a chief reason for the failure of the experiment.[153] He was also critical of the oratorical and administrative abilities of the rabbi. Rabbi Jacob Joseph had been esteemed in Vilna for his preaching ability and scholarship, not for skills in organization or political manipulation. Whether a rabbi expert in these pursuits could have carried off a victory is highly problematical. The situation and conditions militated against success for even the most able in all of the above.

The religious environment that Rabbi Joseph found in America, the faulty planning by the leaders of the association, their disregard of the resident rabbis, the precarious financial structure, engaging in the business of kashrut, the well-nigh impossible goals set for the incumbent, his lack of training and experience for such a program—all these factors combined to bring to an end a project that had seemed to promise so much.

The attempt to establish a chief rabbinate, however, had its lasting effect for the good. It introduced the east European immigrant Jew to communal enterprise. He gained knowledge of the forces shaping the Jewish community and experience in how to direct them toward desired goals. He who was rapidly becoming a dominant factor in that community became conscious of his ability to shape his own destiny. The organization of the association and the enthusiasm it evoked demonstrated the latent vitality of Orthodoxy—a vitality that encouraged Doctor H. Pereira Mendes and his coworkers a decade later to organize the Union of Orthodox Jewish congregations of America, now a century old.

It may well be that the failure of this "noble experiment" was its success, for it taught the more perceptive leaders of Orthodoxy that, in the long run, what was needed to "keep the next generation faithful to Judaism" was not a few great European-trained rabbinic authorities but a corps of American-trained Orthodox rabbis. Within the decade, in 1897, the foundation was laid with the establishment of the Rabbi Isaac Elchanan Theological Seminary, flourishing a century later as the heart of Yeshiva University.

PART THREE

A Pluralistic Religious Community

Reform Judaism, 1869:

> During the last years Jewish religious life in our country has advanced most satisfactorily. Spurred by the blessings of freedom, the reform of Judaism has become a power. . . . The only thing needed to strengthen this power . . . is an understanding of like-minded rabbis concerning the principles—not the forms—of a new ritual and of the solutions of various practical and religious questions.
>
> Dr. Samuel Adler
> Dr. David Einhorn

Orthodox Judaism, 1879:

> The open and flagrant desecration of the Sabbath, the neglect of dietary laws and regulations . . . are signs of the times to which we can no longer be blind and which all the glare and glamour of costly synagogues and temples cannot conceal. We have been slumbering too long! The glories of past history, the sacrifices of our fathers, the noble mission of our race are too precious to be disregarded and thrown away.
>
> The Board of Delegates of the United Hebrew Orthodox
> Congregations

Conservative Judaism, 1886:

> The necessity has been made manifest for associated and organized effort on the part of the Jews in America faithful to Mosaic Law and ancestral traditions, for the purpose of keeping alive the true Judaic spirit; in particular by the establishment of a seminary where the Bible shall be impartially taught and rabbinical literature faithfully expounded . . . with the love of the Hebrew language and a spirit of fidelity and devotion to Jewish law.
>
> The Jewish Theological Seminary Association

7   The Tripartite Division

How It Came To Be

The American Jewish community is at one and the same time part of world Jewry and a component of the American nation. It is shaped and influenced by both. It responds to requirements placed on it by world Jewry and the demands made of it by America. The formative period of organized Jewish religious life in America is the century between the Congress of Vienna in 1815 and the outbreak of World War I in 1914. During that century the Jewish population in the United States increased a thousandfold from about 2,500 to some 2.5 million. In 1815 there were some half dozen congregations. By 1914 there was a religious community divided into Orthodox, Reform, and Conservative groupings, each with its rabbinic seminary, congregational union, and rabbinic organizations.

The European Jewish historic experience in that century was largely that of emancipation, enlightenment, and migration. The promise of the French Revolution of *Liberté, Egalité, Fraternité* was carried by Napoleon's conquering armies through Europe. Grudgingly but increasingly, civic and political rights were extended to the Jew. The periods of reaction that followed the Congress of Vienna and the abortive revolutions of 1848 erased many hard-won rights, but not all. The Jew's usefulness to the growing and expanding economy opened heretofore closed doors. He entered these with alacrity. He sensed that the price of admission was a lessening of Jewish national feelings and aspirations, a casting off of the ways that made him distinct and distinguished.

These sentiments were fortified by his experience with enlightenment, the Jew's absorption of and into the general culture of the country and its civilization. Both in its west European form of *Jüdische Wissenschaft* and in its east European expression *Haskalah* (enlightenment), it led to loosening of ancestral ties and restructuring of communal forms and religious usage. In its extreme it led to apostasy, the baptismal certificate considered the ticket of admission to the world beyond the ghetto.

The extension of civic rights in western Europe and the growth of economic opportunity there, coupled with covert repression and overt op- pression in the Russian Empire, led to migrations westward, most of which carried across the Atlantic to the New World and its promise of ever greater freedom and opportunity. Population movement shakes the stability of established institutions, be they of organization or usage.

Emancipation, enlightenment, and migration made the soil fertile for the sprouting and growth of Reform Judaism. Reform in turn brought about the organized opposition of the traditionalists, which made for a consciousness of their own corporate identity as Orthodox. The excesses of Reform led to the turning away of a leading participant, Zacharias Frankel, and his formulation of "positive, historical Judaism," the fore- runner of American Conservative Judaism. A traditionalist accommoda- tion to the challenges of emancipation and enlightenment was Samson Raphael Hirsch's neo-Orthodoxy, which has been a major influence on modern American Orthodoxy.

IN THE NEW WORLD

The American counterpart to the European emancipation, enlighten- ment, and migration was freedom, frontier, and immigration.

The Jesuit scholar, Father Giovanni Antonio Grassi, came to the United States in 1810. From 1812 to 1817 he served as president of Georgetown College. Returning to Italy, he, like so many others, pub- lished a book of his observations. His description of the religious scene is of significance to our considerations: "Nothing is more striking to the Italian at his arrival in America than the state of religion. By virtue of an article in the federal constitution every religion and every sect is fully tolerated, is equally protected, and equally treated in the United States. . . . Every sect there is held as good, every road is correct, and every error as the insignificant weakness of poor mortals. In accordance with such principles, it is not surprising if America gives birth to innumerable sects which daily subdivide and multiply."[1] A few years later Alexis de Toc- queville observed: "The sects which exist in the United States are innu- merable. They all differ in respect to worship which is due from man to his Creator, but they all agree in respect to the duties which are due from man to man. . . . There is no country in the whole world in which the Christian religion retains a greater influence over the souls of men than in America. . . . The Americans combine the notions of Christianity and of liberty so intimately in their minds, that it is impossible to make them conceive the one without the other."[2]

Grassi, the priest, is struck by the proliferation of sects, which free- dom permits. The layman, de Tocqueville, noting the same, understands that freedom that permits division on matters of doctrine unites men in their esteem of religion as a beneficial force in the service of liberty and democracy. In a word, democracy needs religion, freedom permits religions. De Tocqueville continues: "I have known of societies formed by the Americans to send out ministers of the Gospel into the new western states to found schools and churches there, lest religion should be suffered to die away in those remote settlements, and the rising states be less fitted to enjoy free institutions than the people from which they emanated."[3] The Presbyterian schoolmaster-minister, the Baptist farmer-preacher, and the Methodist circuit rider were familiar figures on the frontier, their calling appreciated and the institution that they represented esteemed.

Throughout the nineteenth century, America was a moving frontier. On the frontier the value of the church as a civilizing, "culturizing," stabilizing force was understood and appreciated. At the same time, the free, often iconoclastic, spirits who were drawn there made the frontier hospitable to proliferating sects espousing new religious forms and doctrines.

Moses Hart, scion of the leading pioneer Jewish family of Canada, then residing in New York, attempted to fashion a new religion for America early in the century. He felt that the existing religions "are strongly chequered with . . . dangerous and disrespectful principles, which ought to be plucked from the fair soil of America." In his *Modern Religion* he issued a call: "Americans, your rapid progress in free principles and toleration, have drawn forth the smiles of applause from Europe, Asia, and Africa. One task remains, may you soon bury their religious superstition in the vast ocean which separates you from them. The author is humbly offering for your adoption a system of religion, styled Modern Religion."[4]

In 1844 I. Daniel Rupp published his *An Original History of the Religious Denominations at Present Existing in the United States.* What is noteworthy is that the accounts were written "expressly for the work by eminent theological professors, ministers and lay-members of the respective denominations," as its editor states in his introduction. No less than forty-three denominations are represented. Mainline Protestant Baptist, Presbyterian, Episcopal, and Congregationalist leaders had no objection to having their denominations listed and described along with the Mennonites, the Amish, the Millenarians, the Shakers, the Schwenkfelders, the Latter Day Saints, and the Jews. The listing is in alphabetical order. The length of the essays was determined by the authors. There being no established church, each denomination felt the equal of any other.

Some forty million immigrants came to America during the century. They brought with them their religious ways and established institutions to serve and perpetuate them. Immigration itself made for the proliferation of sects.

The nineteenth-century professional Jewish traveler I. J. Benjamin II visited America from 1859 to 1862. He lists twenty-three congregations in New York City. In each instance he notes the ritual or ethnic composition of the congregation, e.g., "Polish ritual," "this is a Dutch congregation," "Bohemian ritual," "German ritual," "organized in 1859 by French Jews," and so on.[5]

Many immigrants, in their desire for instant Americanization, sought out what seemed to them to be native American religious groups. Thus there were not only many religious denominations but also ready movement from one denomination to another. The Jewish immigrant, no less than any other and more than most, desired to become an American the moment he set foot on American soil. To him, more than to any other, America was a refuge and a chance at a full free life that the land of his birth had denied him. He soon found that America esteemed religion and encouraged the establishment of religious institutions.

Isaac Leeser, who wrote the article "The Jews and Their Religion" in the aforementioned *History of the Religious Denominations,* stated: "When we endeavor to trace the origin of the civilization which rules with its benignant sway the mightiest nations of modern times, and none more so than the people inhabiting the United States of America, we shall soon discover that it must be ascribed to a great *moral* influence which had its birth in the gray ages of antiquity. . . . This source of light we call divine revelation, and it is contained for us, who live at this day, in the pages of that priceless book which we call the Bible."[6]

To be the people of *The Book* was a source of strength and pride, a patent of nobility to the recently arrived immigrant, now making his way with pack on back. The ancient patrimony could not be easily cast aside even by the less than pious. America was a new world, which esteemed the "Old Faith," and it was a free world that permitted forms of that old faith.

AN AMERICAN JUDAISM

Initially attempts were made to fashion an American Judaism. The first attempt at a national religious union had its roots in a far-off anti-Jewish outrage, the so-called Damascus affair. Following the disappearance of a Catholic priest there in February 1840, the Jews of Damascus were accused of his murder "in order to take his blood for use in their unleavened bread." Scores were imprisoned, children were seized and held as hostages, and a wide-scale massacre was imminent. Jewish communities the world over were shocked and aroused, and those who dared organize and speak protest did so. The news from Syria in 1840 galvanized the Jews of America into action. The Jews of New York, Philadelphia, Cincinnati, and Richmond united in communal expression of horror, sympathy, and indignation. Participation in a common cause that so excited the emotions brought the scattered and disparate elements of the American Jewish community together in a communion of spirit and concern. It has been suggested that modern Jewish history dates from the Damascus affair. Certainly the American Jewish community had its beginnings as a self-conscious entity in the activity precipitated by "the massacre of Damascus."

A number of Philadelphians, distressed with the anarchy that marked Jewish life in 1840 America but heartened by the example of Jews of different congregations uniting for common effort, decided to attempt a Union of American Israelites. If the Jews of America, they reasoned, can unite to protect their brother's body, would they not join together for the enhancement of their own children's souls? In July 1841 a circular was sent to the congregations of the United States. "The Israelites of Philadelphia" sent "greetings" and invited fellow American Jews: "In the full confidence that you will favorably entertain our plan for a general union, we, on the part of the Israelites of this vicinity, affectionately invite you to deliberate well on the proposition and regulations which accompany this, and to elect without delay suitable persons for delegates, to meet us in general convention, on the first Sunday in November, being the 7th of the month, corresponding with the 23rd day of Marcheshvan, 5602, at Philadelphia."[7] The accompanying "proposition and regulations" detailed plans for a national religious authority, a system of elementary and higher Jewish education, and a Union of American Jewish Congregations.

Later, Leeser ruefully reminisced: "The circular, with the preliminary adopted constitution, was sent to the few congregations then existing in the country; but, in brief, the conference did not meet; no rabbinical authority was instituted, no school was erected, no union was established, and the incipient division and strife were permitted to take what shape they pleased."[8]

A second attempt to forge an American Israel was through a conference in Cleveland, Ohio, in October 1855. It sought to unite the traditionalist and liberal forces that were rending American Jewry into two religious camps. The leaders of the respective groups, Isaac Leeser and Isaac Mayer Wise, put aside differences that had led to animosity for the sake of Jewish religious unity. Leeser's contribution was his attendance, thus giving recognition to rabbis of the Reform school. Wise's offering on the altar of unity was ideological. He accepted the proposition: "The Talmud contains the traditional, legal and logical exposition of the biblical laws which must be expounded and practiced according to the comments of the Talmud."[9]

The conference and its principles drew opposition from the right and from the left. Rabbi David Einhorn and members of his Har Sinai Congregation of Baltimore published a protest, declaring that "The said platform would condemn Judaism to a perpetual stagnation."[10] Isaac Leeser, after initial exultation at what he considered a triumph for traditionalism, took a second look and did not like what he saw. Wise's acceptance of the statement on Talmudic law was not, as Leeser first hailed it, "a son of Israel . . . repentantly revok[ing] the rebellion he had uttered" but a strategic move to establish a united American Israel to which he, Wise, would give leadership and which would adopt the prayer book he had prepared.

The prayer book was titled *Minhag America*, "The American Rite." The title page bore the legend that it was revised and translated by the Liturgical Commission of the Cleveland Conference. It was moderate Reform in content and on its publication came to be known as the "Wise Prayerbook."

The Cleveland Conference did not heal the breach between reformers and traditionalists. It led to further division, causing a breach within Reform itself: the practical Reform of Isaac Mayer Wise and the ideological Reform of David Einhorn.

A threefold division in American Jewish religious life was noted in 1871 by W. M. Rosenblatt. In an article in the *Galaxy* he divided American Jewry into Orthodox, Conservative, and Radical.[11] Wise and company were the Conservatives; the Einhorn group were the Radicals.

The divisions in American Jewry were pronounced, the polemics sharp, and the controversies continuous. The pages of the contemporary Jewish press, the *Occident*, the *Israelite, Sinai*, and the *Asmonean*, are replete with attack and counterattack, accusation and refutation. Religious controversy, polemics, and wounding accusations were part of the nineteenth-century American religious scene. Religious controversy was rife in European Jewry as well. American Jewry, being part of both scenes, took example from both. Among public rabbinic disputes, we note those of Isaac M. Wise and David Einhorn; Wise and Isaac Leeser; Marcus Jastrow and Samuel Hirsch; Alexander Kohut and Kaufmann Kohler—controversies "for the sake of Heaven" on matters of religious doctrine and usage.

The death of Isaac Leeser in 1867 left the traditionalist forces without an effective leader or spokesman. The field was open wide for the spread of Reform, and spread it did. Virtually all the leading congregations soon were in its fold, and almost all leading rabbinical personalities were in its camp. An attempt was made in 1869 to unite Reform Jewry, the first step of which was a rabbinic conference held in Philadelphia.

The convener of the conference and its leading spirit was David Einhorn. Isaac Mayer Wise was in attendance, but the Seven Resolutions adopted pronounce Einhorn's ideology: Diaspora is not punishment but divinely ordained opportunity for the Jews to fulfill "their high priestly task to lead the nations in the true knowledge and worship of God." The one "practical" plank declared that because Hebrew has become "incomprehensible for the overwhelming majority of our present-day co-religionists . . . in the act of prayer Hebrew must take second place behind a language which the worshippers can understand."[12]

A quarter of a century earlier, Zacharias Frankel had left the Frankfurt Conference and Reform Judaism on the issue of the place of Hebrew in worship. Wise was not ready to go that far, but he must have bridled at this anti-Hebrew plank. Only a year earlier in his introduction to his *Hymns, Psalms and Prayers* he had written: "The Hebrew language in our public worship is the medium of our synagogal union. Dispersed as the house of Israel is in all lands, we must have a vehicle to understand each other in the house of God, so that no brother be a stranger therein; and this vehicle is the Hebrew."[13]

Wise returned to Cincinnati sobered and humbled. He recognized Radical Reform as a divisive rather than uniting force. His essential commitment was not to Reform Judaism but to an American Judaism. At the conference he was a participant, not a leader. Though he continued formal participation with the rabbinic body that had met in Philadelphia, he knew that this was not a vehicle for the fashioning of an American Judaism.

The eastern seaboard was dominated by the proponents of Radical Reform. Wise's influence was strong in the West and South. Gifted organizer that he was, he understood that congregations could be united through participation in a project rather than through agreement on resolutions. A "Jewish Theological Institute" to educate an American Jewish ministry was the vehicle. To establish and maintain such an institution, a call was issued by the congregations of Cincinnati: "To all congregations of the West and South for a Congregational Convention to form a 'Union of Congregations' under whose auspices a 'Jewish Theological Institute' shall be established, and other measures adopted which will advance the prosperity of our religion."[14]

It is an appeal to *all* congregations. There is no mention of Reform. It is to "advance the prosperity of our religion." It was to be a "Union of American Hebrew Congregations" of all views and all hues.

The union prospered, and the Hebrew Union College was launched and maintained. Wise was able to attract to the enterprise even so staunch a traditionalist as Sabato Morais, hazzan minister of the Mikveh Israel Congregation, Philadelphia. Morais addressed the fourth annual session of the council in 1877 and served on the Examining Committee, signing a report that read in part: "The College in Cincinnati may unequivocally be pronounced an object deserving the support of all Israelites who wish that attachment to the ancestral faith be founded upon a knowledge of its precepts, and an extensive acquaintance with the national literature."[15]

In 1880 the dream of a united American Jewish religious community seemed not only attainable but well on the road to fulfillment. There was little strength or vitality in Orthodoxy. Einhorn's death in 1879 left a void of leadership in the Radical forces. Wise's union and college were prospering and attracting ever larger and ever more diversified affiliation and support.

THE DECISIVE DECADE

The bomb that took the life of Alexander II, "Czar of all the Russias," in March 1881 ushered in a new era in American Jewish life. Until then Jewish immigration to America had been steady but moderate and largely from western and central Europe. The pogroms and restrictive "May Laws" of 1882 touched off a mass migration of east European Jews, which was brought to an end for the Russian Jew by the revolution of 1917 and for Polish Jews by the immigration law of 1924.

In the decade 1880–1890, some 200,000 east European Jews came to America, doubling the Jewish population. In the next decade the number doubled again. A new community was in the making, of a different ethnic composition, having new religious views and needs that found expression in a religious, ideological, and structural realignment.

Three events took place in the middle of the ninth decade of the nineteenth century that concretized the division of the American Jewish religious community into the present groupings of Orthodox, Conservative, and Reform. In 1885 nineteen leading Reform rabbis met in Pittsburgh and adopted a declaration of principles that remained the operative, though unofficial, platform of Reform Judaism for more than half a century. A year later a group of scholarly rabbis and traditionally oriented laymen founded the Jewish Theological Seminary of America. Two years after that the Orthodox congregations of New York brought to these shores Rabbi Jacob Joseph to serve as their chief rabbi.

The platform adopted in Pittsburgh begins with a statement of purpose: "In view of the wide divergence of opinion and of the conflicting ideas prevailing in Judaism today, we, as representatives of Reform Judaism in America, in continuation of the work begun in Philadelphia in 1869, unite upon the following principles."[16] The principles, eight in number, were of such radical nature that they brought forth immediate criticism and denunciation and roused those who were critical to concrete counteraction. Sabato Morais stated that "the platform reveals an unwarrantable antagonism to the five holy books (the Pentateuch)." His fellow Sephardi minister, H. Pereira Mendes, declared: "They may give up . . . the doctrine of a restoration in Palestine if they like. But I prefer Isaiah, Jeremiah, Ezekiel. . . . Forgive me again, if I prefer His voice to the voices of these ministers." The action they jointly undertook was to found a new seminary.

Establishment of the Jewish Theological Seminary of America in 1886 laid the foundation for what was later to become the Conservative movement. Like many religious movements, Conservative Judaism had its beginnings in protest. In 1883, at the banquet held in celebration of the first graduation of the Hebrew Union College, then the only rabbinical seminary in America, the food served was pointedly not kosher. Suspicions that had been smoldering for some time about the college now burst into open flame, and the traditional elements in American Jewry began to think of establishing an Orthodox theological seminary. Two years later the tone of the Pittsburgh platform aroused the misgivings and opposition of a group of moderate Reform rabbis who had long suspected that American Reform had permitted itself excesses that were as dangerous as they were drastic. The "dinner" and the "platform" brought together two forces who now found common ground in their opposition. They united in protest against the Hebrew Union College and the Pittsburgh Conference and gave constructive expression to their disapproval through the founding of a seminary that would chart a new course for American Israel.

The antecedents for the Conservative tendency institutionalized in the seminary were twofold. Sabato Morais, the seminary's first president, was the minister of Mikveh Israel, the Sephardi congregation of Philadelphia. Another of the seminary's founders, H. Pereira Mendes, was the spiritual head of Shearith Israel, the Spanish and Portuguese synagogue in New York. Their coworker, Bernard Drachman, was rabbi of an Orthodox congregation in New York of the west European mode. All three were Orthodox. Cofounders Alexander Kohut, Marcus Jastrow, and Benjamin Szold were rabbis of moderate Reform congregations and ideologically committed to the "positive historical" view of Judaism of Zacharias Frankel, president of the Jewish Theological Seminary of Breslau.

"Positive historical Judaism," as formulated by Frankel and his disciples, became the intellectual/spiritual cornerstone for the rising edifice of Conservative ideology. It viewed Judaism as the product of historical development and called for a positive attitude of reverence and understanding toward traditional Judaism. The complex of values, practices, and ideals of traditional Judaism were not to be lightly surrendered for the sake of convenience, conformity, or material advantage. The specifically Jewish elements in Judaism, as, for example, the Hebrew language, were considered essential to the preservation of its character and vitality.

From the beginning, the leaders of the seminary looked to the dramatically emerging east European Jewish community in America as a source for students and for congregations for its graduates. Conservative Judaism was a "threefold cord" whose strands were the scientific study of Judaism of the "positive historical" school, the congregational manner and mode of Sephardi and west European synagogues, and the piety and zeal of east European Orthodoxy.

The east European Orthodox community did not respond with support for the seminary. It had a plan and project of its own: to organize itself into the Association of the American Hebrew Congregations and bring a chief rabbi to these shores. A call, issued April 1888, tells the purpose, the project, and the hope.

> In this land, where we are at liberty to observe our religion, to study, teach, observe, perform and establish our Law, we find that our religion is neglected and our Law held in light esteem. . . . Rouse yourselves and let not the mistake be repeated and continued by which Orthodox Judaism has lost so many who should be enlisted under its banner. Certain congregations have united in order to create an intelligent orthodoxy, and to prove that also in America can be combined honor, enlightenment and culture, with a proper observance of religious duty. After much care in the choice of a Chief Rabbi, we have selected the learned and pious Rabbi Jacob Joseph of Vilna. He is to be the leader in the battle which must be waged to keep the next generation faithful to Judaism in spite of educational, social and business influences which, in America, are so powerful to make our sons and daughters forget their duty to the religion in which their ancestors lived, and for which those ancestors died.[17]

The rabbi was greeted with all hope and enthusiasm. The press was full of his doings. Although after a brief flush of success the whole endeavor disintegrated into a debacle, the attempt had a lasting effect. It introduced the east European immigrant Jew into communal activities and religious organization. The organization of the association and the enthusiasm it evoked demonstrated the latent vitality of Orthodoxy, which had now declared and established itself as an independent self-conscious religious movement. After these events there was no turning back.

Each movement's project was appropriate to its philosophy of Judaism and in answer to its immediate and future needs. Reform had been largely rejection; a statement of affirmation was needed. Because each rabbi felt free to act as he saw fit and to espouse what he alone felt right, the movement was fragmented. It needed agreement on basic principles and cohesion in views and ways. A declaration of principles, a commonly accepted platform was the need and at Pittsburgh became the reality. Conservative Judaism, faithful to traditional ways and open to development and change, needed a clergy expert in the tradition yet part of the contemporary scene. A seminary was therefore established to train American young men in the tradition that they would then expound in contemporaneous, meaningful fashion and adapt to the spiritual needs of their congregants. For Orthodoxy the truth of word and deed was in the Tradition as received and transmitted. What was needed was an authority to expound it, apply it, enforce it—a rabbi respected for his scholarship and therefore accepted as *the* authority.

By 1890, the pattern was set for American Judaism. Reform was armed with an ideology and was maintained by a network of institutions and congregations. Conservative Judaism had its struggling seminary and the hope that its graduates would fashion a "way" for American Israel. Orthodoxy, having flexed its organizational muscles, felt ready for and looked to an ever increasing immigration to bring it adherents and the strength they provide.

8 A Century of Conservative Judaism

Conservative Judaism, the movement in American Jewish religious life that has attracted the largest number of adherents, celebrated in 1986 the one-hundredth anniversary of the founding of its mother institution, the Jewish Theological Seminary of America. The movement is a product of both the ideological ferment in nineteenth-century Jewish life and the sociological realities of twentieth-century America. The former brought about the coalition of acculturated Orthodox and moderate Reform rabbis and laymen that founded the seminary in 1886; the latter influenced the distinctive mission and program of the Conservative synagogue.

For half of its first century, Conservative Judaism thought of itself as the historically authentic expression of traditional Judaism, believing that it alone could stay the corrosive influences of Reform that the insulated, isolating form of Orthodoxy transplanted from eastern Europe could neither confront nor defeat. The mother institution, the seminary—conservative as institutions are wont to be—felt comfortable and secure in its self-proclaimed status as guardian of authentic traditionalism. At the same time, its children, the rabbis it ordained, increasingly proclaimed the Judaism they espoused to be a distinct movement within the American Jewish religious community. Seeking to blend Orthodoxy's devotion to tradition with the open-mindedness of Reform, adherents of Conservative Judaism proclaimed themselves—in the words of Louis Finkelstein—"the only group in [American] Israel with a modern mind and a Jewish heart, prophetic passion and western science."[1]

Although the post–World War II era saw the ascendancy of Conservative Judaism as the preferred religious affiliation of over 40 percent of American Jewry, its history has been marked by a constant groping for an ideology that would adequately define and effectively direct the movement. Having its historic origin as a protest against both the excesses of Reform and the insularity of Orthodoxy, Conservative Judaism has suffered from the same malady as other protest movements: strong in negation, imprecise in affirmation. Holding a centrist position, it has operated as a coalition movement in which agreement is reached through consensus. This posture has made it vulnerable to accusations from both the right (Orthodoxy) and the left (Reform) that it is a movement lacking in conviction, a halfway house for timid Reformers and compromising Orthodox. The centrist position has, however, permitted Conservative Judaism to claim to be the authentic voice and path of the golden mean, espousing faith tempered by reason, reason uplifted by faith, and a reasonableness that surrenders neither heart nor mind.

In his presidential address to the United Synagogue of America in 1918, Professor Louis Ginzberg said, "Nothing is easier, but nothing is more dangerous than definitions; I shall attempt a description."[2] Writing to Rabbi Herman H. Rubenovitz in 1939, Professor Robert Gordis asserted that "the activity of Conservative rabbis and Conservative congregations [rather than the written word] is a far better index to what Conservatism is."[3] Based on these observations, this study focuses in the main on the activities of Conservative rabbis and congregations. At the same time, following Solomon Schechter's admonition that "a life without guiding principles and thoughts is a life not worth living," attention is given to the continuous quest for an ideology, and its formulation in different eras.

BEGINNINGS

Roots: European

The twofold experience of enlightenment and emancipation that permitted Jews to enter the modern world provided them with opportunities, but also confronted them with the challenge to justify their continued corporate existence in a world that welcomed their assimilation. One response was that of Reform Judaism, which posited a God-given mission as mandate for survival and which viewed Jewish historic experience as a mandate to alter traditional belief and forms in conformity to the most progressive demands of the larger world the Jew was now entering. Declared Samuel Hirsch, rabbi in Germany and America and Reform's philosopher: "The need of the time is the highest law of Judaism. . . . The Jews of the present day must, before all else, participate in the work of the age with all their powers; for their work is the object of Jewish history. Yes, it is the be-all and end-all of Judaism."[4] While German Reform leader Abraham Geiger advocated evolutionary change in the Judaism fashioned by the rabbis, Samuel Holdheim demanded radical reform of biblical Judaism itself. The emphasis of both, however, was on change.

Samson Raphael Hirsch, the founder of neo-Orthodoxy, articulated the response of those who rose to defend tradition against the onslaught of change. Jewish law, biblical and rabbinic, is eternal and unchangeable, he argued. The revealed word and will of the eternal God is manifested to His people Israel in the Torah—the written and oral law—"an eternal code set up for all ages by the God of eternity."[5] Reform's allegiance was to the world and its needs; neo-Orthodoxy's to God and His demands. Samuel Hirsch urged the Jew to alter the tradition as service to the world would require of him; Samson Raphael Hirsch demanded that the Jew direct his life in steadfast loyalty to the total demands of the tradition.

Hewing a middle path between these two positions was Zacharias Frankel, the learned rabbi of Dresden, later head of the Jewish Theological Seminary at Breslau. Though he instituted moderate reforms, such as the abolition of the recitation of the *piyyutim* (liturgical poems), he insisted that only changes that were not in conflict with the spirit of "positive-historical Judaism" should be permitted in the ritual.[6]

What was the "positive-historical Judaism" advocated by Frankel, or, more important to our discussion, how was this concept understood by the architects of Conservative Judaism? Professor Louis Ginzberg, who as the leading figure on the faculty of the seminary had a significant influence on the shaping of Conservative Judaism, wrote:

> The best illustration of his conception of Judaism is the instance which induced Frankel to leave the Frankfort Conference [of Reform rabbis in 1845], on which occasion he, for the first time, made use of the expression "positive-historic" Judaism. The matter at hand was a discussion of the question of whether and to what extent the Hebrew language should be retained in the Synagogue, and when the majority decided that Hebrew must be kept there only out of consideration for the old generation, Frankel took his departure. . . . The underlying principle at stake was this: *does the essence of Judaism lie exclusively in the Jewish religion, that is, ethical monotheism, or is Judaism the historical product of the Jewish mind and spirit?* The Hebrew language is of course not a religious factor, and even from the strictest standpoint of the *Shulhan Aruk* it would be difficult to adduce any fundamental objection to the use of any other language of prayer. Still it is true that in the long development of the synagogue service the Hebrew tongue became . . . the language of the Jewish spirit, and [therefore] an essential component of our devotional sentiment. . . . The recollection that it was the Hebrew language in which the Revelation was given, in which the Prophets expressed their high ideals, in which generations of our fathers breathed forth their sufferings and joys makes this language a holy one for us.[7]

Ginzberg saw in Frankel's views the origins of the Conservative definition of Judaism as "the historical product of the Jewish mind and spirit." Central to Judaism, then, is the Jewish people itself, possessors of that mind and spirit. In the unfolding development of Judaism, Frankel maintained, norms must obtain as to what may be altered and who may determine what needs to be changed. In the words of Ginzberg, "That which the whole community has adopted and recognized may not be repealed . . . [and] only those who recognized the Law as specifically Jewish, could have the right to decide what portions of it had incorporated themselves into the national consciousness."[8]

More recently, Ismar Schorsch has argued that the term *positive-historical Judaism*

> immediately suggests the opposite of "negative," and, often enough in his writing Frankel condemned the program of radical Reform for being utterly negative. . . . But the word "positive" also carried a well-established technical connotation, implying either law in general or posited law as opposed to natural law. . . .
>
> By choosing the adjective "positive" to describe his conception of Judaism, Frankel defiantly reasserted its fundamental legal character and rejected any effort to dilute it.[9]

At the heart of Judaism is a legal system. Among those who adhere to this concept of Judaism, however, there are those who place the emphasis on the historical integrity of the tradition and those who stress its evolutionary character.

Frankel's concept of positive-historical Judaism was adopted and adapted by students and disciples who came to America: graduates of the Jewish Theological Seminary in Breslau, such as Alexander Kohut and Frederic de Sola Mendes; Benjamin Szold, who spent his formative years in Breslau; and men like Marcus Jastrow, Aaron Wise, and Aaron Bettelheim who chose to be identified with the historical school. Frankel's followers practiced a moderate form of Reform Judaism and cooperated with Reform colleagues and institutions until these veered off to radical Reform. Then the moderates turned for religious camaraderie and joint enterprise to acculturated Orthodox colleagues. Together they founded the seminary and thus laid the foundation for Conservative Judaism.

Roots: American

By the middle of the nineteenth century, American Jews already had the option of identifying with either of two religious tendencies, traditionalist or Reform, whose spokesmen were, respectively, Isaac Leeser and Isaac Mayer Wise. Leeser, a German immigrant who served Sephardi congregations in Philadelphia, had the faith that traditional Judaism could flourish in the New World if American Jewry willed it and matched will with enterprise. Through his publication the *Occident* he advocated loyalty to Torah and *mitzvot* (religious commandments). At the same time, through the introduction of the English sermon, a supplementary

Jewish school system, popular religious literature in the vernacular, and the like, he sought to make traditional Jewish living compatible with social and cultural integration into the larger society.

Wise, an energetic and optimistic religious leader from Bohemia who was to become the architect of Reform Judaism in America, believed that Judaism would in time become the religion of all enlightened modern people. First, however, it had to be modernized and democratized or, as he advocated, "Americanized." He became the exponent of a moderate, pragmatic Reform Judaism, responsive to the pressures and practical necessities of living in an integrated society in the modern age. Thus, while Leeser issued the traditional prayer book with his own English translation, the only change being the incorporation of "A Prayer for a Republican Government," Wise published *Minhag America,* an abridged liturgy that eliminated all references to the restoration of sacrifices, the coming of the messiah, and the return to Zion. Reform and traditionalist elements joined together at a conference in Cleveland in 1855, but the conference led not to unity but to further subdivision, a rift between the moderate, practical Reform of the West and the radical, ideological Reform of the East that was to divide that movement for three decades.

As early as 1866, Jonas Bondi—rabbi, publisher, and editor—noted that there had developed in American Jewish religious life a "golden middleway" that was termed "orthodox" by the left and "heterodox or reformer" by the right and was apparently making such progress that it "is hated on both sides."[10] He identified this movement with "positive historical Judaism . . . [that] contains all the ideas of the development of Judaism.[11] Sigmund Hecht described the distinctive religious pattern of this third group as he saw it operating on the American scene in 1882: "Conservatism seeks to reconcile the differences of opinion, to harmonize the written Law (Torah) and the oral law (tradition) with the claims of this advanced age, to maintain venerable institutions, although purified and rendered more attractive, and to impart more sanctity and devotion to the divine service, not by discarding the traditional mode entirely, but by retaining it in the main and only removing those features that are antagonistic to its purpose."[12]

Because the three religious tendencies—they could not yet be called movements—that existed in the late 1860s and 1870s were still in the formative stages, the definition of each was far from clear.[13] Simon Wolf, for example, after worshiping in Philadelphia's Rodef Shalom during the High Holy Days of 1869, was surprised to learn that its rabbi, Dr. Marcus Jastrow, was called Orthodox. "To say that the Reverend Jastrow is Orthodox was doing him a great injustice," Wolf noted, "for a minister who is in favor of a temple, an organ, pews . . . cannot be considered as reflecting the ideas of the past."[14]

Wolf would have agreed fully with the unanimous designation of Jastrow's Philadelphia colleague Reverend Sabato Morais, of K. K. Mikveh Israel, as Orthodox. Yet in the early 1870s Morais put forth this seemingly radical plan for the ritual and liturgy of the American synagogue:

> The demand is for a simpler prayer-book. . . . Expurge, then, what relates to the ordinances followed by the ancients in the performances of sacrificial rites; strike out what belongs to Mishnic and Talmudic lore . . . avoid, as far as practical, the reiterating of supplication, confession or sacred song . . . compare philologically long-established rituals . . . select what is more chaste in style, more exalting in ideas . . . then endeavor to fill up a portion of the space made empty by the expurgatory process with compositions suited to our existing wants, the printed and unedited writings of our philosophers and poets can supply a vast deal, the learning of our modern Rabbis may also be of service.[15]

The religious radicalization of Reform and the growing insularity of Orthodoxy brought men with centrist tendencies closer together. Those from the right carried a commitment to Jewish law and its ritual and the synagogal mode of westernized traditional Jews—decorum, the sermon, and the use of the vernacular; those from the left contributed an ideology expressive of the positive-historical Judaism of Frankel.

The founding of the Jewish Theological Seminary came in response to the religiously radical platform adopted by the conference of Reform rabbis meeting in Pittsburgh in November 1885 and in reaction to the rapid retreat from the tradition by the Union of American Hebrew Congregations, established in 1873 as a synagogal union for *all* congregations, and its Hebrew Union College, whose purpose was to provide rabbis for *all* American synagogues. The UAHC had its roots in a moderate Reform outlook that held that a line should be drawn beyond which Reform should not venture,[16] but it was a line that dissolved fairly quickly.

Any adherence to the dietary laws fell in the summer of 1883 at the banquet celebrating the eighth annual meeting of the council of the UAHC and the first graduating class of the Hebrew Union College. No less than four varieties of forbidden shellfish were served, causing two rabbis to leave the banquet. But the other 198 diners remained. Wise, president of the college, refused to take responsibility for the menu, but did not dissociate himself from those responsible, attacking instead the critics with jeering references to "kitchen Judaism."

Two years later, Alexander Kohut, newly arrived to the pulpit of New York's Ahavath Chesed, raised the alarm against the kind of Reform he found in America: "A reform which seeks to progress without the Mosaic rabbinical tradition, such a reform is a deformity: is a skeleton of Judaism without flesh and sinew, without spirit and heart. . . . Only a Judaism true to itself and its past, only a Judaism which does not disown the character of its worthy antiquity, but is receptive of the ideas of the present, and accepts the good and the beautiful from whatever source it may come; only such a Judaism can command respect and recognition."[17]

Kohut's lecture was translated into English and published in the *American Hebrew*. Kaufmann Kohler, rabbi of Temple Beth El in New York, who had inherited from his father-in-law, David Einhorn, the mantle of spokesman for radical Reform, was quick to respond: "There is a novelty offered to our New York Jews in the appearance of a new rabbi of renown who, with laudable courage and independence, gives free utterance to his rigid conservatism, boldly challenging Reformed Judaism by the open declaration, that he who disowns the statutes and ordinances of Mosaico-Rabbinical Judaism on principle has forfeited the name Jew."[18]

The controversy continued, the antagonists mounting vigorous attacks that, unlike other rabbinic confrontations, never descended to personal invective. The issue was joined: positive-historical Judaism, which the Breslau-ordained Kohut professed, or radical Reform, which Kohler advocated—which would become the Judaism of the American Jew?

It was more the conviction that the UAHC (despite its protestations) had become a Reform organization and that the Hebrew Union College would produce rabbis espousing radical Reform, than the Pittsburgh conference itself, that caused the coalescing of forces that founded the seminary. A number of leading rabbis and laymen were eager to set a new course. A half century later, H. Pereira Mendes, minister of New York's Shearith Israel, America's oldest congregation, recalled:

> Calm and thoughtful conservative and Orthodox Rabbis . . . Doctors Alexander Kohut, Aaron Wise, Henry S. Jacobs, F. de Sola Mendes, Moses Maisner, Bernard Drachman of New York met for consultation. . . . Doctors Sabato Morais and Marcus Jastrow in Philadelphia were not idle; and further afield . . . Rabbis [Aaron] Bettelheim, [Henry] Schneeberger, [Shepsel] Schaffer (Baltimore), etc. proclaimed their sympathies. Prominent laymen gathered about them, Doctors Cyrus Adler, Aaron and Harry Friedenwald, S. Solis Cohen . . . the Honorables Mayer Sulzberger . . . Adolphus Solomon, Joseph Blumenthal. . . . Their numbers grew.
>
> One day, Dr. Morais called on me, to propose changing our action of meetings, debates, press-communications, accusations, recriminations . . . with no tangible results, into something that would advance the cause so dear to us both, the preservation of Historical and Traditional Judaism, by establishing a Jewish Institute of Learning, by educating, training and inspiring teachers, Rabbis who would stand *la Tora v'lat'udah*, "for the Torah and the Testimony."[19]

Half the rabbis mentioned by Mendes—Morais, Drachman, Maisner, Schneeberger, Schaffer, and Mendes himself—were proponents of traditional (Orthodox) Judaism; the rest were identified with the moderately Reform historical school. The leader of the former group was Morais, who, though hazzan-minister of an Orthodox congregation, had for many years been participating with Reform colleagues in communal and religious activities and communal enterprises. The spokesman for the latter group was Alexander Kohut.

The "Institute of Learning" proposed by Morais was created at a meeting held at Shearith Israel on January 31, 1886. Its aim was to train rabbis and teachers "in sympathy with the spirit of conservative Judaism." Morais was named president of the faculty.[20]

The Seminary

The founders of the new institution described it as a "seminary where the Bible shall be impartially taught and rabbinical literature faithfully expounded, and more especially where youths, desirous of entering the ministry, may be thoroughly grounded in Jewish knowledge and inspired by the precept and the example of their instructors with the love of the Hebrew language and a spirit of fidelity and devotion to the Jewish law."[21] Morais took active charge of the day-to-day affairs of the school, but it was Alexander Kohut who determined the fundamental character of the seminary. When, for example, the question of the name of the new institution arose, Morais suggested that it be called the "Orthodox Seminary," but Kohut influenced him to call it the "Jewish Theological Seminary." It was Kohut who expressed the purpose of the seminary at its inaugural exercises: "In the new Seminary a different spirit will prevail, different impulses will pervade its teachings and animate its teachers. This spirit will be that of *Conservative Judaism,* the conserving Jewish impulse which will create in the pupils of the Seminary the tendency to recognize the dual nature of Judaism and the Law; which unites theory and practice . . . acknowledges the necessity of observing the Law as well as studying it."[22]

The newly founded school held its first session on Monday, January 3, 1887, in the vestry room of the Shearith Israel Congregation. "Ten pupils were enrolled in the [preparatory] class," Joseph Blumenthal, president of the Jewish Theological Seminary Association, reported to its first biennial convention, "and the tuition was for a time imparted by various members of the Advisory Board."[23] Of the ten students in the preparatory class, four had been born in New York, three in Hungary, and three in Russia. The four New Yorkers and two of the students from Hungary were attending the City College of New York; the others, recent arrivals, were enrolled in public schools. Their average age was fifteen. There were also four students in a junior class—aged seventeen, nineteen, twenty-five, and twenty-seven—who had recently arrived from Russia. Of the total enrollment of fourteen students, only one continued on until ordination—Joseph Herman Hertz, who eventually rose to the position of chief rabbi of the British Empire.

The delegates also heard President Sabato Morais's vision of the seminary's mission:

> Our Seminary has created itself a church militant, to fight skepticism arrayed against the history and traditions that have rendered Israel deathless. . . .
>
> Well-meaning, but unwise orthodoxy, tells us that by keeping altogether aloof from "Reformer" . . . we will guard our children from the effects of teaching subversive to Holy Writ. . . . Isolation is an impossibility. It would be inadvisable if it were possible. . . .
>
> [The seminary] is the laboratory in which we try to mould the minds of men who will mightily battle for the religion. By the moral force of our disciples, synagogues will be stripped of meretricious garments. . . . Pulpits now convened into a nursery for the propagation of heresies, will become strongholds of the written and oral law.[24]

Who the seminary's constituency would be was not clear. Both Sabato Morais and H. Pereira Mendes looked for support to the east European immigrant community in New York. When that community chose instead to channel its funds and energies to the importation of a chief rabbi, Jacob Joseph of Vilna, both men expressed public disapproval. "I am familiar with the manner in which the Hebrews in the place whence he comes are educated," Morais told a reporter of the *New York Herald.* "He does not possess the knowledge nor the literary attainments which a rabbi should possess."[25] Mendes argued that only graduates of an American seminary, speaking the language of the land, would be able to appeal to the younger generation. "Do not give way to false hopes," he warned New York's Lower East Side Jewry, "[since] those who come after you will be Americans, full-blooded Americans like your brethren uptown."[26] The pleas fell on deaf ears. With few exceptions, east European immigrant Jewry ignored the new seminary, though the student body was drawn from that community.

During the first fifteen years of the seminary's existence, 1886–1900, a period in which more than half a million Jews arrived from eastern Europe, the seminary benefitted little from this influx. The immigrants came, transplanted their *shtiblach* (small synagogues), and appointed cantors and traditionally ordained rabbis, who eked out a living largely through kashrut supervision. The seminary and the rabbis it produced or was about to produce—leaders of the east European religious community inveighed—would expose Judaism and the faithful Jews to influences that would destroy both. The group that would later become the seminary's natural constituency—acculturated east European immigrants and their children—had not yet come into being.

The composition of the seminary's Advisory Board of Ministers and the "congregations entitled to representation" reflected the coalitional nature of the constituency that founded the new institution. Five of the rabbis on the board—Sabato Morais (president of the faculty), H. Pereira Mendes, Bernard Drachman, Henry W. Schneeberger, and Abraham P. Mendes—were traditionalists who comfortably termed themselves Orthodox; the others—Alexander Kohut, Marcus Jastrow, Henry S. Jacobs, Frederic de Sola Mendes, and Aaron Wise—had broken with traditional Judaism and considered themselves adherents of historical Judaism at the border of Reform (which side of the border is open to dispute).[27]

Not one member of the Advisory Board of Ministers was succeeded by a graduate of the seminary. The reason lies in the character of the congregations they led, which ranged all the way from the Sephardi Shearith Israel and the Ashkenazi Zichron Ephraim of New York, officially Orthodox and formally traditional, to Ahavath Chesed, Rodeph Shalom, and Shaarey Tefila of New York, then and now in the Reform camp. (Of the founding congregations, only B'nai Jeshurun of New York and Chizuk Amuno of Baltimore have always been and are today Conservative congregations.)

Loyalty to the seminary or what it stood for was virtually nonexistent. Marcus Jastrow, rabbi of Philadelphia's Rodef Shalom, decried his congregation's decision to engage a Reform rabbi in the "Farewell Sermon Delivered on the Occasion of His Retirement" in 1892: "I did forewarn you; I told you that it was impossible for a congregation to be conservative with a minister of radical convictions . . . but you would not listen to my voice, and now the king that has been chosen will soon be among you."[28] The congregation had rejoined the UAHC, and the new "king" came from the religiously radicalized Hebrew Union College. The death of Alexander Kohut in 1894 took from the seminary's ranks the only leader who could marshal support from what remained of its leftist constituency.

The lack of desirable pulpits for its graduates was only one of the obstacles facing the fledgling institution. It is actually surprising that the seminary survived into the twentieth century, lacking as it did the ingredients that gave Hebrew Union College, for example, life and strength: a natural constituency, an ideology that served the felt needs of that constituency, and a charismatic, energetic leader.

The German-Jewish immigrant community had established its synagogues in the middle of the nineteenth century as sanctuaries of faith and portals to America. In the last decades of the century, the Hebrew Union College was needed to provide English-speaking rabbis for the second generation of German Jews, who had rapidly Americanized and were well along in a total emancipatory process. The Pittsburgh Platform, with its expression of broad religious universalism, sanctioned national, cultural, and religious assimilation. Isaac Mayer Wise, who intuited the felt needs of that community, had the imagination, skills, and energy to fashion institutions to meet them. In the space of a quarter of a century he succeeded in enlisting almost every major congregation in America in the Union of American Hebrew Congregations, which then provided ready pulpits for graduates of his Hebrew Union College.

To his credit, H. Pereira Mendes continued his leadership after the death of Sabato Morais in 1897, but at best it was a holding action. In an attempt to organize support in the Orthodox community, in 1898 he established the Union of Orthodox Jewish Congregations. The organizational meeting was called by the seminary; it met at Shearith Israel and in attendance were lay leaders and teachers of the seminary. Dr. Mendes was elected president, but within two years the new body was dominated by east European immigrants whose loyalty was to Yeshivah Etz Chaim (from which Yeshiva University eventually emerged), not the seminary.

As early as 1890 Morais had recognized the need for a younger, more charismatic leader. Dr. Solomon Solis-Cohen of Philadelphia recalled that "in the year 1890, I had the privilege of bearing a message from Sabato Morais and his colleagues of the Jewish Theological Seminary . . . asking Schechter to consider the possibility of joining the teaching staff of that institution."[29] For a dozen years thereafter, sporadic attempts were made to bring to America Solomon Schechter, reader in rabbinics at Cambridge University, author of scholarly works written in elegant English, a man of great energy and unmistakable charisma. A product of Romanian and Galician yeshivahs, he had continued his studies in Vienna and Berlin, adding Western scientific order and method to the knowledge he had amassed in the East. His subsequent "discovery" of the Cairo *genizah* (storeroom for discarded sacred writings) brought him international fame. In the early nineties, Dr. Cyrus Adler and Judge Mayer Sulzberger visited him in England. They were impressed with the man and convinced that America should be his field of activity. Together with fellow Philadelphian Solomon Solis-Cohen they corresponded with Schechter and in 1895 brought him for a series of lectures to the newly established Gratz College. America had its appeal for Schechter, as he wrote to Sulzberger in 1898: "In your country I can hope to 'make school' and leave students . . . useful to the cause of Judaism."[30]

THE SCHECHTER ERA (1902–1915)

In the first years of the new century a group of American Jewish leaders joined forces to bring Solomon Schechter to these shores to head a reorganized Jewish Theological Seminary, born again April 14, 1902. Philadelphia provided the intellectual leadership and persuasive powers of Cyrus Adler, Mayer Sulzberger, and Solomon Solis-Cohen, while New York contributed the philanthropic generosity of Jacob H. Schiff, the Lewisohns, and the Guggenheims.[31]

The moneyed elite exacted certain conditions in helping to revive the seminary: Solomon Schechter was to serve as president of the faculty; Cyrus Adler was to function as chief executive; Louis Marshall would become chairman of the executive committee; and the elected board of the Jewish Theological Seminary Association would be replaced by a new, essentially self-perpetuating board. In order to demonstrate continuity with the previous administration, the second article of the bylaws of the old Seminary Association was incorporated into the new one, pledging the seminary's continued adherence to "historical Judaism, as ordained in the Law of Moses, and expounded by the prophets and sages of Israel in Biblical and Talmudical writings."

Despite such an assurance, a new type of seminary was, in fact, coming into being, reflecting the personality and religious views of the new faculty president. Morais, Mendes, and Drachman, the chief administrators of the "old" seminary, had designated themselves as Orthodox. Schechter, though pious and observant, was a proponent—if not altogether an adherent—of the positive-historical school. This had already been noted by Rabbi Morris Joseph in his review of Schechter's *Studies in Judaism*, published in 1896. The review dwelled at length on the introduction, in which the author presented the positive-historical position, which, the reviewer wrote, was "formulated by men who were at once liberal in their opinions and conservative in practice." Although Schechter wrote with obvious approval of this religious stance, Joseph lamented, "Mr. Schechter is more content to expound the theory of the historic school than adopt it."[32]

Schechter brought with him the requisite background to fashion a school that would train a scholarly rabbinate that would wield great influence on the new generation of American Jews. A devotee of *Jüdische Wissenschaft* and the positive-historical school, he had learned as a resident in England the need for standards in congregational affairs and dignity in worship. Schechter gathered about himself a faculty that, through its scholarly activities, succeeded in laying a strong intellectual foundation for the movement while creating a major center for higher Jewish learning. Louis Ginzberg charted new paths in rabbinic scholarship, employing a critical method that made use of the disciplines of sociology, economics, and comparative religion, demonstrating how Judaism remained alive by reinterpreting its ideas and practices. Alexander Marx's contributions were in the fields of history and bibliography. The seminary library that he fashioned became the center for the scientific study of Judaism in the United States. Israel Friedlaender was a biblical scholar, religious thinker, and communal leader who advocated the cultural creativity and spiritual Zionism that became hallmarks of Conservative Judaism. Israel Davidson laid open the rich treasures of medieval Jewish literature. No man had greater impact on Jewish religious thinking in America than Mordecai M. Kaplan, a seminary graduate, to whom Schechter entrusted the directorship of the Teachers Institute in 1909.

The course of study that was adopted reflected Schechter's pledge to draw up a curriculum that would include in it almost every branch of Jewish literature: "The Bible; Talmud of Babylon and Jerusalem; Jewish History and the History of Jewish Literature; Theology and Catechism; Homiletics, including a proper training in Elocution and Pastoral work; and Hazanuth . . . optional with the students of the Senior Class."[33] The requirements for ordination called for the successful completion of four years of postgraduate studies. The admission requirements, in addition to "the Degree of Bachelor of Arts . . . from a university or college of good standing," included knowledge of the Hebrew language, the ability to translate and interpret at sight any portion of the Pentateuch, stated selections from the books of Judges, Isaiah, the Psalms, and Daniel, most of *Seder Moed* of the Mishnah, and the first thirteen pages of *Gemara Berakhot,* as well as a knowledge of the prayer book and Jewish history.

Schechter sought to produce a learned rabbinate committed to the disciplines of Judaism but also open to its multifaceted ideological composition. As he told the students:

> You must not think that our intention is to convert this school of learning into a drill ground where young men will be forced into a certain groove of thinking, or, rather not thinking; and after being equipped with a few devotional texts, and supplied with certain catchwords, will be let loose upon an unsuspecting public to proclaim their own virtues and the unfallibility of their masters. . . . I would consider my work . . . a complete failure if this institution would not in the future produce such extremes as on the one side a roving mystic who would denounce me as a sober Philistine, on the other side, an advanced critic, who would rail at me as a narrow-minded fanatic, while a third devotee of strict Orthodoxy would raise protest against any critical views I may entertain.[34]

Schechter's expectation that the seminary would produce religious diversity was fulfilled in his own lifetime. Mordecai M. Kaplan and Jacob Kohn were among the first of the "advanced critics," while C. E. Hillel Kauvar and Herman Abramowitz called themselves Orthodox.

The Rabbis

During the incumbency of Solomon Schechter as president of the seminary—1902 to 1915—the Conservative rabbinate developed a character of its own and began to play an influential role in the religious life of American Jewry. In 1901, when the Alumni Association of the Jewish Theological Seminary was organized, fifteen graduates and former students were considered eligible for membership.[35] By 1916 the Alumni Association's membership had grown to sixty-one rabbis occupying pulpits or engaged in related activities. Conservative rabbis could be found in New York, Boston, Syracuse, Rochester, Buffalo, Toledo, Columbus, Detroit, Chicago, Minneapolis, Sioux City, Denver, Spokane, Dallas, Kansas City, Montgomery, Louisville, Greensboro, Pittsburgh, Altoona, Baltimore, and Newark.

What did a newly ordained seminary rabbi face? The experiences of two young rabbis illustrate the nature of synagogue life in that period. Paul Chertoff became rabbi of Congregation Beth Israel, Rochester, New York, an Orthodox synagogue that had separate seating of men and women, fully traditional Sabbath and weekday services, a cantor facing the ark, and an all-male choir. In contrast, his contemporary and colleague Herman H. Rubenovitz introduced the use of the organ and a mixed choir to his Conservative congregation, Mishkan Tefila, Boston.

Rubenovitz described what he found when he arrived in Boston in 1910:

> Assimilation was rampant, and its leading exponent was . . . the Rabbi of Reform Temple Israel, the wealthiest and most socially prominent Jewish congregation in New England. Hebrew had been practically eliminated from its service . . . the traditional Sabbath had been made secondary to the Sunday service. Even intermarriage between Jew and gentile was openly advocated. But what was even more menacing to the future of Judaism hereabouts, was the fact that by far the greater part of the Sunday morning Congregation which Rabbi Charles Fleischer addressed,[36] was made up of the sons and daughters of Orthodox Jewish parents. The Orthodox . . . synagogue worship . . . was, with few exceptions, utterly devoid of decorum, and its spiritual quality all too often lost in noise and confusion . . . and alienated the youth. When . . . these young people purchased seats for the High Holidays, they saw little of the interior of the synagogue, but instead mostly congregated on the sidewalk outside. . . . Religious instruction of the boys—the girls were completely neglected—was conducted in dark and dingy vestries or by itinerant rebbes . . . teaching the Bar Mitzvah chant and the Kaddish prayer. Little congregations sprang up like mushrooms. . . . Every other

day the community was rocked by some new scandal connected with the administration of Kashrut.[37]

The natural constituency for the Conservative rabbi was the sons and daughters of the east European immigrant community, some of whom Rubenovitz saw either filling the pews at the Sunday services of the Reform temple or socializing in front of the Orthodox synagogues on the holiest days, but with the majority turning away from all religious mooring. Rubenovitz reminisced: "Wherever I went I appealed to the younger generation to accept a new synthesis of tradition and modern spirit; to provide well-housed and properly graded Hebrew schools; to participate actively in the upbuilding of Zion; to create a comprehensive program of adult education."[38] Rabbi Rubenovitz remained at Mishkan Tefila for the remainder of his life and saw it become the leading Conservative congregation in New England.

More typical of the challenges facing a seminary graduate in the early years of the twentieth century was the tenure of Rabbi Paul Chertoff at Congregation Beth Israel, Rochester. Founded in 1874 as an Orthodox synagogue for Rochester's growing community of east European immigrants, the congregation was forced by its younger, more acculturated members to engage seminary-ordained Nathan Blechman in 1906 as "preacher and teacher." The title "rabbi" was reserved by the congregation for the communal Orthodox rabbi. In 1911, seminary-ordained Paul Chertoff was elected to serve as preacher "to deliver lectures and teach in daily school at a salary of $1,200, for one year trial by a vote of 35-16." During his tenure, Rabbi Chertoff instituted a broad program of education through the congregational school and youth clubs. His Hebrew school and Sunday school ledger lists thirty students in the weekday Hebrew school and thirty in the religious (i.e., Sunday) school. The rabbi was principal of the school and taught the most advanced classes, "Hebrew translation and writing, Abbreviated Humash and Jewish Biblical History and Religion."[39]

The congregation was in constant financial difficulties. In addition, it was split by the issue of rov versus preacher, which was but an indication of a more deeply rooted division between adherence to Orthodoxy and a growing tendency toward Conservative Judaism among younger members. Rabbi Chertoff encouraged the latter, a group of whom left in 1915 to organize a Conservative congregation, Beth El; he himself departed a year later.

The Conservative rabbi in the first decades of the century perceived himself as standing in confrontation with Orthodoxy, whether he was a liberal like Rabbi Rubenovitz—in conflict with members of his congregation opposed to his program of changes in synagogue ritual—or a traditionalist like Rabbi Chertoff—chafing at the denial of rabbinic status by the Orthodox communal rov and his followers. Schechter saw things differently. To him the real confrontation was with Reform, which, he charged, asserted that the destruction of the Law is its fulfillment. He feared that the Conservative rabbi would be tempted to emulate his visibly successful Reform colleague.

Schechter felt strongly about the importance of continued study for the rabbi. "It is hardly necessary to remark," he noted wryly in his inaugural address in 1902, "that the Jewish ministry and Jewish scholarship are not irreconcilable." Six years later, having observed that in the American rabbinate scholarship and success were not synonymous, he urged his graduating students to "engage in some scientific work, publishing occasionally a learned article."[40] Believing the study of the Torah to be a transforming sacrament without which the rabbi would become a mere technician, Schechter urged rabbis to become exemplars of an enlightened piety based on learning.

The United Synagogue of America

As demonstrated by Rabbi Chertoff's experience in Rochester, early graduates of the seminary often served congregations that did not accord them full rabbinic status (whether in title or in fact) and that were almost always in financial straits as well as in ideological conflict. Clearly, what was needed, a growing number of rabbis felt, was a national organization of like-minded congregations that would recognize the rabbinic status of seminary ordination, help strengthen the individual congregations through programmatic aid, and help fashion the ideological stance of Conservative Judaism.

In the fall of 1909, Rabbi Rubenovitz suggested to Rabbi Charles I. Hoffman, president of the Alumni Association of the Jewish Theological Seminary, that the graduates of the seminary take the lead "in the establishment of a union of conservative forces in America." At its annual meeting, the association voted unanimously to sponsor the launching of "a Union of Conservative Congregations." Some of the purposes of such a union would be "to print an inexpensive prayerbook; to prevent the isolated man [i.e., rabbi] and the isolated synagogue from being swallowed up; to see that our views are fairly represented in the Jewish press; to have a regular traveling representation; to have a Sabbath observance department."[41] The leaders of the Alumni Association urged that the organization be a union of *Conservative* congregations, but the more traditionally oriented rabbis and the leaders of the seminary insisted that it be directed, as Cyrus Adler expressed it, to the sixteen hundred congregations remaining outside the fold of Reform. Schechter argued that, traditionalist and liberal forces having joined to found the seminary, the same should obtain in establishing the union of congregations.

A "union for promoting traditional Judaism" had long been a dream of Schechter. As coworkers in his endeavor he sought out those lay leaders of the seminary who were traditional Jews, chief among them Cyrus Adler, to whom he wrote, in the summer of 1909, that such an organization was of signal importance to the American Jewish community. Nearly four years later, Schechter and the converts to the cause among his friends, together with the disciples in the rabbinate whom he had trained and inspired, were ready to bring their dream to fruition.[42]

On Sunday, February 23, 1913, Schechter welcomed delegates of twenty-two congregations in Baltimore, Boston, Detroit, Montreal, New York, Norfolk, Philadelphia, Rochester, and Denver as well as some "thirty rabbis, the faculties of the Seminary, Dropsie College and Gratz College and a number of prominent laymen" to the large assembly hall of the seminary and invited them to join "the United Synagogue of America, which is entering upon its existence this day, [upon which] depends the continuance and the survival of traditional Judaism in this country."[43]

The meeting began in an auspicious way when the seminary's first graduate, the Reverend Dr. Joseph H. Hertz, who had just been elected chief rabbi of the British Empire, was called on to say a prayer. The afternoon session was devoted to discussing the platform of the newborn organization. As formulated in the preamble of the proposed constitution, it read:

> RECOGNIZING the need of an organized movement for advancing the cause of Judaism in America and maintaining Jewish tradition in its historical continuity, we hereby establish the United Synagogue of America, with the following ends in view:
>
> TO ASSERT and establish loyalty to the Torah and its historical exposition,
>
> TO FURTHER the observance of the Sabbath and the Dietary Laws,
>
> TO PRESERVE in the service the reference to Israel's past and the hopes for Israel's restoration,
>
> TO MAINTAIN the traditional character of the liturgy, with Hebrew as the language of prayer,
>
> TO FOSTER Jewish religious life in the home, as expressed in traditional observances,
>
> TO ENCOURAGE the establishment of Jewish religious schools, in the curricula of which the study of the Hebrew language and literature shall be given a prominent place, both as the key to true understanding of Judaism, and as a bond of holding together the scattered communities of Israel throughout the world.[44]

How the platform would be understood and applied would depend on the nature of the congregations that this "union" was meant to serve.

Dr. Judah L. Magnes, who had left the pulpit of the country's leading Reform congregation to enter the ranks of Conservatism, brought the matter to the floor. Speaking as a "layman" who was neither Orthodox nor Reform, he expressed a desire to see the new organization make itself the representative of a new third trend. The sense of the meeting, the *American Hebrew* observed, was evidently against this suggestion, and the principle was laid down that the new movement should combine the tendencies common to both Orthodox and so-called Conservative congregations. Schechter underscored this sentiment in his keynote address: "This United Synagogue has not been called into life with any purpose of creating a new division." He envisioned the United Synagogue as an organization broad enough to encompass congregations called Orthodox, as well as "such congregations as have not accepted the Union Prayerbook nor performed their religious devotions with uncovered heads."[45]

Schechter's words heartened the traditionalist rabbis, who could continue to call themselves Orthodox. The rabbis of liberal orientation, though unhappy with Schechter's stance, accepted it as a necessary compromise for the time. In practical terms, Schechter's position virtually guaranteed that the ferment within the congregations would continue, with the rabbis pulling and being pulled either to the right or to the left. At the conclusion of the founding session, Schechter was elected to the presidency of the United Synagogue, and a board of twenty-one members was chosen to work with him.

At the second annual meeting of the United Synagogue, presided over by Dr. Cyrus Adler, Schechter's chosen successor, Mordecai M. Kaplan, head of the seminary's Teachers Institute, presented a report of the Committee on Education. A total of 4,481 students (2,385 boys, 2,096 girls) were enrolled in the religious schools of the twenty-four congregations affiliated with the United Synagogue. The congregations, Kaplan pointed out, "have to maintain a double system of schooling in order to meet the wishes of the two classes of members that are usually to be found in every congregation, namely, those whose slogan is 'more Judaism,' and those who ask for 'less Judaism.' Most congregations, therefore, maintain both a Sunday School and a Hebrew School."[46] The textbooks were "beneath criticism," Kaplan asserted, and the teacher situation was not better. Some teachers possessed "no qualifications beyond the ability to read beforehand the lesson in some elementary textbook used by the children." Only one-third of the children attended more than once a week, and there was no uniform curriculum, no grading system, and hardly any advanced classes. He challenged the United Synagogue to help "create a demand for more Jewish education" and urge its extension to those below and above the school age through kindergartens, junior congregations, and uniform standards for bar mitzvah and confirmation practices and children's services.[47]

The Sabbath Observance Committee devoted itself to "furthering legislation on the observance of the Sabbath, in issuing calendars, and in bringing to the attention of the people the need of a great Sabbath observance." The Committee on Propaganda sent visiting speakers and organizers to congregations needing guidance and direction. The Committee on Religious Observance concerned itself with finding work for "men and women who desire to observe the Sabbath . . . with work among university students . . . the publication of a book of sermons . . . and efforts . . . to secure the observance of Jewish law by Jewish institutions."[48]

The fourth annual convention, meeting on July 9–10, 1916, mourned the loss of its "founder, master and beloved friend," Dr. Solomon Schechter, who, three years before the founding of the United Synagogue, had written of the proposed organization: "This will be the greatest bequest which I shall leave to American Israel."[49]

Schechter's Legacy

Schechter's bequest was greater, however, than the synagogal union he had established. It was a religious movement emanating out of a theological seminary that in a dozen years had developed into one of the primary centers of *Jüdische Wissenschaft*; a growing body of congregations and rabbis hewing out a new path in American Judaism; and an emerging ideology, as yet unarticulated, but sharply focused.

When Schechter arrived in America, as Cyrus Adler noted, he saw a vision of creating a theological center which would be all things to all men, reconciling all parties and appealing to all sections of the community. It did not take him long, however, to recognize that the radical nature of Reform and the insular stance of Orthodoxy would permit, at best, only competitive cooperation. He was convinced that neither could secure the future of a living Judaism in America. Radical Reform's attempt to dispense with the sacred language and to emphasize the universal elements at the expense of the ceremonial law and its national aspects, he was certain, must result in disaster. Orthodoxy was a reservoir of piety and learning but stagnant, and therefore, as Schechter observed, subject to a process of constant attrition which must become dangerous if the tide of immigration should be stopped for a few years. The tide did come to an end less than a decade after Schechter's death. By that time, the children of the immigrants who had arrived found that the institutions that Schechter had fashioned and the disciples he had trained and inspired presented to them a Judaism that better served their spiritual needs as Jews and as Americans than Reform or Orthodoxy.

It was Schechter, also, who pointed to the symbiotic relationship of Zionism and Judaism in America. According to Samuel Halperin, "It was Schechter . . . who won for the tiny Zionist following in America [in the early years of the twentieth century] its first great accretion of strength—

the Conservative Movement in Judaism . . . despite the threats and im-
precations of the Seminary's Reform-dominated Board of Directors."[50] In
"Zionism: A Statement," published in the *American Hebrew* in 1906
and circulated as a pamphlet by the Federation of American Zionists,
Schechter proclaimed:

> Zionism declares to the world that Judaism means to preserve its life by
> not losing its life. It shall be a true and healthy life . . . not only for the
> remnant gathered within the borders of the Holy Land, but also for those
> who shall, by choice or necessity, prefer what now constitutes the
> Galuth. . . .
>   The activity of Zionism must not be judged by what it has accom-
> plished *in* Zion and Jerusalem . . . but by what it has thus far achieved
> *for* Zion and Jerusalem, through awakening of the national Jewish con-
> sciousness. . . . Zionism . . . is the Declaration of Jewish Independence
> from all kinds of Slavery, whether material or spiritual. . . . Whilst con-
> stantly winning souls for the present . . . it is at the same time preparing
> for us the future, which will be a Jewish future.[51]

Schechter, Conservative Judaism's foremost personality, did not formulate an ideology for the movement. Rather he determined its parameters,
suggested its agenda, and set its tone.
  The leading ideologist of Conservative Judaism in the Schechter era
and its most active Zionist spokesman was Israel Friedlaender.[52] As a disciple of both Ahad Ha'am and Simon Dubnow, he labored for Jewish national and cultural rebirth in Palestine and for a vital Jewish community
in America, emphasizing the religious component. In 1907, in a lecture
he called "The Problem of Judaism in America," Friedlaender presented
an ideological base and visionary goal for Conservative Judaism:

> Judaism represents the inner characteristics of the Jewish people as
> manifested in its culture, in its mode of living and in its intellectual
> productivity. . . .
>   It was the fatal mistake of the Jews of emancipation, . . . that, in order
> to facilitate their fight for political equality they introduced Judaism not
> as a culture, as the full expression of the inner life of the Jewish people,
> but as a creed, as a summary of a few abstract articles of faith, similar
> in its character to the religion of the surrounding nations. . . .
>   If Judaism is to be preserved amidst the new condition . . . it must
> break the narrow frame of a creed and resume its original function as a
> culture, as the expression of the Jewish spirit and the whole life of the
> Jews. . . .
>   It will have to take in and digest the elements of other cultures . . .
> while it will endeavor to preserve all those features of Jewish practice

which give shape and vigor to Judaism. . . . It will give full scope to our religious genius. . . . It will develop our literature, create or preserve Jewish art in all its functions, stimulate and further Jewish scholarship. . . .

The only place where such a Judaism has a chance of realization is America. For America . . . is fast becoming the center of the Jewish people of the Diaspora. . . . The American Jews are fully alive to the future of their country as a center of Jewish culture.

A full and successful participation in all phases of American life is reconcilable with a deep attachment to Judaism in all its aspects. . . . In the great palace of American civilization we shall occupy our own corner, which we will decorate and beautify to the best of our taste and ability. . . . [53]

THE ADLER ERA (1915–1940)

Cyrus Adler's appointment as head of the seminary, following the death of Solomon Schechter in November 1915, was a temporary measure, since he was neither a rabbi nor a distinguished Jewish scholar. It was wartime, Adler explained, and the board was reluctant to appoint anyone but a native-born American. The logical candidates seemed to be Israel Friedlaender, who had acted in Schechter's stead during his sabbatical in 1911, and Louis Ginzberg, the senior member of the faculty. The board, however, was not enthusiastic about either man: Friedlaender was a communal activist and Zionist spokesman, given to a liberal view of traditional Judaism; Ginzberg's administrative ability was questioned. Still, both men positioned themselves to strengthen their candidacies. Ginzberg accepted the presidency of the United Synagogue when Adler resigned in 1917 and assumed the chairmanship of its Committee on the Interpretation of Jewish Law. For a decade he was, in effect, the movement's chief rabbi. Friedlaender published *Past and Present* in 1919, putting forward a vision of a vibrant Jewish community in America, with scholarship, verve, and imagination. Eventually, however, both men came to realize that their strivings were in vain. Ginzberg returned to his scholarly work; Friedlaender went to communal activity, which led to a martyr's death while he was on a mission of mercy to fellow Jews in the war-devastated Ukraine.

In 1924, after eight years as acting president, Adler was awarded the full title. Born in Van Buren, Arkansas, and raised in Philadelphia, he had been the recipient of the first doctorate in Semitics granted by an American university. During a long and distinguished career of service to the Jewish community, he served as president of Dropsie College, the American Jewish Historical Society, and the American Jewish Committee and as editor of the *American Jewish Year Book*, 1899–1905, and the *Jewish Quarterly Review*, 1916–1940. A proven administrator, a man of prudence and discretion, a devout Jew who moved in the highest circles of both the Jewish philanthropic and American intellectual establishments, Adler gave the seminary able, devoted, and effective leadership until his death in 1940. With the help of the Schiff family, Louis Marshall, and other friends, budgets were met and the buildings that house the seminary to the present day (save the library building dedicated in 1984) were erected. The quarter century of the Adler administration saw the emergence of the Conservative synagogue as a distinctive institution and the maturation of the Conservative rabbinate as it sharpened and refined the tools of its vocation.

Congregations and Schools

Schechter had charged the Conservative rabbinate "to organize new congregations and to raise the old ones from the sloth of indifference and the vice of strife into which they have fallen." The generation of rabbis that issued from what was now called "Schechter's Seminary" set itself to this task.[54] The post–World War I American scene saw a turning away from the ideology of the melting pot to that of cultural pluralism. Within the American rabbinate, Conservative rabbis became the most fervent adherents of the new ideology, taking their cue in this regard from Mordecai M. Kaplan.

Kaplan viewed with alarm the condition of the synagogue as he found it in his day. Noting that it owed its existence "more to the momentum of the past, than to any new forces created in this country," he warned that only the concentration of "all possible material and moral resources" might save the synagogue from "impending doom."[55] He proposed the creation of a new type of synagogue, a Jewish center whose purpose would be to afford its users "pleasures of a social, intellectual and spiritual character."[56] According to Kaplan, such a synagogue-center, a beth am, would include "Jewish elementary school facilities; recreational facilities such as gymnasia, showers, bowling alleys, pool tables, and game rooms; adult study and art groups; communal activities; religious services and festival pageants and plays; [and] informal meetings of friends and associates."[57] This was precisely the kind of synagogue that Schechter had warned against,[58] but precisely the kind of synagogue that might win the second generation Jew to Conservative Judaism. A synagogue so conceived and so fashioned had great appeal to a generation of American Jews, the children of the east European immigrants, who were desirous of maintaining a Jewish identity while intent on integrating fully into the American scene.

Reform temples, Marshall Sklare has written, "hesitated to expand their activities and to gain too many new adherents. . . . They were sus-picious of too much non-religious activity on synagogue premises, which would be an expression of racial consciousness." Moreover, they did not want to attract and serve "the unaffiliated," who were of a lower socio-economic class.[59] For its part, the Orthodox shul viewed expansion as change, and therefore resisted it, since any change was seen as fraught with peril to the faith. The "synagogue center" was solely the creation of the emerging Conservative movement.

How did such a synagogue come into being? In some instances it was established by seceding members of an Orthodox synagogue; more often it resulted from the transformation of an existing Orthodox synagogue. Thus, for example, in 1915 a group of young members of the Orthodox Beth Israel synagogue in Rochester, New York, left to form a new con-gregation that would better answer their needs. They issued a call: "Rec-ognizing that it is our duty as Jews to bear witness to the truths of our Faith in our days and generation as our Fathers did in theirs . . . we hereby constitute ourselves a Jewish congregation for the purpose of conserving Judaism." Their new synagogue, which they later named Beth El, pro-vided the following: family pews for men and women; prayers in Hebrew and English, conducted by a rabbi, cantor and Jewish choir; head covering and tallith; congregational singing without an organ; daily services, with special services on Friday evening, Saturday morning, and holidays; and daily and Sunday school.[60]

Within a year the group purchased and adapted for synagogue use the Park Avenue Baptist Church and by 1922 could boast of having the largest Jewish congregational school—270 pupils. In the 1920s and 1930s Beth El's sisterhood, men's club, junior congregation, Boy Scout troop, youth clubs, and athletic teams made it the "established coequal" of Re-form Temple B'rith Kodesh, long the city's largest, wealthiest, and most prestigious congregation.[61]

Rabbi Ralph Simon described the first steps in transforming the Or-thodox Rodef Sholom synagogue in Johnstown, Pennsylvania, into a Con-servative congregation in the 1930s:

This congregation was a traditional Orthodox synagogue which was founded by East European immigrants about the year 1885. I was the first Seminary rabbi to serve them. . . . The decision to invite a Conser-vative rabbi came as a result of the insistence of a younger group who correctly believed that the next generation would join the Reform temple unless the synagogue was modernized. The older generation was suspi-cious of innovations. . . . The rabbi had to walk a narrow line in order to remain on good terms with the elders as well as to satisfy the rebellious young people. . . . Very few changes [were made] in the Sabbath and holidays Synagogue service. It was only in Friday evening late service that changes could be made, since the leaders of the older group did not attend and did not recognize it as an authentic service. The major changes were sermons in English, insistence on decorum and interpretation of the liturgy. One activity which won the elders over to a trust in the new rabbi was the formation of a Talmud study group.

The major area of change was in the cultural and social program. All the activities envisioned in the synagogue-center program of Dr. Kaplan were introduced. Adult education classes were organized. A good Hebrew school was conducted. There was an active Men's Club, Sisterhood and Youth Group. There were frequent programs of music, a new choir, dramatic presentations and guest speakers.

The unique aspect of the new Conservative rabbi was his multifaceted role. He was the preacher, pastor, teacher, executive and communal figure. . . . One activity of the rabbi was received with great approval by practically the entire Jewish community. He began to appear before church and civic groups who welcomed an erudite Jewish spokesman. As the rabbi became popular with the non-Jewish community, his popularity increased with the Jewish community.[62]

Traditionalist Conservative rabbi Israel H. Levinthal, whose Brooklyn Jewish Center offered the entire gamut of synagogue center activities, was aware of the accusation that "Synagogue Centers have tended to detract from the centrality of religion in Jewish life."[63] In 1926 Levinthal wrote in defense of the institution: "If the Synagogue as a Beth Hatefilah has lost its hold upon the masses, some institution would have to be created that could and would attract the people so that the group consciousness of the Jew might be maintained. The name center seems to work this magic with thousands who would not be attracted to the place if we simply called it Synagogue or Temple. . . . The Center is a seven-day synagogue. From early morning to late at night its doors should be open. It is true that many will come for other purposes than to meet God. But let them come."[64]

Most congregations, of course, could not afford a full program of religious, cultural, social, and athletic activities. For them, "synagogue-center" meant that it aimed to serve the religious and cultural needs of the majority of its congregants by fulfilling a threefold function as *beth ha-tefillah* (house of worship), *beth ha-midrash* (house of study), and *beth ha-knesset* (house of assembly).

At the heart of each congregation, old or new, were the services of worship—daily, Sabbaths, and holidays. Conservative innovations included the incorporation of English into the traditional service, insistence on decorum during prayers, and the introduction of the late Friday night service. The following account by a "successful professional man who had the usual Orthodox upbringing" demonstrates the magnitude of change represented by the Conservative synagogue:

> The biggest shock of all to me was the temple services on New Years and Yom Kippur. . . . I was born and bred in an orthodox shul with the accompanying multitudinous prayers, jams of people and children all joined together in a cacophonous symphony of loud and sometimes raucous appeals to the Almighty. Here it was so different. A large group of Jews, men and women, sitting quietly together for hours at a stretch, subdued prayers, no mass movements, no rustling and bustling, no weeping and wailing, no crying children, just the music of the choir and cantor being the only loud sounds heard. Truly it was a revelation to me. I looked around the congregation and saw a large number of younger people sitting intently and reverently reading their *Machzors* [holiday prayer books]. They supplied you with a talis and yarmelke [skullcap] at the door. No carrying packages. The Machzor was clear, concise and arranged in order so as to be easily followed when the rabbi announced the page numbers. I soon immersed myself in the prayers and responsive readings. I listened to the sermons and understood what it was all about. . . . It is so different for me. Like another world.[65]

The late Friday night service was an innovation that evoked mixed responses. Rabbi Louis M. Levitsky explained the rationale for the practice and shared his misgivings about it in the *United Synagogue Recorder* in 1927:

> The late Friday night services are an attempt to satisfy what we have been hoping are the spiritual needs for public worship for the vast preponderant majority of our men and women who because of economic pressure cannot be with us on Shabbos morning. Were it not for these late Friday night services by far most of the members of our congregations would not be found in the synagogue between Yom Kippur and Rosh Hashonah. With the further weakening of the Shabbos atmosphere at home, it becomes all the more necessary to bring into the lives of our men and women a little of the Shabbos spirit. This we hope to accomplish by the late Friday services.
>
>   But the problems that we face are several and serious. We must face a congregation tired from a day's business and anticipating the Saturday business for which they prepare most of the week. To this physical weariness and preoccupied mind is added the drowsiness that follows a heavy meal. Add to this the very small initial interest in religious worship and we can readily see where the weather (either good or bad), and now the radio, have become obstacles to people attending Friday night

services. But if the speaker is one whose name is familiar or the topic promises to be thrilling, they may succeed in overcoming these difficulties. For after all, most of our people come to the late Friday night services to listen to the address and hardly to worship. The older people have worshipped at sunset, and among the rest we find many who cannot follow interestingly, or not at all, the Hebrew of our services. We must therefore make the worship part of these services interesting by means of elaborate choirs, and thus make a concert out of the service. I believe that few of us delude ourselves with believing that any of these or all combined give the worshipper a sense of reverence.

Rabbi Levitsky urged that the pulpit not be used, as it too often was, for "book reviews, dramatic criticisms and political orations," but rather for the "instruction of the congregation . . . to teach Jewish history, Jewish theology, or Jewish ethics," arguing that "once the congregation will feel that the rabbi utilizes his time in the pulpit toward real spiritual ends and constructive teaching they will in time be infected with the spirit."[66]

In the emerging Conservative synagogue, great emphasis was placed on the youth element—the congregational school and clubs. A 1938 report on the Beth El religious school in Rochester, New York, prepared by Dr. Ben Rosen, indicated the problems facing the Conservative congregational school of that period. The Beth El school had a Sunday department and a weekday department. Of the 275 pupils, 144 attended one day a week for two hours, 76 twice a week for one hour each, 42 three times a week for a total of five and a half hours, and 13 four times a week. Only 20 percent of the pupils, then, received more than two hours of instruction per week. Rosen found that the curriculum "was not well formulated . . . nor strictly adhered to; nor in terms of the purposes of a school of this type . . . sufficiently rich in content or broad enough in scope. . . . The educational achievement . . . falls below the standard of better congregational schools of this size in other communities." Compared with the total Jewish school population in Rochester, Beth El's students attended fewer hours but for a longer span of years. Almost one-third of the former received instruction five times a week, but only 9 percent were in the high school department; at Beth El, where less than 5 percent attended four days a week, 35 percent were students in the older preconfirmation and confirmation classes (meeting two hours a week).[67]

Since it was generally recognized that the hours per week and the number of years spent in the classroom were inadequate, supplementary education through club activities was offered by almost all Conservative congregations. The program at New York's B'nai Jeshurun Synagogue in 1923 was as follows:

There are six such Junior Clubs, the Z'eire Yisroel of boys between 10–12, B'nai Am Chai of boys between 12–14, the Girl Scout Troop of girls between 10–12, the Emmunoh Club of girls between 12–14, the Beta Alpha and the B'nai Jeshurun Juniors. The existence of these clubs has been a wonderful asset for the Religious School, because of the splendid group spirit which they have created. . . .

Center Clubs have also been organized for a group of adolescents between the ages of 14–17. There is a group of "Scrolls and Quills," consisting of boys between the ages of 14–16. There is an Alumni Association consisting of boys and girls of the ages from 15–18, who were formally [sic] members of the Religious School, and from whom come some of the leaders of the younger groups.[68]

The United Synagogue

The fifth annual convention, held on July 1–2, 1917, marked the coming of age of the United Synagogue. Delegates heard that a Kosher directory listing three hundred eating places in 107 cities had been prepared; that textbooks were in the offing; that regional units had been established and were functioning; that twenty-six congregations had affiliated during the year; and that Rabbi Samuel M. Cohen had been appointed full-time supervising director. Particularly significant was the establishment of a "standing Committee of the United Synagogue to be known as the Committee on the Interpretation of Jewish Law."[69] This was in response to Dr. Adler's call a year earlier to reverse the "semi-anarchy" that had developed because of the "absolute independence and autonomy of every congregation" by appointing "some sort of Rabbinical authority, which, fully basing itself upon the Jewish law and tradition, can interpret at least for the people of the congregations whom we have brought together in union."[70]

The committee's creation marked a step forward in the transformation of the United Synagogue from an association of "non-Reform" congregations to the representative body of a self-consciously emerging movement within American Jewry. The Committee on the Interpretation of Jewish Law, consisting of "five members learned in the Law" and chaired by Professor Louis Ginzberg, issued responses written by the chairman, covering a broad range of issues. Among them were: May a synagogue sell its old building for commercial purposes to use the money for the building of a new one? May a part of the lower floor of a synagogue be set aside as a social center and be used for prayers as well? A vexing issue that rent many congregations was that of mixed seating.

Question: Would family pews be a departure from traditional Judaism?
Answer: The earliest reference to separating the sexes in the houses of worship is found among the Jews Therapeutae of which Philo tells us

that the women were separated from the men by a wall three to four cubits in height so that they might listen to the service without infringing the rules of modesty becoming to women. As we otherwise do not lead the life of these Jewish "monks and nuns" there does not seem to be any valid reason why we should attempt to imitate their synagogue regulations. . . . In Talmudic times the sexes were separated in the synagogue . . . not by a partition, only that the men had their places on one side and the women on the other. . . . The women's gallery is, comparatively speaking, a modern invention. Taking into consideration the conditions of today, I do not see any reason for insisting on continuing the women's gallery, but the separation of the sexes is a Jewish custom well established for about 2,000 years and must not be taken lightly.[71]

When the convention turned to consider the plight of Jewry abroad, an issue developed that was vigorously debated before culminating in a historic decision. The Resolutions Committee proposed that the United Synagogue join with the Zionists throughout the world in voicing the claim "for a Jewish homeland in Palestine." Despite the opposition of a determined minority led by Cyrus Adler himself, a rephrased resolution was adopted that affirmed Dr. Friedlaender's assertion that "unless Zionism is realized, there is no hope for Judaism here or elsewhere" and that Conservative Judaism could not possibly fulfill its highest function "unless Zionism is realized." The resolution read:

> WHEREAS, the present world crisis opens a new vista for the realization of the ever-cherished hope of the Jewish people for the rehabilitation of the land of our forefathers,
>
> BE IT RESOLVED, that the United Synagogue of America reaffirms its faith in the fulfillment of our ancient Zionist hope in the early restoration of Palestine as the Jewish homeland as the means for the consummation of the religious ideas of Judaism.[72]

What gave added importance to this resolution was the fact that organized Reform Jewry was zealously anti-Zionist.

From the inception of the United Synagogue, its annual conventions brought together seminary faculty, rabbis, and laymen. The first three presidents—Schechter, Adler, and Ginzberg—were members of the faculty; the next two—Elias L. Solomon and Herman Abramowitz—were rabbis. It was only in 1927, with the election of S. Herbert Golden, that the tradition of lay presidents began.

Golden's election reflected the growing assertiveness of the organization's lay leadership. A reporter commenting on the 1926 convention stated that the rabbis did too much of the speaking, though outnumbered ten to one. Two years later, the newly elected lay president stated diplomatically but firmly what the division of responsibilities would hence-forth be: "By drafting the *baalebatim* (lay leaders) into the administrative tasks of the organization, we can leave the rabbis free to devote them-selves to the religious and educational phases of our program."[73]

The Rabbinical Assembly

An alumni association of the Jewish Theological Seminary had been organized in 1901. In 1918 it took a more appropriately descriptive name—the Rabbinical Assembly of the Jewish Theological Seminary. In 1933, in recognition of the growing number of non-seminary graduates on its roster, and in order to establish a position of independence and parity in the triad of Conservative Judaism with the seminary and the United Synagogue, it changed the designation from "of the Jewish Theo-logical Seminary" to "of America."

As the Rabbinical Assembly grew, reaching 158 members in 1922, its annual convention came to serve a number of important functions. It was the forum where the central concerns of the movement could be voiced and ideological differences debated. It also offered rabbis an opportunity to air professional problems and frustrations. Rabbis com-plained, for example, that most of their time and energy had to be given to the management of struggling synagogues rather than to intellec-tual activity. At the same time, however, they recognized the necessity of the administrative function. They had to create new synagogues or strengthen frail, struggling ones by filling their membership rolls, estab-lishing their schools, initiating their activities, and securing their bud-gets. They also had to build new buildings and then worry lest the leaders of the congregation decide that a new building needed a new rabbi.

Jacob Kraft described his duties as rabbi of Beth Shalom Congrega-tion, Wilmington, Delaware, in the 1930s: "This rabbi acted as a *kol bo* [all-purpose functionary], taking charge of the services, preaching weekly, explaining Torah portion on Sabbath morning. He supervised the school, taught, took care of assemblies, visited the sick several times a week, the hospitals, visited the home during shivah period and conducted services, taught some converts of Judaism (about 3 or so during the 30's) etc., etc."[74] What kept rabbinic morale alive was the conviction that what they were doing was of crucial importance to the future of Judaism in America, that they were engaged in creating something new, and that even "managing" a synagogue called for a high order of creativity. They were also strengthened by two of their teachers at the seminary, Morde-cai M. Kaplan, who, as one rabbi phrased it, "opened a new world to me," and Louis Ginzberg, whose towering scholarship validated their tradi-tionalist tendencies. Ginzberg provided solid roots; Kaplan gave them wings.

Schechter's expectation that the seminary training would make for an ideologically diverse Conservative rabbinate was prophetic. Such was the diversity that at the 1927 annual meeting of the Rabbinical Assembly, vice-president Louis Finkelstein felt impelled to present a paper on "The Things That Unite Us."[75] Still, while conservatives and liberals might disagree on the content of the tradition and the dynamics making for change, they were united in the view that, as Rabbi Norman Salit put it, "Orthodoxy has our yesterday, and Reform our to-day, [but] Conservatism has our to-morrow."[76] Finkelstein was even bolder in asserting this point: "We are the only group in Israel who have a modern mind and a Jewish heart, prophetic passion and western science. . . . And it is because we are alone in combining the two elements that can make a rational religion, that we may rest convinced that, given due sacrifice and willingness on our part, the Judaism of the next generation will be saved by us. Certainly it can be saved by no other group. We have before us both the highest of challenges and the greatest of opportunities."[77]

At the 1928 conference, president Max Drob was proud to announce as "the greatest accomplishment of the year" the organization of a committee on Jewish law to replace the United Synagogue committee that, for its ten-year tenure, had been dominated by Louis Ginzberg. The R. A. committee, reflecting the diversity within the movement, consisted of four members representing the liberal tendency—Mordecai Kaplan, Jacob Kohn, Herman Rubenovitz, and Solomon Goldman; four representing the conservative tendency—Max Drob, Louis M. Epstein, Louis Finkelstein, and Julius H. Greenstone; and two others—Harry S. Davidowitz and Morris Levine—chosen by the eight. A unanimous opinion would become authoritative; lacking unanimity, "the opinions of the minority as well as the majority" were to be submitted to the questioner. Chairman Drob hailed the creation of the law committee as the first step toward the organization of an American "Beth Din Hagadol . . . which will study the problems arising in our new environment, and solve them in the spirit of our Torah. . . . The time is not too far distant when all ritual and domestic problems will be brought to us for solution."[78]

The question of how contemporary problems were to be addressed and solved and the ideological underpinning of the procedure to be pursued were considered in the three major papers presented at the 1929 R. A. conference. Max Drob, calling his address "A Reaffirmation of Traditional Judaism," spoke as follows: "As to the content of Judaism, there is really no difference between the Traditional Judaism as it was taught at the Seminary and Orthodox Judaism. We believe in the divine revelation and the duty to practice the Laws of Judaism as promulgated in the Torah, as interpreted by the Talmud and as codified by the Sages of Israel." Referring, no doubt, to Mordecai Kaplan's God concept, he asserted, "I certainly shall not accept the mandate to create a God pleasing to certain elements. My God cannot be made to order." And to the colleague who ten years earlier had pleaded, "If the young must dance, let them dance in the Synagogue; if they must play, let them play in the Synagogue; if they must swim, let them swim in the Synagogue," his response was that they *have* danced, played, and swum in the synagogue, "but they still have to pray in the Synagogue. . . . It is about time that we and not the laymen's committee on Ritual decide whether the prayers are to be retained or not." Emphasizing his uncompromising loyalty to the received tradition, Drob climaxed his exhortation by citing Cyrus Adler's words, "What has been preserved for four thousand years, was not saved that I should overthrow it."[79]

Drob's successor to the presidency of the Rabbinical Assembly, Louis Finkelstein, titled his presidential address "Traditional Law and Modern Life." In it he argued that the religious "restrictions which bore easily on our ancestors of the ghettos, can be observed by us only with great difficulty. . . . It is impossible to expect the mass [of American Jews] to give the greater part of the holiday to Synagogue and prayer and at the same time to maintain that they are enjoying the festival." He asked: "Have we, rabbis, any authority to deal with the problem of Jewish custom and Law so as to bring our observance more in conformity with the ideals of Judaism than it is under the general practice today?" The solution, he argued, was to be found in legislation through reinterpretation:

> The position that has been held before us by all the great scholars of our people . . . is that recognized authorities may take it upon themselves to accept, for the purposes of interpreting the law, the lenient principles established by ancient scholars rather than the more severe opinions that may accidentally have crept into general practice. We shall, where facts warrant it, seek to take advantage of such leniencies as the law permits and such adjustments as it warrants. . . .
>
> Once more, after many years, a group of rabbis are prepared to deal with the problems of Jewish Law and life not merely from a technical and repressive attitude, but from one of worldly wisdom and mature understanding.[80]

Eugene Kohn, speaking for the religious liberals in the Rabbinical Assembly, questioned whether "judicial interpretation is a sufficient method for the adjustment of Law to life."

> When man had the conception of the Law as a perfect and sufficient rule of life, the search for a hidden meaning of the Law that would reconcile it with their vital interests was an honest search for something that they believed to exist. . . . It is unwarranted aspersion on the honesty of our forefathers to assume that they deliberately created legal fictions in order to circumvent a law. From our modern point of view, however, which

regards as a human institution . . . a search for something that we do not believe to exist and the devising of a legal fiction . . . ceases to be honest interpretation and becomes legislative amendment masquerading as interpretation. . . .

Dr. Finkelstein being impressed with the danger of spiritual anarchy . . . has chosen to preserve the formal method of Orthodoxy even while discarding the naive theology by which alone that method can find legitimate moral sanction.

Admitting that the attitude advocated by him and his colleagues, disciples of Mordecai M. Kaplan, would be considered dangerous by more traditionally minded colleagues, Kohn argued that "the crisis which confronts Judaism at the present time is an unprecedented one and reliance on the precedents of the past will not suffice for the present emergency . . . in which life itself has put Judaism in a position where it must live dangerously or die." He urged acceptance of the viewpoint of Dr. Kaplan's disciples:

At the present time the Torah functions in our life not in any strict sense as Law, but rather as lore, as a nexus of inherited habits and attitudes that we honor because of their inherent value and because of their emotional associations, but that we do not either in theory or practice accept as an infallible guide in all the situations of life and that we cannot by any means impose on our fellow Jews. Under such conditions, it seems impossible to escape from the necessity and responsibility of exercising a large measure of individual judgment and allowing a large measure of individual liberty in applying the principles of our Torah. . . .

We conceive of God's guidance being exercised in other ways than by juridic interpretation of the received Torah and do not shudder with fear at the thought that the Jewish Nation may have to assume a consciously creative share in the development of the Torah by which its conduct is to be guided.[81]

By the time that the Rabbinical Assembly met for its fortieth annual convention in June 1940, its membership had grown to 282, which represented an increase of about 40 percent during the preceding decade. The Committee on Jewish Law reported deliberating on a broad range of issues: the use of an organ at Sabbath and festival services; consumption of cooked vegetables and broiled fish in nonkosher restaurants; autopsies; civil marriage; birth control; whether a physician may act as a mohel; and the question of relief for the *agunah* (a woman whose husband has disappeared or abandoned her without having granted her a Jewish divorce), a problem that had been troubling the assembly since the first years of its existence.

The convention theme, the state of the rabbinate, afforded an opportunity for serious self-examination. Rabbi Morris Adler of Congregation Shaare Zedek in Detroit reminded his colleagues:

> Whereas in our day of specialization every profession has contracted the area of its intensive study and operation, the office of the rabbi has, on the contrary, assumed new and multiple duties. . . . He is, or is expected to be, at once scholar, teacher, priest, pastor, preacher, administrator, communal-leader, social worker and ambassador of good-will. To him come many and diverse appeals for assistance, for counsel, for . . . leadership. . . . In the brief span of a fortnight a rabbi, to give a concrete example, has been approached on behalf of the Yiddish Scientific Institute, the Zionist organization, the publication of a Biblical encyclopedia, a B'nai B'rith project, the Federation of Polish Jews and the Agudath Israel. Nor is the appeal exclusively for financial aid. The rabbi is urged to take part in the leadership of these numerous causes.

Adler argued that the rabbi could not remain aloof from "the multitudinous manifestations of Jewish life in the community" nor "from the social and cultural movements of American society. . . . In the desire to preserve the character and strength of the synagogue [the rabbi] must seek to guide, to channel and inform with something of his spirit, the streams of Jewish life that course outside of the synagogue."[82]

Given the reality of the expanding responsibilities of rabbis, Mordecai Kaplan proposed a division of labor:

> It will not be possible for the rabbi, whose official duties bind him to the synagogue, to keep up with the growing needs of Jewish life. . . . The principle of division of labor would have to be applied to the function of the rabbi. Some rabbis would serve congregations, others would specialize in educational work, and still others in the various types of communal endeavor. . . . It will be necessary for men with a rabbinic training and outlook to serve in administrative capacities in every phase of Jewish activity. . . . When Jewish institutions come to prefer as administrators those who have had an intensive Jewish training, the entire trend of Jewish life will be transformed from one of decline to one of ascent.[83]

The Quest for an Ideology

Cyrus Adler saw the seminary as an institution "for the teaching and promotion of Jewish learning . . . to create a learned Rabbinate who will use this learning to a religious purpose—the promotion and practice of Traditional Judaism. . . . The Seminary has not modified its prayerbook, it has not changed the calendar, it has not altered the dietary laws . . . and although some of its founders and some of its graduates have, without protest from the Seminary, attempted changes in the ritual, the Seminary itself has never adopted or approved of any of these changes." While Adler accepted Schechter's view that "the Seminary must always shelter men of different types of mind," he expressed the hope that what had happened to Schechter would happen to those who came forth from the school: "At one time in his life, [Schechter] was accounted a Liberal, [but] as the years passed [he] became more conservative."[84]

While some seminary graduates may indeed have become more conservative, with the passage of time the greater number became more liberal. This tendency was due only in part to the cultural climate of twentieth-century America and the demands of congregants. By far the greatest influence on seminary students and graduates in terms of their liberalization was the teachings of Mordecai M. Kaplan. During his one-year tenure (1932–1933) as president of the Rabbinical Assembly, Kaplan delivered an address to his colleagues on the subject "The Place of Dogma in Judaism," in which he urged them to reorient their thinking from the past to the present and future:

> If we want to render the Jewish religion articulate and communicable, nothing could be so pointless as to state the beliefs we hold concerning the Jewish civilization of the past. . . . [They cannot] serve as a definition of what the Jews really mean to do with their Judaism. That can only be set forth in terms of "wants" on which all Jews can unite. . . . The affirmations of Judaism would no longer have to be assent to facts, the truths of which are often challenged by reason. . . . Rather they would set forth what [they] expect of [their] civilization, if it is to inspire [them] to perpetuate it, to enrich it, and to make it a source of blessing to mankind.[85]

Samuel Rosenblatt, among the most traditionalist of Conservative rabbis, maintained that "Judaism may be a civilization as Professor Kaplan describes it" but that "belief in God and his Torah . . . is the center of gravity which cannot be disturbed without danger to the entire structure." Asserting that the lack of a "clearly formulated creed" was the cause of Judaism's weakness at present, he exhorted his colleagues to clarify their views, "the dogmas we subscribe to." He concluded: "There are few thinkers as eminently fitted to this task as Professor Kaplan."[86]

Kaplan did define his views in his magnum opus, *Judaism as a Civilization*, published in 1934, but they were hardly to Rabbi Rosenblatt's liking. A work that exerted singular influence on Conservative rabbis and laymen, it came in for wide-ranging criticism as well. In analyzing "The Current Versions of Judaism" in the volume, Kaplan gave no place of its own to Conservative Judaism, discussing it only as "the right wing of Reformism" and again as "the left wing of Neo-Orthodoxy." He completely ignored the considerable body of Conservative literature fashioned by his colleagues—papers delivered at United Synagogue and Rabbinical Assembly conventions, articles in periodicals, discussions, and correspondence in which he himself had participated. The views of Israel Friedlaender received but fleeting notice; those of Louis Ginzberg, Louis Finkelstein, Jacob Kohn, Eugene Kohn, Israel Levinthal, and Louis Epstein, none at all!

Rabbi Max Arzt, who identified himself as "a disciple of Dr. Kaplan," hailed the volume as a "courageous, comprehensive analysis of the complex problems facing Jews and Judaism in our day," expressing the belief "that no creative reconstruction of Jewish life will come unless we reckon with the basic issues so splendidly formulated and analyzed therein." Still, Arzt criticized Kaplan's ambivalence toward religion and its place in Jewish civilization, warning that "Judaism becomes an empty shell" without the religious dimension. Arzt was also critical of Kaplan's demoting "the mitzvot to the primitive status of folkways," an act whose effect was to "destroy their main sanction and purpose as forms of group expression dedicated to God and uniting Israel with its God." Arzt went on to summarize the dominant centrist position in Conservative Judaism as he saw it:

> Dr. Kaplan says that revision of the entire system of Jewish custom is imperative. . . . What we need is not an official revision but rather some agreement as to what forms of observance we should emphasize. . . . Conservative Judaism aims to do just this thing. It does not announce its negations. It proclaims its affirmations. It stresses Sabbath observance, the dietary laws, the retention of Hebrew in prayer and in Jewish education, and the restoration of Palestine. There is so much in our law that is vital, soul-stirring and full of aesthetic possibilities that we should not be concerned about the inevitable obsolescence of a few mitzvot. . . .
>
> Judaism is essentially Halachic in its nature and development. . . . Judaism will always demand of the individual to exert all efforts to order his life according to the Torah rather than order the Torah to fit exactly into his personal desires and tastes. Therefore, I differ with Dr. Kaplan who would eliminate the concept of Law from Mitzvot. Such a suggestion would violate the criteria which he himself suggests. It would destroy Judaism's continuity, its individuality and its organic character.[87]

The most representative and comprehensive formulations of Conservative Judaism in its period of early maturation (1920–1945) were provided by two young seminary-trained rabbis: Louis Finkelstein, who went on to become the head of the movement during the period of its greatest growth (1940–1972), and Robert Gordis, who became Conservative Judaism's most articulate ideologist. In 1927 Finkelstein focused on those elements that he saw as common to all Conservative Jews:

1. *The Concept of God.* We are a unit in our understanding of the ultimate basis of all religious life and insist that only in our faith, which is frankly based on our emotions and intuition, but which we seek to formulate with proper recognition of the scientific facts which have been established, is there room for the conception of God that can remain living and effective in our children's minds.

2. *Our Attitude Toward the Torah.* Judaism is a developing religion, which has undergone an historical and definable change through the periods of the prophets and the rabbis; this change was not one of deterioration and ossification but of growth, self-expression, and foliation. . . . Because we regard the Torah as prophetically inspired . . . the legalism of the rabbis as the finest and highest expression of human ethics, we accept the written and oral Law as binding and authoritative. . . . But we are entirely unwilling to cajole or intimidate our following or our children into being loyal to the Torah through threats and the fear of punishment.

We are drawn to the Torah [by] love for its ceremonies, its commandments, its rules, and its spirit. We delight in its study, and find in it comfort and consolation, discipline and guidance.

3. *Our Attitude Toward Change in Ceremonial.* If the shifting of values and the introduction of new devices will actually bring Jews back to God, to the Torah, and to the Synagogue, they will doubtless be accepted. . . . As to the proposed innovations and new interpretations, there is none of us so bigoted as to refuse to cooperate with those who are attempting them, provided always that the ultimate purpose of change is to strengthen the attachment of Israel to the whole of the Torah, and that it does not defeat its own end by striking at the fundamentals of Judaism.

4. *Our Attitude Toward Israel.* Israel is a great and ancient people, it has done great things and there is no reason for doubting its ability to create further. We love it as our people. We recognize that it has weaknesses. . . . Our loyalty to it does not depend on our belief in its singular excellence. We decry any attempt to establish loyalty to it on such basis. . . .

5. *Our Attitude Toward Palestine.* We want to see Palestine, . . . for which we have an intuitional, unreasoning and mystic love . . . rebuilt as the spiritual center of Israel. . . . We want Eretz Israel established as a Jewish community; if possible as an autonomous one.

6. *Our Attitude Toward the Hebrew Language.* We are entirely sympathetic to the establishment of Hebrew as the language of conversa-

tion, Jewish literature and learning. . . . We find ourselves in opposition to those who have permitted the excision of Hebrew from their prayerbook, and have dropped it as a subject for instruction in their schools. A Hebrewless Judaism we conceive to be an impossibility.

7. *The Seminary.* Through it we have become not only comrades in arms, but also brothers. . . . Within our ranks there is wide difference of opinion . . . [which should not] justify any separation in our ranks, in view of our substantial unity of outlook and the difficulty in serving our cause even when we are together. . . . We are all of us "Seminary Men."[88]

Fourteen years later, Robert Gordis presented his formulation of Judaism as "A Program for American Judaism," a chapter in his book *The Jew Faces a New World.*[89] Conceding that Conservative Judaism's critics were not altogether unjust in calling it a watered-down Orthodoxy or a timid Reform because it lacked a platform, Gordis attributed this lack to the American character of the movement, which was "pragmatic rather than theoretical." He then went on to point to a number of thinkers who had shaped his own understanding of Conservative Judaism: Zacharias Frankel, Solomon Schechter, Ahad Ha'am (Asher Ginzberg), Israel Friedlaender, Louis Ginzberg, and Mordecai M. Kaplan. The influence of Kaplan is clearly discernible in many of Gordis's formulations, particularly in his definition of Judaism as the evolving religious civilization of the Jewish people:

> The evolving character of Judaism: Judaism has never been static; it has always adapted itself to new thought and new conditions. . . .
>
> Judaism is the culture or civilization of the Jewish People. It is not merely a religion, in the sense of a few articles of belief or a handful of practices, as Reform teaches, or a longer list of beliefs and practices, as maintained by orthodoxy. It is a complete culture or civilization, possessing all the varied attributes of language and literature, art, music, customs and law, institutions and history. . . .
>
> Since it is the civilization of the Jewish people, Judaism must have a locale, one corner of the world where it can grow and flourish. . . . Therefore, Palestine, as the center of the Jewish people, must be the living center of Judaism, and the more strongly and firmly Jewish life is established in the Homeland, the richer Jewish life will everywhere be. . . .
>
> Judaism has many aspects, but religion is primary. The recognition of God in the world and the drive for ethical perfection are the two great Jewish contributions to the world—two that are really one. . . .
>
> Jewish nationalism and religion are the body and soul of a living organism.
>
> Jewish nationalism without religion is in danger of becoming . . . destructive and brutal. . . . Jewish religion without nationalism is a disem-

bodied ghost, without vitality and staying power. . . . Judaism as the evolving religious civilization of the Jewish people—therein lies the distinctive attitude of Conservative Judaism that makes it . . . the most vital and promising tendency for the future, if it adheres to its program with intelligence.[90]

THE FINKELSTEIN ERA (1940–1972)

Following Cyrus Adler's death in 1940, the man chosen to succeed him was Louis Finkelstein, a professor of Talmud and theology who had become Adler's assistant in 1934 and provost of the seminary three years later. Finkelstein was born in Cincinnati and grew up in Brooklyn, the son of a respected Orthodox rabbi who provided him with his early talmudic education. Finkelstein went on to earn a B.A. from the College of the City of New York and a Ph.D. from Columbia University, as well as ordination from the seminary. A charismatic personality, Finkelstein made the seminary the fountainhead of Conservative Judaism, while he himself became the acknowledged leader of the Conservative movement. The years of his stewardship saw Conservative Judaism emerge as the largest Jewish religious grouping on the American scene, with its influence extending into the community at large.

The factors leading to the growth of the Conservative movement were closely linked to social forces that were at work in American life in the years following World War II. The postwar phenomenon of suburbanization greatly affected Jews, drawing them in large numbers to new communities. The need to establish roots and secure status, combined with the elevated prestige of religion in general, produced a climate conducive to the establishment of new synagogues.

The Conservative synagogue, which by the late 1930s had become a "synagogue-center" offering religious, cultural, and social programming for the entire family, was ideally suited to meet the needs of Jews in the rapidly growing suburban communities. The Conservative mode of worship was one that returning Jewish servicemen had experienced in the armed forces, and Conservatism's broad ideological framework made it appealing to young families coming from a variety of religious backgrounds. In addition, as the Jewish religious movement that had had the longest and strongest identification with Zionism,[91] Conservative Judaism benefitted from American Jewry's identification with the new State of Israel.

Congregations and Schools

In March 1949, 365 congregations were affiliated with the United Synagogue; by 1954 that number had reached 492—serving a total of more than two hundred thousand Jewish families. The six hundred affiliated sisterhoods had a membership of some 160,000. The Rabbinical Assembly saw its membership grow from 282 in 1940 to 600 strong in 1954.

At the center of most suburban synagogues stood the congregational school. As the result of an aggressive program carried out by the Commission on Jewish Education of the United Synagogue, directed by Abraham E. Millgram, the complexion of Conservative Jewish education changed dramatically in the course of a decade. Curricula were planned, tested, evaluated, and published. A steady flow of publications included textbooks in Hebrew and in English that reflected modern pedagogical methods as well as a Conservative religious orientation; preschool materials; parent education guides; audiovisual aids; and school-administration manuals. With the cooperation of the Teachers Institute of the Seminary, which had been educating teachers for religious schools since 1909, a teacher-training program for nursery schools was established. Sunday school education was eliminated (save for the first two grades), replaced by the congregational or Hebrew school meeting two or more afternoons as well as Sunday.

The highly successful United Synagogue Youth movement (USY) first developed in the Midwest, as did Camp Ramah, which was established by the Chicago Council of the United Synagogue. In describing the camp, Rabbi Ralph Simon, chairman of the camp's Program and Operations Committee, said: "Creative self-expression will be the goal of the camp program, and the religious approach of Conservative Judaism will pervade the spirit of the camp." The official language of the camp was Hebrew, and the program included classes in Bible and Hebrew literature as well as athletics and the arts; services were conducted daily and on the Sabbath.

The first Conservative Jewish day school, offering Judaic as well as secular studies, opened in 1950 in Rockaway Park, New York, organized by Rabbi Robert Gordis. This was the beginning of a nationwide effort to provide a more intensive Jewish education than could be offered in the congregational supplementary schools, an effort that produced the network of Solomon Schechter Day Schools.

There were important developments in the area of liturgy during this period. In 1946, the Joint Prayer Book Commission of the Rabbinical Assembly and the United Synagogue published the *Sabbath and Festival Prayer Book* edited by Rabbi Morris Silverman. Robert Gordis, chairman of the commission, identified the three fundamental principles that had guided the work of editing and compilation: continuity with tradition; relevance to the needs and ideals of the present generation; and intellectual integrity. In conformity with the first principle, the prayer book followed traditional liturgy. The second principle found expression in the modern translation and the expansion of the liturgy to include responsive readings and hymns culled from various sources, both ancient and modern. In obedience to the last principle, a number of minor changes were made, such as referring to sacrifices as a past rather than a future obligation and switching from a negative to a positive formulation in the preliminary blessings—from "thou hast not made me a woman . . . slave . . . gentile" to "thou hast made me in thy image . . . free . . . an Israelite."

The Rabbis

The 1950s and 1960s were the golden age of the American rabbinate. Religion was esteemed as a significant force in American life, and the synagogue was universally recognized as the preeminent institution of the Jewish community. Rabbis, therefore, were accorded wide respect and were able to exert influence far beyond their congregations.

The American rabbi became an extraordinarily busy man, and particularly so the Conservative rabbi. While the Orthodox rabbi preached on Saturday morning and the Reform rabbi on Friday evening, the Conservative rabbi preached at the two major services. The Orthodox rabbi dealt with b'nai mitzvah and the Reform rabbi with confirmands, but the Conservative rabbi dealt with both. The Conservative rabbi needed to work hard to retain his status in the institutions serving the most parochial Jewish interests, e.g., the *vaad hakashrut* (communal committee on kosher food), where the credibility of his Orthodox colleague was not in question even as he struggled for acceptance as a significant participant in interfaith activities in which his Reform colleague had long been the recognized spokesman for the Jewish community.

Here is how one Conservative rabbi serving a large congregation in the northeast described his activities in 1964:

> *Preacher.* Two sermons weekly at the late Friday evening and the Sabbath morning services, as well as at all holiday services.
>
> *Teacher.* Mondays: Men's Club Downtown Study Group, at noon. Subject: "The Living Talmud."
>
> Tuesdays: Confirmation class and post–Confirmation class. Subjects: "Conservative Judaism"; "History of Religions."
>
> Wednesdays: Three six-week semesters of Adult Education Institute, two courses each session. Subjects: "The Legacy of Solomon Schechter—Conservative Judaism"; "The Wisdom Literature of the Bible."
>
> Saturdays: Talmud study group, the tractate Berakhot. Monthly young-marrieds discussion group. Biweekly Sabbath-afternoon LTF study group.
>
> Sundays: Jewish current events discussion groups at post–minyan breakfasts.
>
> *Administrator.* The congregation dedicated its new synagogue building in June 1962 after four years of planning, fund raising, and building, in

all of which the rabbi participated.

Attended meetings of congregational board, Ritual Committee, School Committee, Adult Education Committee. Conducted weekly staff meetings. Wrote weekly column for congregational bulletin.

Ecclesiastical functionary. Officiated at forty-two weddings and thirty-nine funerals, all in the congregational family. Premarital interviews; attendance at wedding receptions, visited with bereaved families before funeral, officiated at one or more services at mourners' home, conducting a study session. Attended daily morning services on Sunday, Monday, and Thursday mornings. Officiated at unveilings, *Brit Milah,* and *mezuzah* (scriptural passage placed on doorpost) ceremonies in new homes.

Jewish community activities. On boards of Jewish Community Federation, Jewish Family Service, Israel Bonds, Day School, *Vaad Hakashrut.*

Community activities. Member, Mayor's Advisory Board; Committee on Religion and Race; boards of Association for the United Nations, Friends of the Public Library.

Weekly radio program, *From a Rabbi's Study.*

National activities. Member Executive Council, Rabbinical Assembly; Editorial Board, *Conservative Judaism;* Rabbinic Cabinet, Jewish Theological Seminary; Executive Council, American Jewish Historical Society; Publications Committee, Jewish Publication Society.

Pastor. Congregants felt free to call upon the rabbi for counseling at all hours.[92]

While the postwar period was one of dynamism and growth for Conservative Judaism, there were problems as well. Rabbi Max Gelb of White Plains, New York, for example, saw his congregation grow fourfold within a short period of time. "I have had to adjust myself to a new congregation . . . every few years," he told colleagues at the 1949 Rabbinical Assembly convention. More disturbing to him than increased numbers, however, was the impact of the suburban milieu: "The pull of the Christian environment is very powerful. Every Christmas presents a crisis in our school. There are scores of homes in which children experience a Christmas tree and parents argue with the rabbi whether it is a national or religious holiday."[93]

The task of winning over members to religious observance and genuine commitment called for unceasing effort, as the experience of Rabbi Reuben J. Magil of Temple Beth El in Harrisburg, Pennsylvania, testifies. His congregation held services on a daily basis—morning and evening—conducted Hebrew and Sunday schools, and had the usual gamut of congregational activities, but creative efforts were required to maintain it all. Thus, even though breakfast was served after the morning service to help assure a daily minyan, members still had to be drafted by the brotherhood's minyan committee. The Saturday morning service had an abridged *musaf* (closing section of Sabbath and holiday services), and the junior congregation was brought in to participate. Simhat Torah was revived by the introduction of a consecration service for children beginning their Hebrew studies. To assure a respectable attendance at the Megillah reading, a "sort of supper and carnival, the Annual Family Party" was inaugurated. Finally, to attract increased attendance, the Hebrew school graduation was moved from Sunday to the final Friday evening sermon service.[94]

A source of deep frustration to many Conservative rabbis was the relative disinterest of synagogue members in worship, unless it was linked to social activity, such as a bar mitzvah. A 1950 survey conducted by the United Synagogue was very revealing in its documentation of members' attitudes.[95] Some 60 percent of the respondents considered the Friday night prayers to be the "main Sabbath service." Nonetheless, the survey noted, attendance at Friday night services "is at an appalling disproportion with congregational membership." As for Saturday morning services, only 17 percent of respondents attended "quite regularly or often," while 77 percent attended "never or once in a while."

Another problem area in many Conservative synagogues was the absence of dignity in congregational demeanor and in relations with rabbis. This problem had existed since the earliest immigrant days, but the postwar move to suburbia and the proliferation of congregations made it all the more acute. Well-meaning men and women, new to congregational leadership, were often unaware of their responsibility for the maintenance of congregational dignity. At its 1952 convention, the United Synagogue asked its affiliated congregations to adopt a "Proposed Guide to Standards for Congregational Life." Among the standards adopted were those pertaining to rabbinic authority, Sabbath observance, kashrut, rites and ceremonies, dignity in fund-raising, and relationships with other congregations and the community.

The Seminary and the Movement

Throughout this period, Louis Finkelstein was the undisputed central figure of the Conservative movement. While his views (which, like Schechter's, became even more traditional) were often challenged, none could gainsay his scholarship, his administrative skills, and his contributions toward developing an ideology for Conservative Judaism. Finkelstein's appointment to national commissions by Presidents Eisenhower and Kennedy and his appearance on the cover of *Time* magazine helped to make him the most widely known and respected Jewish religious leader in America.

Chancellor (his title after 1951) Finkelstein not only believed that Conservative Judaism was the authentic expression of traditional Judaism and that "the Judaism of the next generation will be saved by us" but also was convinced that Judaism had a vital message for all of America. It was in that light that he launched the Conference on Science, Philosophy and Religion in order to give Judaism a platform in the academic world and the Institute for Religious and Social Studies to provide an ecumenical setting in which Judaism could join with the other great faiths in helping to establish the moral climate of America. The *Eternal Light* programs on radio and *Frontiers of Faith* programs on television depicted the riches of the Jewish tradition to a broad general audience. The prestige that accrued to the seminary from the success of these programs gave strength to the movement as a whole and status to its associated congregations.

Finkelstein attracted gifted coworkers, chief among them Rabbis Simon Greenberg, Max Arzt, and Moshe Davis. Greenberg came to the seminary from Philadelphia, where he had fashioned Congregation Har Zion as the model Conservative synagogue, noted especially for its educational system. As provost and vice-chancellor, his most notable contribution was the geographic expansion of the seminary: the founding of the University of Judaism in Los Angeles and the American Student Center and the Schocken Institute for Jewish Research in Jerusalem. Moshe Davis, the first American student to receive a doctorate from Hebrew University, was chosen, on his ordination from the seminary, to strengthen and expand its program of education. As dean of the Teachers Institute and provost, he created and expanded programs for disseminating Hebrew language and culture, including the flourishing Camp Ramah network and special programs in Israel. The Jewish Museum became an important component of New York's cultural life and, through traveling exhibits, extended its program nationwide. Max Arzt left his flourishing congregation in Scranton, Pennsylvania, to build the financial base for the seminary's and the movement's expansion. The joint campaign that he launched was seminary centered and reached out to the Conservative constituency through the congregations. Arzt succeeded not only in establishing a sound fund-raising vehicle but also in developing a cadre of Conservative lay leaders who were devoted to the seminary as the heart of Conservative Judaism.

Finkelstein focused on rebuilding the faculty. To the Schechter-chosen senior professors—Louis Ginzberg, Alexander Marx, Mordecai M. Kaplan—he added H. L. Ginsberg, Robert Gordis, Boaz Cohen, and Hillel Bavli. Finkelstein brought Saul Lieberman from Jerusalem, Shalom Spiegel from the Jewish Institute of Religion, and Abraham Joshua Heschel from Hebrew Union College.

In addition to the Rabbinical School, the Teachers Institute, and the College of Jewish Studies, the seminary expanded its mandate to include the Cantors Institute, the College of Jewish Music, and a graduate school offering master's and doctoral programs in all areas of Jewish studies. Offshoots of the professional schools were the Educators Assembly, which brought high professional standards to the field of Jewish education, and the Cantors Assembly, which transformed the American cantor from a pulpit-riveted leader of prayer to a clergyman engaged in the educational, cultural, and pastoral activities of the congregation.

Within the organizational structure of the movement itself a struggle for parity was waged between the seminary, the United Synagogue, and the Rabbinical Assembly. The posture of the seminary administration and faculty was staunchly traditionalist (Kaplan always excepted), with the more liberal members yielding to the authority of the chancellor and the rector, Saul Lieberman, who succeeded Louis Ginzberg as head of the Talmud faculty. The course of study emphasized rabbinics, and the Rabbinical School remained central to the institution.

The explosive growth of the United Synagogue in the postwar years under the imaginative leadership of Rabbi Albert I. Gordon was welcomed and aided by the seminary. But when Gordon accorded a central role to lay leaders in a projected formulation of an ideology for Conservative Judaism, his attempt was frustrated by the seminary administration. Finkelstein argued that ideological formulation should be the exclusive concern of rabbis and scholars who had adequate training in the Judaic sources. When similar confrontations led to Gordon's resignation, Simon Greenberg assumed his post while also retaining his position in the seminary administration.

Similarly, in 1952, when the Rabbinical Assembly began to pursue vigorously a solution to the problem of the agunah that the traditionalists on the Seminary faculty considered a departure from strict *halakhic* (legal) process, Finkelstein insisted that the seminary be given a partnership role in the endeavor. The resultant Joint Law Conference succeeded in removing decision making in this matter from the rabbinic group. It was only when the conference was dissolved in 1968 that the Rabbinical Assembly adopted what it considered an adequate solution to the problem.

In a movement that had from its inception accepted and permitted diversity and was committed to both tradition and change, the seminary's self-chosen role was that of upholder of the tradition and restraining influence on those impatient for change. Perhaps the greatest contribution of the seminary in the Finkelstein years was to demand spiritual content and halakhic discipline of a movement growing at so rapid a pace that sociological needs threatened to overwhelm theological imperatives. And perhaps its gravest mistake was doing this in so imperious a manner as to inhibit the evolutionary expansion of halakhic parameters in the 1940s, 1950s, and 1960s.

Within the Rabbinical Assembly itself, the question of halakhic development continued to engender controversy, with the mainline Conservative rabbis refusing to go beyond interpretation and the progressives urging "legislation." The disciples of Mordecai M. Kaplan proclaimed ever more aggressively their belief that Judaism had entered a post–halakhic age in which standards rather than laws obtained. The renaming of the Committee on Jewish Law as the Committee on Jewish Law and Standards in 1948 had been a symbolic accommodation to this view, though to the frustration of the Reconstructionists no substantial changes had ensued. The controversy came to a head at the 1958 Rabbinical Assembly convention at which Rabbis Jack Cohen, Jacob Agus, and Isaac Klein presented papers on "Theoretical Evolution of Jewish Law"[96] from left, centrist, and rightist positions respectively. Rabbi Cohen recommended that the Rabbinical Assembly "declare publicly that ritual can no longer be a matter of law" and that synagogue members be "encouraged to participate in an effort to develop standards for the entire community." Rabbi Klein reacted strongly: "Rabbi Cohen's paper is a philosophy of halachah to do away with halachah. . . . We have no common platform." For his part, Rabbi Agus attempted to mesh both viewpoints—halakhah and standards—into an integrated whole. The issues were highlighted but remained unresolved.

The first full-scale study of Conservative Judaism, published by sociologist Marshall Sklare in 1955, identified sources of strength, as well as shortcomings, in the movement. Sklare's probing analysis, which viewed social and economic factors as more significant determinants of behavior than theology or ideology, caused discomfort to many Conservative leaders, who were all too aware of the unresolved tensions within the movement. Sklare's basic argument was as follows:

(1) Conservatism represents a common pattern of acculturation—a kind of social adjustment—which has been arrived at by lay people. It is seen by them as a "halfway house" between Reform and Orthodoxy. It possesses no ideological system in the usual sense of the term. (2) The lack of ideology does not constitute a serious problem for most laymen, but it has harassed many rabbis. (3) There has been a somewhat greater interest in recent years in ideological problems. This is traceable to the operation of social forces, and to organizational trends in the Jewish community. (4) The resistances and obstacles to ideological clarification are formidable. (5) The rabbis have been very hesitant about officially sanctioning any departures from Jewish tradition. . . .

Although a few attempts have been made by the rabbis to develop a distinctive Conservative ideology and to obtain consensus, such endeavors have met with only very limited success. They have hardly been able to describe what is actually in existence in the Conservative movement, or to relate present realities to theoretical principles. The functionaries have not succeeded in spreading the few ideas which they have evolved among the laity. The concepts which they have presented are largely improvised. They express the needs and training of the religious specialists rather than of the mass of Conservative Jewry. The "ideology" has not as yet reached the stage of justifying—with any degree of sophistication—various institutional imperatives, although this is its present aim.[97]

Sklare paid tribute to Conservative Jewry for having made a "notable contribution to survivalism and . . . providing a significant institutional framework for a possible revivified Judaism." "Perhaps," he concluded, "Conservatism will not rest upon this accomplishment but will come to play a new and as yet unforeseeable role in the Jewish life of the future."[98]

THE COHEN ERA (1972–1985)

On his retirement, Louis Finkelstein was succeeded as chancellor by Gerson D. Cohen, a seminary graduate and professor of history at the seminary and at Columbia University. Important changes were taking place at the seminary and in the movement at the time of Cohen's accession. A new faculty, the majority American-born, seminary-educated, was replacing the European-trained giants. For rabbis this spelled the end of a special attitude of reverence for teachers who were "masters" and its replacement by one of simple respect for colleagues who were also scholars.

A new kind of student was entering the Rabbinical School. In earlier days the great majority had come from Orthodox backgrounds, while in the post–World War II era an increasing number came from Conservative homes, products of Camp Ramah and day schools—not an insignificant number of them sons of Conservative rabbis. The late 1960s brought a new group. Of the thirty students in the class of 1969, only four had attended a day school through high school, and only one had attended a yeshivah while in college. A member of the class described them as "virtually unfamiliar with the intensity of Jewish tradition, its complex web of law and custom, its texts . . . until [they] reached the Seminary."[99]

Tradition and Change

In the classic expression of the Conservative commitment, "tradition and change," the old administration had given nearly all emphasis to tradition. Under Chancellor Cohen, change was elevated to a position of parity, and the liberal elements in the faculty felt free to express their views. The primary focus of this new posture was the role of women in Judaism, especially their participation in public worship and ritual. On the congregational level, pressure for equal participation of women was growing, and the issue was being vigorously debated throughout the movement. A 1955 ruling of the Rabbinical Assembly had already made it possible for women to participate in the Torah service. Supporters of women's equality were further strengthened when the Rabbinical Assembly law committee issued a ruling *(takkanah)* in 1973 allowing women to be counted to a minyan.

It was not surprising, therefore, when the 1973 United Synagogue convention adopted a resolution urging admission of women to the Rabbinical School of the seminary. Four years later the Rabbinical Assembly convention called on Chancellor Cohen to appoint a committee to study the matter. He did so, establishing the Commission for the Study of the Ordination of Women as Rabbis, with himself as chairman and fourteen commission members drawn from the faculty, rabbinate, and laity representing the gamut of views in the Conservative movement. Regional meetings at which opinions were aired and testimony taken disclosed wide-ranging support for the admission of women to the Rabbinical School. The commission's report, issued in 1979, argued that there were no halakhic barriers to women's ordination. The vote of eleven to three in favor of ordination was an appeal to the faculty to follow suit, for it was the faculty's legal prerogative to make the decision.[100]

Cohen assumed personal leadership in the struggle to win approval from a faculty that was so bitterly divided on the issue it took four years for the crucial vote to take place. On October 24, 1983, with some of the traditionalists absenting themselves, the faculty voted thirty-four to eight, with one abstention, to admit women into the rabbinical program of study. In May 1985 Amy Eilberg became the first woman to receive ordination from the seminary; a month later, at its annual convention, the Rabbinical Assembly accepted her to membership.

Calling the faculty decision "one of our proudest achievements," Cohen spelled out its significance in a letter to colleagues.

> It is important because this faculty had the courage to confront directly what had become to many a challenge to the relevance of halakhah in the contemporary world. . . . Perhaps, most important, this decision provides a paradigm for the way halakhah evolves within Conservative Judaism. The method is not new—countless examples can be found in the deliberations over the years of our Committee on Jewish Law and Standards—but it took an issue on which public opinion was so strong, and so divided, to familiarize our laity with the procedure, and with the flexibility within limits which it permits our movement. Most important, it enabled the Seminary to assert its authority as a leading force in determining the direction of Conservative Judaism.[101]

A group of rabbis and laymen of a traditionalist bent, who regarded the ordination decision as a deviation from halakhah in both substance and process, organized themselves as the Union for Traditional Conservative Judaism. But the great majority of rabbis and lay people accepted Cohen's assertion: "Our decision to ordain women is a prime example of the evolution of halakhah. Without controverting Jewish law, we have adapted it to the religious and ethical norms of a new generation. . . . I believe deeply that . . . we behaved as our ancestors did on occasion when they found new forms of response for new challenges."[102] Robert Gordis evaluated the decision and its consequences this way:

> If history is any guide at all, it is clear that this move, important as it is, will prove neither as world-shaking as its proponents believe, nor as catastrophic as its opponents maintain. . . .
> However welcome this accession of new strength and idealism may be, [the ordination of women] will not drastically transform the character and function of the rabbinate. . . .
> One important by-product of women's ordination will be the beginning of the end of the psychological reign of terror exerted by contemporary Orthodoxy over some rabbis and laymen in the Conservative movement. . . . By this act Conservative Judaism will have demonstrated that the Jewish tradition is truly viable and as sensitive to human needs and aspirations in the present as it has been in the past.[103]

In 1979 the seminary had published *A Guide to Jewish Religious Practice* by Rabbi Isaac Klein, the leading traditional scholar in the movement. The book grew out of a course on "Laws and Standards for Religious Observance" that Louis Finkelstein had invited Rabbi Klein to conduct beginning in 1959. The volume, which Chancellor Cohen described in his foreword "as written in the authentic spirit of the Conservative Movement," was intended, its author stated, as a "guide for those congregations that are affiliated with the United Synagogue and the World Council of Synagogues, as well as for individuals in accord with their principles." In spirit and form, the *Guide* followed the classic codes of the Jewish legal tradition. However, as the author noted, "in preparing this work I insisted on the authority of our Conservative Scholars and on the validity of the practices of our Conservative Congregations."[104]

Cohen continued the seminary tradition of devotion to Jewish scholarship and commitment to excellence. Under his leadership a new library building was completed, thus making the seminary's rich resource of books and manuscripts more easily available to students and scholars. Among graduates of the seminary who did not enter the pulpit rabbinate were young scholars who joined the faculties of leading universities in the United States and Israel. In 1985 members of the seminary faculty received significant honors: David Weiss-Halivni, professor of Talmud, was awarded the Bialik Prize (the Israeli equivalent of the Pulitzer Prize) for his completed four volumes of a ten-volume series, *Sources and Traditions;* David Roskies received a Guggenheim Fellowship; and Ivan G. Marcus was appointed chairman of the History of Judaism section of the American Academy of Religion.

The United Synagogue

In the immediate post–World War II era, the United Synagogue had played a central role in the expansion of Conservative Judaism, helping to establish new congregations in suburbia and providing them with guidance in administration, programming, and education. Its joint Commission on Jewish Education, working with the Rabbinical Assembly, had developed curricula, published textbooks, and made the afternoon Hebrew school the central educational institution of the movement. By the 1970s, however, the excitement had spent itself. What remained were mundane realities—retaining congregational loyalties (and dues) and trying to meet growing demands for service with a limited budget. Attracting lay leadership of a high caliber became increasingly difficult, and weakened morale was not helped by the realization that the United Synagogue had been relegated to the status of the least influential component of the triad of Conservative Judaism. Although it continued to participate with the Rabbinical Assembly and the seminary in addressing the challenges that faced the movement, it remained essentially a synagogue service agency.

Functioning as an effective service agency was a challenge of no small proportion, however. By 1985 a total of 830 congregations, most with men's clubs, sisterhoods, and youth organizations affiliated with the national movement, were being served through twenty regional offices. The number of synagogues in the Sunbelt states was on the rise—sixty-five in California, forty-eight in Florida—many of them young congregations in new areas, asking for extra guidance and service. The Solomon Schechter Day School Association had sixty-five affiliates, and United Synagogue Youth claimed the largest membership of any Jewish youth organization in the country.

A mere listing of the United Synagogue's departments and services demonstrates the range of its concerns: Programs; Synagogue Administration; Regions; Education; Israel Affairs and Aliyah; Youth Activities; Community Relations and Public Policy; the Joint Commission on Social Action; Tour Service; Book Service; Committee on Congregational Standards; and the *United Synagogue Review.*

Perhaps the greatest challenge facing the United Synagogue in the eighties was deciding how to respond to the demographic and social changes that were taking place in the Jewish community and in American society at large. Individual congregations were attempting to solve problems posed by growing numbers of divorced and single persons and single-parent families, the mobility of a salaried professional class, and the high rate of intermarriage. The national organization was beginning to coordinate and disseminate the programs and approaches created in the field and to provide guidance in these areas.

The Rabbinical Assembly

Between 1955 and 1985 membership in the Rabbinical Assembly increased threefold—from some four hundred to well over twelve hundred. In that period more than six hundred Orthodox and Reform rabbis applied for membership, while fewer than ten left for other rabbinic associations. In 1980 the Rabbinical Assembly counted 94 members in Israel, 29 in Canada, 11 in Latin America, and 7 in Europe.

New problems and challenges faced the rabbi of the 1980s and 1990s. Congregations grown large in the 1960s were seeking ways to humanize and personalize religious experience. The havurah, a product of the Jewish student counterculture movement of the 1960s, was seized on by a large number of synagogues as one hopeful approach. As noted earlier, Rabbi Harold M. Schulweis, who pioneered the use of havurot in Congregation Valley Beth Shalom, Encino, California, addressed his colleagues about the matter at the 1973 Rabbinical Assembly convention:

In our congregation, a havurah is comprised of a minyan of families who have agreed to meet together at least once a month to learn together to celebrate together and hopefully to form some surrogate for the eroded extended family. I know what it means for children to see [their fathers] with hammers and saws helping to build a sukkah . . . the havurot plan their own Sedarim . . . they wrestle with the Haggadah and the decision to add and delete . . . The havurah offers the synagogue member a community small enough to enable personal relationships to develop. It enables families to express their Jewishness. . . . Hopefully the synagogue itself will gradually be transformed into . . . a Jewish assembly [of] havurot. . . . My grandfather came to the synagogue because he was a Jew. His grandchildren come to the synagogue to become Jewish.[105]

Changing times and perceptions called for a new—or at least revivified—approach to liturgy as well. An ambitious publishing program was undertaken, with Jules Harlow, the Rabbinical Assembly's staff liturgist, as editor. The *Mahzor for Rosh Hashanah and Yom Kippur,* published in 1972, hewed to the tradition but widened the parameters to include modern readings and poems that touched more immediately on the contemporary historical experience of the Jewish people and the existential needs of the modern Jew. A similar eclecticism informed the contents of *Siddur Sim Shalom*, a prayer book for Shabbat, festivals, and weekdays, published in 1985, some four decades after the first Conservative prayer book appeared.[106] Also made available was a Haggadah with modern commentaries and liturgies for *S'lihot*, Tisha B'av, and Purim.

The seventy-fifth anniversary year of the Rabbinical Assembly—1975—was designated as a time for professional self-appraisal. Rabbi Wolfe Kelman, who had served for almost a quarter of a century as the organization's chief executive officer, urged an end to the unwarranted self-flagellation that had characterized such undertakings in the past. He was particularly perplexed, he told his colleagues at their annual convention, by the "internal and external chorus of anxiety and despair" that had accompanied the phenomenal growth of the Conservative movement. About Conservative rabbis, he asserted: "No other group of committed Jewish professionals in recent Jewish history has been more successful in achieving those goals to which it has been unequivocally committed."[107]

Not everyone shared Kelman's optimistic assessment. When Marshall Sklare took a second look at Conservative Judaism some twenty years after his original research, he found that the "group's progress in the 1950s and 1960s was so rapid that Conservatism overtook Orthodoxy and Reform and went on to achieve primacy on the American Jewish religious scene." However, noted Sklare, with all its apparent success, "the morale of the Conservative movement is on the decline. . . . Leaders are less satisfied with their movement . . . less sanguine about its future." Discontent and doubt, he said, were expressed particularly by the rabbis, who "have a special sensitivity to its problems."[108]

Already in 1965, in his presidential address to the Rabbinical Assembly, Rabbi Max Routtenberg had confessed: "During the past decades we have grown, we have prospered, we have become a powerful religious establishment. I am, however, haunted by the fear that somewhere along the way we have become lost; our direction is not clear, and the many promises we made to ourselves and to our people have not been fulfilled. We are in danger of not having anything significant to say to our congregants, to the best of our youth, to all those seeking a dynamic adventurous faith that can elicit sacrifice and that can transform lives."[109]

One cause for the crisis of morale in the Conservative rabbinate, Sklare suggested, was its misreading of the future of Orthodoxy in America. Routtenberg disclosed that he and his friends studying in yeshivah had "decided to make the break and become Conservative" because they despaired that Orthodoxy could hold the next generation of Jews to Judaism. "We loved the Jewish people and its heritage" and, seeing "both threatened, we set out to save them" through Conservative Judaism, the wave of the future.[110] But the unanticipated resurgence of Orthodoxy brought into question the old justification for turning to Conservatism—to secure Judaism's future.

Another cause for the crisis in morale was what Sklare described as "Conservatism's defeat on the ritual front, which can be demonstrated in almost every area of Jewish observance."[111] A study published in 1970, for example, disclosed that in Har Zion Congregation, Philadelphia, long regarded as the model Conservative synagogue, only 52 percent of members lit Sabbath candles, only 41 percent purchased kosher meat, and only 33 percent kept separate dishes for meat and dairy foods.[112] A 1979 study of Conservative Jews found that while 29 percent kept kosher homes, only 7 percent claimed to be "totally kosher."[113] Sixty-five percent attended synagogue less than once a month, and only 32 percent recited kiddush on Sabbath eve. There was little confidence among Conservative rabbis that the erosion of observance among Conservative Jews was reversible. They remembered the campaign for the revitalization of the Sabbath in the early 1950s with embarrassment. Hopes had been high; special rabbinic dispensation had been granted to drive to synagogue; an imaginative and far-reaching campaign was launched with great enthusiasm. Still, the measurable results were nil.

There was no lack of reasons adduced for the failure to elicit sacrifice, transform lives, and win widespread adherence to Torah and mitzvot. Some blamed the movement—and themselves. Rabbi Gilbert Rosenthal stated: "Despite our movement's official espousal of mitzvot . . . the pattern of personal observance among the bulk of our congregants is barely distinguishable from that of their Reform neighbors. . . . We have missed the boat in not making demands on our people . . . we have followed the outmoded and naive view of Schechter . . . that we must make a virtue of nonpartisanship. . . . He who seeks to be all things to all men, ends up being nothing to too many." Rabbi Jordan Ofseyer added: "Many of our people . . . have become Conservative for reasons of compromise rather than conviction. Can we reasonably expect them to evince excitement or enthusiasm? . . . Should we expect anything but a decline in the level of observance when congregants are not asked to make any . . . commitment to mitzvot?"[114]

Some blamed the seminary for failing to prepare rabbis in a realistic manner. Sklare observed that the seminary's curriculum, "centered about the study of the Jewish legalistic system," was appropriate for the training of rabbis who would be serving congregations made up of observant Jews, but was not relevant to the actual situation in most Conservative congregations. Moreover, Sklare noted, the emphasis on halakhah in rabbinic training apotheosized a rabbinate of authority. How then could a rabbi respect himself when he functioned in a world in which, as Sklare put it, "the sanction of a rabbi is no longer required for the correct practice of Judaism"?[115]

The Direction of the Movement

For the first third of its existence, Conservative Judaism was seen by many rabbis and laymen as synonymous with a modernized Orthodoxy. In the second third, it became a distinct movement, but one that still shared the "same neighborhood" with Orthodoxy, sociologically and ideologically. In the last three decades, however, there has been a clear move away from Orthodoxy and toward a rapprochement with Reform. This is due more to changes that have taken place within Orthodoxy and Reform than to changes within Conservatism itself. Two examples will illustrate.

In the early years of the State of Israel an approach was made to the Orthodox Hapoel Hamizrachi by some members of the Rabbinical Assembly who felt that a socially progressive Orthodox religious movement would make an ideal partner in the enterprise of nation building. Nothing resulted from the overture except the knowledge that cooperation with Orthodoxy, even its liberal branches, was not possible. For the past quarter of a century, in matters pertaining to the State of Israel, cooperation has been with Reform Judaism, which has become enthusiastically Zionist in its outlook.

For four decades Conservative Jewish scholars labored on the problem of the agunah. In the 1930s Rabbi Louis Epstein, a halakhic authority, attempted to cooperate with the Orthodox rabbinate on this matter, but to no avail. In the early 1950s there was talk of a joint beth din with the Orthodox Rabbinical Council of America. Professor Saul Lieberman and Rabbi Joseph B. Soloveitchik, it was reported, were in consultation. As soon as word of possible joint action reached the Orthodox establishment, however, all talks ceased.

While the commitment of Conservative Judaism to halakhah remained constant, the utilization of the halakhic process itself became more adventurous. The new boldness was most dramatically expressed in the area of religious enfranchisement of women. While liberal rulings in this area caused dismay in some quarters, they were seized on eagerly by substantial segments of the rabbinate and the laity. The rapid acceptance of change was documented in a 1983 survey of congregations that compared current practices with those in 1975: *aliyot* (being called to the Torah to recite blessings) for women equally with men—(1975) 29.3 percent, (1983) 59.4 percent; aliyot for women regularly or on some occasion—(1975) 49.8 percent, (1983) 76.7 percent; women included in minyan—(1975) 37.1 percent, (1983) 59 percent.[116]

The view that the liberal rulings on women signaled a definite shift in thinking about the parameters of the halakhic process was expressed by Seymour Siegel, professor of theology and ethics at the seminary, chairman of the Committee on Jewish Law and Standards, and the movement's most widely respected ideologist on halakhic matters. Siegel, who in 1977 had asserted that "the observance of Jewish law had been the main aim of the Conservative movement since its very beginning,"[117] expressed a modified view in 1985: "When Jewish law makes us insensitive, less human and more prone to withhold human rights from our fellow men, then it has lost its primacy in Jewish life. . . . Halacha is a means, not an end in itself. The means should be judged by the ends." Relating this specifically to the emergence of the women's movement, Siegel said:

> Try as one would, I am convinced that strict adherence to the demands of halacha would not permit the important changes in synagogue life which the past period has brought about. I am not bothered by that now. For it is clear in my mind, at least, that if strict halachic conformance frustrates our highest and best human instinct, then the halachic considerations should be secondary and yield to ethics and *menshlichkeit* (civility). . . . It is not the exact halachic norms that should be primary but the goals of the Law, indeed of Judaism, which are to follow the *derekh Hashem* (the way of the Lord), *laasot tzedakah umishpat* (to do righteousness and justice).[118]

A friendly critic, Orthodox scholar Michael Wyschogrod, in surveying the American Jewish religious scene in 1985, wrote: "While for a long time Conservative Judaism has been taking liberties with halacha that I could not approve, one still had the feeling that the movement was anchored in loyalty to Torah. In spite of everything it was not difficult to distinguish it from Reform Judaism. This is becoming far less the case."[119] He expressed the fear that if Conservative Judaism continued in the direction it was moving, "the fusion of the two movements cannot be too far in the future" and warned that "the absorption of Conservative Judaism by Reform . . . can only lead to tragic results." As if to confirm Wyschogrod's fear, Rabbi Alexander M. Schindler, president of Reform's Union of American Hebrew Congregations, claimed that Conservative Judaism was following Reform's lead: "It usually takes them about 10 years—like on the woman's issue," he stated, referring to Conservative Judaism's decision to ordain women rabbis, which Reform had been doing since 1972.[120]

For his part, Gerson Cohen was well aware that expansion of the halakhic "creativity" was fraught with problems as well as promise. In a message to members of Ometz, the organization of Conservative university students, he stressed the importance of "developing halakhah within the movement" in a manner that reflects "our approach to halakhah, which differs from the traditional approach of the Orthodox." At the same time, he called for "a renewal of halakhic observance . . . and for the generation of renewed halakhah." It was essential, he emphasized, "to establish limits to pluralism. Just as liberty must not give way to license, pluralism does not mean that everything is acceptable."[121] Whether Conservative Judaism was ready to be led in such a direction was the chief question confronting it as it entered its second century.

Dr. Cohen announced his retirement in 1985. In discussing the future of Conservative Judaism, he urged fellow Conservatives to view their movement "as the dynamic and developing phenomenon which it is," instead of allowing themselves to be defined "by what we are not."

In comparison with its sister movements, Conservative Judaism has proven to be remarkably cohesive and consistent. The extremes in beliefs and life-style in Conservative Judaism are much closer than the extremes in Orthodoxy; Conservative rabbis and congregations of the 1920s and 1980s are much more similar in ideology and practice than their counterparts in the Reform movement. Solomon Schechter would be more comfortable in a Conservative synagogue today than his contemporaries Dr. Kaufmann Kohler in a Reform temple or Rabbi David Willowsky in an Orthodox synagogue affiliated with the Union of Orthodox Jewish Congregations.

In the matter of continuity and change, the "center has held." The changes over the past century have been pronounced, but the continuity more so. The continuing quest for an ideology and the persistent enterprise of making the tension between tradition and change a vitalizing force characterize Conservative Judaism today as they did a century ago and in all the years between.

As Conservative Judaism enters its second century, the mood within the movement is one of concern and apprehension—concern about its vitality as it confronts the buoyant élan of Orthodoxy and apprehension about its long-range viability as it reads demographic projections that Reform will soon overtake Conservatism as American Jewry's "movement of choice."

Stocktaking marked by concern and apprehension has been a constant in the movement's centennial experience. In 1927, Rabbi Israel Goldstein asked, "As Orthodoxy becomes more de-Ghettoized and Reform more conservatized, what is left for the Conservative Jew to do?"[122] A quarter of a century later, Rabbi Theodore Friedman confronted this question: "Is Conservatism, viewed in historical perspective, merely a stopover for Jews on the way from Orthodoxy to Reform?"[123] Historically speaking, it needs to be noted that these disturbing questions were posed when Conservative Judaism was beginning to experience its two periods of greatest growth—in numbers, creativity, and influence.

Postscript

Between Fear and Faith

Rabbi Solomon Schindler came to the pulpit of Boston's leading congregation, Temple Adath Israel, in 1874 from a small Orthodox shul in Hoboken. In the next two decades, he led his congregation from traditionalism to radical Reform.

Rabbi Jacob David Willowsky (known by his acronym *Ridbaz*), author of a classic commentary on the Jerusalem Talmud, first came to America in 1900. When he returned three years later, the organization of Orthodox Rabbis, *Agudas Harabonim*, conferred on him the title *Z'kan Harabonim* (senior rabbi). Elected chief rabbi of Chicago, he nevertheless called himself "Jacob David, of the City of Slutsk, a guest in Chicago."

Dr. Israel Friedlaender, born in Poland, educated at the Universities of Berlin and Strasbourg, served as professor of Biblical Literature and Exegesis at the Jewish Theological Seminary of America. As an ideologist of Judaism he introduced to the American Jew the concepts of Diaspora Nationalism of Simon Dubnow and Cultural Zionism of Ahad Ha-am.

Each of the three wrote perceptive comments on American Jewry. The first two reacted to America, the melting pot, with Schindler yielding to it and the *Ridbaz* rejecting it. Friedlaender's vision for America was as a land of cultural pluralism in which the Jewish community could flourish.

Arthur Mann, biographer of Temple Adath Israel's rabbis, wrote:

It is doubtful that Solomon Schindler's aspirations were ever identical to those of his congregants. The latter wished to retain their Jewish identity; Schindler wished to destroy it. For him, Reform . . . was a first step toward a non-sectarian religion that would include the highest ethics in the Jewish Christian tradition. . . . Twenty-five years after his arrival in Boston, Solomon Schindler was a confessed Socialist and agnostic. . . . In September 1893 he and his congregants agreed to part, he to continue in free thought and socialism but later to return to Orthodoxy, they to hold fast to humanist Judaism.[1]

Schindler's successor, Charles Fleischer, continued in the ways of his predecessor and went beyond them. He called for an ethical humanism based on democracy to replace the traditional faiths—a new religion to be proclaimed by a new prophet like "Jesus, Isaiah." By 1908, he advocated intermarriage for America's Jews to build "a new nation to emerge from the melting pot." As Fleischer was moving from the ancestral faith toward a "free and natural religion" that would replace Judaism and Christianity, Schindler was returning to the ways of his ancestors, a return to traditionalism that he explained to his former congregation in late March 1911 in a sermon titled "Mistakes I Have Made":

> When I came to Boston I was confronted with one great problem which I was expected to solve; namely, how to get people into the synagogue. . . .
>
> I tried reform. . . . Neither the family pew, nor the choir and the organ, nor the abolishment of rites and rituals would fetch the neighbor. . . .
>
> I tried sensationalism—sensational lectures which the newspapers would publish. I went to the very verge of a yellow pulpit. . . . Christians came to hear me. They praised me for what I said. But while they filled the temple, my congregation remained absent.
>
> Reform should have meant merely a change of form, but not the destruction of the form. But in my shortsightedness . . . I did away with rituals and ceremonies. . . . I took away whatever symbolism there was.
>
> I believed in making the Jew like the Gentile. He was to be like [the] Gentile in appearance, in thoughts, in ceremonials, in everything. The more he became near to that ideal being like his Gentile fellowmen, the more I believed success would crown my work. It was a great mistake. There must be a difference. . . . The Jew we shall have in years to come will be something different. The melting pot will not melt him. Assimilation, in which I believed, is a failure.
>
> Fifty years ago we seemed near assimilation. Then a cloud out of the East brought here to us two millions of people . . . different from us in appearance and habits . . . and they brought a new spirit amongst us. . . . This great army strong in the old ideals acting upon and changing our mode of thought, demanding from us change—this was the hand of God.
>
> The Jew should differ from his neighbor. He can be on the same terms with him in politics, can be socially his friend, and he can do business with him from morning to night, but he must be, in his religion, a different person.
>
> We can never unite mankind into one great body. We can only unite them into groups.
>
> That was something I have learned, only too late.
>
> You may take a lesson from my experiences, and I pray to you to avoid the mistakes, which I made.[2]

Fleischer answered with a sermon in which he proclaimed: "I have gladly made the seeming mistake of encouraging assimilation." Before a half century had passed, the congregation of Temple Israel was far closer in spirit to the repentant Schindler than to the assimilationist Fleischer.

The *Ridbaz* first arrived in America at the end of 1900 and was accorded a royal welcome by the Orthodox Jewish community. Within five months he had obtained a sufficient number of subscriptions for his edition of the Palestinian Talmud and set sail for home. He returned in 1903 and made his home in Chicago.

In 1904, he wrote about and to the Jews of America, in the introduction to *Nimukei Ridbaz,* a commentary on the first two books of the Pentateuch.

The Jews came to the United States, a land blessed with prosperity. Here they prospered, and are honored among peoples. But the ways and customs of this land militate against the observance of the laws of the Torah and the Jewish way of life. For example, the rule that boys and girls must attend public school. A boy will spend most of his day in the public school where he learns the ways of the gentiles and becomes estranged from Judaism. Even when his father hires a tutor to teach him for an hour, all he will be able to learn is the prayers, and no more. Most boys of 13 and 14 don't even know to say their prayers.

Sabbath observance is very difficult for one who is not truly pious, for by violating the Sabbath he can earn more money. . . .

There are many God-fearing Jews in this land. When they see what is happening to their children, they curse the day they came to this land. I have also seen many Jews, who violate the Sabbath, yet whose hearts still ache, and who would flee if only they could. . . .

Brothers and friends! When I came to this land to visit my brethren . . . I responded to their pleas . . . and decided to settle among them, to try to remedy the situation. I felt moved to accept their entreaties, for I saw that they were strong and sincere in this desire. So I said to myself, perhaps I'll be able to establish here a great Yeshiva, and bring here fine students from Europe. American Israel will be built only through the study of Torah. It has happened often in our history that Torah was introduced into a land by but a few scholars.

If I do not succeed in my hopes for Torah, why remain a rabbi here?

My advice and urging is:

Even though the laws of this land make it obligatory for the father to send his son to school, permission is granted to a Jewish community or a congregation to establish its own school, where the boys can study Torah, as well as those subjects which are taught by "teachers." The Poles who have come to this country have done so. They have established schools in their churches, to preserve and foster their faith. Why should we not do the same for our children?

If we do not bestir ourselves now, I am sore afraid that there will be no Jew left in the next generation.[3]

To the Zionists of America, in convention assembled in Pittsburgh in 1903, he urged the establishment of day schools as the only answer to the dangers of assimilation: "Give your attention to the education of your sons, for most of them have so assimilated among the population . . . that in twenty years there may not be Jews or Judaism left in this land. . . . Establish a school in every synagogue, in which half the time will be for God [religious studies] and half for you [secular studies]. . . . Dear brothers: This letter is written with heart's blood and not with ink."[4]

Despairing of a future for Jew and Judaism in America, the *Ridbaz* left for the Holy Land in 1905, settling in Safed. A half century later the network of day schools that he urged began to become a reality.

Israel Friedlaender labored for national and spiritual rebirth in Palestine and for the fashioning of a vital Jewish community in America. He went further, emphasizing the religious component in Jewish nationalism and culture. "Judaism was essentially a *national* religion," he maintained; "the Jewish people was, first and foremost, a religious nation." Such a Judaism, stressing both its national and its religious character, he argued, is possible in America as nowhere else in the Diaspora. He put forth his thesis in "The Problem of Judaism in America," a lecture delivered before the Mikveh Israel Association of Philadelphia on December 8, 1907.

It was the fatal mistake of the Jews of emancipation . . . that, in order to facilitate their fight for political equality they introduced Judaism not as a culture, as the full expression of the inner life of the Jewish people, but as a creed, as a summary of a few abstract articles of faith, similar in its character to the religion of the surrounding nations. . . . Judaism became a church, the rabbis became priests and the Jews became a flock. . . . Jewish education . . . dwindled down to Sunday school experiments. . . .

If Judaism is to be preserved amidst the new condition . . . it must break the narrow frame of a creed and resume its original function as a culture, as the expression of the Jewish spirit and the whole life of the Jews. . . .

The only place where such a Judaism has a chance of realization is America. For America . . . is fast becoming the center of the Jewish people of the Diaspora. . . . America has every chance of also becoming the center of Judaism, of the spiritual life of the Jewish people in the dispersion. . . . The freedom enjoyed by the Jews is not the outcome of emancipation, purchased at the cost of national suicide, but the natural product of American civilization. . . . The true American spirit understands and respects the traditions and associations of other nationalities.

He who feels the pulse of American-Jewish life can detect, amidst numerous indications to the contrary, the beginnings of a Jewish renaissance. In the great palace of American civilization we shall occupy our own corner, which we will decorate and beautify to the best of our taste and ability, and make not only a center of attraction for the members of our family, but also an object of admiration for all the dwellers of the palace.

A vision unfolds itself before our mind's eye presenting a picture of the future American Israel. We perceive a community great in numbers, mighty in power, enjoying life, liberty and the pursuit of happiness; actively participating in the civic, social and economic progress of the country, fully sharing and increasing its spiritual possessions and acquisitions; yet deeply rooted in the soil of Judaism, clinging to its past, working for its future, true to its traditions, faithful to its aspirations, one in sentiment with their brethren wherever they are, attached to the land of their fathers as the cradle and resting place of the Jewish spirit; men with straight backs and raised heads, with big hearts and strong minds, with no conviction crippled, with no emotion stifled, with souls harmoniously developed, self centered and self-reliant; blending the best they possess with the best they encounter; adding a new note to the richness of American life, leading a new current into the stream of American civilization; a sharply marked community, distinct and distinguished, trusted for its loyalty, respected for its dignity, esteemed for its traditions, valued for its virtues, a community as the Prophet of the Exile saw it in his vision: "And marked will be their seed among the nations, and their offspring among the peoples. Everyone that will see them will point to them as being a community blessed by the Lord."[5]

Friedlaender did not live to see the renaissance whose beginnings he limned. He died a martyr's death in 1920 in the Ukraine while on a mission of mercy to the Jewish communities of that war-devastated land.

AND AT THE END OF THE CENTURY . . .

In the first decade of the twentieth century, Rabbi Solomon Schindler called for a radical change of direction for Reform Judaism: back to tradition! Rabbi Jacob David Willowsky urged the establishment of Jewish day schools. Dr. Israel Friedlaender envisioned a wide-ranging cultural and spiritual renaissance.

Were they afforded a glimpse of Jewish life in America in the last decade of the century, they would behold a Reform Judaism that has embraced a rediscovered traditionalism; a network of day schools that is radically reforming the Jewish educational scene, and wide evidence of a cultural and spiritual renaissance. They would be heartened by the presence of Jewish studies on the campuses of America's leading universities, by the continually expanding student bodies of the seminaries, by the quantity and quality of Jewish scholarly activity, and by the growing numbers of highly educated young Jews in halakhically committed communities and in congregations seeking spiritual fulfillment in sacred Jewish texts, ritual, and celebration.

And yet, they would hear a rising chorus of lament about the future, no less urgent in the last decade of the century than in the first. The more pessimistic would point to the demographic crisis of most serious magnitude brought on by a rate of intermarriage and a degree of assimilation unmatched in the Jewish historic experience. The more optimistic would explain that such crises are to be anticipated in a free and open society, that this has been the experience of every generation of Jews in America and will no doubt continue in the future but that American Jewry has over the years built up an arsenal of ideologies and institutions and has personnel motivated and trained to stand up to the challenge of survival. All admit that there will be casualties, among whom will be too many of our best and brightest, but new heroes of the spirit will also arise.

Who is to say what the future will bring? The long history of the Jews bears testimony to the proposition that when it comes to survival, the only certainty is uncertainty.

Israel Friedlaender offers guidance for a creative vision of the future of American Jewry:

There is an old rabbinic saying that after the destruction of the Temple the gift of prophecy passed over to children and fools. True, prophecy without inspiration, which predicts the future as a matter of fact, is childish and foolish, because no human eye can perceive and no human mind can calculate the innumerable and imponderable effects of the concatenation of human events. But prophecy as a matter of hope, the prediction of the future not as it will be, but as it ought to be, is indispensable for all who have, or desire to have, a clear conception of their duties towards the coming generations.

To Schindler's warning, to Willowsky's plea, to Friedlaender's vision, we add the challenge of this century's premier Jewish historian, Salo Baron:

One thing may be confidently asserted: If American Jewry turns from quantity to quality, if it builds its communal co-existence less upon the quantitative criteria of financial success, statistically measurable memberships or school attendance and costly and outwardly impressive buildings and institutions, and devotes more attention to the cultivation of the genuinely creative personality and of the substantive and enduring values in religion and culture, the new type of American Jewry will be a cause of pride and satisfaction.

To put it bluntly, if someone were to guarantee that in the next generation American Jews will harbor one hundred truly first-rate scholars; one hundred first-rate writers and artists; one hundred first-rate rabbis; one hundred first-rate communal executives and one hundred first-rate lay leaders—the total number would not exceed five hundred persons, a negligible and statistically hardly recognizable segment of the Jewish population—one could look forward confidently to American Judaism's reaching new heights of achievement.[6]

NOTES

PREFACE

1. *Publications of the American Jewish Historical Society* [hereafter cited as *PAJHS*] 18 (1909): 73–74.
2. W. M. Rosenblatt, "The Jews, What They Are Coming To," *Galaxy* 13, no. 1 (January 1872).
3. Jacob David Willowsky, *Nimukei Ridbaz* (Chicago, 1904).
4. Winthrop S. Hudson, *Religion in America* (New York, 1973), 441.
5. Simha Assaf, *L'Korot Ha-Rabbanut* (Jerusalem, 1922).
6. Association of the American Hebrew Orthodox Congregations, Circular (New York, 1888).
7. Cited in Abraham J. Karp, "The Origins of Conservative Judaism," *Conservative Judaism* 19, no. 4 (summer 1965): 39.
8. Henrietta Szold, *The Russian Jew in the United States,* ed. Charles Bernheim (New York, 1905), 18.

INTRODUCTION: QUEST FOR A VIABLE IDENTITY

1. W. Gunther Plaut, *The Rise of Reform Judaism* (New York, 1963), 138.
2. Michel Guillaume Jean de Crèvecoeur, *Letters from an American Farmer* (London, 1782).
3. Israel Zangwill, *The Melting Pot* (New York, 1909), 198–99.
4. Louis B. Wright, *Culture on the Moving Frontier* (New York, 1961), 168.
5. Joseph L. Blau and Salo W. Baron, *The Jews of the United States, 1790–1840: A Documentary History,* vol. 2 (New York, 1963), 576.
6. W. Gunther Plaut, *The Growth of Reform Judaism* (New York, 1965), 34.
7. *Maccabean* 1, no. 2 (November 1901): 66.
8. Emma Felsenthal, *Bernhard Felsenthal* (New York, 1924), 233.
9. Israel Friedlaender, *Past and Present* (Cincinnati, 1919), 159–84; and "The Problem of Judaism in America," a lecture before the Mickveh Israel Association, Philadelphia, December 8, 1907.
10. Chaim Zhitlowsky, *Gesamelte Schriften,* vol. 2 (New York, 1912), 187–286. Anarchist leader Emma Goldman wrote of Zhitlowsky in *Living My Life:* "An ardent Judaist, he never tired of urging upon me that as a Jewish daughter I should devote myself to the cause of the Jews" (370).
11. Horace M. Kallen, "Democracy *Versus* the Melting Pot," *Nation,* February 18 and 25, 1915; reprint, *Culture and Democracy in the United States* (New York, 1924), 124–25 (page citations are to the reprint edition).

12. Mordecai M. Kaplan, "Judaism as a Civilization: Religion's Place in It," *Menorah* 15, no. 6 (December 1928): 511.

13. Mordecai M. Kaplan, *Judaism as a Civilization* (New York, 1934), 513.

14. Ibid., 182.

15. Milton Steinberg, *To Be or Not To Be a Jew* (New York, 1941), in *Common Ground* (spring 1941): 15.

16. C. Bezalel Sherman, *The Jew within American Society* (Detroit, 1961), 208.

17. Will Herberg, *Protestant—Catholic—Jew* (New York, 1955), 201–2.

18. Sherman, *The Jew within American Society*, 223.

19. See Abraham J. Karp, "The American Jewish Community—Union Now or Ever?" *Proceedings of the Rabbinical Assembly of America*, vol. 25 (New York, 1961), 55–66.

20. Winthrop S. Hudson, *Religion in America*, 2d ed. (New York, 1973), 440–41.

PART ONE: THE SYNAGOGUE IN AMERICA

1. Salo Wittmayer Baron, *The Jewish Community*, vol. 1 (Philadelphia, 1942), 5.

1. THE SYNAGOGUE IN AMERICA: A HISTORICAL TYPOLOGY

1. Samuel Oppenheim, "The Early History of the Jews in New York," *PAJHS* 19 (1909): 73–74.

2. Ibid., 21.

3. Ibid., 75.

4. Ibid., 76.

5. See the statement of Jacob de la Motta in the introduction.

6. Jacob R. Marcus, *The Colonial American Jew, 1492–1776*, vol. 2 (Detroit, 1970), 857.

7. Jacob R. Marcus, *American Jewry—Documents* (Cincinnati, 1959), 88–92.

8. Ibid., 859, 856.

9. Franklin Hamlin Littell, *From State Church to Pluralism* (New York, 1962), 13, 14.

10. *PAJHS* 21 (1913): 4.

11. David De Sola Pool and Tamar De Sola Pool, *An Old Faith in the New World* (New York, 1955), 39.

12. *PAJHS* 39, no. 2 (December 1949): 194.

13. Charles Reznikoff and Uriah Z. Engelman, *The Jews of Charleston* (Philadelphia, 1950), 56.

14. Edwin Wolf II and Maxwell Whiteman, *The History of the Jews of Philadelphia* (Philadelphia, 1957), 143–44.

15. Jacques J. Lyons and Abraham De Sola, *A Jewish Calendar for Fifty Years* (Montreal, 1854).

16. Cited in *The Voluntary Church*, ed. Milton Powell (New York, 1967), 81.

17. Joseph L. Blau and Salo W. Baron, *The Jews of the United States, 1790–1840: A Documentary History*, vol. 1 (New York, 1963), 13.

18. Wolf and Whiteman, *History of the Jews of Philadelphia*, 225ff.

19. Israel Goldstein, *A Century of Judaism in New York* (New York, 1930), 52.

20. [I. J.] Benjamin II, *Three Years in America*, trans. Charles Reznikoff (Philadelphia, 1956), 76–77.

21. Simon Cohen, *Shaaray Tefila* (New York, 1945), 1–14.

22. Isaac Leeser, "The Jews and their Religion," in *An Original History of the Religious Denomination in the U.S.*, ed. I. Daniel Rupp (Philadelphia 1844), 368.

23. Ibid.

24. *Israelite* 3 (December 26, 1856): 196.

25. Ibid.

26. Leon A. Jick, *The Americanization of the Synagogue, 1820–1870* (Hanover, N.H., 1976), 174, 193.

27. Joseph Krauskopf, "Half a Century of Judaism in the United States," *The American Jews' Annual for 5648 A.M.* (New York, 1888), 72.

28. Reznikoff and Engelman, *Jews of Charleston*, 139–40.

29. W. Gunther Plaut, *The Growth of Reform Judaism* (New York, 1965), 9.

30. Isaac M. Fein, *The Making of an American Jewish Community* (Philadelphia, 1971), 65.

31. David Einhorn, [*Olath Tamid*] *Gebetbuch für Israelitische Reform—Gemeinden*, 2d ed. (Baltimore, 1862), 396–97.

32. Myer Stern, *The Rise and Progress of Reform Judaism* (New York, 1895), 41.

33. Ibid., 28–29.

34. Ibid., 41.

35. Isaac A. Wile, *The Jews of Rochester* (Rochester, N.Y., 1912), 12.

36. Ibid.

37. *Ritual for Jewish Worship* (Rochester, N.Y., 1885), v–vi.

38. Isaac M. Wise et al., *Hymns, Psalms and Prayers* (Cincinnati, 1866), 3.

39. *Extracts from Proceedings of Chicago Sinai Congregation at Its Annual Meeting, March 26, 1885, and Special Meeting, April 9, 1885* (Chicago, 1885), 2–7.

40. J. D. Eisenstein, "The History of the First Russian-American Jewish Congregation," *PAJHS* 9 (1901): 64.

41. Abraham Joseph Ash, "The Beth Hamidrash, New York," *Occident* 15, no. 12 (March 1857): 600.

42. Ibid.

43. Eisenstein, "History of the First Russian-American Jewish Congregation," 74.

44. Moshe Weinberger, *Jews and Judaism in New York* (New York, 1887), 2.

45. Oscar Handlin, *The Uprooted* (Boston, 1951), 124.

46. *Constitution and By-Laws of the Beth Hamidrash Hagadol of the City of New York*, revised and adopted at a special meeting, March 20, 1887 (New York, 1887).

47. *Constitution of the Congregation Kahal Adas Jeshurun with Anshe Lubtz* (New York, 1913), 15.

48. *Constitution Fun Shul Anshei Sefarad* (Yiddish) (n.p., 1918).

49. See Abraham J. Karp, "An East European Congregation on American Soil," in *A Bicentennial Festschrift for Jacob Rader Marcus*, ed. Bertram W. Korn (New York, 1976), 263–302. For an extended history of Beth Israel, see chapter 2.

50. *Occident* 13, no. 9 (December 1855): 467.

51. *Rochester Democrat and Chronicle*, September 20, 1886.

52. *Rochester Union-Advertiser*, April 5, 1895.

53. *Constitution of Agudas Achim Nusach Ari* (Yiddish) (Rochester, N.Y., 1911), art. 3, p. 3.

54. *Congregation Vaad Hakolel, Constitution and By-Laws* (Yiddish) (Rochester, N.Y., 1915), art. 2, p. 4.

55. *Constitution and By-Laws of the Congregation of Beth Israel* (Rochester, N.Y., 1906), art. 3, p. 1.

56. *Constitution of the Congregation Kahal Adas Jeshurun with Anshe Lubtz* (New York, 1913), sec. 5, p. 3.

57. See *The Jewish Communal Register of New York City, 1917–1918* (New York, 1918), 111–285.

58. Ibid., 111–12.

59. Ibid., 121–22.

60. *American Hebrew* (March 22, 1918).

61. Mordecai M. Kaplan, *Judaism as a Civilization* (New York, 1934), 428.

62. Mordecai M. Kaplan, "The Way I Have Come," in *Mordecai M. Kaplan: An Evaluation*, ed. Ira Eisenstein and Eugene Kohn (New York, 1952), 311.

63. Henry Kalloch Rowe, *The History of Religion in the United States* (New York, 1924), 142, 152.

64. Herbert S. Goldstein, a graduate of the Jewish Theological Seminary but an orthodox rabbi, founded the Institutional Synagogue in Harlem, then a place of residence of economically and socially upwardly mobile Jews; it provided full facilities for religious, cultural, and social activities, including athletics and day camp.

65. See Abraham J. Karp, "Ideology and Identity in Jewish Group Survival in America," *American Jewish Historical Quarterly* 65, no. 4 (June 1976): 310–34.

66. Marshall Sklare, *Conservative Judaism* (New York, 1972), 131.

67. It must be noted, however, that two of the most prominent "synagogue centers" were Orthodox: the Jewish Center and the Institutional Synagogue. The former was founded by Mordecai M. Kaplan, on the faculty of the Conservative Jewish Theological Seminary, and the latter was organized by a graduate of that school.

68. Rabbi Chertoff taught the advanced classes. Among the subjects listed were "Hebrew Translation and Writing," "Abbreviated Humash," and "Jewish Biblical History and Religion."

69. *Minute Book of Temple Beth El*, Beth El Archives, Rochester, N.Y.

70. Ibid.

71. Stuart E. Rosenberg, *The Jewish Community of Rochester, 1843–1925* (New York, 1954), 179.

72. Cited in Abraham J. Karp, "The Conservative Rabbi—'Dissatisfied but Not Unhappy,'" in *The American Rabbinate*, ed. Jacob Rader Marcus and Abraham J. Peck (Hoboken, N.J., 1985).

73. *United Synagogue Recorder* 3, no. 5 (April 1923): 14. Conservative congregations in the East generally called themselves temple; in the Midwest they called themselves synagogue.

74. Ibid.

75. David De Sola Pool, "Judaism and the Synagogue," in *The American Jew*, ed. Oscar I. Janowsky (New York, 1942), 54.

76. Abraham J. Feldman, "The Changing Functions of the Synagogue and the Rabbi," in *Reform Judaism: Essays by Hebrew Union College Alumni*, ed. Bernard J. Bamberger (Cincinnati, 1949), 212.

77. Cited by Marshall Sklare, "Conservative Judaism," in the *United Synagogue Recorder* 6, no. 4 (October 1936): 136.

78. *American Jewish Year Book* [hereafter cited as *AJYB*] 5699 (Philadelphia, 1938), 61; *AJYB* 5701 (Philadelphia, 1940), 217.

79. *AJYB* 55 (Philadelphia, 1954), 81.

80. *AJYB* 57 (Philadelphia, 1956), 191.

81. *AJYB* 59 (Philadelphia, 1958), 125, 131.

82. *New York Times*, April 6, 1959.

83. Cited in *AJYB* 62 (Philadelphia, 1961), 130.

84. *AJYB* 65 (Philadelphia, 1964), 75.

85. *AJYB* 67 (Philadelphia, 1966), 176.

86. Albert I. Gordon, *Jews in Suburbia* (Boston, 1959), 85–119.

87. Ibid., 88.

88. Ibid., 96, 97.

89. Ibid., 116–19.

90. Eugene Borowitz, *A New Jewish Theology in the Making* (Philadelphia, 1968), 45, 46, 53, 54.

91. Gordon, *Jews in Suburbia*, 127.

92. Harold M. Schulweis, "Restructuring the Synagogue," *Conservative Judaism* 27, no. 4 (summer 1973): 19–23.

93. *Young Israel Viewpoint* 24, no. 5 (January 1984): 13.

94. *Young Israel Viewpoint* 24, no. 7 (March 1984): 19.

95. *Jewish Communal Register of New York*, 122.

2. THE AMERICANIZATION OF CONGREGATION BETH ISRAEL, ROCHESTER

1. *The Minute Book of the Beth Israel Congregation*, Abraham and Deborah Karp Collection of American Judaica, Library of the Jewish Theological Seminary of America, MS. The *Minute Book* consists of three volumes. Contemporary paginated ledger books were used. Since the minutes are in Yiddish, and the pagination is from right to left whereas the ledger numbers are from left to right, the pagination is in reverse order. Nine secretaries inscribed the 1,115 pages of minutes of 845 meetings over the course of thirty-eight years. Vol. 1, pp. 256–2, June 28, 1874–September 10, 1882; vol. 2, pp. 384–7, October 1, 1882–October 20, 1894; vol. 3, pp. 498–15, October 24, 1894–September 30, 1912. Hereinafter referred to as *MBBI*.

2. For the history of the Rochester Jewish community, see Stuart E. Rosenberg, *The Jewish Community in Rochester, 1843–1925* (New York, 1954).

3. *Occident*, 13, No. 9 (December 1855): 467.

4. *MBBI*, July 4, 1874.

5. Ibid., July 26, 1874.

6. Ibid., August 30, 1874.

7. Ibid., August 23, 1874.

8. Ibid., March 10, 1878.

9. Ibid., May 5, 1878.

10. Ibid., November 24, 1878.

11. Ibid., December 1, 1878.

12. Ibid., April 10, 1879.

13. Ibid., June 2, 1879.

14. Ibid., August 17, 1879.

15. Ibid., August 31, 1879.

16. Ibid., July 4, 1875.

17. Ibid., August 3, 1879.

18. Ibid., October 3, 1880.

19. Ibid., April 24, 1881.

20. Ibid., May 8, 1881.

21. Ibid., June 5, 1881.

22. Ibid., July 17, 1881.

23. Ibid., February 5, 1882.

24. Ibid., August 20, 1883.

25. Still in existence in 1996.

26. It seems most likely that the issue that caused the split in the congregation was cemetery versus synagogue. In a preface to the *Minute Book of the Beth Haknesses Hachodosh*, Mr. Meir Nusbaum is lauded for his efforts: "Mr. Meir Nusbaum worked hard for the *hevra* that everything should be in order, that there should be a cemetery. In the second year Mr. Meir Nusbaum bought land for a cemetery, on the third year he had a fence built."

27. *MBBI*, special trustees meeting, September 23, 1883.

28. Ibid., October 21, 1883.

29. Moshe Weinberger, *Hayehudim veha-Yahadut b'New York* (New York, 1877), 4.

30. See Abraham J. Karp, "New York Chooses a Chief Rabbi," *PAJHS* 44, no. 3 (March 1955): 129ff.

31. *Rochester Union-Advertiser*, April 5, 1895, p. 10.

32. *MBBI*, September 3, 1883.

33. Ibid., November 25, 1883.

34. Ibid., December 1883.

35. Ibid., July 7, 1884.

36. Ibid., July 19, 1885.

37. Weinberger, *Hayehudim veha-Yahadut b'New York*, 2.

38. *MBBI*, February 5, 1882.

39. Ibid., March 10, 1884.

40. Ibid., May 11, 1884.

41. Ibid., June 1, 1884.

42. Ibid., March 7, 1886.

43. Ibid., March 28, 1886.

44. *Rochester Democrat and Chronicle*, June 28, 1886, pp. 6 and 7.

45. Ibid., September 20, 1886.

46. Reproduced as written by J. Rosenbloom. Inserted in *MBBI*, vol. 2, between pp. 227–26. J. N. Smith was the "contractor for the building of said house of worship."

47. The *Pinkas of the Hevra Mishnayes* is in the Library of the Jewish Theo-

logical Seminary of America. It is written in Hebrew and contains the rules and regulations; the list of founding members; and one hundred pages listing individual members and data (e.g., offices held and date of death). Three rabbis of Beth Israel are listed: Rabbi Abba Hayim b. Yitzhak Isaac (Levinson); Rabbi Abraham Abba b. David (Rosen); and Rabbi David b. Rabbi Yitzhak Isaac (Ginsberg).

48. The *Jewish Tidings* was founded in 1887 by two young members of the German Jewish community, Samuel M. Brickner and Louis Wiley. The former was a twenty-year-old senior at the University of Rochester, who later became a prominent physician in New York City. The latter was only eighteen at the time but already displayed the ability that later elevated him to the position of business manager of the *New York Times*. The journal advocated radical reform but reported on the broad spectrum of Jewish activities in Rochester and in the nation. By the end of 1888 it claimed in a banner headline under its masthead: "The *Jewish Tidings* has the largest circulation of any Jewish paper in the country." See Rosenberg, *Jewish Community*, 99ff.

49. *Jewish Tidings*, September 24, 1887.

50. Ibid., October 8, 1887.

51. Ibid., October 15, 1887.

52. See, for example, minutes in English of December 8, 1886; his letter to the *Jewish Tidings*, October 8, 1887; and his statement to a *Rochester Union-Advertiser* reporter, April 5, 1895.

53. *MBBI*, June 3, 1888.

54. Ibid., November 4, 1888.

55. Ibid., May 5, 1889.

56. Ibid., August 11, 1889.

57. The three were Beth Israel, Beth Haknesses Hachodosh, and Hevra Tillim.

58. Aaron Nusbaum had been a founding member of Beth Israel and served as its president in 1878–79 and 1882–83. Together with his brother he led a group out of Beth Israel to form B'nai Aviezer (named for his father), which took the name of Beth Haknesses Hachodosh when its building was built. It was popularly known as the Nusbaum Shul.

59. The Beth Haknesses Hachodosh.

60. *Jewish Tidings*, November 1, 1889.

61. *MBBI*, May 17, 1891.

62. Ibid., October 12, 1895.

63. Incorporated April 14, 1896, as Rochester Hebrew Religious School. Rosenberg, *Jewish Community*, 261.

64. *MBBI*, October 1, 1899.

65. *Jewish Tidings*, December 28, 1888.

66. Rabbi Leeser Anixter later became a leading rabbi in Chicago, serving congregation Ohave Emuno. Morris A. Gutstein writes in his *A Priceless Heritage: The Epic Growth of Nineteenth-Century Chicago Jewry* (New York, 1953), "Rabbi Anixter was widely famed for his profound Talmudic scholarship, his piety and his devotion to the cause of Orthodox Judaism in Chicago" (130). He was also a Hebraist and author of *Hidushei Ari.*

67. *Jewish Tidings*, April 3, 1891.

68. *MBBI*, July 31, 1892.

69. Ibid., July 8, 1894.

70. Ibid., July 29, 1894.

71. Ibid., July 15, 1895.

72. *Rochester Union-Advertiser,* April 2, 1895.

73. Ibid., April 4, 1895.

74. Ibid., April 6, 1895.

75. *MBBI,* June 4, 1896.

76. Ibid., September 24, 1896.

77. *Rochester Democrat and Chronicle,* July 14, 1895.

78. *MBBI,* July 20, 1890.

79. Ibid., August 2, 1891.

80. Ibid., May 1, 1892; August 14, 1892.

81. Ibid., August 20, 1892; February 19, 1893; March 21, 1893; April 23, 1893; April 30, 1893; May 7, 1893; May 13, 1893; May 14, 1893.

82. Ibid., May 19, 1895.

83. *Jewish Tidings,* July 18, 1890.

84. Library, Jewish Theological Seminary, ledger containing printed contracts, "indentures," signed by members of the congregation and authorized by the commissioner of deeds of Monroe County.

85. *MBBI,* May 7, 1893.

86. The July 19, 1889, issue of *Jewish Tidings* reported, as its headline proclaimed, "A Noteworthy Event." The subhead read: "First English Sermon in Leopold Street Temple . . . Able Address by Rev. Dr. S. S. Kohn." The synagogue was filled almost to capacity to hear the rabbi's address in English. It was reported in the *Rochester Democrat and Chronicle* (July 14, 1889), but no mention of it is found in the minutes of Beth Israel. Self-censorship was apparently applied by the secretaries and leadership of Beth Israel on matters that might call into question the traditionalism of the congregation. The minutes may not fully reflect the process of acculturation and Americanization taking place in the congregation.

87. Rosenberg, *Jewish Community,* 261–62.

88. It is estimated that in 1890 the Jewish population in Rochester numbered five thousand, of whom two thousand were from eastern Europe. At the turn of the century the number had grown to seven thousand, of whom four thousand were east European Jews. Rosenberg, *Jewish Community,* 148.

89. Louis Lipsky's father, Jacob Lipsky, was a founder of Beth Israel, as was his uncle Isaac. His grandfather, Judah, was a member and served for a brief period as *shamash.* Jacob Lipsky served as president when the synagogue was built in 1886 and when the first English-speaking preacher-teacher was engaged in 1906. Louis Lipsky describes his childhood in Rochester in *Memories and Profiles* (Philadelphia, 1975), 11ff.

90. *MBBI,* October 15, 1899; December 17, 1899; April 1, 1900; September 30, 1901.

91. Ibid., July 1, 1900.

92. Ibid., August 26, 1900.

93. Ibid., August 25, 1902.

94. Ibid., January 21, 1903.

95. Ibid., June 5, 1904.

96. Ibid., October 2, 1904; December 11, 1904; January 15, 1905.

97. Selig Adler and Thomas E. Connolly, *From Ararat to Suburbia* (Philadelphia, 1960), 159.

98. *MBBI,* January 28, 1906.

99. Ibid., January 31, 1906.

100. Ibid., July 1, 1906.

101. Rosenberg, *Jewish Community,* 169.

102. *MBBI,* August 27, 1907; September 10, 1907.

103. The *Universal Jewish Encyclopedia* states that he was awarded a Ph.D. at Goettingen; the *Encyclopedia Judaica* states only that he studied there.

104. As early as 1889, a group of Rochester *Maskilim* (devotees of modern Hebrew culture) had set up a Hebrew and Yiddish library, first called the Slonimsky Library and later called the Hebrew Free Library. Among the volumes in the library was found a number of *haskalah* volumes bearing the ownership stamp of A.D. Joffe, a leader of Beth Israel.

105. In the spring of 1908 the name of the education committee was changed to board of education, an indication of the further growth of the independence of its status. Officially it had power over all matters pertaining to the school, save finances.

106. *MBBI,* August 2, 1908.

107. Ibid., November 30, 1908.

108. Ibid., June 20, 1909.

109. Ibid., August 16, 1909.

110. We shall use the term *Rov* to refer to the communal and *Rabbi* to refer to the congregational spiritual leaders.

111. Rabbi Jacob S. Minkin, a graduate of the Jewish Theological Seminary, who later served as second rabbi of Congregation Beth El, Rochester.

112. Probably Rabbi Mordecai M. Kaplan, who was then already on the faculty of the seminary.

113. *MBBI,* December 31, 1910; February 25, 1911; March 14, 1911; April 27, 1911; May 16, 1911; May 30, 1911; June 18, 1911; July 24, 1911.

114. See Arthur A. Goren, *New York Jews and the Quest for Community,* (New York, 1970).

115. *MBBI,* June 18, 1911.

116. See Isaac A. Wile and Isaac M. Brickner, *The Jews of Rochester* (Rochester, New York, 1912), 43.

117. "Congregation Beth Israel Hebrew School and Sunday School," Karp Collection, Library of the Jewish Theological Seminary of America.

118. *MBBI,* November 12, 1911.

119. Ibid., September 29, 1912.

120. *Report of the Second Annual Meeting of the United Synagogue* (New York, 1914), 20.

PART TWO: THE AMERICAN RABBINATE

1. Mordecai M. Noah, *Discourse Delivered at the Consecration of the Synagogue Shearith Israel in the City of New York* (New York, 1818).

2. *Documentary History of the State of New York* (New York, n.d.), 3: 434.

3. Charles S. Liebman, "The Training of American Rabbis," cited in the *American Jewish Year Book 1968* (Philadelphia, 1967).

4. Broadside issued by the Association of the American Orthodox Hebrew Congregations (April 1888).

3. EXPANDING THE PARAMETERS OF THE RABBINATE: ISAAC LEESER OF PHILADELPHIA

1. Henry S. Morais, *Eminent Israelites of the Nineteenth Century* (Philadelphia, 1880), 195–96. The "sketch," as the author calls it, first appeared in the *Jewish Record* of Philadelphia in 1879.

2. To be expected of a writer not yet twenty years old, a Philadelphian writing for a Philadelphia audience about its leading figure, who had passed away but a decade earlier.

3. Leeser dedicated *The Jews and the Mosaic Law* (Philadelphia, 1833) to Rabbi B. S. Cohen, principal of the Jewish Institute at Münster, to whom he writes, "The sentiments, imbibed in part under your excellent instruction . . . are yet remembered and cherished by me." Leeser dedicated his *Discourses Argumentative and Devotional* (Philadelphia, 1837) to "the Right Rev. Abraham Sutro, Chief Rabbi of the Diocese of Münster and Mark," of whom he states, "To you it is chiefly due that I ever ventured to undertake the task of public teacher."

4. *The Jews and the Mosaic Law*. As Leeser notes in his address to the reader, "This book, now for the first time published, was composed more than four years ago." The preface is dated "Richmond, Va. Sivan 9th [June 10) 5589" (1829).

5. Ibid., v.

6. The reader is directed to Maxwell Whiteman's excellent "Isaac Leeser and the Jews of Philadelphia," in *PAJHS* 48, no. 4 (1959), for a full listing and appreciation of Leeser's religious, cultural, and communal accomplishments.

7. *The Jewish Encyclopedia* (New York, 1904), 8: 663, s.v. "Isaac Leeser."

8. *Instruction in the Mosaic Religion*, trans. Isaac Leeser (Philadelphia, 5590 [1830]), vi.

9. Ibid., 7.

10. Isaac Leeser, *The Form of Prayers According to the Custom of the Spanish and Portugese Jews* (n.p., 1838), 1: 7, 8.

11. The *Occident* appeared for twenty-five years under the editorship of Leeser and for another year under Mayer Sulzberger. With the exception of volumes 17 (1859–60) and 18 (1860–61), when it appeared weekly, the publication was issued monthly.

12. The preface is dated January 7, 1856.

13. Preface to 1853 edition (reprint, 1859 ed.), 8.

14. *United States Gazette*, letter dated January 31, 1835.

15. Isaac Leeser, *Discourses on the Jewish Religion* (Philadelphia, 1867), vol. 1.

16. Ibid., 7

17. Ibid.

18. Quoted in Mordecai Waxman, *Tradition and Change* (New York, 1958), 53.

19. In the European community a regular weekly sermon was not part of the service of the traditional synagogue. In eastern Europe the communal rabbi would preach (a lengthy legal discourse) on the Sabbaths preceding Passover and the Day of Atonement only. The discourse would be delivered not during the morning service but in the afternoon.

20. *Occident* 25, no. 12 (March 1868): 595.

21. Gunther Plaut, *The Growth of Reform Judaism* (New York, 1965), 20.

22. "Founded upon" Dr. Edward Kley's *Catechismus der Mosäischen Religion* (Berlin, 1814). It is of interest that Leeser chose a catechism written by a German Reform rabbi.

23. Isaac Leeser, *The Hebrew Reader,* 4th ed. (Philadelphia, 1856), 3.

24. Isaac Leeser, *Catechism for Jewish Children,* 3d ed. (Philadelphia, 1856), 10.

25. Isaac Leeser, *Second Annual Examination of the Sunday School* (Philadelphia, 1840), 5.

26. In "To the Jewish Inhabitants of Philadelphia," two-page circular, Philadelphia, 1835.

27. *Charter and By-Laws of the Hebrew Education Society of Philadelphia* (n.p., n.d.), 2–3.

28. Ibid.

29. *Occident* 25, no. 5 (August 1867): 223.

30. Ibid., 223.

31. Ibid., 228.

32. Ibid., 223.

33. *Occident* 25, no. 12 (March 1868): 598.

34. The current Jewish Publication Society of America is the third to bear the name and was organized in 1888. The second was the American Jewish Publication Society (1873–76).

35. "To the Friends of Jewish Literature," circular, Philadelphia, 1845, broadside.

36. Yehoseph Schwarz, *A Descriptive Geography . . . of Palestine,* trans. Isaac Leeser (Philadelphia, 1850). "The execution of the whole," Leeser states in the translator's preface, "in a mechanical point also, will no doubt give satisfaction the more so, as the whole is the work of Jewish writers and artists, the drawings being executed by Mr. S. Shuster, a lithographer belonging to our nation, and whose work cannot fail to please."

37. *Jewish Encyclopedia,* 8: 597.

38. Isaac Leeser, "History of the Jews and Their Religion" in I. Daniel Rupp, *History of All the Religious Denominations in the United States* (Philadelphia, 1844), 368.

39. *Occident* 17, no. 14 (June 30, 1859): 80–81.

40. Ibid., 81.

41. Ibid.

42. Ibid., 83.

43. Moses A. Dropsie, *Panegyric on the Life, Character and Services of the Rev. Isaac Leeser* (Philadelphia, 1868), pp. 8–10.

4. FROM CAMPUS TO PULPIT: SIMON TUSKA OF ROCHESTER

1. Max Lilienthal, in the *Israelite* (Cincinnati) 17, no. 29 (January 13, 1871): 9.

2. *Occident* 12, no. 3 (June 1854): 167.

3. *Rochester Daily Democrat,* August 27, 1851, p. 2, col. 6

4. Tuska's commencement address, delivered July 9, 1856, was in Greek.

The manuscript copy in his own hand is preserved at the University of Rochester Library.

5. *Rochester Daily Union and Advertiser,* January 11, 1871, p. 2, cols. 4 and 5.

6. *Israelite* 17, no. 28 (January 6, 1871): 9.

7. Simon Tuska, *The Stranger in the Synagogue* (Rochester, N.Y., 1854).

8. *Occident* 12, no. 6 (September 1854): 319–20.

9. *Occident* 12, no. 3 (June 1854): 167–68.

10. Letter (manuscript), Isaac Leeser to Simon Tuska, May 21, 1855, American Jewish Archives.

11. Letter (manuscript), Isaac M. Wise to Simon Tuska, January 15, 1855, American Jewish Archives.

12. *Israelite* 3, no. 7 (August 1856): 53.

13. Ibid.

14. Ibid.

15. *Israelite* 5, no. 3 (July 23, 1858): 20.

16. *Israelite* 17, no. 28 (June 6, 1871): 9.

17. Ibid.

18. Ibid.

19. *Israelite* 5, no. 6 (August 13, 1858): 44.

20. *Israelite* 17, no. 28 (January 6, 1871): 9.

21. Ibid.

22. *Israelite* 5, no. 15 (October 15, 1858): 118.

23. *In Geschichte des jüdisch-theologischen Seminars: (Fraenckel'sche Stiftung)* in Breslau: *Festschrift zum Fünfzigjährungen Jubiläum der Anstalt,* by Dr. M Brann (Breslau, 1904), a list of students who attended the Breslau Jewish Theological Seminary and their writings is given on pages 140–209. On page 199, the name of Tuska is recorded as follows: "Tuska, Simon, geboren in Rochester (Nordamerika) 1835, im Seminar 1858–1860, Rabbiner in Amerika."

24. *Israelite* 5, no. 31 (February 4, 1859): 243. Benjamin Szold was not a student at the Jewish Theological Seminary in Breslau. He was attending the University of Breslau at the time. He was, however, in close contact with the faculty and students at the seminary. In a letter from Tuska to Szold, dated Memphis, December 22, 1870, we find that Tuska questions Szold as to "whether you still keep up communication with the professors of the Seminary." In the letter, the word "our" is crossed out and replaced by the word "the."

25. *Israelite* 5, no. 10 (September 10, 1858): 76.

26. *Israelite* 5, no. 31 (February 4, 1859): 242.

27. Letter (manuscript), I. M. Wise to Simon Tuska, Cincinnati, April 21, 1859, American Jewish Archives.

28. *Israelite* 17, no. 28 (January 6, 1871): 9.

29. Letter (manuscript), Simon Tuska to M. B. Anderson, LL.D., Memphis, Tennessee, July 19, 1860, University of Rochester Library.

30. *Rochester Daily Union and Advertiser,* January 11, 1871, p. 2, col. 5.

31. Letter (manuscript), Simon Tuska to M. B. Anderson, July 19, 1860, University of Rochester Library.

32. *Israelite* 17, no. 29 (January 13, 1871): 9.

33. *Israelite* 17, no. 28 (January 6, 1871): 9.

34. Benjamin Tuska, "Biography of Simon Tuska," typescript, files of the Library of Congress, Washington, D.C.

5. AMERICAN RABBIS FOR AMERICA: SOLOMON SCHECHTER COMES TO THE SEMINARY

1. Cyrus Adler, ed., *The Jewish Theological Seminary of America* (New York, 1939), 10.

2. *Students' Annual, Jewish Theological Seminary of America, Schechter Memorial* (New York, 1916), 61.

3. Norman Bentwich, *Solomon Schechter* (Philadelphia, 1938), 167.

4. Cyrus Adler, "Solomon Schechter," *American Jewish Year Book, 5677* (Philadelphia, 1916), 37.

5. *Publications of the Gratz College* (Philadelphia, 1897), 9.

6. Adler, "Solomon Schechter," 37.

7. Ibid.

8. *Students' Annual*, 96.

9. *American Israelite*, February 14, 1895, p. 5.

10. *American Hebrew* 56, no. 11 (January 18, 1895): 320.

11. Ibid.

12. Adler, "Solomon Schechter," 40.

13. Letter, Schechter to Sulzberger, May 9, 1897, Library of the Jewish Theological Seminary of America [hereafter cited as LJTSA].

14. Adler, ed., *Jewish Theological Seminary*, 10.

15. Letter, January 14, 1898, LJTSA.

16. Letter, March 8, 1898, LJTSA.

17. Letter, June 26, 1898, LJTSA.

18. Ibid.

19. *American Hebrew* 64, no. 11 (January 13, 1899).

20. *American Hebrew* 64, no. 17 (February 24, 1899).

21. *American Hebrew* 65, no. 1 (May 5, 1899): 9, and following issue.

22. Letter, October 20, 1899, LJTSA.

23. *Jewish Exponent*, October 6, 1899.

24. *American Hebrew* 65, no. 24 (October 13, 1899).

25. Letter, October 25, 1899, LJTSA.

26. Letter, November 16, 1899, LJTSA.

27. Bentwich, *Solomon Schechter*, 168.

28. Ibid.

29. Ibid., 169.

30. Ibid.

31. Ibid.

32. Letter, March 5, 1900, LJTSA.

33. Letter, March 15, 1900, LJTSA.

34. Letter, December 9, 1900, LJTSA.

35. *Jewish Exponent*, October 20, 1899.

36. *Jewish Exponent*, October 27, 1899, p. 4.

37. As quoted *Jewish Exponent*, December 27, 1899, p. 4.

38. Ibid.

39. *Jewish Exponent*, January 5, 1900, p. 4.

40. Adler, ed., *Jewish Theological Seminary*, 9–10.

41. Letter, April 17, 1901, LJTSA.

42. Letter, June 14, 1901, LJTSA.

43. Letter, December 24, 1901, LJTSA.

44. *Students' Annual*, 161.
45. Letter, December 24, 1901, LJTSA.
46. *American Hebrew* 65, no. 8 (June 23, 1899).
47. *Jewish Exponent*, June 12, 1896.
48. Letter, October 31, 1895, LJTSA.
49. Letter, December 9, 1900, LJTSA.
50. Letter, June 26, 1898, LJTSA.
51. Letter, December 21, 1899, LJTSA.
52. See, for example, letter to Sulzberger, January 24, 1901, LJTSA.
53. *Jewish Exponent*, October 20, 1899, p. 7.
54. Adler, "Solomon Schechter," 52.
55. *Students' Annual*, 161.
56. Letter to author, April 12, 1963.
57. *American Hebrew* 65, no. 8 (June 23, 1899): 231.
58. Ibid., 224.
59. *American Hebrew* 70 (March 8, 1902): 484.
60. Letter, November 5, 1901, LJTSA.
61. *American Hebrew* 65, no. 22 (April 18, 1902): 656.

6. NEW YORK CHOOSES A CHIEF RABBI: JACOB JOSEPH OF VILNA

1. Isaac Leeser, "Spiritual Authority," *Occident* 2, no. 12 (March 1845): 571.

2. Abraham Rice, "Editorial Correspondence," *Occident* 2, no. 12 (March 1845): 599–600.

3. *Occident* 3 (1846): 576. In the *Allgemeine Zeitung des Judenthums* 10 (1845): 98, there was a report published that "Dr. Lilienthal, Chief Rabbi of Russia, will give a lecture." The term *chief rabbi* was a loose one, flexibly used to designate the rabbi either of a group or association of congregations or applied variously to the rabbinical head of a Jewish community in a city, province, or country. The titles *Oberrabbiner* and *Rav Ha-Kolel* are not always identical and not synonymous with the term chief rabbi, though they are sometimes so translated in the English language. The title *Oberrabbiner* was sometimes applied to a local rabbi, and a *Rav Ha-Kolel* in an eastern European Jewish community should be distinguished from a chief rabbi, say, of a west European community, who may have had a university training. Concerning Lilienthal, see David Philipson, *Max Lilienthal, American Rabbi* (New York, 1915), 51.

4. "Rabbinical Authority," *Occident* 23, no. 5 (August 1865): 193ff.

5. Judah D. Eisenstein, "The History of the First Russian-American Jewish Congregation," *PAJHS* 9 (1901): 69.

6. *Minute Book of the Beth Hamedrash Hagadol*, manuscript written in Yiddish for the year 1879. Subsequent references are to other minutes of the same congregation. The minute books are in the archives of the YIVO Institute for Jewish Research, New York City. Hereinafter they will be referred to as *MBHH*. In this study, we use the spelling of the name of the congregation that occurs in other sources as Beth Hamidrash Hagadol, although the former occurs in its *Constitution and By-Laws* (New York, 1887).

7. *Jewish Encyclopedia* 8: 276; J. D. Eisenstein, *Ozar Israel* 6 (1911): 214.

8. *New York Herald*, August 4, 1879, p. 7.

9. For the full text of the "Call," see Karp, "New York Chooses a Chief Rabbi," 188. The title "Dr." was conferred by the writer of the "Call."

10. *Jewish Record*, August 22, 1879.

11. *American Israelite*, August 29, 1879.

12. Ibid., September 5, 1879.

13. The figures are for Russia, Austria-Hungary, and Romania. See Samuel Joseph, *Jewish Immigration to the United States* (New York, 1914), 93.

14. Judah D. Eisenstein, "History of the Association of American Orthodox Hebrew Congregations," *Ner Ha-Ma'aravi* [Hebrew], 1, no. 11 (1897): 4.

15. Ibid.

16. Moses Weinberger, *Ha-Yehudim veha-Yahadut be-New York* [Jews and Judaism in New York] (New York, 1887), 1.

17. Ibid., 2–5.

18. Ibid., 17ff.

19. Ibid., 203. The name very likely was United Hebrew Orthodox Association. I could find no record of it.

20. Ibid., 98–106.

21. Ibid., 107–8.

22. *MBHH*, May 23, 1887.

23. Ibid., June 12, 1887.

24. Ibid., July 17, 1887.

25. For full text of the letters and replies, see Eisenstein, "History of the Association of American Orthodox Hebrew Congregations," 9ff.

26. Ibid.

27. Ibid., 10.

28. Ibid.

29. Ibid.

30. Ibid.

31. Ibid., 11

32. Ibid.

33. Ibid., 11–12.

34. Ibid., 12–13.

35. Ibid.

36. *MBHH*, January 3, 1888.

37. Six years as the period of contractual obligation is found in many rabbinic contracts. It was the maximum period. This was based on the biblical tradition that made six years the period of servitude of a Hebrew servant.

38. For the complete text of the charter, see *PAJHS* 44 (March 1955): 189–90.

39. *MBHH*, December 18, 1887, and January 3, 1888.

40. *American Israelite*, December 16, 1887.

41. *American Hebrew* (February 24, 1888).

42. See Menahem G. Glenn, *Israel Salanter: Religious Ethical Thinker* (New York, 1953), 69, 90–92.

43. Jacob Joseph, *Le-Bet Ya'akob* (Vilna, 1888).

44. Abraham Cahan, *Bleter fun Mein Leben*, vol. 2 (New York, 1926), 402–3. The author states that this is a paraphrase of the letter, which, although not exact in form, conveys its content and spirit.

45. *American Israelite*, February 3, 1888, p. 5.

46. *Ha-Meliz,* March 10, 1888.
47. *American Israelite,* March 30, 1888.
48. For complete text of the Call, see Karp, "New York Chooses a Chief Rabbi," 191–92.
49. Only one of the constitution's thirteen articles, article VII, deals with the chief rabbi.
50. See full text of article VII, *infra,* 195.
51. Certifications of character.
52. Rabbinical approbations that the product conforms fully with the dietary laws.
53. For the complete text of the "Constitution of the Association of the American Hebrew Orthodox Congregations," see PAJHS 44:192–98. Cf. Jeremiah J. Berman, *Shehitah: A Study in the Cultural and Social Life of the Jewish People* (New York, 1941), 294ff., 321–23.
54. *Jüdisches Tageblatt* (New York Yiddish daily newspaper), July 1, 1888.
55. *Ha-Zefirah,* 22 Tammuz, 5648, no. 136 (July 1, 1888), 13.
56. *Jüdisches Tageblatt,* July 2, 1888.
57. *American Israelite,* July 13, 1888.
58. J. D. Eisenstein in *Ha-Zefirah,* 16 Ab, 5648, no. 155 (July 24, 1888).
59. *Jüdisches Tageblatt,* July 8 and 16, 1888.
60. *American Hebrew* (July 13, 1888): 150.
61. *Jewish Messenger,* July 13, 1888.
62. *Jewish Exponent,* July 13, 1888.
63. *Ha-Meliz,* 26 Adar, 5648 (February 9, 1888).
64. *American Israelite,* December 23, 1887.
65. *Jewish Tidings,* August 17, 1888.
66. Ibid., August 24, 1888, quoted from Stuart E. Rosenberg, *The Jewish Community in Rochester* (New York, 1954), 68.
67. *American Israelite,* March 30, 1888.
68. *New York Herald,* July 21, 1888. The article was headed, "Will He Be an Autocrat?"
69. Ibid.
70. Ibid.
71. *New York Sun,* August 12, 1888, p. 5.
72. *Ha-Zefirah,* 3 Elul, 5648, no. 170 (August 10, 1888).
73. J. D. Eisenstein, in his version of the rabbinic contract in *Ner Ha-Ma'arabi* 1, no. 11 (New York, 1895): 27–28, sets down $2,500 as the yearly salary "payable in equal monthly installments." This is the correct sum; the sum as stated in the Buchhalter article is either an error or a wilful exaggeration.
74. Section F is not found in J. D. Eisenstein's version of the rabbinic contract.
75. Judah Buchhalter in *Ha-Zefirah,* 3 Elul, 5648 (August 10, 1888).
76. Rabbi Ash's salary in 1879 was $200 a year, and it was $400 in 1887, the year in which he passed away.
77. *New York Sun,* April 1, 1888.
78. *Jewish Messenger,* July 27, 1888.
79. For a full description of the "day's activities," see the *New York Sun,* July 22, 1888, p. 10.
80. Rabbi Joseph spoke briefly at the morning service as well. See the *New York Herald,* July 22, 1888, p. 9.

81. *Jewish Exponent,* July 27, 1888. The "German" referred to was, of course, Yiddish.

82. For full text of English translation of the sermon, see *American Hebrew* (July 27, 1888): 183–85. An excerpt of the sermon appeared in the *New York Sun,* July 22, 1888, p. 10. It was translated by Mr. Jacob Judelsohn at Rabbi Joseph's request.

83. *Ha-Meliz,* 17 Ab, 5648, no. 152 (July 25, 1888).

84. Ibid., 7 Elul, 5648 (August 14, 1888): 169.

85. *American Israelite,* August 3, 1888.

86. Ibid., July 22, 1888, p. 10.

87. *American Hebrew* (August 10, 1888): 9.

88. *Jewish Messenger,* August 10, 1888.

89. Ibid., July 27, 1888.

90. *American Hebrew* (August 10, 1888): 2.

91. *Jewish Messenger,* September 14, 1888.

92. *American Israelite,* November 16, 1888.

93. *American Hebrew* (September 28, 1888): 121.

94. *Jewish Messenger,* March 1, 1889.

95. *Hamelitz,* 9 Elul, 5678, no. 181 (August 16, 1888).

96. Eisenstein in *Ner Ha-Ma'arabi* 1, no. 12: 42.

97. *American Israelite,* October 5, 1888; for Yiddish proclamation, see *Der Volksadvokat* 2, no. 9 (September 19, 1888).

98. *Der Volksadvokat,* August 24, 1888.

99. Ibid., August 31, 1888; translated from the Yiddish.

100. A minor religious functionary, not a rabbi, who specialized as a marriage performer and sometime preacher.

101. For an account of the meeting, see *Der Volksadvokat,* September 26, 1888.

102. Ibid., October 5, 1888.

103. *American Israelite,* October 19, 1888.

104. *Jüdisches Tageblatt,* October 15, 1888.

105. The three sermons were published in a pamphlet issued by the office of the chief rabbi, titled *Sefer Toledot Ya'akob Yosef be-New York* [The History of Jacob Joseph in New York] (Kislev-Tebet, 5649). The title page bears the date 1889.

106. Ibid., 6–7.

107. Ibid., 14.

108. *American Hebrew* (October 5, 1888): 130.

109. *Jewish Messenger,* February 22, 1889.

110. *American Hebrew* (January 11, 1889).

111. Ibid., April 12, 1889.

112. Ibid.

113. In a letter that Rabbi Jacob Joseph sent from New York to "My brethren, my people of Vilna," he tells how difficult it was for him to leave Vilna, the metropolis of Jewish life, "but I could do naught else, for my financial position so deteriorated that I had to seek help from afar . . . so I came here." *Ha-Meliz,* 7 Tishri, 5648, no. 191 (August 31, 1888).

114. Ibid. This title appeared under his signature in his letter to Vilna.

115. For a description of Jewish educational facilities on the Lower East Side

in 1887, see Weinberger, *Ha-Yehudim veha-Yahadut be-New York*, 17ff; Cf. Jeremiah J. Berman, "Jewish Education in New York City, 1860–1900," *Yivo Bleter* [Yiddish], 38 (New York, 1954): 208–35. Berman's paper was also published in English in the *Yivo Annual of Jewish Social Science* 9 (New York, 1954): 247–75.

116. *Jüdisches Tageblatt*, July 27, 1888.

117. *Sefer Toledot Ya'akob Yosef*, 17.

118. See Karp, "New York Chooses a Chief Rabbi," 191.

119. *American Hebrew* (February 24, 1888): 41.

120. See Karp, "New York Chooses a Chief Rabbi," 194–95.

121. *New York Herald*, July 8, 1888.

122. *Jewish Exponent*, July 13, 1888.

123. *Ha-Meliz*, 23 Tammuz, 5648 (July 2, 1888).

124. Followers of the pietistic movement, known as Hasidism and initiated by the Baal Shem Tov.

125. *American Israelite*, July 28, 1888.

126. Father of Professor Mordecai M. Kaplan of the Jewish Theological Seminary of America.

127. Letter from Rabbi Jacob Joseph to Dr. Simon P. Burstein of Cleveland, Ohio, May 1895, in possession of Rabbi Abraham Burstein, son of Dr. Simon P. Burstein and father-in-law of the author.

128. As chief rabbis increased in number, so the title decreased in value. In 1893, Rabbi Hayyim Jacob Vidrowitz came to New York from Moscow, gathered a few small hasidic *shtiblach* (prayer rooms) under his control, and hung out a shingle that bore the legend "Chief Rabbi of America." When asked, "Who made you Chief Rabbi?" he replied with a twinkle in his eye, "The sign painter." "And why the Chief Rabbi of America?" he was asked. "Because it would be well nigh impossible for all of America to gather together to depose me," he would answer with a chuckle. Albeit the title could be made the butt of a joke, when it referred to Rabbi Jacob Joseph it carried a considerable degree of weight and authority. He was *the* chief rabbi.

129. *Der Volksadvokat*, October 26, 1888. Although the announcement bore the caption, "Announcement of the *Beth Din Hagadol* of New York," the rabbis did not sign it as was their custom in other announcements. It was signed by the officers of the Butchers Association. This was apparently either too strong or too wrong an accusation to make, and they did not want to be associated with it, even though they had permitted it.

130. *Jewish Messenger*, January 18, 1889.

131. *Jewish Exponent*. The congregation that emerged was *Zikhron Ephraim*, under the spiritual leadership of Rabbi Bernard Drachman.

132. *MBHH* discloses that on October 21, 1888, it voted to give Rabbi Joseph a gift of $50 and that the delegates of the other congregations who had met on the eve of Hoshanah Rabbah had promised that their congregations would also send gifts to the rabbi. Subsequently the Beth Hamidrash Hagadol sent gifts to the rabbi for almost every holiday, but in decreasing amounts.

133. *Jüdisches Tageblatt*, March 11, 1889.

134. Eisenstein, *Ner Ha-Ma'arabi* 1, no. 12: 43.

135. Benjamin L. Gordon, *Between Two Worlds* (New York, 1952), 142.

136. Manuscript in possession of Rabbi Abraham Burstein; now at the Jewish Theological Seminary of America library.

137. *MBHH*.

138. Ibid.

139. Ibid.

140. A very small number for a special meeting of this congregation.

141. *MBHH.*

142. Letter from Rabbi O. N. Rapeport, dayyan of the chief rabbi, to the Reverend Judah Berman and his son-in-law, Dr. Simon P. Burstein, April 17, 1895. Reverend Berman was a shohet as well as an ordained rabbi, and Dr. Burstein was an ordained rabbi and physician (courtesy of Rabbi Abraham Burstein).

143. Letter from Rabbi Jacob Joseph to Dr. Simon P. Burstein (courtesy of Rabbi Abraham Burstein).

144. *Jewish Daily Forward* 5, no. 1660 (July 29, 1902).

145. *Jewish Gazette,* English supplement, vol. 27, no. 33 (August 15, 1902).

146. Ibid.

147. Ibid. See also the editorial in *American Hebrew* 71, no. 11 (August 1, 1902): 291; "Riot at a Jewish Funeral in New York," *Jewish Chronicle* (London), August 1, 1902, p. 19, and "The Riots in New York," *Jewish Chronicle,* August 8, 1902, p. 17. Cf. the article on the role of Rabbi Jacob Joseph on the American scene, in five installments, by S. Judson in *The Day* [Yiddish], August 31 and September 2, 5, 9, and 13, 1951. Although in the initial installment passing reference is made to the funeral that took place on Wednesday, July 30, 1902, Judson devotes the last installment to "The Historic Funeral of New York's Chief Rabbi, Rabbi Jacob Joseph" (*The Day,* September 13, 1902, pp. 7–8).

148. *PAJHS* 44 (March 1955): 191.

149. Ibid., 192.

150. *American Israelite,* March 30, 1888.

151. *Ha-Meliz,* 18 Nisan, 5648 (March 3, 1888).

152. *Der Volksadvokat,* October 12, 1888.

153. Eisenstein, *Ner Ha-Ma'arabi* 1, no. 12: 46.

7. THE TRIPARTITE DIVISION: HOW IT CAME TO BE

1. *This Was America,* ed. Oscar Handlin (New York, 1949), 147–50.

2. Alexis de Tocqueville, *Democracy in America,* vol. 1 (New York, 1899), 308, 311.

3. Ibid.

4. Moses Hart, *Modern Religion* (New York, 1824), 11.

5. I. J. Benjamin II, *Three Years in America,* vol. 1 (1956), 50ff.

6. I. Daniel Rupp, *An Original History of the Religious Denominations at Present Existing in the United States* (Philadelphia, 1844), 350.

7. Judah L. Hackenburg, Lewis Allen, Isaac Leeser, et al., Circular (Philadelphia, 1841).

8. *Occident* 17, no. 14 (June 30, 1859), 80.

9. Gunther Plaut, *The Growth of Reform Judaism* (New York, 1965), 20.

10. Protest, November 6, 1855, signed by Dr. David Einhorn, Rabbin [sic] of the Har Sinai Verein and A. Nachman, president (Baltimore, 1855).

11. *Galaxy* 13, no. 1 (January 1872), 47ff.

12. Plaut, *Growth of Reform Judaism,* 29–30.

13. Isaac M. Wise et al., *Hymns, Psalms and Prayers* (Cincinnati, 1868).

14. *Proceedings of the Union of American Hebrew Congregations,* vol. 1 (Cincinnati, 1879), 4.

15. Ibid., 524.
16. Plaut, *Growth of Reform Judaism*, 33.
17. Karp, "New York Chooses a Chief Rabbi," 191.

8. A CENTURY OF CONSERVATIVE JUDAISM

1. "The Things That Unite Us," *Proceedings of the Rabbinical Assembly, 1927*, 53.
2. Louis Ginzberg, *The United Synagogue of America* (New York, 1918), 6.
3. Herman H. Rubenovitz and Mignon L. Rubenovitz, *The Waking Heart* (Cambridge, 1967), 156.
4. David Philipson, *The Reform Movement in Judaism* (New York, 1931), 351–52.
5. Cited in Mordecai M. Kaplan, *Judaism as a Civilization* (New York, 1934), 534.
6. *Encyclopedia Judaica*, vol. 7 (Jerusalem, 1972), 80.
7. Louis Ginzberg, *Students, Scholars, Saints* (Philadelphia, 1928), 203–4.
8. Ibid., 209.
9. Ismar Schorsch, "Zacharias Frankel and the European Origins of Conservative Judaism," *Judaism* (summer 1981): 345–46.
10. *Hebrew Leader* 8 (June 29, 1866): 4.
11. *Hebrew Leader* 9 (February 8, 1867): 4.
12. Sigmund Hecht, *Epitome of Post-Biblical History* (Cincinnati, 1882), 113.
13. W. M. Rosenblatt, in "The Jews, What They Are Coming To," *Galaxy* (January 1872): 47, consigned "Dr. Wise, Dr. Huebsch and Dr. Mielziner" to the Conservatives.
14. *Jewish Times* 1 (October 22, 1869): 5.
15. Cited in Moshe Davis, *The Emergence of Conservative Judaism* (New York, 1963), 163–65.
16. *Proceedings of the Union of American Hebrew Congregations* (1879), i, ii.
17. Alexander Kohut, *The Ethics of the Fathers* (New York, 1885), 12–13.
18. Kaufmann Kohler, *Backwards or Forwards?* (New York, 1885), 7.
19. H. Pereira Mendes, "The Beginnings of the Seminary," in *The Jewish Theological Seminary of America*, ed. Cyrus Adler (New York, 1939), 36–38.
20. *American Hebrew* 25 (February 5, 1886): 200–201. Cited in Davis, *Emergence of Conservative Judaism*, 237–38.
21. From the preamble of the constitution of the Jewish Theological Seminary Association, adopted at its founding convention, May 9, 1886.
22. *American Hebrew* 29 (January 7, 1887): 137. Cited in Davis, *Emergence of Conservative Judaism*, 239.
23. *Proceedings of the First Biennial Convention of the Jewish Theological Seminary Association, held in New York on Sunday, March 11, 1888* (New York, 1888), 6.
24. Ibid., 19–20.
25. *New York Herald*, July 21, 1888. Cited in Karp, "New York Chooses a Chief Rabbi," 153.
26. *American Israelite*, March 30, 1888. Cited in Karp, "New York Chooses a Chief Rabbi."

27. On the ideological orientation and identification of the rabbinic founders of the Jewish Theological Seminary, see Davis, *Emergence of Conservative Judaism*; Charles S. Liebman, "Orthodoxy in Nineteenth Century America," *Tradition* 6, no. 2 (spring-summer 1968): 132–40; and Abraham J. Karp, "The Origins of Conservative Judaism," *Conservative Judaism* 14, no. 4 (summer 1965): 3–48. See also the opening section of Jeffrey S. Gurock, "Resisters and Accommodators," in *The American Rabbinate*, ed. Jacob R. Marcus and Abraham J. Peck (Hoboken, N.J., 1985).

28. Marcus Jastrow, *The Warning Voice* (Philadelphia, 1892), 8.

29. *Students' Annual, Jewish Theological Seminary of America, Schechter Memorial* (New York, 1916), 61.

30. Letter, June 26, 1898, LJTSA.

31. See chapter 5, "American Rabbis for America: Solomon Schechter Comes to the Seminary."

32. *Jewish Chronicle* (London), May 15, 1896, pp. 22–23.

33. Solomon Schechter, *Seminary Addresses* (Cincinnati, 1915), 20.

34. Ibid., 22.

35. *American Hebrew* (April 11, 1902): 635–36.

36. For the radical nature of Rabbi Fleischer's religious views, see Arthur Mann, *Growth and Achievement: Temple Israel* (Cambridge, 1954), 63–83.

37. Rubenovitz and Rubenovitz, *Waking Heart*, 27–28.

38. Ibid., 30.

39. See chapter 2, "The Americanization of Congregation Beth Israel, Rochester."

40. Schechter, *Seminary Addresses*, 131.

41. Rubenovitz and Rubenovitz, *Waking Heart*, 46.

42. See Herbert Rosenblum, "The Founding of the United Synagogue of America, 1913," (Ph.D. diss., Brandeis University, 1970); Abraham J.Karp, *A History of the United Synagogue of America, 1913–1963* (New York, 1964).

43. *United Synagogue of America Report* (New York, 1913), 14.

44. Ibid., 9.

45. Schechter, *Seminary Addresses*, 20.

46. *United Synagogue of America Report of the Second Annual Meeting* (New York, 1914), 34.

47. Ibid., 32–40.

48. Ibid., 32–46; 23–27.

49. *United Synagogue of America Fourth Annual Report* (New York, 1916), 15.

50. Samuel Halperin, *The Political World of American Zionism* (Detroit, 1961), 102.

51. *American Hebrew* (December 28, 1906): 191–94.

52. See Baila Round Shargel, *Practical Dreamer: Israel Friedlaender and the Shaping of American Judaism* (New York, 1985).

53. Israel Friedlaender, *Past and Present* (Cincinnati, 1919), 159–84.

54. This designation, or simply "Schechter's," was the popular name for the Jewish Theological Seminary in the east European Jewish community until World War II.

55. *The Jewish Community Register of New York City, 1917-1918* (New York, 1918), 121–22.

56. *American Hebrew* (March 22, 1918).

57. Kaplan, *Judaism as a Civilization*, 428.

58. In his last public address at the commencement exercises of the seminary, June 6, 1915, Schechter had warned against "the Institutional Synagogue [i.e., a synagogue center] in which the worship of God must become in the end subordinated to the material service of man and his amusements" (*Seminary Addresses*, 252).

59. Sklare, *Conservative Judaism*, 131.

60. *Minute Book of Temple Beth El, Rochester, N.Y.*, Beth El Archives, unpaged.

61. Stuart E. Rosenberg, *The Jewish Community of Rochester, 1843–1925* (New York, 1954), 179.

62. Cited in Karp, "The Conservative Rabbi," 126.

63. Abraham J. Feldman, "The Changing Functions of the Synagogue" in *Reform Judaism: Essays by Hebrew Union College Alumni* (Cincinnati, 1949), 212.

64. *United Synagogue Recorder* 6, no. 4 (October 1926).

65. Sklare, *Conservative Judaism*, 112.

66. *United Synagogue Recorder* 7, no. 4 (October 1927): 11.

67. Mimeo and typescript, June 22, 1938. In possession of the author.

68. *United Synagogue Recorder* 3, no. 2 (April 1923).

69. Cited in Karp, *History of the United Synagogue*, 25.

70. *United Synagogue of America Fourth Annual Report*, 17.

71. Karp, *History of the United Synagogue*, 45.

72. Ibid., 29.

73. Ibid., 59.

74. Cited in Karp, "Conservative Rabbi," 126.

75. *Proceedings of the Rabbinical Assembly, 1927*, 42ff.

76. Ibid., 18.

77. Ibid., 53.

78. *Proceedings of the Rabbinical Assembly, 1928*, 21–22.

79. *Proceedings of the Rabbinical Assembly, 1929*, 43–50. The address was also published in the October 1929 issue of the *Jewish Forum*, an Orthodox periodical.

80. Ibid., 18–30.

81. Ibid., 31–39.

82. *Proceedings of the Rabbinical Assembly, 1940*, 89–92.

83. Ibid., 288, 289.

84. *United Synagogue Recorder* 3, no. 4 (October 1923).

85. *Proceedings of the Rabbinical Assembly, 1930–1932*, 305–6.

86. Ibid., 309–10.

87. Max Arzt, "Dr. Kaplan's Philosophy," *Proceedings of the Rabbinical Assembly, 1939*, 195–219. For an appreciation of the enduring impact of *Judaism as a Civilization*, see Myer S. Kripke's article in *Conservative Judaism* (March/April 1981): 17–23: "[It] was certainly a (if not the) highwater mark in American Jewish self-study. . . . [Its] critique of Reform was one of the reasons . . . a major one, for the drastic change in Reform in the last 40 years or so. . . . Conservative Judaism particularly bears the imprint of his teaching, his thought, his progressivism, his bold encounter with the realities of Jewish life at every significant point, ritual, ideology, instruction and organization. But Conservative Judaism did not become Reconstructionist. Where he had most earnestly hoped

to succeed, his central theological ideas were held at intellectual arm's length, even though his influence was readily acknowledged." For a critique of Kaplan's theology by his most gifted disciple, Milton Steinberg, see *Proceedings of the Rabbinical Assembly, 1949,* 379–80.

88. *Proceedings of the Rabbinical Assembly, 1927,* 42–53.

89. Robert Gordis, *The Jew Faces a New World* (New York, 1941), 195–214. The chapter served as the basis for Gordis's widely read *Conservative Judaism: An American Philosophy,* published for the National Academy of Adult Jewish Studies of the Jewish Theological Seminary by Behrman House in 1945. In the foreword, Gordis stated: "For a variety of reasons, [Conservative] scholars and leaders have until recently been loath to elaborate its philosophy. . . . Even this modest attempt to present a survey of Conservative Judaism has been a difficult and challenging task, with few sources and virtually no precedents to guide the writer."

90. Ibid.

91. See Abraham J. Karp, "Reactions to Zionism and the State of Israel in the American Jewish Religious Community," *Journal of Jewish Sociology* 8, no. 2 (December 1966): 150–74.

92. See Karp, "The Conservative Rabbi," 148–49. The rabbi was Abraham J. Karp, Temple Beth El, Rochester, New York.

93. *Proceedings of the Rabbinical Assembly, 1949,* 178–80.

94. Ibid., 169–73.

95. "Report on the Findings of the National Survey on Synagogue Attendance, Children's Jewish Education, Adult Jewish Education, and Youth Work in Conservative Congregations," United Synagogue of America, 1950.

96. *Proceedings of the Rabbinical Assembly, 1958,* 81–117.

97. Sklare, *Conservative Judaism,* 229, 241.

98. Ibid., 250, 252.

99. Martin N. Levin, "2001: Blueprint for the Rabbinate in the Twenty-First Century," *Proceedings of the Rabbinical Assembly, 1979,* 115–16.

100. For more on women's ordination see *Conservative Judaism* (summer 1979): 62–80; *Proceedings of the Rabbinical Assembly, 1979,* 217–51; Robert Gordis, "The Ordination of Women," *Midstream* (August-September 1980). The most comprehensive presentation of the issues is in "Women as Rabbis—A Many-Sided Examination of All Aspects," *Judaism* (winter 1984): 6–90.

101. Gerson D. Cohen, typed letter, August 26, 1985, pp. 1, 4.

102. Ibid., p. 3

103. Robert Gordis, "The Ordination of Women—A History of the Question," *Judaism* (winter 1984): 12.

104. Isaac Klein, *A Guide to Jewish Religious Practice* (New York, 1979), xxi, xxiv.

105. Harold M. Schulweis "Restructuring the Synagogue," *Conservative Judaism* 27, no. 4 (summer 1973): 13–23.

106. *Festival Prayer Book,* edited by Professor Alexander Marx, was published by the United Synagogue in 1927, but it was a classically traditional *mahzor.*

107. *Proceedings of the Rabbinical Assembly, 1975,* 14–16.

108. Marshall Sklare, "Recent Developments in Conservative Judaism," *Midstream* 18, no. 1 (January 1972): 3–19.

109. *Proceedings of the Rabbinical Assembly, 1965,* 23.

110. Ibid.

111. Sklare, "Recent Developments," 13–14.

112. Samuel Z. Klausner and David P. Varady, *Synagogues without Ghettos* (Philadelphia, 1970).

113. Charles S. Liebman and Saul Shapiro, "A Survey of the Conservative Movement and Some of Its Religious Attitudes," mimeo, 1979.

114. "Morale and Commitment," *Conservative Judaism* (fall 1972): 12–26.

115. Sklare, *Conservative Judaism,* 177–78.

116. *Rabbinical Assembly News,* February 1984, pp. 1, 8. The survey was conducted by Rabbi Stephen C. Lerner and Dr. Anne L. Lerner.

117. Seymour Siegel, "The Meaning of Jewish Law in Conservative Judaism: An Overview and Summary," in *Conservative Judaism and Jewish Law,* ed. Seymour Siegel (New York, 1977), xiii.

118. Seymour Siegel, "After Fifteen Years—My Mind," *Sh'ma* 15/300 (November 1, 1985): 155.

119. Michael Wyschogrod, "After Fifteen Years-*My World,*" *Sh'ma* 15/300 (November 1, 1985): 153.

120. *New York Times,* July 2, 1985, section A, p. 11.

121. Gerson Cohen, *Ometz Shaliach* 1, no. 1 (winter 1984): 1.

122. *Proceedings of the Rabbinical Assembly, 1927,* 35.

123. Theodore Friedman, "Jewish Tradition in Twentieth Century America—The Conservative Approach," *Judaism* (fall 1954): 320.

POSTSCRIPT: BETWEEN FEAR AND FAITH

1. Arthur Mann, *Growth and Achievement: Temple Israel, 1854–1954* (Cambridge, Mass., 1954).

2. *American Hebrew and Jewish Messenger* 88, no. 23 (April 7, 1911).

3. Jacob David Willowsky, *Nimukei Ridbaz* (Chicago, 1904).

4. Quoted in Zev Shraga Kaplan, *Edut B'Yaakov* (Warsaw, 1904).

5. Israel Friedlaender, *Past and Present* (Cincinnati, 1919).

6. Leo W. Schwarz, ed., *Great Ages and Ideas of the Jewish People* (New York, 1956).

GLOSSARY OF TERMS

agunah	woman abandoned without Jewish divorce
aliyah (pl. *aliyot*)	going up to the Torah to recite blessings
beth am	house of the people
beth din	religious court
beth haknesseth	house of assembly
beth hamidrash	house of study
beth hatefilah	house of worship
bimah	synagogue platform
dayyanim	religious judges
halakhic	legal (referring to halakhah, Jewish religious law)
haskamah (pl. *haskamot*)	approbation; recommendation
hazzan	cantor; in Sephardic tradition, head synagogue functionary
heder	private school for religious instruction
heksher (pl. *heksherim*)	rabbinical approbation, specifically for kosher food
hevra (pl. *hevrot*)	mutual interest group; congregation
Hevra Mishnayes	Mishnah (q.v.) study group
havurah (pl. *havurot*)	group joined for religious fellowship
karobka	Russian government tax on kosher meat
kashrut	dietary laws
Kehillah	(Jewish) community
landsmanshaft	society of immigrants from one European city or town
maggid	preacher
maskilim	intelligentsia; students of modern or general culture

matzah (pl. *matzot*)	unleavened bread
melamed (pl. *melamdim*)	teacher
mikvah	ritual bath
minhag	rite
minyan	quorum of ten for public prayer
Mishnah (pl. *Mishnayot* or *Mishnayes*)	ancient legal code, redacted c. 200 C.E.
mitzvah (pl. *mitzvot*)	religious commandment
mohel	circumciser
plumbe	lead seal denoting kosher poultry
Prediger	preacher (German or Yiddish word)
Rav or *Rov*	Orthodox rabbi
Sephardi (pl. *Sephardim*)	descendants of Spanish and Portuguese Jews
shamash (sometimes *shammes*)	sexton
shehitah	ritual slaughtering of cattle and fowl
shohet (pl. *shohatim*)	ritual slaughterer
shul	synagogue (usually Orthodox usage; Yiddish)
tallit (talith, tallis)	prayer shawl
Torah	(1) parchment scroll of the Pentateuch (first five books of the Bible) read at services of worship; (2) the Pentateuch; (3) the totality of Jewish religious tradition
trefah	nonkosher
yeshiva (pl. *yeshivot*)	school of higher religious learning

INDEX

Abrahams, Abraham I., 18
Abramowitz, Herman, 216, 231
Adath Yeshurun (Syracuse, N.Y.), 92
Adler, Cyrus, 132, 136, 138, 140, 143, 210, 215, 219, 221, 224, 225, 231, 241
Adler, Felix, 168
Adler, Leibman, 24
Adler, Morris, 236
Adler, Nathan Marcus, 145
Adler, Samuel, 26, 129, 191
Agudas Achim Synagogue (Rochester, N.Y.), 33
Agus, Jacob, 248
Ahad Ha'am (Asher Ginzberg), 223
Ahavat Chesed (New York), 209
Alexander, Moritz, 170
Alumni Association of the Jewish Theological Seminary, 219
American Hebrew (New York), 168, 169, 177
American Israelite (Cincinnati), 116, 147, 156, 157, 163, 168
Americanization, 196
American Jewish Publication Society, 118
American Society for Meliorating the Condition of the Jews, The, 113
American Student Center (Jerusalem), 246
Anderson, Martin B., 122
An Original History of the Religious Denominations at Present Existing in the United States (Rupp), 195, 196
Anshe Chesed Congregation (New York), 22
Anshei Sefarad Synagogue (Manchester, N.H.), 31

Anshe Russia, Congregation (Newark, N.J.), 33
Arzt, Max, 238, 246
Ash, Abraham Joseph, 28, 146, 148, 149, 151, 171
Assaf, Simha, x
Assembly of Jewish Notables, 2
Association of the American Orthodox Hebrew Congregations, xi, 150, 171, 178, 202

Bardin, Kalman, 32, 45, 46, 53, 59, 81
Baron, Salo Wittmayer, 15, 264
Bavli, Hillel, 246
Benai David, congregation (Rochester, N.Y.), 76
Benjamin II, I. J., 22–23, 196
Berlin, Hayyim, 151, 152, 154
Beth Din Hagadol, 181
Beth Din Zedek, 174
Beth El (Buffalo, N.Y.), 91
Beth El (New York), 210
Beth El (Rochester, N.Y.), 36, 105, 226
Beth El Emet (Philadelphia), 119
Beth Haknesses Hachodosh (Rochester, N.Y.), 81, 99. *Also see* B'nai Aviezer
Beth Hamedrash Hagadol (Rochester, N.Y.), 102, 104
Beth Hamidrash Hagadol (New York), 29, 146, 147, 149, 151, 170, 183, 184
Beth Hamidrash Hagadol Anshe Ungarn (New York), 175
Beth Hamidrash Halchei Yousher (New York), 146
Beth Israel Bikkur Holim (New York), 181

Beth Israel Congregation (New York), 22

Beth Israel Congregation (Rochester, N.Y.), 31–32, 35, 45–105; cantors, 64; cemetery, 84; dedication of synagogue 56–57; early years, 45–61; Friday evening gatherings, 95; Hanukkah concerts, 84; Hevra Kadisha, 83–98; from hevra toward congregation, 61–87; the making of an American congregation, 87–105; Purim Ball, 83–84; rabbis, 70–82; Sunday school, 95; youth, 85

Bettelheim, Aaron, 207

Binkowitz, Zundel, 64, 65

Blechman, Nathan, 94, 95, 96

Blum, Abraham, 83

Blumenthal, Joseph, 138, 140, 210

B'nai Aviezer: also known as Beth Haknesses Hachodosh, also known as Nusbaum Minyan, also known as Nusbaum Shul, 51

B'nai Israel (Rochester, N.Y.), 55

B'nai Jeshurun, Temple (Cincinnati), 27

Bnai Jeshurun Congregation (New York), 22

Board of Delegates of American Israelites, 119

Board of Delegates of United Hebrew Orthodox Congregations, 146, 191

Bondi, Jonas, 208

Book of Daily Prayers for Every Day in the Year According to the Custom of the German and Polish Jews, The (Leeser), 113

Brickner, Isaac M., 104

Brith, Kodesh, Temple (Rochester, N.Y.), 27, 104, 127

Brodsky, H., 173

Brooklyn Eagle, 186

Brooklyn Jewish Center (New York), 37–38

Buchhalter, Judah, 150, 165, 169

Burstein, Simon, 183

Butkowsky, Moses, 149

Cairo Genizah, 135

Call to Israel, 146

Cambridge, University of, 132, 134

Caminsky, David Solomon, 45

Campanall, Valentin, 19

Cantor, Samuel Joseph, 79–80, 84

Cantors Assembly, 246

Cantors Institute, The (J.T.S.A.), 246

Caplan, Isaac, 99

Carigal, Haim Isaac, 20

Catechism for Jewish Children (Leeser), 116

Chertoff, Paul, 35, 102, 103, 105, 217, 218

Chief Rabbi for New York, 145–90, 202

Chuck, Henry, 150, 153, 158, 170, 182

Cleveland Conference, 115–16, 197, 198

Cohen, Arthur A., 12

Cohen, Benjamin, 110

Cohen, Boaz, 246

Cohen, G. M., 26

Cohen, Gerson D., 249, 250, 251, 257, 258

Cohen, Jack, 248

Cohen, Jacob, 83

Cohen, Max, 103

Cohen, Samuel M., 230

College of Jewish Studies (J.T.S.A.), 246

Collegiate Institute at Brockport, 125

Commission for the Study of the Ordination of Women as Rabbis, 250

Committee on Jewish Law and Standards (Rabbinical Assembly), formerly Committee on Jewish Law, 248, 256

Conference on Science, Philosophy and Religion, 246

Conservative Judaism, xii, 201, 204–58; Adler era (1915–1940), 224–40; —, education, 225–30; —, ideology, 236–41; Cohen era (1972–1985), 249–58; —, tradition and change, 249–52, 256–58; Finkelstein era (1940–1972), 241–49; —, congregations, schools, 241–43; —, rabbis, 243–45; —, the seminary, 246–47; Morais era (1887–1897),

210–14; Rabbinical Assembly of America, 232–36, 253–55; roots, American, 207–11; roots, European, 205–7; Schechter era (1902–1915), 214–19; —, rabbis and congregations, 217–19; synagogues, 35–42; United Synagogue of America, 219–22, 230–32, 252–53. *See also* Jewish Theological Seminary of America; Rabbinical Assembly of America; United Synagogue of America
Conservative responsum (Louis Ginzberg), 230–31
Council of Jewish Federations and Welfare Funds, 11
Cowen, Philip, 134
Crèvecoeur, Michel Guillaume Jean de, 3
Cultural pluralism, 7, 225

Davidowitz, Harry S., 233
Davidson, Israel, 216
Davis, Moshe, 246
Damascus Affair, 196
Deborah Nursery (New York), 146
De Cordova, R. J., 26
de la Motta, Jacob, 4, 22
De Lucena, Abraham, 107
Dembitz, Lewis N., 136
De Rossi, Giovanni, 118
Descriptive Geography . . . of Palestine, A (Schwartz), 118
De Sola, Meldola, 136
Dictionary of Hebrew Authors (De Rossi), 118
Discourse Delivered at the Consecration of the Synagogue Shearith Israel in the City of New York (Noah), 107
Discourses, Argumentative and Devotional on the Subject of the Jewish Religion (Leeser), 112
Discourses on the Jewish Religion (Leeser), 115
Diskin, Joseph Duber, 151
Drachman, Bernard, 157, 176, 210, 213, 215
Drob, Max, 233
Dropsie, Moses A., 121

Dual-image identity, 11
Dubnow, Simon, 223
Dutch West India Company, ix, 17

Educators Assembly, 246
Egelson, Joshua, 103
Eilberg, Amy, 250
Einhorn, David, 25, 27, 191, 197
Eisenstein, Judah D., xi, 28, 158, 189
Emancipation, 1, 3, 194, 205
Emanu-El, Temple (New York), 26
Emerson, Ralph Waldo, 3
Emma Lazarus Club, 35
Enlightenment, 1, 3, 193, 194, 205
Epstein, Louis M., 233, 256
Eternal Light, The (radio), 246
Etz Hayyim, Yeshivat (New York), 178
Evening Post (New York), 170

Federation of American Zionists, 223
Feldman, Abraham J., 37
Felsenthal, Bernhard, 5, 8
Female Hebrew Benevolent Society, The (Philadelphia), 112
Fernandes, Benjamin Dias, 114
Finkelstein, Louis, 204, 233, 238, 239–40, 241, 245, 246, 247, 249, 251
Fleischer, Charles, 260, 261
Form of Prayers According to the Custom of the Spanish and Portuguese Jews, The (Leeser), 112
Frankel, Frieda, 103
Frankel, Zacharais, 127, 128, 198, 201, 206, 207
Franklin, Benjamin, 21, 111
Freeman, Meyer, 149, 154
Friedlaender, Israel, 6, 8, 9, 216, 223, 224, 231, 259, 262, 263, 264
Friedman, Theodore, 258
Frontiers of Faith (television), 246
Furtado, Abraham, 2

Geiger, Abraham, 2, 129, 205
Gelb, Max, 244
Ginsberg, David, 70, 77–78, 81, 82, 86, 88, 93, 96, 97, 98, 99, 100
Ginsberg, H. L., 246
Ginsburger, Ed, 103

Ginzberg, Louis, 205, 206, 207, 215, 224, 230, 232, 246
Goldman, Solomon, 233
Goldstein, Israel, 258
Gomez, Horatio, 147
Gordis, Robert, 205, 239, 240–41, 242, 246, 251
Gordon, Albert I., 39, 247
Grassi, Giovanni, 194
Gratz, Barnard, 111
Gratz, Hyman, 111, 133
Gratz, Michael, 111
Gratz, Rebecca, 111, 116
Gratz College (Philadelphia), 136
Greenberg, Simon, 246, 247
Greenstone, Julius H., 233
Grund, Francis, 21
Guggenheim, Daniel, 140
Guggenheim, Solomon, 140
Guide to Jewish Religious Practice, A (Klein), 251
Gutheim, James K., 145

Halperin, Samuel, 222
Hamburg Temple, 128, 129
Ha-Melitz (St. Petersburg), 162
Hamilton, Alexander (Annapolis, Md.), 20
Hansen, Marcus L., 10
Hapoel Hamizrachi, 256
Harlow, Jules, 253
Harrison, Eva, 103
Har Sinai Congregation (Baltimore), 197–98
Hart, Moses, 195
Har Zion Congregation (Philadelphia), 255
Haskalah, 193
Havurah, 43
Ha-Zefirah (Warsaw), 160, 163, 165
Hazzan (Sephardi), 18, 19
Hebrew Charitable Fund of Philadelphia, 118
Hebrew Education Society (Philadelphia), 117
Hebrew Free School, The (New York), 178
Hebrew Free School (Rochester, N.Y.), 68

Hebrew Poultry Butchers Association, 173, 174
Hebrew Reader, The (Leeser), 116
Hebrew Ritail [sic] Butchers Union, 161
Hebrew Tales (Hurwitz), 118
Hebrew Union College, 199, 201, 208, 213
Hecht, Sigmund, 208
Heller, Max, 136
Herberg, Will, 10
Hershberg, I., 83–84
Hertz, Joseph Herman, 92, 212, 220
Heschel, Abraham Joshua, 246
Hevra B'nai Shalom (Rochester, N.Y.), 45
Hevra Chayateem (Rochester, N.Y.), 87
Hevra Mishnayes, Beth Israel (Rochester), 62 passim
Hevra Sheves Ahim (Rochester, N.Y.), 45
Hevra Tillim (Rochester, N.Y.), 81
Hildesheimer, Azriel, 150, 154
Hirsch, Emil G., 28, 139
Hirsch, Samson Raphael, 205, 206
Hirsch, Samuel, 198, 205, 206
Hirschel, Chief Rabbi (Solomon), 111
History of Religion in the United States, The (Rowe), 34
Hoffman, Charles I., 140, 219
Holdheim, Samuel, 2, 205
Hudson, Winthrop S., x, 12
Hymns, Psalms and Prayers (Wise), 199

Institute for Religious and Social Studies, 246
Instruction in the Mosaic Religion (Leeser), 111
Interpretation of Jewish Law, Committee on (Conservative), 230, 235
Isaacs, Samuel M., 23

Jacobs, Henry S., 210, 213
Jalomstein, Mordecai, 168, 189
Jarmulowsky, Sender, 150, 158
Jastrow, Marcus, 207, 208, 213
Jellinek, Adolf, 129

Jerusalem (Mendelssohn), 118
Jew Faces a New World, The (Gordis), 240–41
Jewish Benevolent Society (Beth Israel, Rochester, N.Y.), 81
Jewish Calendar of 1854 (Lyons-De Sola), 21
Jewish Center, The (New York), 34
Jewish Chronicle (London), 137, 142
Jewish Community, The (Baron), 15
Jewish Daily Forward, 185
Jewish Encyclopedia, 97
Jewish Exponent (Philadelphia), 137, 162, 168
Jewish Foster Home (Philadelphia), 118
Jewish Gazette, 185
Jewish Hospital of Philadelphia, 118
Jewish Messenger (New York), 139–40, 162, 163, 177
Jewish Record (Philadelphia), 147
Jewish Theological Seminary Association, The, 91
Jewish Theological Seminary at Breslau, 127, 128, 206, 207
Jewish Theological Seminary of America, The, 35, 92, 94, 102, 105, 132, 163, 200, 204, 211–16, 245–47
Jewish Tidings (Rochester, N.Y.), 64
Jews and Mosaic Law, The (Leeser), 112
Jews in Suburbia (Gordon), 39
Jews of Rochester, The (Wile and Brickner)
Jick, Leon A., 24
Joffe, Abraham D., 90, 93, 100, 102
Johachimsen, Philip J., 169
Jones, Dramin, 149, 150, 158, 161
Joseph, Jacob, 107, 145–90; arrival in New York, 160–62; chief rabbi of United Congregations, 156; communal preacher, Vilna, 155–56; death and funeral 185–86; decline and dissolution, 182–85; first sermon and reaction, 167–69; kashrut, problems and pitfalls, 170–75; mismanagement, 175–78; projects, 178–82; prospects, 178–82; rab-
binic contract, 165–66; rivals, 178–82; "what is he to do?" 162–67
Joseph, Morris, 215
Judaism as a Civilization (Kaplan), 8, 237, 238
Jüdisches Tageblatt, 156, 168
Jüdische Volkszeitung, 164
Jüdische Wissenschaft, 193, 215

Kahal Adas Jeshurun (New York), 31, 33
Kallen, Horace M., 7, 8, 9
Kaplan, Israel, 180
Kaplan, Mordecai M., 8, 9, 34, 44, 101, 143, 144, 216, 221, 225, 232, 234, 236, 237, 246
Karobka, 172
Kauvar, C. E. Hillel, 216
Kelman, Wolfe, 254
Kertzer, Morris N., 39
Kirszenbaum, Raye, 103
Klein, Isaac, 248, 251
Kohler, Kaufmann, 170, 198, 210, 258
Kohn, Eugene, 102, 234, 235
Kohn, Jacob, 216, 233
Kohn, S. S., 92
Kohut, Alexander, 133, 198, 209, 210, 211, 213
Kraft, Jacob, 232
Krauskopf, Joseph, 25

Landsberg, Max, 27, 48
Lass, H. ("Yezner Rav"), 173
Lauterbach, Jacob Zallel, 96–100
Lavater, Johann Casper, 2
Leeser, Isaac, xi, 23, 109–21; birth and education, 109–10; communal endeavors, 119–21, 123, 124; educational endeavors, 116–18; hazzan minister of Mikveh Israel, 110; institutional endeavors, 118–19; literary endeavors, 111–15; on orthodoxy, 115, 145, 146, 196, 197, 207; religious endeavors, 115–16
Levi, Harris, 48
Levine, Morris, 233
Levine, Nathan, 150
Levinson, Abba Hayim, 52, 54, 70, 71, 81
Levinson, Elijah, 151, 154

Levinthal, Israel H., 37
Levitsky, Louis M., 228–29
Levy, Abraham, 83
Levy, Morris, 173
Lewisohn, Leonard, 139, 144
Lieberman, Saul, 246, 247, 256
Liebman, Charles S., 107
Lifschitz, Hillel, 150, 153
Lilienthal, Max, 145
Lipschitz, Jacob Halevi, 147–48, 154
Lipsky, Jacob, 53, 66, 67, 68, 93
Lipsky, Louis, 86
Little, Franklin Hamlin, 19
London Quarterly Review, 110
Lopez, Mosses, 19
Louis, Harris, 51
Louzanda, Hannah, 18
Lower East Side, New York, 148; Orthodox congregations, 150

Maccabean, The, 5
Magil, Reuben J., 244
Magnes, Judah, 33, 221
Mahzor for Rosh Hashanah and Yom Kippur (Harlow, ed.), 253
Maimonides College, 117
Malbim, Meir Loeb, 146, 147
Mann, Arthur, 259
Mannheimer, Isaac Noah, 129
Marcus, Ivan G., 252
Marcus, Jacob R., 18, 19
Marshall, Louis, 139, 215, 225
Marx, Alexander, 215, 246
Megapolensis, Johann, 17
Meisels, Elijah, 150, 152, 154
Melting Pot, The (Zangwill), 3
Memoirs of Moses Mendelssohn, 118
Mendelssohn, Moses, 2, 118
Mendes, Frederic de Sola, 207, 210, 213
Mendes, H. Pereira, 157, 163, 164, 169, 176, 188, 190, 200, 201, 210, 212, 213, 214
Mendes, Mrs. H. Pereira, 144
Merzbacher, Leo, 26
Michaels, Levi, 18
Mikveh Israel Congregation (Philadelphia), 19, 110, 119
Millgram, Abraham E., 242

Minhag America (Wise) 24, 27, 198, 208
Minkowski, Pinhos, 30
Minsky, Joseph, 45, 60
Modern Religion (Hart), 195
Montefiore, Claude G., 134
Morais, Henry S., 109
Morais, Sabato, 133, 164, 199, 200, 201, 209, 210, 212, 213
Mt. Hope Cemetery (Rochester, N.Y.), 89

Nation, The, 7
New Amsterdam, ix, 17
New Yorker Yiddsche Zeitung, xi
New York Herald, 146, 161, 162, 164
New York Sun, 164
New York Times: on post–World War II synagogue in New York, 39
Nimukei Ridbaz (Willowsky), 261
Noah, Mordecai M., 107
Nusbaum, Aaron, 51, 55, 59, 68, 81

Occident and American Jewish Advocate, The (Leeser), 112
Ofseyer, Jordan, 255
Olat Tamid (Einhorn), 25, 27
Ometz, 257
Orthodox Judaism: Beth Israel (Rochester, N.Y.) (1874–1913), 45–105; chief rabbi for New York, 145–90; congregations in America, 18–24, 28–34, 43–44; in Europe, 150–54, 205, 206

Past and Present (Friedlaender), 224
Philadelphia Conference (1869), 4, 198, 199, 200
Pittsburgh Conference (1885), 4, 200, 201
Pittsburgh Platform, 200, 201
Pool, David de Sola, 37
Portalis, Joseph Marie, 2
"Positive historical Judaism," 201

Rabbiner Seminar für das Orthodox Judenthum, 97
Rabbinical Assembly of America, The, 232–36, 247, 248, 250, 253–55

Rabbinical School (JTSA), 247, 249
(Rabinovich) Zvi Hirsch, 153, 154
Ramah, Camp, 246, 249
Rapeport, Osher Noah, 180
Rapoport, Solomon Judah, 129
Reidfei Zedek Anshe Ritove, Congregation (New York), 33
Reform Judaism: congregations, 22, 26, 27, 28, 42, 104, 127–29, 197, 198, 210; mission idea in Europe, 2; Philadelphia Conference (1869), 4, 91, 200; Pittsburgh Platform (1885), 44, 200, 201; rabbis, 2, 24–28, 37, 52, 54, 58, 70, 71, 81, 124, 125, 129, 136, 145, 147, 162, 170, 191, 197–99, 205–10, 214, 257, 261, 263; Reformed Society of Israelites (1825), 2; Union of American Hebrew Congregations, 121, 199, 214
Rehine, Zalma, 110, 111
Reicher, Nathan, 83
Religion in America (Hudson), x
Rice, Abraham, 145
Richmond Whig (newspaper), 110
Rifkind, Simon H., 109
Rochester, University of, 122
Rochester Daily Advertiser, 122
Rochester Daily Democrat, 122
Rochester Hebrew School, 68
Rodef Shalom Congregation (Philadelphia), 22
Rodef Sholom, Congregation (Johnstown, Penn.), 36
Rosen, Abraham Abba, 70–71, 81, 99
Rosen, Ben, 229
Rosenberg, Eliezer, 83
Rosenblatt, Samuel, 237
Rosenblatt, W. M., ix, 198
Rosenbloom, Jacob, 53, 65, 68, 81
Rosenthal, Gilbert, 255
Roskies, David, 252
Rothstein, Joshua, 150, 182
Routtenberg, Max, 254
Rowe, Henry Kalloch, 34
Rubenowitz, Herman H., 205, 217, 218, 219, 233
Rupp, I. Daniel, 195
Rush, Benjamin, 111

Russian Jew in the United States, The (Bernheimer), xii

Sabbath and Festival Prayer Book (Silverman, ed.), 242
Sadowsky, Solomon, 101, 102, 103
Salwen, Asher, 153
Sawyer, Adolph L., 164
Schechter, Solomon, xi, 92, 132–44; American Israelite on, 134; education of, 134; in England, 133, 134; greeted by the "establishment" in America, 140, 141; greeted by the press in America, 139, 140; and mission of the seminary, 216, 258; president of Jewish Theological Seminary of America, 214–19; reasons for coming to America, 141, 142; visits America, 135, 214
Schiff, Jacob H., 132, 139, 140, 141, 215
Schindler, Alexander M., 257
Schindler, Solomon, 259, 260, 263
Schocken Institute for Jewish Research (Jerusalem), 246
Schorsch, Ismar, 207
Schulweis, Harold M., 43, 253
Schwartz, Yehoseph, 118
Sefer Toledot Ya'akob Yosef (Joseph), 179
Segal, J(oshua), 173, 180
Seixas, Isaac B., 110, 116
Selikovitch, Getzl, 164, 172
Semuel Bar Meyr, 19
Series of Letters on the Evidences of Christianity, A (Fernandes), 114
Shaarey Zedek Congregation (New York), 22
Shaare Zedek (Detroit), 236
Shearith Israel Congregation (New York), 19, 211, 213
Sherman, C. Bezalel, 10
Siegel, Seymour, 256, 257
Silverman, Morris, 242
Silverstein, Shalom Joseph, 162, 173
Simon, Ernst, 15
Simon, Joseph, 93
Simon, Ralph, 226, 242
Simon, Shevah, 83

Sinai Congregation (Chicago), 27
Sklare, Marshall, 35, 225, 248, 249, 254, 255
Society for the Education of Poor Children, The (New York), 112
Solis-Cohen, Solomon, 132, 136, 139, 143, 210, 214, 215
Solomon, Adolphus, 210
Solomon, Elias L., 231
Solomon, Gotthold, 129
Solomon, J. P., 146
Solomon Schechter Day Schools, 242
Soloveitchik, Joseph B., 256
Spektor, Isaac Elhanan, 77, 82, 148, 150, 152, 154
Spiegel, Shalom, 246
Spirit of Judaism, The (Aguilar), 118
Standard Union (Brooklyn), 186
Stephen S.Wise Temple (Los Angeles), 42
Stern, Julius, 113
Stranger in the Synagogue (Tuska), 123
Strashun, Simon, 182
Stuyvesant, Peter ix, 17
Sulzberger, Mayer, 115, 117, 118, 133, 136, 138, 143, 144, 215
Sulzer, Solomon, 129
Sunday School of Religious Instruction of Israelites of Philadelphia, 113
Sutro, Abraham, 110
Sutro, Max, 25
Swartzberg, M. N., 160
synagogue in America, x, 15–44; Orthodox shul, 28–34; Reform temple, 24–28; rite congregations, 21–24; synagogue-center (suburban), 38–44; synagogue-center (urban), 34–38; synagogue/community, 17–21
Szold, Benjamin, 128, 207
Szold, Henrietta, xii, 137

Talmud Torah (Rochester, N.Y.), 68
Teachers Institute (The Jewish Theological Seminary), 216, 246
Temkin, Sefton D., 39
Temple Beth El (Harrisburg, Penn.), 244

Temple Israel (Scranton, Penn.), 36–37
Tocqueville, Alexis de, 194
Tuska, Mordecai, 122
Tuska, Simon, 122–31; aspirations for the rabbinate, 125, 126; at the Breslau seminary, 127, 128; education, 122–23; to Europe for rabbinic training, 126; literary efforts, 124; rabbi in Memphis, Tennessee, 130, 131; return to America, 129, 130; visits to Europe's leading rabbis, 128, 129
Twenty-four Books of the Holy Scriptures: Carefully Translated According to the Massoretic Text, The (Leeser), 113

Union for Traditional Conservative Judaism, 251
Union of American Hebrew Congregations, 121, 199, 214
Union of American Israelites, 119, 197
Union of Orthodox Jewish Congregations, 38, 190, 214
Union Prayerbook, 27
United Hebrew Orthodox Association (U.H.O.A.), 148
United Synagogue of America, The, 105, 220, 242, 250, 251, 252, 253
United Synagogue Recorder, 228
United Synagogue Review, 252
University of Judaism (Los Angeles), 246
Unterberg, Peretz, 59, 60, 83

Va'ad Ha-Kashrut (New York), 179
Vaad Hakolel Synagogue (Rochester, N.Y.), 33, 87
Volksadvokat, Der (New York), 164

Washington, George, 19
Weinberger, Moshe, 30, 52, 54, 148, 149
Weinshel, Hayim, 78–79
Weiss, Moshe, 49
Weiss, S. ("Vizaner Rav"), 173
Weiss-Halivni, David, 252
Werner, Julius, 147
Wile, Isaac A., 104

Willowsky, Jacob David ("Ridbaz"),
  ix, 90, 258, 259, 263
Wise, Aaron, 207, 213
Wise, Isaac Mayer, 24, 27, 109, 115,
  122, 123, 124, 125, 147, 162, 197,
  198, 199, 207, 208, 214
Wolf, Simon, 208
World Council of Synagogues, 251
Wright, Louis B., 4
Wyschograd, Michael, 257

"Yom Kippur Ball," 181
Young American Zionist Club (Rochester, N.Y.), 88

Young Israel, 33
Young Israel of East Northport, New
  York, 44
Young Israel of New Rochelle (N.Y.), 43
Young Judea, 35
Youth program (B'nai Jeshurun, New
  York), 229–30

Zangwill, Israel, 3, 139
Zhitlowsky, Chaim, 7, 8
Zichron Ephraim (New York), 213
Zinsler, Leopold, 174
Zionism, 222, 231
Zovchei T'mimim (New York), 148

ABOUT THE AUTHOR

Abraham J. Karp is Emeritus Professor of History and the Philip
S. Bernstein Professor Emeritus of Jewish Studies, the University
of Rochester, and the Joseph and Rebecca Mitchell Research
Professor of American Jewish History and Bibliography, the
Jewish Theological Seminary of America. He has taught at
Dartmouth College and the Hebrew University, Jerusalem, and is
past president of the American Jewish Historical Society. A
historian of the American Jewish experience, he is the author of
such works as *Haven and Home: A History of the Jews in
America* and *From the Ends of the Earth: Judaic Treasures of the
Library of Congress* and editor of *The Jewish Experience in
America* (five volumes) and *The Jews in America: A Treasury of
Art and Literature.*